A summer cruise, a careless sail
That gives material for a careless tale.

THE CRUISE OF THE BREEZE

The Journal, Art and Life of a Victorian Soldier in Canada

Marc Seguin

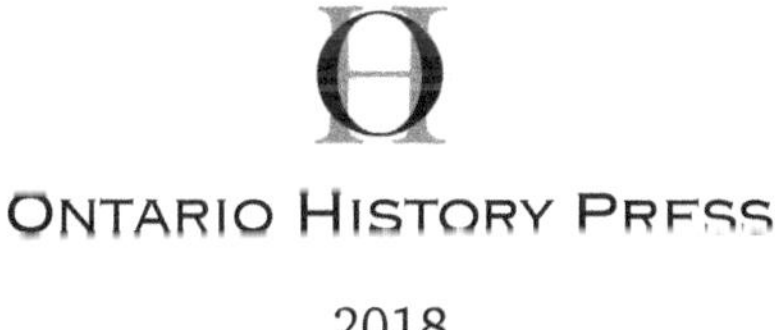

ONTARIO HISTORY PRESS

2018

ISBN: 978-0-9940106-1-2 (paperback)

ISBN: 978-0-9940106-2-9 (hard cover)

As a result of the dynamic nature of the Internet, any web addresses or links contained in this book may have changed since publication and may no longer be valid.

Cover design by Dan Seguin Designs   danseguindesigns@telus.net

Ｏ
ONTARIO HISTORY PRESS
358 Edward Drive
RR 3 Consecon, ON
CANADA
K0K 1T0

Order this book online at   www.ontariohistory.ca

Also available through most booksellers.

Also by Marc Seguin.
For Want of a Lighthouse:
Guiding Ships Through the Graveyard of Lake Ontario
1828-1914

TABLE OF CONTENTS

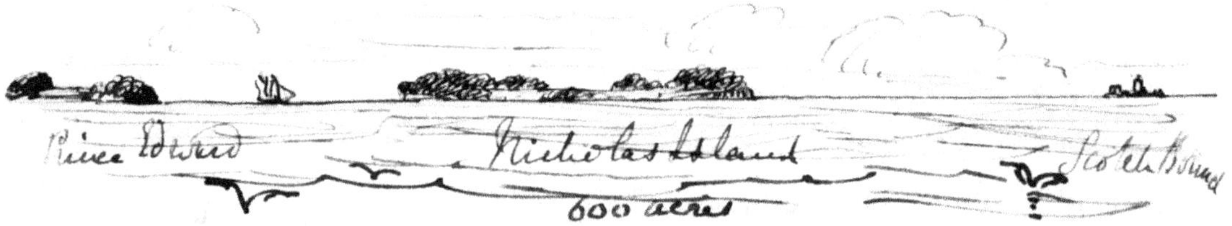

Prince Edward
Nicholas Island
600 acres
Scotch Bonnet

PREFACE

It was a simple seascape drawn in 1863 — a distant panorama of an island, a lighthouse, and a broad expanse of Lake Ontario all quickly captured in a pen-and-ink sketch — this was my introduction to the journal, artwork, and life, of the Victorian soldier and artist Henry Edward Baines.

That tiny drawing so piqued my curiosity that I followed a long and circuitous trail from one archival collection to another, until I found the source of the sketch: the artist's original illustrated manuscript entitled "A Month's Leave or The Cruise of the *Breeze*," locked away in the vault of a secure conservation facility outside of Ottawa, Canada.

The manuscript was in the form of a scrapbook and consisted of Henry Baines' personal journal compiled while he was living in Toronto, Canada. The journal detailed the activities of his twenty-five day pleasure cruise around Lake Ontario in August, 1863.

But it was more than just a written diary. When I finally saw the original manuscript in person, I was surprised to find that, in addition to several other pen-and-ink sketches, the journal contained two-dozen beautiful watercolour paintings depicting the Canadian and American towns around the shores of Lake Ontario that Baines visited, and scenes of the adventures that he had that summer aboard the private yacht, *Breeze*.

I realized then what a unique treasure I was looking at, and that is when I determined to have Henry Baines' illustrated journal transcribed, annotated and published; to give this document the attention it deserves as a remarkable visual and written glimpse into a little-known period of mid-19th Century North American history.

As I began my research into the life and art of this young soldier-artist, I was saddened to discover that, after being transferred to Quebec City, he was tragically killed in the performance of his duty; saving the city's General Hospital during the Great Fire of 1866. He was twenty-six years old.

Undeterred by this surprizing finding, I continued my search, from city to city, for more of Henry's artwork and for more clues to his life in Canada. The chance discovery of a substantial collection of his paintings held by a private art gallery in the United States led me to New York City to view that collection with the idea that I would raise the funds to purchase and repatriate many of these paintings. In Toronto and Hamilton, Ontario, I was given access to several museum collections to see more Henry Baines paintings. In Quebec City, where Henry spent his final months, I saw the barracks where he lived, the venues that he painted and the hospital that he saved while fighting the Great Fire; the very hospital where he spent his last days. I also visited Henry's gravesite where, with my family, I planted a memorial flag in honour of the 150th anniversary of his tragic death.

Later, I had the good fortune to meet some of the Canadian descendents of Henry's sister Isabelle, who had cherished and kept family keepsakes of their Uncle Henry, along with some of his artwork. Their willingness to meet with me and show me these family heirlooms helped to bring his story to life.

Henry Baines was a talented young man who was among the last of the British Army officer-artists who painted scenes of early Canada. To date, one hundred of his paintings and drawings and sketches, mostly Canadian scenes, have been identified; the vast majority of which have been seen by only a handful of people since the artist first rendered them more than 150 years ago.

With his unique illustrated journal as the centre-piece, I am pleased to present the story of the life and sacrifice of Henry Edward Baines — Victorian soldier, artist, yachtsman and hero.

Marc Seguin
Prince Edward County, Ontario, Canada
January, 2018

ACKNOWLEDGEMENTS

In compiling this account of the life, the writing and the art of Henry Edward Baines, I have had the kind and invaluable assistance of numerous individuals and several institutions:

Krista Richardson, County of Prince Edward Archives, who was my first point of contact in my quest to find Henry Baines' journal;

Jean Matheson, Library and Archives Canada, Ottawa, who had a copy of the original journal made for me and who provided me with a very useful transcription of its contents;

Beverley Darville, Royal Canadian Yacht Club, Toronto, who pointed me in the direction of several valuable sources of information;

Shane McCord, Library and Archives Canada, Gatineau, Quebec, who patiently showed the original manuscript journal to me and assisted with the repatriation of twenty of the Henry Baines watercolours from the United States to Canada;

Sheldon Lapierre, formerly with the Gerald Peters Gallery in Santa Fe, and Alexandra Polemis Vigil, Gerald Peters Gallery New York City, who assisted with the repatriation of the Henry Baines paintings;

Diane Laundy and Ellen Boddington, of Ottawa, Canada, who helped me locate some of the living relatives of Henry Baines;

Ariane Blanchet-Robitaille, Audrey Julien and Genevieve Piché, Archives du Monestere, Quebec, who researched the original Henry Baines documents in their collection and enthusiastically shared their findings with me;

Carol Baum, Arlene Gehmacher and Melissa Maltby, Royal Ontario Museum, Toronto, who enabled me to view the Henry Baines watercolours in the museum's collection;

Christine Braun, Art Gallery of Hamilton, Ontario, who showed me the Henry Baines watercolours in the gallery's collection;

Mary Margaret Johnston Miller, Library and Archives Canada, Gatineau, Quebec, who helped to fill in many of the details of the Baines and Rice family genealogies;

Verna Hollingshead, Parish of St. Andrews and St. Michael, London, UK, who provided assistance with research in Britain;

Barbara Boddington Selkirk, who freely gave of her time to answer my questions and show me many of the cherished family keepsakes related to her Great-Grand-Uncle Henry;

June Boddington, grand-niece of Henry Baines, who welcomed me into her home to view her collection of her ancestor's beautiful watercolours;

William Henry, master of S.V. *Saorsa II*, Port Whitby, Ontario, a long-time friend and a yachtsman with decades of experience sailing the waters of Lake Ontario, who provided technical consulting on the sailing details in the journal;

Kamille Parkinson, principle of Upper Canada Art Consultants, Kingston, Ontario, whose expertise in Canadian art history and review of portions of the text was invaluable,

and Marjorie Seguin, my wife and editor, herself an artist and writer, who joined me in my travels to find out more about the art and life of Henry Baines, and who contributed her artist's perspective and editing experience to help make this book a readable narrative of the life, journal and art of Henry Edward Baines.

Without the assistance of all of you, this book would not have been possible.

Thank you.

Marc Seguin

INTRODUCTION

Dawn was just breaking as the Royal Mail Steamship *Asia* sailed into the calm waters of Halifax harbour in the early morning hours of December 31, 1861. In spite of the early hour, most of the *Asia*'s five hundred passengers could be found excitedly lining the ship's rails, straining to catch a glimpse of the faint outlines of the city's houses and shops with their snow-covered roofs dotting the slope of Citadel Hill which rose from the water's edge to the masonry fortress guarding the city. This would be their first sight of land after a stormy nine-and-a-half day crossing of the Atlantic Ocean and, for the majority of the passengers, this would be their first tantalizing view of British North America, the place that they would call home for the next several years.

Most of those disembarking at the Halifax wharf were soldiers; part of a contingent of thousands of troops that had been hastily dispatched to Canada by the British government, fully kitted out with rifles, artillery, ammunition and special winter clothing, all in preparation for a war with the United States which, just weeks earlier, appeared to be all but inevitable.

Among the soldiers was a twenty-one year old lieutenant, Henry Edward Baines; by profession an army officer in the Royal Regiment of Artillery; by vocation a writer, poet and artist.

From Halifax, Baines, along with hundreds of other soldiers, would embark on a perilous overland winter journey to Toronto where he would spend three years in a quite, peacetime garrison enjoying the social activities and artistic opportunities that his new home afforded. While in Toronto, Henry also became an enthusiastic yachtsman. In August, 1863, he embarked with a group of friends on a sailing cruise around Lake Ontario. During this summer pleasure cruise, Henry kept a notebook which he later compiled into a journal, "A Month's Leave or The Cruise of the *Breeze*", which included numerous watercolour and pen-and-ink sketches, all of which are reproduced here.

From Toronto, Lieutenant Baines was posted to Quebec City where he continued his artistic endeavours painting scenes of the picturesque countryside. In 1866, just months before his brigade was to leave Canada, the Great Fire of Quebec swept through the city's suburbs. While fighting the fire to prevent the imminent destruction of the city's General Hospital, Henry was badly hurt and soon afterwards died as a result of his injuries. The grateful citizens of Quebec embraced him as a fallen hero and recognized his valour with memorial plaques and monuments in Quebec and in Great Britain.

Largely forgotten until now, the legacy that Henry Baines has left us includes his vibrant and detailed watercolour paintings, his simple pen and ink sketches and his descriptive and amusing journal which, taken together, give us a glimpse into the life of this soldier, artist, yachtsman, and hero, and bring a unique perspective to a fascinating period of Canadian and American history.

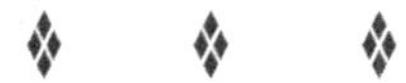

Part 1

THE SOLDIER

The hallmarks of Victorian Britain were already being indelibly stamped on the world when Henry Edward Baines was born in 1840. A rising middle-class in Great Britain was becoming firmly established thanks to increased industrialization at the centre of an expanding British Empire. The British Army, supported by the world's most powerful naval force, the Royal Navy, proudly protected imperial interests around the globe to ensure Britain's continued prosperity.

These were exciting times to be growing up at the centre of Queen Victoria's Empire. A quarter-century after Napoleon had been defeated at Waterloo by the British and allied armies, memories of the glorious victories of the Duke of Wellington were still fresh in peoples' minds. By the time Victoria ascended to the throne in 1837, an era of almost continuous warfare throughout Britain's global sphere of influence had begun. It has been observed that, "there was not a single year in Queen Victoria's long reign (1837-1901) in which somewhere in the world her soldiers were not fighting for her and her empire... to repel a provoked attack; to save an Englishman in distress; to avenge an insult; to suppress a mutiny or rebellion by those who did not understand the benefits of British rule; to move into a power vacuum; or to prevent Russia from extending her empire."[1] In 1840 alone, the year Henry Baines was born, British soldiers were fighting in Afghanistan and in China. Three years later, the British in India conquered the Sindh province of what is now southern Pakistan, followed by campaigns in the Indian provinces of Gwalior and the Punjab. In the 1850's, the threat of war with Napoleon III's France resulted in much excitement at home. Army enlistments were increased, new forts were built and existing fortifications all around the British Isles were strengthened. By the time he was nineteen, Henry Baines would be making his own contribution to the security of the Empire as a soldier in Queen Victoria's army.

Henry's path towards a military career was, perhaps, a natural one for him to take; undoubtedly influenced both by his parents' personal backgrounds and by the times in which he lived.

Henry's mother, Mary Rice, was a member of the branch of the Rice family from greater London that had produced no fewer than seven prominent military men: four uncles, two cousins and a brother, including two captains in the Royal Navy and five officers in the British Army, two of whom were colonels who had been decorated for meritorious actions while on active service in defence of the Empire.[2]

Henry's father, Dr. Philip Ottey Egerton Baines (known as Egerton), son of a clergyman from Shropshire, had served in the army of the Honourable East India Company in Bengal, India, before Henry was born. After graduating from the London Medical College in 1835, Dr. Baines had entered the service of "John Company's Army" as an assistant-surgeon.[3]

The East India Company was a private corporation that had its own army which was used to control and protect the British Empire's most valuable commercial asset: India. On leaving the Indian Army in 1838, perhaps due to ill health,[4] Egerton made his way back to London where he married Mary Rice. The young couple moved to Shropshire where Egerton started a medical practice with his brother James. Egerton and Mary were a well-respected middle-class couple. Egerton was known as a passionate amateur ornithologist[5] and Mary was a talented watercolour artist.[6] Two years later, Henry was born at Shrewsbury, the county seat of Shropshire, on April 4, 1840.

Eight years later, the Baines family, now with two young children — Henry and his sister Emma Elizabeth (known as Bessie, born in 1843) — had moved from the landlocked English county of Shropshire to the tiny island of Alderney in the English Channel just off the coast of France. This move may have been an attempt to improve Egerton's health by relocating to a place with a milder climate.[7] While living in the Channel Islands, the Baines family was further augmented, in 1848, by the birth of another daughter, Isabelle Frances.

As a result of the French invasion scare in 1852, Alderney was flooded with military engineers who were constructing a series of massive forts around the island. Soon, hundreds of artillerymen arrived to man the more than 200 cannons sent from the foundries of England to arm the forts. Soldiers marching, bands playing, forts under construction, artillery practice along the coast — any twelve year old boy could not help but be impressed with all of this military activity on Alderney, added to which was a visit, in 1854, by Queen Victoria herself.[8]

Henry's first-hand exposure to soldiers and forts and cannons may have combined with his long family tradition of military service to ultimately influence his decision to pursue a career as an officer in the British Army.

By 1854, the French invasion scare had passed. The British and French had resolved many of their differences and, allied with the Ottoman Empire, began to actively oppose Russian expansion in Europe and Asia. The result was the Crimean War. By the time the war ended in 1856, the Baines family had moved back to England, probably as a result of the deteriorating health of Henry's father. Mary Baines would have wanted family support while caring for her ailing husband and, since most of her family was then living in the Gloucestershire town of Cheltenham, 150 kilometers north-west of London, it is likely that the Baines family chose this town in which to settle because of the proximity of many members of Mary's family.

Sadly, Dr. Egerton Baines died at Cheltenham in February, 1856, leaving his widow to provide for her three children: fifteen-year-old Henry, twelve-year-old Bessie, and eight-year-old Isabelle. As a middle-class widow at age thirty-eight with limited means, little prospect of gainful employment, and three children to care for, Mary Rice Baines may have had to rely on the Rice family for financial support. For Henry, the death of his father may also have meant that he would have to give up any notion he might have had of joining the army as a officer. Given the great cost of purchasing an officer's commission,[9] plus the additional clothing costs and mess expenses that all officers were expected to incur, a career as an army officer now appeared to be out of Henry's reach.

Fortunately, though, his mother had numerous family connections in military circles, and some of them were quite wealthy. From fragments of correspondence eight years later between Henry Baines and his mother's cousin, retired army officer Colonel Augustus Thomas Rice,[10] it appears that the colonel, who also lived in Cheltenham, may have become young Henry's mentor and financial sponsor after the death of Egerton Baines.

Col. Rice was a decorated officer of the 51st Regiment of Foot (King's Own Yorkshire Light Infantry). He had fought with distinction in Burma where, as a captain, he had commanded a company of the regiment. In 1852, during the 2nd Burma War, he had been severely wounded at the battle of Bassein. After he recovered from his wounds, Capt. Rice was granted a field promotion to the rank of major and then given the honorary rank of lieutenant-colonel before retiring from the army in 1854.[11] As a reward for his meritorious service, Augustus Rice was given the further honorary rank of colonel and allowed to retire on the full pay of that higher rank; giving him an annual pension of £480 (the equivalent of more than US$65,000 in 2016 dollars). On retiring from the army, he also would have sold his captain's commission for at least £1,800 (the 2016 equivalent of almost US$250,000), adding a sizeable sum to his retirement fund. When he died in 1888, Augustus Rice left an estate valued at more than £70,000 (US$9.5 million in 2016).[12] In all, Col. Rice was considered to be a wealthy man.

He never married and had no children of his own. One of Henry Baines' cousins, Percy Thornton, described their Uncle Augustus as,

> The bravest of soldiers and tenderest of relatives.... That he never married
> may in some degree be considered a loss to the world, but then possibly
> more distant kinsmen might not have seen and known so much of his warm-
> hearted and sympathetic nature which under any possible circumstances
> must have coloured the lives of those most intimate with him.[13]

One of those "more distant kinsmen" may have been his cousin Mary's son, Henry Baines. Not only might Uncle Augustus have encouraged Henry to enter the army, but he also may have given his protégé financial support to obtain an officer's commission. It is unlikely that Henry's entry into the army as an officer could have been effected without such financial assistance.

The cost of obtaining a commission in the British Army in the 1850's was substantial. Until 1871, officers' commissions up to the rank of lieutenant-colonel were usually purchased, and even a commission as a lowly ensign in a common infantry regiment, priced at £450 in 1856 (the equivalent of more than US$60,000 in 2016 dollars), would have been such an expensive proposition that Henry Baines' mother likely could not have afforded to finance her son's entry into the army as an officer.

Whether because of the high cost of a commission or because of his interest in the more technical aspects of the military profession, Henry decided to seek a commission as an officer in one of the army's technical branches, the Royal Engineers or the Royal Artillery, where commissions were not purchased. Instead, candidates for commissions in these branches of the service attended the Royal Military Academy (RMA) at Woolwich, near London, where cadets were trained for up to

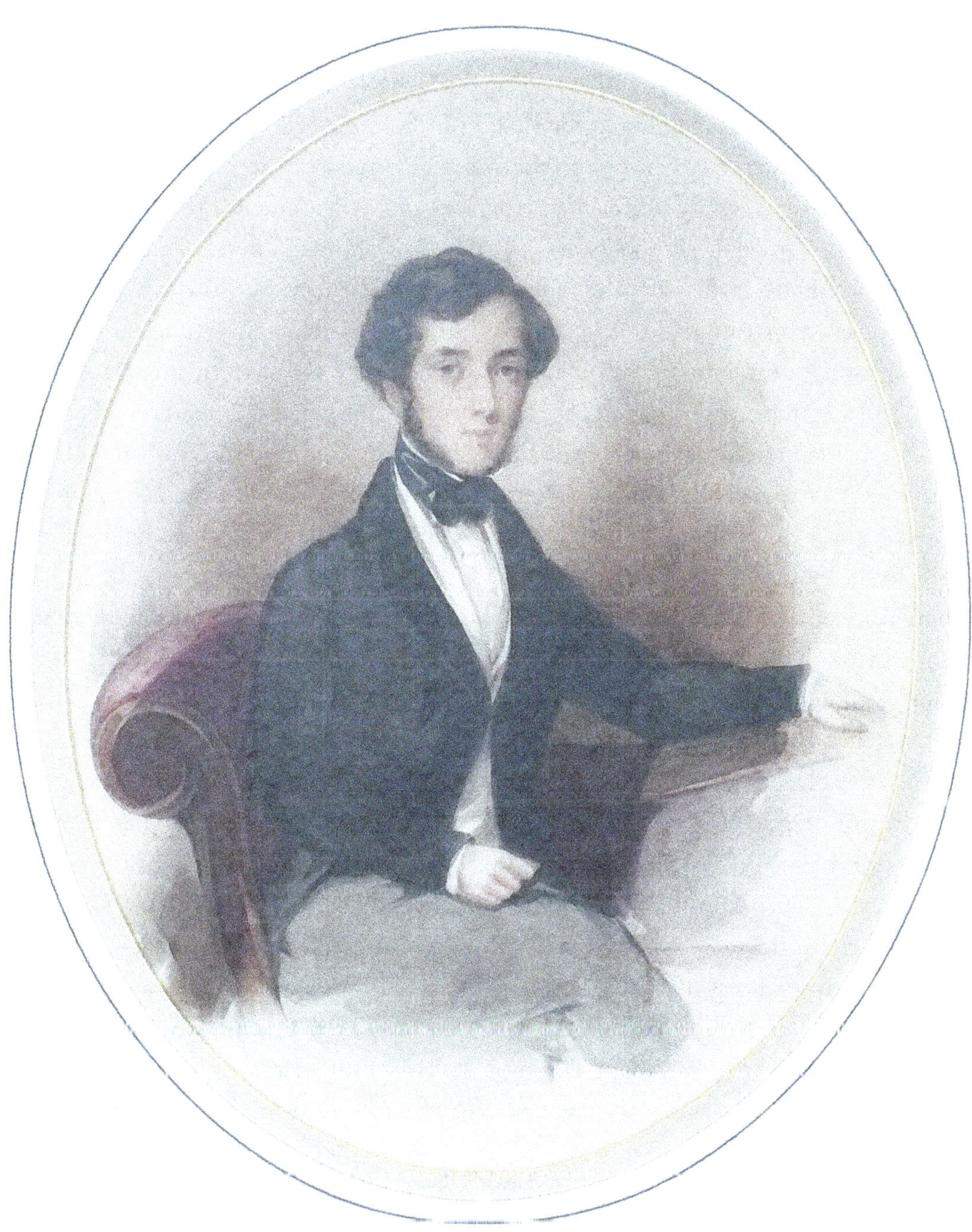

Untitled (self-portrait)
Attributed to Henry Edward Baines, c.1856
[Courtesy of J. Boddington, Toronto, Canada]

thirty months. On graduation, if the army needed to fill vacancies in the officer ranks of the artillery or engineers, the graduates would be offered a commission.

Until 1855, the Royal Artillery along with the Royal Engineers belonged to a separate part of Britain's military, the Board of Ordnance, which reported not to the army's Commander-in-Chief, but to the Master-General of the Ordnance. Military reforms brought about by serious logistical and chain-of-command problems during the Crimean War led to the abolition of the Board of Ordnance and the amalgamation of these technical corps with the rest of the British Army. Within two years, the system of selecting candidates for the Royal Military Academy was changed. The old practice of appointment to the Academy based largely on favouritism was ended. This was a system under which, as described by one writer, "... cadets obtained admission as competitors for the two scientific branches of our army, not so much in virtue of their own abilities, as by the influence, moral or political, of a male or female patron, invisible to the public, who might possibly be careless, ignorant, or both, of the requirements necessary for either corps.".[14] This system of patronage had often resulted in unqualified cadets as young as fourteen being admitted to the Academy, and officers with insufficient technical knowledge or leadership skills being commissioned and given command.[15] By 1857, this practice had been replaced with a system based solely on merit as demonstrated at a series of exams for admission to RMA Woolwich.

Even though his officer's commission would not have to be purchased upon graduation from the Academy, being an officer in any branch of the British Army was an expensive proposition. All officers were considered to be gentlemen and, as such, a certain standard of behavior was expected of them. It was also expected that they could afford a very high standard of living. That standard included lavish dining with copious amounts of food and expensive wines, as well as certain gentlemanly pastimes including fox hunting, shooting and theatre subscriptions, all of which cost much more than the inadequate pay that officers received from the government.

In addition, officers were required to purchase their own uniforms, of which each officer had several, as well as their own swords, pistols and other accoutrements. This could amount to well over £100 (US$13,000 in 2016).[16] There were also various regimental fees to be paid including mandatory mess dues and regimental band sub-scriptions. A junior artillery lieutenant was paid just over £100 per year from which he would have to pay for his own accommodations when not in barracks, as well as for his own food and clothing.[17] This was supplemented by "field allowance" of one extra shilling (US$7.00) per day when on active service.[18] However, it was estimated that young subalterns (the term used for all army officers under the rank of captain; i.e., ensigns, cornets and lieutenants) required an additional £60 to £100 per year just to cover their extra messing and other regimental expenses.[19]

Even before sitting the RMA entrance exams, most candidates would have to incur the added expense of a course of study at a preparatory school in order to have any hope of making the grade. A good grounding in Classics and Drawing was useful, and an excellent knowledge of Mathematics was essential. Under the new merit system of entry to the Royal Military Academy, there was considerable competition for the few seats available every year. Before the Board of Ordnance was abolished, it had established a preparatory school at Carshalton House for boys who were seeking admission to RMA Woolwich and it remained in operation until 1859. British universities (including Oxford and Cambridge) and public schools (such as Eton and Rugby) also created special academic programs after 1855 just to prepare their students for the Academy's entrance exams and the chance for a few of their students to gain a prestigious position in the army as a military engineer or artillery officer. Numerous private schools had also sprung up across Britain with curricula designed specifically for those students who desired to sit the RMA entrance exams. Tuition fees at any of these schools could cost several hundred pounds sterling (tens of thousands of dollars in 2016 terms).

If a candidate were successful at gaining admission to RMA Woolwich, there were still fees to pay: £22 10s. to cover the cost of uniforms and books, plus £62 10s. per term in academic fees. With two terms per year and up to two-and-a-half years of study required, the total fees were not inconsiderable and could amount to as much as £335 (more than US$45,000 in 2016) if a cadet required the full five terms of instruction.[20]

These were some of the financial barriers that Henry Baines had to overcome if he wanted to become an army officer in his chosen field. This is where an inheritance or the patronage of a wealthy benefactor would have been essential.

As a cost-cutting measure in 1858, Britain's War Office proposed that by the end of that year students would no longer be admitted directly to the Royal Military Academy at Woolwich. Instead, all prospective officers would first have to pass a two-year course of general military instruction at the army's Royal Military College at Sandhurst. Those Sandhurst graduates who chose to enter the Royal Artillery or

Royal Engineers would then be required to apply for admission to the Woolwich academy for further technical training. As this could greatly lengthen the time and the expense of gaining a commission, competition for the few available seats at Woolwich would have been particularly fierce in 1858, the year in which Henry Baines finished his prep school studies and sat the exams for the Academy.[21]

In May 1858, the War Office announced that up to thirty new students would be admitted to RMA Woolwich to offset those who were graduating that year.[22] At the July 1858, entrance examinations held at Kings College, London, eighty candidates, Henry Baines among them, presented themselves to vie for the thirty available seats at the Academy. After first being pronounced physically fit by a medical officer, the candidates were examined over the course of nine days in several branches of Mathematics along with four other subjects of their choosing, among which were English, French, German, Classics, Experimental Sciences, Natural Sciences and Drawing.[23] Of the eighty candidates who wrote the entrance exams that summer, only twenty-nine achieved a score high enough to secure admission to the Academy. Henry Baines was one of them; ranking seventeenth of the twenty-nine.

On August 11, 1858, Henry Edward Baines was officially appointed to the Company of Gentlemen-Cadets at "The Shop", as the Royal Military Academy at Woolwich was known. Located on the banks of the Thames River, just downstream from central London, one contemporary chronicler described the town of Woolwich and the Academy as they appeared in the mid-19th Century:

> Barracks, military hospitals, stores of ammunition, and of arms — all these give it a warlike stamp, which contrasts with the peaceful appearance of the majority of English towns. The town itself dominated by the high brick chimneys of the dockyard and of the arsenal, huddled between the walls of those two great war manufactories, traversed by monotonous streets, which grow dingy as they decline towards the Thames, has nothing gay nor attractive; but in front of the barracks there is an immense open plain. To the right of this plain (Woolwich Common) a tent-shaped edifice is erected, the Rotunda. To the left, at the extremity of the plain, stands the Royal Military Academy.
>
> The centre consists of a solid square building, with four turrets, crowned with octagon domes, and two wings, which extend on each side in a straight line. Before the front extends Woolwich Common behind the wooded rises of Shooter's Hill.[24]

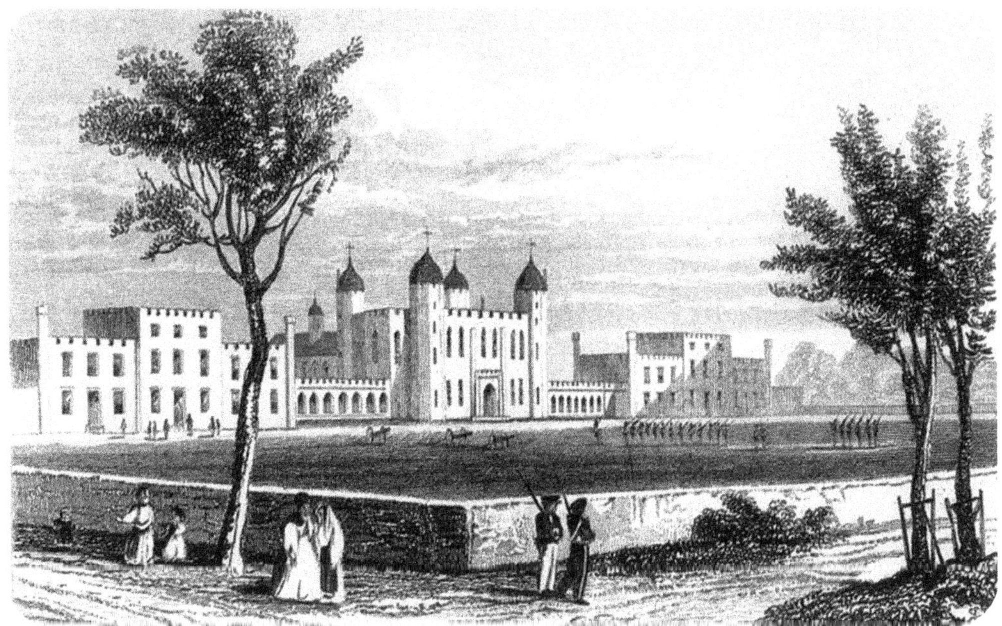

Royal Military Academy, Woolwich.
Wood engraving. Thomas Dugdale, 1845.
[Author's collection]

It was into these new surroundings that Henry Baines stepped to begin his career as a professional soldier. Like all "neux" or "snooks" or "snookers", as new cadets were called, Henry started in the Theoretical Class where he was instructed in academic subjects such as Mathematics, French, German, Chemistry, Geology and Astronomy, in addition to learning the standard foot drills and small-arms drills of the 19th Century British soldier. Although the gentlemanly courses of fencing and dancing had been dropped from The Shop's curriculum some years earlier, as gentlemen all British Army officers were required to ride, so equestrian instruction at the Royal Artillery Riding Establishment was also part of the course of study. In addition, there were several courses in drawing: geometrical drawing, military plan drawing, surveying and sketching, and landscape drawing. These art subjects were more than just an attempt at imparting gentlemanly refinement to the cadets. In an age before portable cameras were readily available and aerial reconnaissance was largely unknown, painting and drawing were often the best ways for military observers to produce an accurate image of the ground to illustrate a potential defensive position or a possible battlefield location which might be used by commanding officers to deploy their troops with greater effect.[25] Based on the later evidence of the artwork that he produced, Gentleman-Cadet Baines likely excelled in these drawing courses.

Some aspects of life as a new cadet at the Royal Military Academy at the time that Henry was a student there are described by a graduate, Captain F.G. Guggisberg, in his book, *The Shop*:

> Those were the days of bullying, and the 'snookers' — as the two junior batches were termed — had a very hard time of it. There were four cadets in each room, the corporal, or 'head of the room', being in charge; the poor snookers had often a terrible time of it, and were fagged and unmercifully thrashed with belts and tennis-bats.
>
> The baths were in the yards, supplied with cold-water taps only; in the winter these froze, and we 'snookers' had to fill the baths in the mornings with 'tosh-cans' from the pumps — a dreadfully cold business when it was freezing or snowing, and one had only a pair of trousers and dressing-gown and slippers on! In summer, we also bathed at the cadets' pond near the Repository, and were taught to swim more or less by repeated duckings. We also went to the Repository for heavy gun drill and mortar practice; and used actually to fire at a mark placed on the upper part of the Common, notwithstanding that a cadet had some years before been killed by one of the bursting shells.
>
> We were very hard-worked, the régime being about as follows: Study 8 to 11; drill 11.15 to 1; study 2 to 4.30; drill for an hour, and study 6 to 8.[26]

A cadet's time in the Theoretical Class usually consisted of three six-month terms or "half-years". After only two half-years, however, Gentleman-Cadet Baines was promoted to the Practical Class where he received hands-on instruction in military engineering, fortifications and artillery gunnery. A shortage of engineer and artillery officers in 1859 had prompted the authorities at the Royal Military Academy to begin an accelerated program of instruction.[27] As a result, within six months of joining the Practical Class, Gentleman-Cadet Baines was selected to sit for the public examinations for graduation from The Shop. Henry passed the examinations, ranking forty-second of the fifty-three successful candidates. The top eighteen cadets were offered commissions in the Royal Engineers. The other thirty-six cadets, including Henry Baines, were selected for the Artillery. On December 22, 1859, after only seventeen months at the Royal Military Academy, the Duke of Cambridge,

Commander-in-Chief of the British Army, commissioned Henry Edward Baines as a lieutenant in the Royal Regiment of Artillery.

In 1859, the British Army was on active service in several places on the fringes of the Empire including China, New Zealand and the North-West Frontier of India. Among the cadre of newly commissioned officers were many who must have been hoping for an immediate posting to one of these hotspots in hopes of seeing action and achieving the fame and recognition sought by many Victorian soldiers, believing, as they did, in the words of the great patriotic English poet, Alfred Lord Tennyson, that, "The path of duty was the way to glory."[28]

If Henry were among those seeking immediate glory fighting in a foreign land, he would have been disappointed. After kitting himself out with the Artillery's distinctive royal blue uniform tunic with its red trim and gold officer's braid, adorned with a regulation pattern artillery officer's sword and topped off by the standard "busby" fur hat (all purchased at his own expense), he was given a domestic posting to the Channel Islands. There, in January 1860, Lieut. Baines joined Captain Lennox's No. 5 Battery of the 10th Garrison Artillery Brigade which was then stationed at

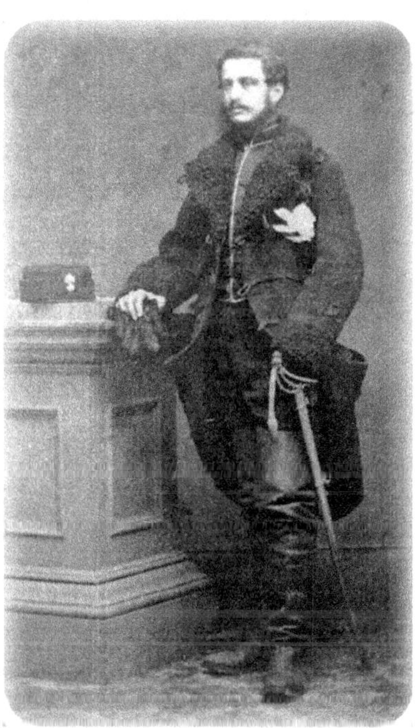

Portrait of Lieut. Henry E. Baines, Royal Artillery.
Photographer unknown, c.1860.
[From a photograph appearing in, *That Thy Days May Be Long*, Garnet Gibson, 1975.]

one of the many forts which ringed the island of Alderney. Here, the newly-minted nineteen-year-old officer took command of three gun detachments consisting of some thirty men, with orders to maintain his guns and care for his gunners.

The Royal Regiment of Artillery is the branch of the British Army responsible for all of the military's land-based cannons, howitzers and mortars, collectively known as artillery pieces or ordnance. The longest artillery pieces, the cannons, are usually referred to as "guns" by the artillerymen, themselves referred to generically as "gunners". While any soldier in the Royal Regiment of Artillery could be referred to as a gunner, this was also the title used for the lowest ranking artilleryman, equivalent to a private in an infantry regiment.

The Royal Artillery of the 1860's was organised into several Brigades, each of which performed one of three principle functions: they were either a Horse Artillery Brigade with their light cannons mounted on highly manoeuverable, horse-drawn carriages so that the guns, ammunition and gunners could be deployed very quickly to support the cavalry on the battlefield; or they were a Field Artillery Brigade, also known as the Foot Artillery, with heavier, longer-range cannons and ammunition wagons pulled by draught horses which followed behind the infantry and which were used tactically to bombard enemy troop concentrations and field fortifications; or they were Garrison Artillery, sometimes called the Siege Artillery, like Baines' 10th Brigade, manning the largest guns, howitzers and mortars which were usually mounted permanently in fortresses, citadels and coastal forts positioned at strategic locations throughout the British Empire.[29] Brigades were commanded by a lieutenant-colonel, and each Brigade was divided into eight smaller units known as Batteries. Each Battery was commanded by a major or captain and assisted by a number of 2nd-captains and lieutenants. These officers were each responsible for a division of the Battery usually comprising three 10-man gun detachments consisting of the sergeants, corporals, bombardiers (lance-corporals) and gunners (privates) who maintained and fired the ordnance. Each Garrison Battery consisted of about 120 rank and file and up to five officers.[30]

As a lieutenant commanding the three gun detachments in his division of No. 5 Battery, Lieut. Baines would have been well versed in gunnery practice for large cannons such as 32-pounders and 68-pounders (so-called because of the weight of the solid cast iron cannon balls that they fired), and 8-inch, 10-inch and 12-inch shell guns (the size determined by the diameter of the shells fired), as well as other ordnance such as carronades, howitzers and mortars and the variety of solid shot,

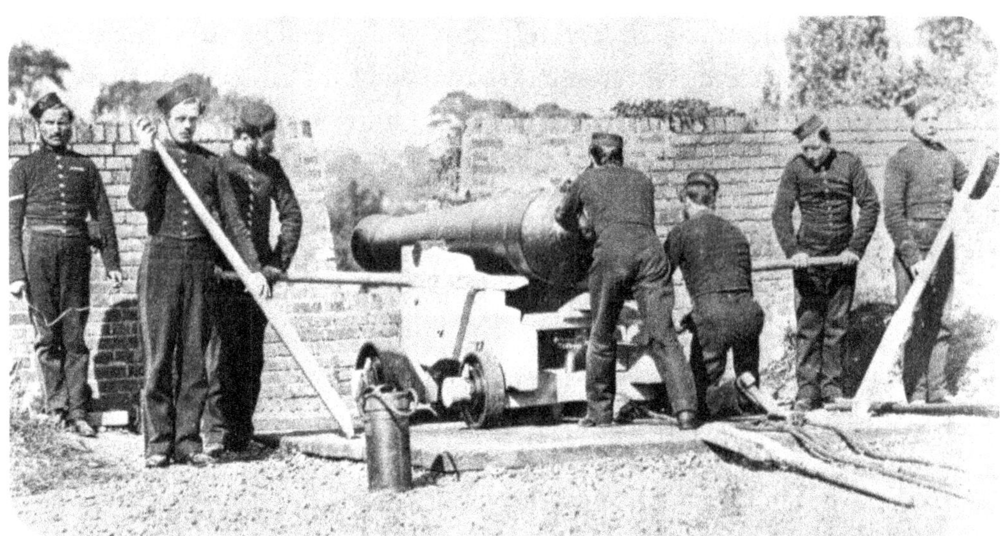

Gun detachment of a garrison artillery battery at drill with a 68-pounder.
British Army official photographer, c.1865.
[Courtesy of the Royal Artillery Institution, Woolwich, U.K.]

case shot and exploding Shrapnel shells used by each. Unlike the Field Artillery which had just adopted the state-of-the-art Armstrong rifled breech-loading guns with their high rate of fire and exceptional accuracy, the Garrison Artillery was still using the outdated smooth-bore, muzzle-loading cannons that had changed little over the previous 200 years.

In 1860, the official size of the British Army was set by Parliament at 240,000 soldiers — cavalry, infantry, marines, artillery, and support corps — including some 70,000 local militiamen in Britain.[31] The actual number of officers and soldiers in the army at any given time was usually significantly below the official number. Of the more than 170,000 regular soldiers of the British Army available for active service, almost 60,000 were retained in Britain for local defence, nearly 70,000 were assigned to India (the East India Company had been dissolved in 1858), and the remaining 40,000 were thinly spread across numerous strategic stations and countless detached posts scattered over five continents in more than twenty different colonies, protectorates and dependencies.

The force that effectively held this widely scattered Empire together was the Royal Navy, with two-thirds of its 250 ships usually on foreign stations at any given time.[32] This was an era in which the classification of a warship was determined by the number of guns it carried; the strength of a navy determined by the number of ships in its fleet, and a country's global power determined by the power of its navy. By that measure alone, Britain was the most powerful country in the world with its huge fleet of mostly iron-hulled, steam-powered ships carrying a combined total of more 6,300 guns (many of them state of the art rifled, breech-loading canons), with the capability to outnumber and out-gun any fleet of any other country.

During the decade following the end of the Crimean War in 1856, the British Army was involved in no fewer than forty skirmishes, campaigns, expeditions and minor wars in such far-flung corners of the world as New Zealand, China, Burma, India, Africa and Canada. It was into this environment of never-ending battles and military victories "for the glory of the Empire" that Lieut. Baines proudly took up his role as an officer in the world's most active army supported by the world's most powerful navy.

Joining No. 5 Battery on Alderney in 1860 must have been something of a home-coming for Henry as he had spent several years of his youth on the island. His father had worked there as a surgeon and his younger sister, Isabelle, had been born on the island. The very fort where Henry was stationed was probably built while he looked on as a boy as the walls and barracks were constructed and the heavy artillery pieces placed along the ramparts.

Henry's time stationed on Alderney, however, was short. After less than a year, No. 5 Battery was moved to the nearby island of Guernsey, and it may have been here that Henry's interest in yachting was kindled.

Yachting had been a gentleman's pastime on an unorganized basis since at least the early 18th Century. The first formal yachting organization in the British Isles, the Royal Cork Yacht Club, was established in 1720. The Guernsey Yacht Club itself was established in 1860, the year that Lieut. Baines was stationed on the island, and it is possible that several officers of his Battery, always on the lookout for ways to occupy their time to relieve the boredom of peacetime garrison duty, were involved in the sport, one of the few pastimes in which gentlemen could indulge on a small island where opportunities for activities such as riding, shooting and fox hunting would have been limited. The only record that Henry Baines has left of his time stationed in the Channel Islands is a drawing of a Jersey fruit schooner, the *Aquila*.

In September, 1860, No. 5 Battery was transferred again; this time to Portsmouth, the Royal Navy's principal naval base on the south coast of England, where Lieut.

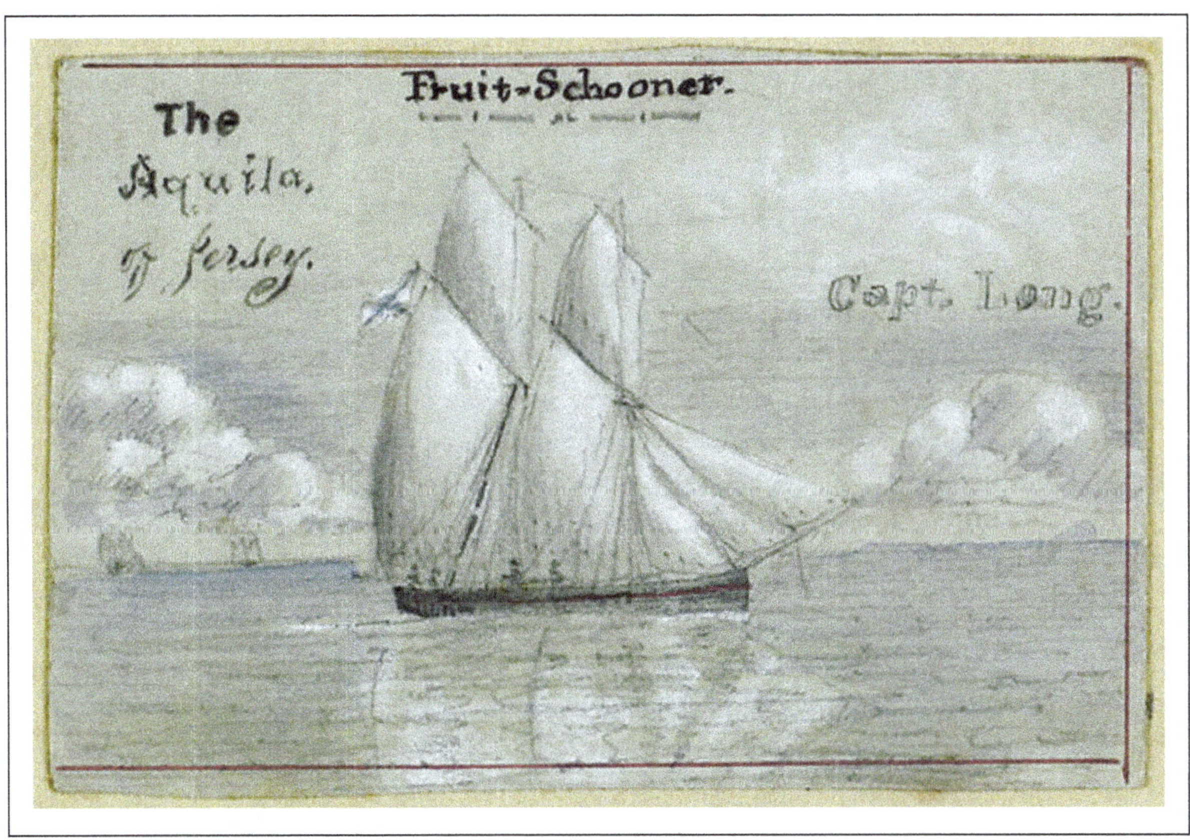

Fruit Schooner. The Aquila of Jersey. Capt. Long.
Henry Edward Baines, c.1861. Watercolour, pencil and ink on paper.
[Courtesy of Library and Archives Canada.]

Baines was stationed at Southsea Castle. Built during the reign of King Henry VIII, the small 16th Century castle, strategically located at the entrance to Portsmouth harbour, had been converted to a fortified artillery battery in 1814 and then upgraded with 10-inch muzzle-loading shell guns in 1850.

Civil War in America

It was while stationed at Portsmouth in February, 1861, that Henry would have read the news in the *Portsmouth Times and Naval Gazette* that, in the United States of America, seven Southern states had seceded from the Union (later increased to eleven states) and that the secessionists had declared their Confederate States of America an independent country. Only two months later, in April, 1861, further shocking news from America announced the outbreak of armed rebellion. The American Civil War had begun:

> Saturday, April 20, 1861. We regret to see from the latest accounts from America that but little prospect now remains of an arrangement, indeed there is every reason to fear that war has actually begun on the part of the Southerners. No news having been received for some days from Fort Pickens [at Pensacola Florida, then under siege by Confederate forces] led to the belief that communication had been cut off by the Southern troops. Major Anderson had been called upon to evacuate Fort Sumter [at Charleston, South Carolina] within 48 hours. Surely for the sake of humanity, if from no higher principle, the time is come when we and other nations may interfere with friendly Councils to prevent the horrors of Civil War.[33]

In fact, seven days earlier, Fort Sumter had been evacuated by its Union defenders after the United States Army commander, Major Anderson, surrendered to the Confederate attackers at the end of a relentless two-day bombardment, while Pensacola's Fort Pickens successfully withstood the rebel siege until relieved by Union forces. The delay in reporting the news was a result of the time it took for dispatches to be transported by ship across the Atlantic Ocean. While telegraph lines ran to most points in the United States and British North America, including an underwater cable connecting New York City with Cape Race, Newfoundland, it was not until 1866 that a trans-Atlantic telegraph cable was successfully laid between Newfoundland and Ireland.[34] Until then, all news had to travel across the Atlantic by ship, resulting in delays averaging more than twelve days in each direction.

The siege of Fort Pickens and the bombardment of Fort Sumter marked the beginning of a civil war in America that would last for more than four years. Those first hostile acts thousands of kilometers away on the other side of the Atlantic Ocean subsequently triggered a series of events that would eventually lead to Lieut. Henry Baines arriving in Halifax, Nova Scotia, eight months later.

News of the American Civil War elicited mixed reactions in Great Britain. While most Britons abhorred the continued use of slave labour on the cotton plantations of the Southern states, many were also aware that it was cheap Southern cotton that fed the textile mills of England, and this was a major driver of the British economy of the mid-19th Century. At the same time, in the United States there was a widespread yet largely unfounded perception that the British secretly hoped that the Confederates would be successful in their attempt to tear apart the Union which had been created by armed rebellion against Britain's King George III during the American War of Independence almost a century earlier.

Officially, relations between the United States and Great Britain just prior to the onset of the American Civil War had been cordial, if not outright friendly. In September and October of 1860, Queen Victoria's son, Edward Albert, the Prince of Wales and heir to the British throne, had paid an unofficial visit to the United States during which he had been welcomed enthusiastically by hundreds of thousands of Americans. While visiting Washington, the Prince had even stayed at the White House as a guest of President Buchanan. At the end of 1860, relations, official and otherwise, between the United States and Great Britain had never been better. Any ill feelings between the two countries over the American War of Independence (1775-83) or the later War of 1812 (1812-15) seemed to have completely dissipated. However, only six months after the prince's visit, in the aftermath of the beginning of armed hostilities between Union forces of the North and Confederate forces of the South, a string of seemingly unrelated developments would combine to build tensions between the United States and Great Britain to such an extent that, before the end of 1861, the two countries were brought to the brink of war.

The first of these developments came in April, 1861, just days after the surrender of Fort Sumter to Confederate forces. The newly elected president, Abraham Lincoln, proclaimed a naval blockade of Southern ports:

> Whereas an insurrection against the Government of the United States has broken out in the States of South Carolina, Georgia, Alabama, Florida, Mississippi, Louisiana, and Texas, [later, Virginia, North Carolina, Tennessee and Arkansas were added to this list] ...
>
> I, Abraham Lincoln, President of the United States, have deemed it advisable to set on foot a blockade of the ports within the States aforesaid, in pursuance of the laws of the United States, and of the law of Nations.... For this purpose a competent force will be posted so as to prevent entrance and exit of vessels from the ports aforesaid....Washington, 19 April 1861.[35]

The president's decision to impose a blockade rather than to declare the Southern ports "closed" meant that, in terms of international law, he was treating the Confederate States of America as an independent belligerent power rather than as an internal rebellious faction. This also meant that the United States Navy would have the right to seize all ships entering or leaving any port that was being "effectively" blockaded.[36] To British commercial interests, a naval blockade would mean a restriction of trade, especially British exports of manufactured goods to the Southern states, and imports of Southern cotton and tobacco. British textile manufacturers were rightly concerned as American cotton made up more than seventy-five percent of all British cotton imports in 1860. By the end of 1862, as a result of the combined effects of the blockade and reduced cotton production in the Southern states because of the war, British imports of American cotton had been reduced to only four percent of their pre-war levels, having dropped from 2.5 million bales in 1860 to less than 100,000 bales by the end of 1862.[37] While Britain was able to make up some small portion of this shortfall by increasing imports of cotton from India, Egypt and other countries, the overall effect of the loss of almost all of the American cotton supply was devastating to manufacturers in British textile centres like Liverpool and Manchester.

While the few ships that the U.S. Navy had available were immediately placed on blockade stations at a small number of Southern ports in May 1861, the wide-scale blockade called for by Lincoln's proclamation was unrealistic due to the lack of ships in the navy's fleet. Initially, there were only fourteen ships dedicated to patrolling some 180 ports along a coastline of more than 5,600 kilometers. Several months would pass before the number of ships was increased by commandeering a large number of merchant vessels,[38] as well as by building new ships and purchasing ships from other countries (including Great Britain) for use on blockade service. Even then, the U.S. Navy's blockade of Southern ports was never truly effective. However, as soon as it was announced, the British government received numerous protests and petitions from textile mill owners and shippers in Liverpool and Manchester calling for the official recognition of the Confederate States of America as an independent nation and for the protection by the Royal Navy of all British merchant ships sailing into Southern ports.[39]

Recognition of the Confederacy by the British government would have pleased the Southern states, but it also would have caused an enormous rift in diplomatic relations between Britain and the Northern states. Instead of bowing to the demands of commercial interests in Britain, the British government decided on a middle course. On May 13, 1861, Queen Victoria issued a Royal Proclamation of Britain's neutrality in the conflict between the Union and the Confederacy:

> Whereas hostilities have unhappily commenced between the Government of the United States of America and certain States styling themselves "the Confederate States of America",
> And whereas we, being at peace with the Government of the United States, have declared our Royal determination to maintain a strict and impartial neutrality in the contest between the said contending parties,
> We do hereby strictly charge and command all our loving subjects to observe a strict neutrality in and during the aforesaid hostilities.[40]

The Queen's proclamation of British neutrality prohibited her subjects from fitting out any transport vessels or arming any ships to be used by either of the hostile parties, and it prohibited British-registered ships from breaking the blockade or carrying any military personnel or war materiel for use by either the Union or the Confederacy. The proclamation also reaffirmed the decades-old "Foreign Enlistment Act" making it an offence for British subjects to join either of the opposing armies or to recruit others to do so. At the same time, the British Admiralty prepared to dispatch ships from the Mediterranean to join the Royal Navy's Halifax-based fleet, the North American and West Indies squadron, commanded by Rear Admiral Sir Alexander Milne. Milne was ordered to keep his ships prepared for any eventuality while patrolling international waters along the American coast and to shadow the U.S Navy's ships to determine whether or not the blockade was truly "effective" as stipulated by international law.[41] As an additional defensive precaution, Britain's War Office began making plans to send some 2,000 troops to reinforce the undermanned garrisons in Canada.[42]

The Southern states, hoping for full diplomatic recognition by Great Britain, were disappointed by the British neutrality proclamation, and the representatives of the Confederacy who were then in London continued in vain to lobby British members of Parliament for full recognition of their new nation. At the same time, the Northern states were outraged by the proclamation. They saw it as granting "belligerent status" to the Confederacy, a status tantamount to full recognition of the Confederate States of America as a legitimate and independent country. This confirmed the belief of many Northerners that Britain secretly hoped that the Civil War would end in a victory for the South.

In a Fourth of July speech in 1861, the popular New York orator, John Jay II, expressed the feeling of many Northerners as he strenuously denounced the British neutrality proclamation:

THE GREAT CONSPIRACY AND
ENGLAND'S NEUTRALITY

The visit of the Prince of Wales [in 1860], who was greeted with the heartiest welcome, seemed to have blotted out the last lingering remnant of ill-feeling, and left, on this side of the Atlantic at least, the belief that henceforth there was a firm alliance between England and America, not based on treaty stipulations, but upon that heartfelt cordiality which springs from mutual regard.

It is with profound regret that we have seen that friendly feeling suddenly converted into one of intense and bitter disappointment by the conduct and tone of the English Government and the ill-judged comments of the English press.

After the proclamation [of neutrality], for an Englishman to serve the United States [in the military] is a crime, and the rebels are elevated into a belligerent power — and this intervention of England, depriving us of a support which her practice permitted, and giving the rebels a status and right they did not possess, we are coolly told is neutrality.[43]

Three days later, on July 7, the British steamship *Great Eastern* arrived at Quebec, followed closely by the troopship *Golden Fleece*, which together disembarked an entire brigade of British troops including more than 2,800 soldiers and a battery of field artillery.[44] From the British perspective, this was simply a prudent measure for the defence of her Canadian colony which shared a very long and largely undefended border with a country where there was a massive build-up of troops occurring as a result of the Civil War. In the opinion of one London newspaper,

> The circumstances which have induced Her Majesty's ministers to dispatch this body of troops to Canada need not excite the slightest apprehension either in the minds of our military economists at home, or in those of our irritated and impulsive friends in the neighbouring Republic [the United States].
>
> Sir Fenwick Williams, the commander-in-chief in Canada, having regard to the disturbed state of the neighbouring Republic, has strongly urged upon the Home Government the necessity of increasing the military defences of the province.
>
> No reasonable man either in this country or the province can ignore the fact that in the Northern States more than two hundred thousand men are in arms – men who misinterpret the neutrality of England, and who would, if it suited their pleasure, just as soon make a raid into Canada as invade the Southern States.[45]

The intent of sending the reinforcements to Canada was strictly defensive. In fact, just a year earlier, in March 1860, some British Army officers had expressed concerns about the depleted state of their North American garrisons which had been stripped of troops during the Crimean War. These concerns, however, were about repelling a potential French invasion rather than about preparing for an assault on American territory.[46] Nevertheless, many Americans believed that the addition of a few regiments to the small British garrison already in Canada, along with the increase in the number of ships in the Royal Navy's North American and West Indies squadron, were simply the first steps towards war with the United States.

Certainly, incendiary editorials in sensationalist newspapers like the *New York Herald* which railed against Britain as well as other colonial powers such as Spain, threatening that the United States would invade their colonies bordering on the United States, only served to increase tensions on both sides of the Atlantic:

The Powers of Europe must beware how they act during the period upon which we are entering. Especially must Spain and Great Britain heedfully refrain from such displays of petulance and want of forbearance, as have characterized many of their past proceedings, unless they would conjure into existence a hurricane of indignation that cannot fail to burst forth with destructive power against themselves, so soon as our domestic struggles are ended. Most of the foreign Powers fail to consider what the attitude of the United States must necessarily be at the close of this civil war. On land, we shall have a thoroughly drilled and disciplined army of five hundred thousand of the bravest troops in the universe. The exigencies of the blockade will compel us to build up a navy, whose armaments, for practical purposes, will fully equal those of either England or France.

It is to be feared that both Great Britain and the government of her Catholic Majesty [Spain], goaded by aristocratic jealousy and hereditary hatred of democratic institutions, will engender fatal animosities against themselves, upon this continent. The inevitable consequence of such a policy will be that, so soon as rebellion is put down, a cry will arise from Maine to California for the annihilation of every trace of their rule on this side of the Atlantic.

The war that is now raging in the United States will have given place to internal tranquility before the lapse of another year. The warlike spirit that has been created by it will not be so easily lulled. Legions, flushed with victory, and accustomed to the din of arms and the excitement of successful conflict, will thirst for a new arena in which to achieve glory and distinction. No fields of action will appear to them more fitting than Canada and Cuba.[47]

More evenly-tempered newspapers such as the Toronto *Globe*, the *New York Times* and the *Philadelphia Inquirer* strove to counter the irresponsible editorials of papers like the *Herald*. A week later, the *Globe* printed this rebuttal:

WAR OR PEACE

We are glad to see that the absurd and mischievous threats of the *New York Herald* against Britain and Spain are being repudiated by the Northern press. In regard to the *Herald*'s prediction that Canada and Cuba would be assailed after the conclusion of the civil war, the *Philadelphia Inquirer* says:

"The whole spirit of the article is without any warrant, either in the state of international affairs or of popular feeling. So far from coveting

Canada, under any pretext, or desiring to lift against it a hostile arm, we are warranted in asserting that the people of the Union are a unit in their desire to witness its prosperity under its own government".[48]

Much of the bombast coming from the *Herald* and other anti-British newspapers in the United States was, in part at least, a reaction to highly contemptuous, anti-American articles appearing in many newspapers in Great Britain. Some of the ill-will reflected in American newspapers may also have been fueled by an overwhelming sense of frustration felt by many Northerners at the ineffectiveness of the generals appointed to command the United States Army and whose indecisiveness had resulted in many months of inaction followed, in July 1861, by a great blow to the morale of the North when Union forces were defeated by the Confederate Army at Bull Run, the Civil War's first major battle.

Hostile feelings between the United States and Great Britain were further heightened well into the autumn of 1861. Much to the annoyance of many Northerners, there were numerous incidents of blockade running by British-registered ships and by Confederate merchant ships arriving from or clearing to British ports; not only ports in the United Kingdom, but also those of British possessions in the West Indies and in North America such as Halifax, Nova Scotia and Saint John, New Brunswick. These incidents occurred on a regular basis in spite of the Queen's neutrality proclamation.

In September, the *New York Times* highlighted one such incident:

> Of the four vessels that were entrapped last week at Hatteras Inlet [North Carolina], two proved to be from Nova Scotia, laden with cargoes of cloth, iron, steel, shoes, etc. It is evident from letters that were found in the possession of the Captains that illicit trade with Southern ports is carried on to an enormous extent from ports in Nova Scotia and New-Brunswick. It seems also that since this traffic has proved so remunerative, the good people of Nova Scotia and New-Brunswick have become ardent Secessionists, and are able to gratify at once their conscience and their love of cash by thus rendering aid and comfort to the enemy.[49]

More than 200 similar blockade-running incidents were recorded in the eight month period from May to December, 1861.[50] Enormous profits could be realized by just a single return trip carrying foodstuffs or weapons into a blockaded Southern harbour and returning with cotton or tobacco. At some of the larger ports such as

Wilmington, North Carolina; Charleston, South Carolina; Mobile, Alabama, and New Orleans, Louisiana, blockade running by Confederate and foreign vessels was virtually a daily occurrence. This was especially true in the first months following President Lincoln's proclamation as the blockade was often only intermittently enforced while the United States Navy scrambled to increase the number of ships in its blockading squadrons.[51]

Not only civilian goods, but shipments of arms and ammunition from Britain with bills of lading marked for European ports or for British overseas possessions, were successfully smuggled into Confederate ports. This further frustrated and annoyed the United States government and the American people even though they too benefitted from similar breaches of British neutrality as military materiel from Britain was also received in Northern ports throughout much of the Civil War. Both the Union and the Confederate armies benefitted from this trade and British shipowners made handsome profits by ignoring the Queen's proclamation.[52] Customs officials in Britain and British diplomatic officers stationed in the United States often chose to ignore these breaches of British law.[53]

While the blockade of Southern ports was never completely effective at any time during the American Civil War, the United States Navy did capture a considerable number of blockade runners, including some thirty British-registered merchant ships in 1861 alone.[54] One estimate puts the total of British-owned blockade runners in the period 1861 to 1865 at more than 100 ships[55] (not including those owned by Southerners but built in British shipyards), many of which undoubtedly ran the blockade numerous times during the course of the war. The seizure of these British ships caused even more friction between Britain and the United States and provided ever increasing levels of rancorous debate in the editorials of newspapers on both sides of the ocean.

After unsubstantiated rumours were printed in some American newspapers that the British were about to send another 25,000 troops to North America, U.S. Secretary of State William Seward recommended that all Northern states bordering on British possessions should immediately strengthen their border defences. In this atmosphere of mounting tensions, even the *New York Times*, usually the voice of reason among that city's newspapers, advised that, "[Since] it would be at the City of New-York, as the heart of the country, the seat and radiating centre of commerce, wealth and intelligence, that the concentrated efforts of the enemy would be directed", the city's eleven forts, then armed with a total of more than 1,000 heavy cannons, should be further strengthened to guard against a possible invasion by the British[56].

The American blockade; British neutrality; British ships breaking the blockade with some being captured and seized as prizes by the U.S. Navy; Britain sending troops and warships to North America; the Northern states fortifying themselves against a possible invasion from Canada — all of these events were part of an escalating tangle of misunderstandings and poorly thought-out actions which triggered unintentional results creating ill-will and hostile feelings between Great Britain and the United States of America. Wading in on the debate, the Toronto *Globe* attempted to deliver a message of measured caution to its readers. On November 16, 1861, the *Globe* reprinted a newspaper article from Oswego, Toronto's neighbour on the New York side of Lake Ontario, where the *Oswego Times* had printed these qualified words of friendship between Canada and the United States:

> We dislike to discuss such a thing as hostilities with the Canadians. They are our friends, and we religiously believe they will continue so. We have no apprehensions now that Great Britain will interfere with our affairs, and we hope for humanity's sake that the descendents of one common stock will never again meet in deadly strife. Nevertheless, it is the part of wisdom, even in times of the most profound peace, to put all our coast and frontier defence in good condition. No wise Government will neglect such provisions.[57]

The editor of the Toronto *Globe* agreed with the writer at the *Oswego Times*, and added his own thoughts:

> We fully reciprocate the feeling of our contemporary of the *Times* in disliking "to discuss hostilities with the Canadians." War between Britain and the United States would be the greatest crime ever committed against Christianity and civilization. It is not to be thought of for a moment. The fact that the Imperial Government has sent out a few thousand troops to Canada affords not the slightest reason for defensive preparations on the American side. The force is not large enough to be a defence against a

movement on the part of the American Government.... Nobody wants to fight on this frontier, but if both sides go to building forts, enrolling volunteers, and storing up arms, a conviction will gradually arise that they are enemies, and then a small spark may kindle a great flame.[58]

Unknown to the *Globe*'s editor, a "great flame" had already been kindled by "a small spark" on the high seas a week earlier: the "Trent Affair" would bring Britain and United States to the brink of war.

The "Trent Affair"

On November 8, 1861, the United States warship, USS *San Jacinto*, commanded by Captain Charles Wilkes, had fired on the unarmed British mail steamer, *Trent*, in international waters between Cuba and The Bahamas, forcing the *Trent* to halt on the high seas. Captain Wilkes ordered a party of U.S. Marines to board the *Trent* to arrest and forcibly remove four Confederate envoys; James Mason, John Slidell, William McFarland and George Eustis, who were known to be on the British steamer making their way to Europe on a diplomatic mission for the Confederate States of America.

The *Trent*'s purser gave a detailed eye-witness account of the high seas' incident in a lengthy letter penned immediately after the event:

> To the Editor of the *London Times*:
>
> I hasten to forward you some particulars of the previous outrage committed to-day against the English flag by the United States steam-sloop *San Jacinto*, Capt. Wilkes. You have probably heard how, some three weeks ago, the little steamer *Theodora*, having on board the Commissioners sent by the Confederate States of America to London and Paris, ran the blockade at Charleston, arriving safely in Havana.
>
> Mr. Slidell, the Commissioner for Paris, was accompanied by his wife, son and three daughters, and also by his secretary, Mr. G. Eustis, with his wife; Mr. Mason, the Commissioner for England, being accompanied by his secretary, Mr. McFarland. It was well known in Havana that berths were booked for the whole party to proceed by this steamer [the *Trent*] to

St. Thomas [in the Virgin Islands, 1,000 kilometers east of Cuba], there to join the homeward West India mail steamship [*La Plata*] for Southampton.

We left Havana yesterday morning, at 8. This morning, about half past 11, we observed a large steamship ahead, and on a nearer approach found her hove to, evidently awaiting us. We were then in the narrowest part of the Bahama Channel, abreast of Paredon Grande lighthouse. As soon as we were well within range, we had the first intimation of her nationality and intentions by a round shot being fired across our bows, and at the same moment by her showing American colors. We were now sufficiently near to observe that all her ports were open, guns run out, and crew at their stations. On a still nearer approach she fired a shell from a swivel gun of large calibre on her forecastle, which passed within a few yards of the ship, bursting about a hundred yards to leeward. We were now within hail, when Capt. Moir, commanding this ship, asked the American what he meant by stopping his ship, and why he did so by firing shotted guns, contrary to the usual custom.

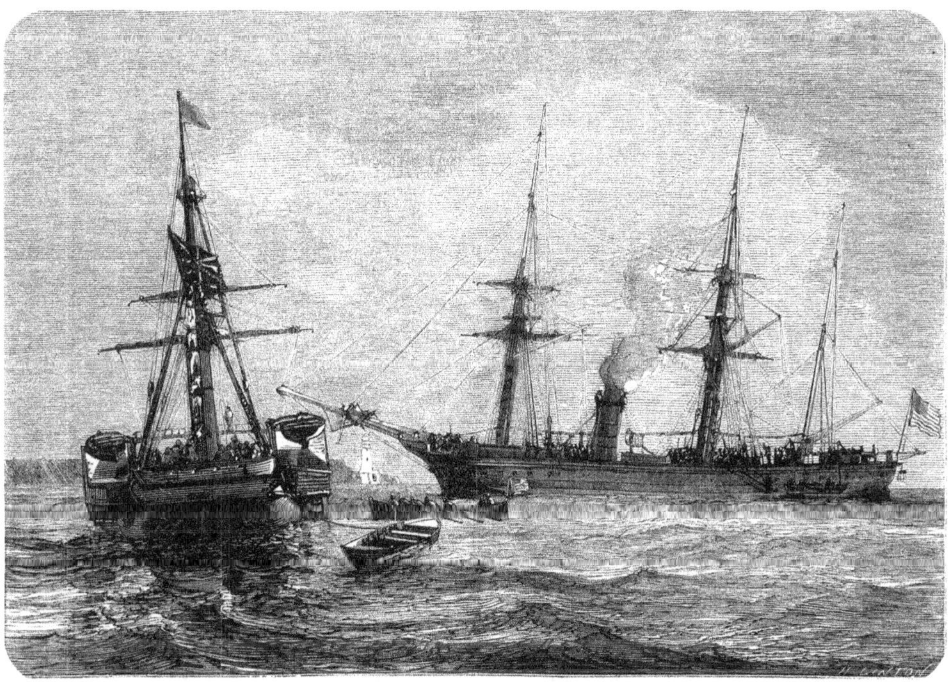

The English packet-steamer *Trent* stopped, November 8, by the American warship *San Jacinto*, in front of the Paradon-Grande lighthouse.
(**Le paquebot anglais** *Trent* **arreté, le 8 novembre, par le navire américain le** *San Jacinto*, **devant le phare the Paradon-Grande.**)
Wood engraving. *Le Monde Illustré*, Paris, 7 Dec.1861.
[Author's collection]

The reply was that he wished to send a boat on board of us. This was immediately followed by a boat putting off from the side of the *San Jacinto*, containing between twenty and thirty men, heavily armed, under the command of the First-Lieutenant [Fairfax], who came up on the quarter deck, and, after asking for Captain Moir, demanded a list of passengers. As his "right of search" was denied, the information required was, of course, peremptorily refused.

He then stated that he had information that Messrs. Slidell, Mason, Eustis, and McFarland were on board, and demanded that they should be given up. This also being indignantly refused, Mr. Slidell himself came forward, and said that the four gentlemen named were then before him, but appealed to the British flag, under which they were sailing, for protection. The Lieutenent said that his orders were to take them on board the *San Jacinto* by force if they would not surrender. He then walked to the side of the ship and waved his hand; immediately three more heavily armed boats pushed off and surrounded the ship, and the party of marines who came in the first boat came up and took possession of the quarterdeck; these, however, he ordered down on the main-deck to take charge of the gangway ports.

Captain Williams, R.N., the naval agent in charge of the mails, who was of course present during this interview, then, in the name of Her Majesty, he being the only person on board directly representing her, made a vehement protestation against this piratical act. During the whole of this time the *San Jacinto* was about 200 yards distant from us on the port beam, her broadside guns, which were still manned, directly bearing upon us. Any open resistance to such a force was, of course, hopeless, although, from the loud and repeated plaudits which followed Captain Williams' protestation, and which were joined in by every one, without exception, of the passengers congregated on the quarter-deck, men of all nations, and from the manifested desire of some to resist to the last, I have no doubt but that every person would have joined heart and soul in the struggle had our commander but given the order. Such an order he could not, under such adverse circumstances, conscientiously give, and it was therefore considered sufficient that a party of marines, with bayonets fixed, should forcibly lay hands on the gentlemen named....

I am, Sir, your obedient servant.
THE PURSER OF THE *TRENT.*
ROYAL MAIL STEAMSHIP TRENT,
AT SEA, Nov. 8. [59]

In an attempt to convince Britain and France to grant official diplomatic recognition to the Confederate States of America, Confederate president Jefferson Davis and his cabinet had dispatched two well-known and respected Southern gentlemen, former United States senators James Mason and John Slidell, and their secretaries William McFarland and George Eustis, as diplomatic envoys to London and Paris. In October, 1861, the Confederate statesmen had run the blockade at Charleston and arrived safely at the neutral Spanish port of Havana, Cuba. From there, Mason, Slidell and their secretaries had boarded the British mail steamer *Trent*, trusting that they would be safe from capture by the U.S. Navy while on board a ship of a neutral country.

It would take nearly a month for news of the "Trent Affair" to reach Britain. It only took ten days, however, for the news of the incident to break in newspapers throughout the United States and Canada. On November 15, the *San Jacinto* stopped at Fortress Monroe, at the entrance to Chesapeake Bay, so that Captain Wilkes could relay his dispatches to Washington before proceeding to Boston where the Confederate prisoners were to be incarcerated at Fort Warren. On November 17, The *New York Times* reported the capture of the "arch rebels":

> The United States steam-frigate *San Jacinto*, Captain WILKES, arrived in the Roadstead [at Hampton Roads, Virginia] at 12 1/2 P.M., having on board the rebel Commissioners, SLIDELL and MASON.
>
> Commodore WILKES came ashore and had a lengthy conversation with General WOOL [the commander of Fortress Monroe]. He expressed his opinion that he had done right, and said that, right or wrong, these men had to be secured, and if he had done wrong, he could do no more than be cashiered for it.
>
> All the documents and papers of Messrs. SLIDELL and MASON were seized. Their families were allowed to proceed.[60]

The story was picked up by newspapers in Toronto the following day. The report printed by *The Globe* was serious but cautious:

> THE MASON AND SLIDELL CAPTURE
> An Event has just occurred which might, if handled intemperately, involve the United States and Britain in very serious complications. An American steam frigate, the *San Jacinto*, has stopped a British mail steamer on the high seas, and compelled the surrender of Messrs. Mason and Slidell, diplomatic representatives of the revolted States on their way to Europe.

> There can be no doubt that the action of the *San Jacinto* commander
> was an outrage on the British flag, and an infraction of International law.
> There can be no possible justification of it. The seizure of Messrs. Slidell
> and Mason was a gross wrong, which can only be repaired by the offer of
> ample apologies by the United States Government, and the liberation of
> the captives.
>
> We have no expectation that the British Government will deal with the
> matter otherwise than temperately, but the collision will strengthen the
> hands of the not uninfluential parties in Britain who are striving to induce
> the Government to interfere in the American quarrel.[61]

With the capture of the four "rebels" from the neutral British ship in international waters, there was much rejoicing in the Northern states. Captain Wilkes was hailed a hero and dinners were given in his honour. He was praised for performing "the most illustrious service that has been rendered since the war began" and he was officially offered the thanks of the Congress of the United States.[62]

At the same time, the news of the "Trent Affair" also raised cheers in the Southern states. Throughout the Confederacy, the general opinion was that the North had committed a virtual act of war against Great Britain and, unless the United States government offered Britain an immediate apology and released the four captives, the British would now surely give the Confederate States of America official recognition as an independent country and go to war with the Northern states, thus guaranteeing the South's separation from the Union.

When he finally arrived in St. Thomas, Captain Moir of the *Trent* communicated the details of the incident to the captain of the British trans-Atlantic steamer *La Plata*, who carried the news to England. *La Plata* arrived at Southampton on November 27, and the details of the "Trent Affair" were immediately telegraphed to London. On receiving the news, Prime Minister Lord Palmerston called an emergency meeting of his cabinet to deliberate about "the outrage on the British flag perpetrated by an United States ship of war."[63]

Within days, there was public outrage all across Britain fuelled by countless fiery newspaper editorials of "Yankee treachery" on the high seas. A litany of indignant editorials was reprinted by London's *Morning Chronicle* on November 29:

> *The Times:* It is clear that the Federal States of America have, in stop-
> ping our mail steamer, been guilty of an act of aggression which could only
> be properly punished by laying an embargo on every American ship in
> British ports, and sweeping their little navy from the seas.

The Morning Herald: We trust that there will be no delay in avenging an outrage unprecedented, even in the annals of American lawlessness. It is the duty of our Government to demand the immediate return of the gentlemen stolen from under our flag, in honourable guise, together with an ample apology for a lawless act of piratical aggression; and to prepare for the rejection of such a demand by dispatching forthwith to the American coast such a naval force as may ensure the total destruction of the Federal navy.

The Sun: Whatever the law of the case, all Englishmen will be slow to regard the seizure of the passengers on board a British mail ship in any light but one – that of a bullying exhibition of what Yankees dare do against unarmed "Britishers". We regard the act as an intentional insult to the British flag, and an insult for which the Government at the North is responsible. The officer in command of the *San Jacinto* was, of course, but their servant; his manner of executing orders might be more or less rude, but the great insult is from Abraham Lincoln.

The Express: We have given no provocation for this outrage. The Washington Cabinet has shown itself sufficiently imbeciles, but to authorize the forcible arrest of gentlemen under the protection of the British flag, is nothing less than madness.

The Western Daily Times: In vulgar but expressive parlance the Federal Government has put its foot in it. By intelligence brought [by *La Plata*], we learn that the bitter feeling which has existed in the Northern States of America with reference to this country ever since we recognized the South as a belligerent Power, has broken out into an overt act.[64]

One of the few voices of reason in Britain was that of the *London Examiner*, whose editor wrote:

This occurrence, however much it may be deplored, involves not the slightest violation of international law. The Americans have only done precisely what, in similar circumstances, we should have done ourselves. The duty of intelligent men is to do their best towards allaying an irrational excitement, founded on no principle, and sustainable by no argument, which might otherwise lead to the most calamitous consequences.[65]

Despite such reasonable advice, "irrational excitement" is exactly what swept across Britain. Two American expatriates writing letters home from Britain gave their own assessment of the mood of the British people:

> [Letter, London to Washington] There never was within memory such a burst of feeling as has been created by the news of the boarding of the *Trent*. The people are frantic with rage, and were the country polled, I fear that 999 men out of a thousand would declare for immediate war.[66]

> [Letter, Edinburgh to New York] The excitement consequent upon the insult to the British flag by the U.S. Frigate, *San Jacinto*, has entirely monopolized the public mind. I have never seen so intense a feeling of indignation exhibited in my life.[67]

The actions of Capt. Wilkes were seen by British officials as a serious breach of international law, and the diplomatic incident that it sparked escalated with great rapidity toward full-scale war.

Without waiting for word from Washington whether Wilkes had acted on his own initiative or on the instructions of his government, Lord Palmerston's cabinet drafted a terse ultimatum to the United States demanding the immediate release of the four diplomats along with an apology for the incident. The British ultimatum required an unequivocal response from the Americans within seven days of it being delivered by Lord Lyons, the British ambassador at Washington, to U.S. Secretary of State William Seward. If there was no response by the seventh day, or if the response were deemed inadequate, then Admiral Milne was under instructions to evacuate the British diplomatic legation as the penultimate step to Britain's formal declaration of war on the United States. In such an eventuality, Milne had further orders to deploy his squadron, now numbering nearly thirty iron-clad warships, to blockade all of the major Northern ports from Maine to Maryland. One of the British war plans went so far as having the British fleet bombard and capture Portland, Maine, the strategic ice-free port that could then be used by the Royal Navy as a coaling and supply station to refuel and refit its steamships.[68] Portland was also important because of its direct rail link to Montreal that would allow the British Army's commanders to send troops and supplies quickly to and from Canada so that they would not have to rely on the St. Lawrence River being ice-free.

British Troops Dispatched to North America

Since the British government's diplomatic dispatches had to cross the Atlantic Ocean by ship, it could take two weeks or more for the ultimatum to reach Washington, and then another two weeks for the reply to get back to London. In the prevailing atmosphere of mistrust and uncertainty, fully expecting that armed conflict was imminent and, at the very least, as a forceful expression to the Americans that their intentions were serious, the British prime minister directed the War Office to take immediate action. More ships were sent to join the Royal Navy's North American and West Indies squadron, and thousands of troops along with tons of arms, munitions and military supplies were ordered to British North America. This was to be the vanguard of a much larger expeditionary force to follow.

In the years before the Dominion of Canada was formed as an independent country in 1867, "British North America" was the term generally used for the collection of British colonies located north of the United States. These included Prince Edward Island, Nova Scotia, New Brunswick and the United Province of Canada, which itself was made up of two distinct portions, Canada East (formerly Lower Canada, which became the Province of Quebec in 1867) and Canada West (formerly Upper Canada, which became the Province of Ontario in 1867).[69] Whenever British officials referred to sending troops to "Canada", they were referring to the reinforcements being sent to the garrisons at Quebec City, Montreal, Kingston, Toronto and London in the "Province of Canada", in what are now the provinces of Ontario and Quebec.

On December 3, 1861, the British diplomatic pouch containing the ultimatum to the American government was taken aboard the steamer *Europa* bound for Boston. It would be fifteen days before the diplomatic courier, Captain Conway Seymour, reached the British Embassy in Washington. In the meantime, the Admiralty ordered an immediate increase in the production and commissioning of warships at Britain's shipyards, the Commander-in-Chief of the army cancelled leave for all soldiers and placed all regiments in Britain on a war footing to quickly bring battalions up to strength by local recruiting, and the War Office scrambled to book every available berth on the regularly scheduled trans-Atlantic passenger steamers and urgently chartered as many other steamships as possible to transport troops and military materiel to North America. In Canada, the local militia regiments were put in a state of readiness and new volunteer companies of infantry, cavalry and artillery were quickly raised.

When the news of the "Trent Affair" arrived in Britain, Lieut. Baines and No. 5 Battery had just been moved from Portsmouth to the Essex town of Shoeburyness seventy kilometers east of London, where the Royal Artillery's practice gunnery ranges were located. This is where gunners were being instructed on the use of the new Armstrong rifled breech-loading guns.

On December 10, No. 5 Battery was quickly ordered to Woolwich, the regimental headquarters of the Royal Artillery. Here, the entire 10th Brigade was gathering, making hasty preparations to embark on overseas service in just ten days' time.

By then, the first troop transport to leave Britain had already sailed for British North America. This was the dilapidated steamer *Melbourne*, which had embarked from the Woolwich dockyard on December 7. In their desperation to find any available transport, the War Office had chartered the *Melbourne* despite being warned that she was "...a well-known 'lame duck', condemned as useless during the Crimean War, known to be a very bad ship at sea, to be very slow, to have unsatisfactory machinery, and, indeed, to be a worthless craft in every way".[70] Under the protection of the Royal Navy's newly launched iron-hulled, 21-gun steam frigate, HMS *Orpheus*, the *Melbourne* began a twenty-nine day voyage to North America with 266 officers and men of "E" Battery of the 4th Field Artillery Brigade along with their new rifled breech-loading Armstrong artillery pieces. Accompanying them was a detachment of commissariat staff officers who were to be the advance logistics party who were to prepare for the reception of the thousands of troops who would soon be crossing the Atlantic Ocean on their way to war.

Within the week, six more ships with a total of more than 5,800 troops — infantry, artillery, engineers, transport, commissariat and medical staff — were scheduled to leave Britain. Before the end of December, an additional eight ships loaded with another 4,800 soldiers along with rifles, Armstrong guns, ammunition and winter clothing would be dispatched to British North America.

In Woolwich, preparations were being made for the transport of the entire 10th Artillery Brigade. Numbers 1, 2 and 3 Batteries would sail on the *Niagara* on December 14. No. 4 Battery would sail on the *Adriatic* on December 19. A command shuffle in Baines' battery, however, was delaying their departure. No. 5 Battery commander, Capt. du Plat, who had replaced Capt. Lennox five months earlier, had just been promoted to a staff position as a lieutenant-colonel with the Royal Artillery's 12th Brigade, so the next in line, Captain Denne, was appointed to command No. 5 Battery. Denne, however, was able to beg off his overseas posting so it fell to Crimean War veteran 2nd-Captain Michael Tweedie to take No. 5 Battery to Canada.[71] The other Batteries of the Brigade would follow shortly afterward.

On December 18, in anticipation of his departure from Britain, and with thoughts of those he was leaving behind, Henry Baines expressed his feelings in a poem:

> Lines in a Holly Bough
>
> Although, Dear, 'tis full early now
>   For Christmas to prepare,
> I would, within this holly bough,
>   Subscribe a Christmas prayer.
>
> For I, when Christmas bells ring free
>   To English ears, my love,
> Far on the wide black-heaving sea
>   With grim gray sky above.
>
> Shall sail with wrath and fire and sword
>   To tame the Yankee's brag,
> Quit many loved and one adored
>   To guard our English flag.
>
> A moment now my thoughts I spare
>   From war and fierce endeavour,
> And give my whole soul to the prayer,
>   "God bless you now and ever."[72]

Henry may have written this poem for his mother, or it may have been for a sweetheart he was leaving behind. Little is known about Henry's personal life or any romantic attachments he may have had. Some hints of a close relationship with a girl on the Channel Islands are revealed in the lines one of Henry's poems that has been preserved:

> For then I stood 'neath the Channel skies
>   Bewitched by the gentle grace,
> Lost in the violet gleam of thine eyes,
>   And the love in thy rose-bud face.[73]

In other poems he writes such lines as, "Thy sweet beauty conquered me", "My life's one object is my love for you" and "Above all others in the land, I love thee."[74] In still another poem, Henry seems to indicate that he is engaged to be married when he writes...

> Take, Lady, this poor ring I send;
>   In Egypt circles used to be
> The emblem of eternity;
>   It means my love will never end....
>
> O regnant angel of my dreams!
>   Sole object of my waking life!
> From whose blue eyes all sunlight beams!
>   My own betrothed wife.[75]

However, in spite of such eloquent expressions of love and affection, no other evidence of any serious relationship or betrothal that Henry may have had has come to light.

In the days preceding Christmas, 1861, 121 officers, non-commissioned officers and gunners of No. 5 Battery, accompanied by seven Headquarters Staff officers of the 10th Brigade, along with some 300 other officers and soldiers of the Military Train and the General Staff, boarded a special train for Liverpool where the Cunard steamship, RMS *Asia*, about to embark on her regular mail run to Halifax, Nova Scotia, was waiting to transport the troops to war.

Farewells were said to family and friends and huge crowds of enthusiastic well-wishers gathered at the railway stations and at the dockyards to cheer the troops on their way. A guardsman in the Scots Fusilier Guards, one of eight infantry battalions being sent to Canada with the first wave of reinforcements, recorded a typical parting scene that was repeated across much of England as troops embarked for British North America throughout the month of December:

> Numbers of ladies, officers, and relations and friends of the men were assembled in the barrack square to see us off. People were continually rushing into the ranks to shake hands, and bid adieu to friends, sweethearts or relations.
>
> We arrived at the Waterloo Station and in a few minutes we were seated on the train. When the train moved off, the scene at the station could hardly be gazed upon; wives and sweethearts were crying fit to break their hearts, their husbands in the train looking a last, fond adieu.

The ladies, dear creatures, waved their white handkerchiefs; the men cheered and waved their hats, the band meanwhile playing the inspiring strain of 'Cheer boys, cheer' and then the melting melody 'Auld lang syne.'[76]

As soon as the train transporting the Royal Artillery's No. 5 Battery arrived at Liverpool, the soldiers were marched to the docks from where they were ferried to RMS *Asia*, which set sail on Saturday, December 21:

The Cunard Company's Royal Mail steamship *Asia*, which sailed from Liverpool on Saturday, for Halifax, carrying the mails for Newfoundland, Nova Scotia, New Brunswick, Canada, and other portions of North America, also took out about 470 military passengers, and 200 tons of warm clothing, camp equipage, &c. The military arrived at Liverpool early on Saturday morning, by special trains, from Woolwich and Aldershott, and they were promptly conveyed in steam tenders to the *Asia*, lying at anchor in the Sloyne. The *Asia* sailed about 11:30 a.m., with an easterly wind, and every prospect of making a rapid passage to Queenstown [Cobh, Ireland].

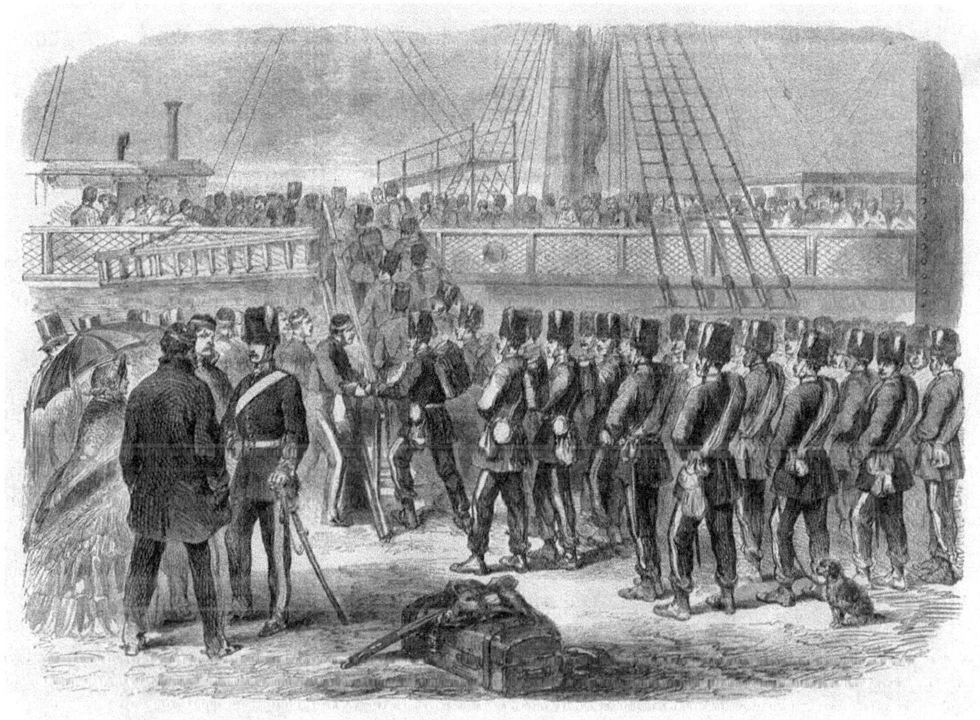

Embarkation of the Royal Artillery for Canada.
Wood engraving. *Illustrated London News*, London, 14 Dec. 1861.
[Author's collection]

Amongst the military passengers there were the staff for the army in Canada, Third Battalion of the Military Train from Aldershott, Headquarters Staff and No. 5 Battery of the 10th Brigade of Royal Artillery from Woolwich.[77]

The Royal Mail Steamship *Asia* was a speedy, side-wheel steamer used by the Cunard Line on their regular trans-Atlantic mail and passenger service from Liverpool to Halifax and New York. With a top speed of more than twelve knots (twenty kilometers per hour), the *Asia* could cross the ocean, including a stop at the port of Queenstown, Ireland, in as little as nine days[78] The wooden-hulled steamer was originally built to accommodate 160 first class passengers, but she had been quickly fitted out with extra berths for this trip to accommodate more than 400 soldiers in addition to a number of regular, paying passengers.[79]

From English ports, most ships bound for Canada in December, 1861, stopped first at Queenstown (now Cobh, Ireland, the port of the city of Cork), before setting a course for the Gulf of St. Lawrence, where they hoped to be able to steam up the St. Lawrence River toward Quebec City. Despite the lateness of the season and the likelihood that the gulf and river St. Lawrence would already be choked with ice, the

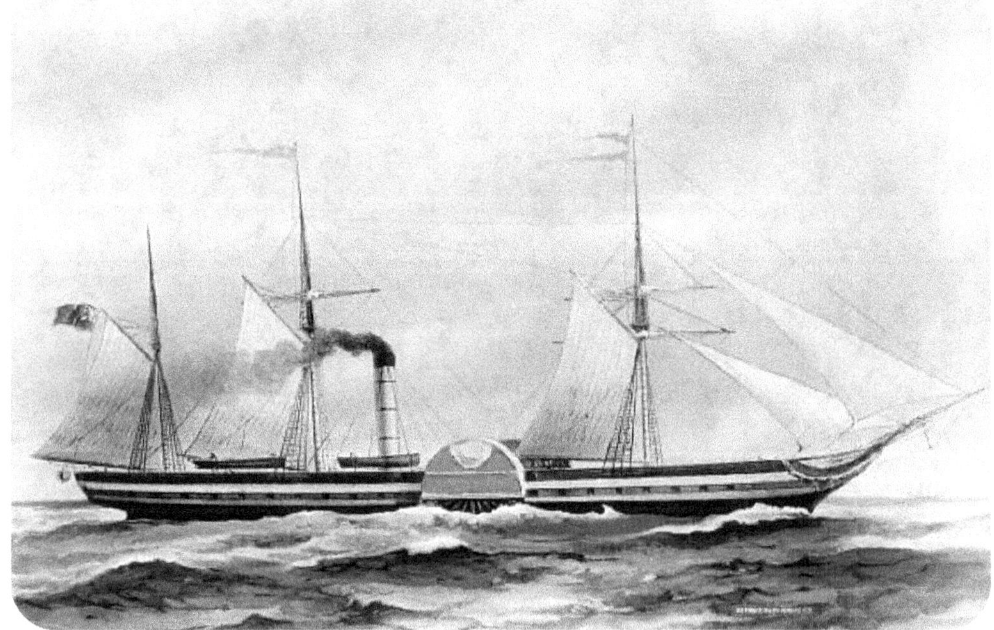

Royal Mail Steamship *Asia*, 1850.
Glass plate photograph of painting. Detroit Publishing Company London, 14 Dec. 1861.
[Courtesy of the United States Library of Congress. LC-D416-28022]

first four ships chartered by the War Office, *Melbourne*, *Persia*, *Parana* and *Adriatic*, were ordered to sail for the St. Lawrence River and to navigate as far as Bic Island or, if possible, Riviere du Loup in Canada East (now the province of Quebec) where the eastern terminus of the Grand Trunk Railway was located. If they were successful in executing such a risky maneuver, the War Office would pay the ships' captains a handsome bonus.[80] Only one ship, the iron-hulled *Persia*, was able to accomplish that feat. Her captain got her as far as Bic Island, just 90 kilometers downstream from Riviere du Loup. Several companies of the 16th (Bedfordshire) Regiment along with "D" Battery of the 4th Field Artillery Brigade were able to disembark before the ice on the river began to close in forcing the *Persia's* captain to quickly set sail for the nearest ice-free port, Halifax, Nova Scotia, 1,300 kilometers away by sea. Subsequently, all other troopships leaving Britain had to be routed directly to Halifax or to Saint John, New Brunswick.

Depending on the weather, crossing the Atlantic Ocean could take several weeks and, making that voyage in winter when storms were often at their worst, could mean a very rough and unpleasant passage. The Scots Fusilier Guards spent twenty-five days aboard the steamship *Parana*, including several days in the Gulf of St. Lawrence when the captain tried to follow the *Persia* to Bic Island but was turned back by ice floes in the river. The common soldier's perspective on that voyage was recorded by a guardsman in his personal diary:

> December 21st. The ship had now begun to roll, and a good many gave
>   their dinner to the fishes.
> December 22nd. The wind blew away a jib. Some of the men sick again at
>   dinner time.
> December 23rd. This was a beautiful morning, there was hardly
>   any wind.
> December 24th. When I got up I found the weather looking very stormy.
>   The wind again began to rise, and by 11 p.m. it had increased to a gale.
> December 25th. The ship was now rolling a good deal and shipping water,
>   which I could hear dashing over the ship above my head. Towards
>   morning the wind shifted and then fell, and by day-light it was quite
>   calm again, the sun shining out beautifully. I had nearly forgotten it
>   was Christmas Day. Thoughts of roast beef and plum pudding floated
>   through my head, but the reality was salt pork and biscuits, hard
>   enough to require a hammer to break them. Because it was Christmas
>   Day we got a double allowance of rum.

> December 26th. About 7 a.m., commenced to blow very hard, and soon
> had increased to a gale. It is very disagreeable to be below in a storm;
> the motion below tends more to sea sickness. There were a great many
> sea-sick today. We had a double allowance of grog to keep out the cold.
>
> December 27th. The gale had abated during the night. About mid-day
> commenced raining, and by evening once more blew a gale of wind; we
> rather liked the gales at first, but we were now heartily tired of them.
>
> December 28th. Very cold frosty morning. It turned out a fine day and
> still finer evening.
>
> December 29th. Sunday morning, cold and raining. A few of us joined
> together and sang some psalms, the time now hanging heavily on our
> hands, and "land", "land" was all the talk, both amongst the officers
> and men.
>
> December 30th. Still foggy and dreadfully cold. There was a man at the
> mast head on the look out for land. When the man at the mast
> head came down he was covered with ice, and nearly insensible for
> the effects of the cold. No land was seen and no change in the
> weather occurred during the day.
>
> December 31st. Land reported in sight; turned out to be a false alarm. I
> went to bed in bad humour with myself, the weather, and things in
> general.
>
> January 1st, 1862. At 7 a.m., land in sight. This was my first glimpse of the
> New World, and most certainly its appearance was not inviting; it rose
> steeply from the water, and was covered with snow; a few stunted trees
> were scattered here and there.[81]

Officers on board the troop transports, even junior officers like Lieut. Baines, had better accommodations and more privileges than the rank and file soldiers, but they too suffered from the tossing, pitching and rolling of the ships. Lieut.-Col. Garnet Wolseley en route to Canada with the Commissariat Department as part of the army's advance party, recorded his recollections of the twenty-nine days he spent aboard the steamer *Melbourne* from Woolwich to Halifax:

> It was bad dirty weather when we steamed out of the Thames into the
> Channel, bound for Plymouth, and it grew worse between that place and
> Cork [Ireland]. From that beautiful harbour we finally started about noon
> on December 14, and pushed out into the great Atlantic. There the sea
> was 'running mountains high.' I do not remember having ever been on a
> sea that looked more angry and, to the landsman's taste, more hateful.

A few of us 'old salts' had our meals as best we could, holding on with one hand as we fed ourselves with the other; but as a rule nearly every one was very sick.

The weather grew worse and worse and our discomfort increased. Occasionally we lay-to, for our wretched engines could make no headway in such terrible weather. How I pitied the non-commissioned officers and men of the field battery we had on board. Their existence must have been simply terrible, for that of the colonels on board the ship was bad enough, as she pitched and rolled, often strained as if she were going to pieces.

In the course of my eventful life I can recall many extremely disagreeable nights and days. Even now the remembrance of them is still fresh in my mind; and amongst them, very high up towards the boiling-point of my past miseries, I place the Christmas Day of 1861 that I spent on board the steamer *Melbourne*. We lay-to most of the daylight, steaming hard to try and keep her inconstant head to the wind, as she plunged and rolled, shipping tons of water as she did so.[82]

Those officers and men of the Royal Artillery's 10th Brigade who were aboard RMS *Asia* were more fortunate than the troops sailing on most of the other ships. While they also had to endure the effects of a number of gales, the *Asia*'s Atlantic crossing was accomplished in a remarkably speedy time of just nine-and-a-half days. During the crossing, Lieut. Baines likely bunked in with one or more of his fellow battery officers, including Lieut. Henry Harvey, and while on board, they would have met fellow passengers Assistant-Surgeon Samuel Woodfull of the 4th Brigade and Captain George Morrison of the Military Train. At the time, none of these men could have imagined another nautical adventure of a very different sort that they would share on Lake Ontario eighteen months later.

Despite their speedy transit of the Atlantic, Henry Baines and his fellow passengers would have been overjoyed to arrive safely in Halifax harbour on the morning of December 31, 1861. Another artillery officer, Lieut. Francis Duncan of the 7th Brigade, writing of an earlier Atlantic crossing, recorded his feelings on arriving at Halifax:

> And then came the morning which saw us steam up the grand harbour of Halifax, a noble specimen of nature's works in America first to greet our eager eyes and never surely did Columbus examine more curiously the features of his newly-discovered continent, than did we those of that part of it where we were destined for a time to reside.[83]

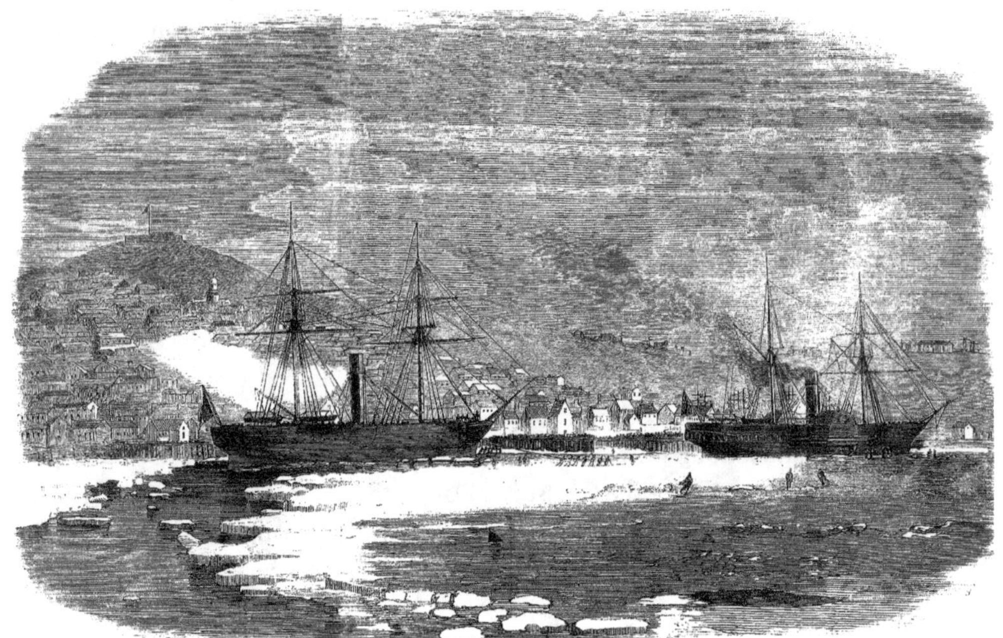

The English and Newfoundland Mail Vessels Making Their Way Through the Ice in Halifax Harbour, Nova Scotia.
Wood engraving. *Illustrated London News*, London, 5 Feb. 1859.
[Author's collection]

The Winter Journey Overland from Halifax to Toronto

On the same day that Lieut. Baines arrived at Halifax on the *Asia*, the first of many groups of soldiers left the city, beginning their long, cold trek to the Province of Canada. Troops who had already been in garrison at Halifax for several years made up this first contingent: the entire 62nd (Wiltshire) Regiment along with a detachment of forty gunners of the 7th Field Artillery Brigade. The soldiers boarded the steamer SS *Delta* bound for the Bay of Fundy port of St. Andrews, New Brunswick. From there, they would take a train to the end of the railway line near the town of Woodstock, New Brunswick, then transfer to a convoy of horse-drawn sleighs which, over the course of several days, would whisk them along snow-covered roads to the Grand Trunk Railway station at Riviere du Loup where they could once again board railway cars destined for garrisons in Canada.

Whenever winter conditions closed off direct access to Canada by the St. Lawrence River, the normal alternative was to disembark passengers from Britain at one of the ice-free American ports such as Portland, Maine or Boston, Massachusetts, from which railway lines connected directly to Montreal. However, given that Britain and the United States were on the brink of war at the end of 1861, moving British military reinforcements through United States territory was not an option. Since there was no railroad connecting Halifax to the Province of Canada, the Commander-in-Chief of British North American forces, Major-General Sir William Fenwick Williams, had no choice but to make alternate plans to route troops and supplies overland through New Brunswick on a risky and potentially dangerous winter march.

Over the course of several decades, there had been much talk of building an inter-colonial railway connecting the Grand Trunk terminus at Riviere du Loup with New Brunswick and Nova Scotia, but lack of cooperation among the separate colonial governments prevented its completion until 1876, almost a decade after Canada became an independent country. In 1861, only a short 125 kilometer section of the New Brunswick and Canada Railway was in operation from Saint Andrews northward towards the Canadian border. To cover the remaining 275 kilometers, the troops would have to be transported in stages by horse-drawn sleigh; a journey of at least six days.

Disaster nearly struck the first contingent of troops travelling by rail to Woodstock. The soldiers almost froze to death when the train they were on was blocked by enormous snow drifts on the track. After enduring two days of sub-zero temperatures in the unheated railway cars with little food, snow plows finally reached the stranded train and the track was cleared.[84] As a result of that near-disaster, the military authorities decided that all further reinforcements for Canada that winter would have to endure the long and hazardous overland march covering the entire 500 kilometer distance from Saint John, New Brunswick to the Grand Trunk railhead at Riviere du Loup, with nine overnight stops in between. Single regiments had accomplished similar feats in the past. The 104th (New Brunswick) Regiment had marched the 1,100 kilometers all the way to Quebec City on snowshoes in 1813, and the 43rd Regiment had been transported across New Brunswick on sleighs in 1838, but never before had such a large body of troops — eventually numbering nearly 7,000 men — made an attempt to travel such an enormous distance through the North American wilderness in the depths of winter.

To coordinate the colossal logistical task of transporting, sheltering, feeding and providing medical care for thousands of men in such a remote area under severe weather conditions, the War Office had dispatched a detachment of commissariat and other staff officers on board the steamer *Melbourne*, the first troop transport to leave England as a result of the "Trent Affair". Unfortunately, the under-powered *Melbourne* not only encountered numerous severe storms, but she also suffered intermittent mechanical problems during her trans-Atlantic journey. By the time she reached the Gulf of St. Lawrence, she was running low on fuel so had to stop for several days at Sydney, on Nova Scotia's Cape Breton Island, to replenish her supplies of coal. There, the *Melbourne*'s captain received orders to divert to Halifax, which was only reached several days after many of the troopships from Britain had already landed their passengers and military materiel. In order to expedite the last leg of their journey to Riviere du Loup from where they could coordinate the logistical effort, the staff officers then sailed onward to Boston from where they proceeded incognito; wearing only civilian clothing, until they arrived at Montreal. From there, they made their way to Riviere du Loup.[85]

Lieut. Baines and No. 5 Battery on board RMS *Asia* were among those who had already disembarked at Halifax; beating the *Melbourne* to port by a full five days. On the day of his arrival, Henry, like many of his fellow passengers, would have been anxious for the latest details of the "Trent Affair". On obtaining the local newspapers, however, he would have would have read the disappointing news:

> *The British Colonist*, Halifax, Sat. Dec. 28
> Latest advices from Washington: "Our Cabinet, looking to the absorbing and paramount issue — the suppression of this Southern rebellion — will yield to the present demand of England as the conditions of her neutrality, even if these demands involve the restoration of Mason and Slidell to the protection of the British flag and a disavowal of and an apology for their seizure by Captain Wilkes.[86]

> *The British Colonist*, Halifax, Tue. Dec. 31
> SLIDELL AND MASON TO BE RELEASED — Washington, Dec. 28. Mason and Slidell are to be surrendered. This and other peaceful indications show that war with England will not take place.[87]

Within a week, the four Confederate envoys, Mason, Slidell, Eustis and McFarland, were on their way to England aboard the Royal Navy's ship, HMS *Rinaldo*.

Although it would take two more weeks for the official dispatches to reach London, the diplomatic incident which had brought Henry Baines to North America, the "Trent Affair", was essentially over. War between Britain and the Untied States had been averted.

The news elicited a mix of reactions. Most civilians were overjoyed. We can only imagine that Henry Baines, as well as many other soldiers who had recently arrived at Halifax anxious to "tame the Yankee's brag" with "wrath and fire and sword", may have shared the disappointment expressed by Royal Artillery officer Francis Duncan:

> Our world in Halifax was thrown into a great state of disturbance a little before Christmas, 1861, by the celebrated *Trent* affair. The excitement and indignation produced by that insolent act of an insolent Government was only equaled by the longing desires of our community that war would spring of it....
>
> As vessel after vessel arrived with their thousands of picked troops, and hoards of munitions of war, the excitement gave way to a feeling of proud satisfaction that our country had proved true to itself....
>
> [When] it was telegraphed from Washington that the Yankees had submitted to give up Messrs. Mason and Slidell, the feelings of disappointment in every breast were almost ludicrous. We never had an exalted opinion — who has? — of the Yankee nation; but we never thought so meanly of them as this....
>
> But although all chance of war was thus dispelled, there was not accommodation in Halifax for the troops already arrived and on their way from England, and it was at the same time desirable that the force in Canada should be augmented, as, in event of hostilities, our great weakness would be found in the immense undefended frontier of that province.[88]

While the immediate threat of war had passed, tensions between Britain and the United States were still high and would remain so until after the end of the American Civil War. On January 1, *The New York Times* lamented the continuation of military preparations in British North America:

> We are told that, in spite of the peaceful solution of the MASON-SLIDELL difficulty, the war preparations of England will still go on. An impression seems to prevail in the British mind that a war between the two countries will inevitably spring from the present troubles, and as long as

such an impression exists, it would be extremely unwise on our part, if we failed to prepare ourselves for the struggle that may or may not come. The surest way to avert a war is to be fully ready to meet it. Great Britain is acting on this principle.[89]

Further reinforcements of troops from Britain, however, were suspended, but most of those already arrived would remain in British North America until such time as relations between Britain and the United States returned to their pre-war status. On January 4, 1862, the *Illustrated London News* summarized the war preparations that had been made over the previous thirty days:

> The arrangements for dispatching the troops selected for service in Canada have now been entirely completed.
>
> More than 10,000 men have been dispatched with extraordinary celerity, and it is gratifying to know that they have left our shores under circumstances which leave no room for doubt as regards their comfort and efficiency. The extra warm clothing, which has not been procured without difficulty, is of the best quality, and perfectly suited to the sharp winter the men will have to encounter.
>
> The number of transports wholly chartered by the Government is thirteen, all powerful screw-steamers; and in several cases troops have been sent by the Cunard mail-steamers to Halifax.[90]

The army's official "Memoranda of Embarkation of Troops to British North America" show that in all, between Dec. 7, 1861 and Jan. 11, 1862, seventeen ships had set sail from Britain carrying a total of thirteen batteries of Royal Artillery, eight battalions of infantry (including two elite Guards battalions), four companies of Royal Engineers, two battalions of the Military Train, and several dozen commissariat, staff and medical officers totaling 11,161 personnel.[91]

Having decided that it would be prudent to continue with the plan to reinforce the garrisons in Canada, Maj.-Gen. Sir Fenwick Williams ordered the army's commissariat department to coordinate the movement of troops from Halifax to their stations in Quebec, Montreal, Kingston, Toronto, Hamilton and London (Canada West) as expeditiously as possible. Over the following two months, groups of soldiers were regularly ferried by ship from Halifax to Saint John, New Brunswick, from where, with the use of hundreds of horse-drawn sleighs in ten stages, they were

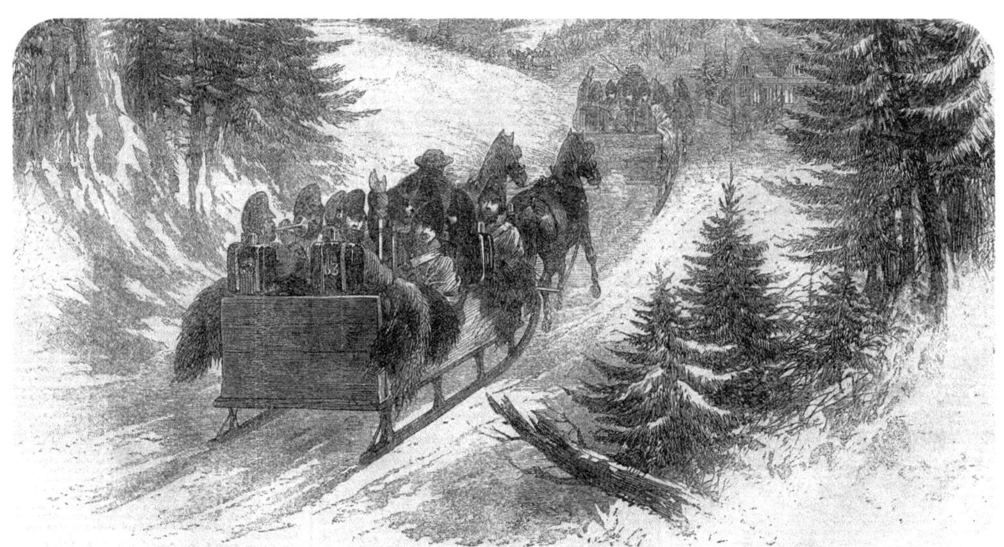

The Reinforcements for Canada Passing Through New Brunswick (detail).
Wood engraving. *The Illustrated London News*, London, 29 Mar. 1862.
[Author's collection]

moved to overnight encampments at Petersville, Fredericton, Tilley's Inn, Woodstock, Florenceville, Tobique, Grand Falls, Little Falls, Fort Ingall and finally to Riviere du Loup where they could board trains for their final destinations at military posts in Canada. At each stage, commissariat staff officers would be on hand to coordinate the accommodation, feeding and the next day's transport of the arriving contingent of troops, and medical officers would look after cases of frostbite and other injuries.

The winter march across New Brunswick operated smoothly, but slowly, and Baines' No. 5 Battery was not scheduled to depart Halifax until early February. As a result, Henry had several weeks to take part in many of the local recreational activities that were popular among the army officers in the city: moose hunting, snowshoeing, skating, sleighing and curling. In addition, as was his habit, Henry explored his new surroundings and made drawings and paintings of local sights in and around Halifax. One of the watercolours he painted there is a view from York Redoubt, a fort at Ferguson's Cove guarding the western entrance to Halifax harbour, where No. 5 Battery was likely in barracks until their departure from the city.

On February 11, Baines and his Battery embarked on the SS *Delta*, sailing the 500 kilometers from Halifax into the Bay of Fundy and landing at Saint John, New Brunswick, two days later. With thousands of soldiers flooding into Saint John, the city "presented a very lively appearance".[92] A bottleneck at this point in the transport system meant that those arriving from Halifax were detained for up to two weeks, so accommodation in Saint John for the transient soldiers was scarce. The town barracks had been hastily expanded from three hundred beds to 1,000, but many of the rank and file had to endure rougher accommodations in empty sheds and warehouses as well as in the government customs house, while the officers were billeted in comfort at Stubbs Hotel.

Soon enough though, No. 5 Battery was on the move again. Lieut. D.T. Irwin, an Artillery officer in No. 1 Battery, left this description of the start of the overland journey in the winter of 1862:

> Got up like the early bird at about 5:30 a.m. this morning, swallowed a hasty hot breakfast, and sallied out of Stubbs' Hotel, to begin our sleigh ride.
>
> We found the sleighs drawn up in line in front of the barracks and soon got them filled with the British gunners. Each sleigh holds eight men besides the driver, the sleigh is a long box, with boards across the top for the men to sit upon. We (the officers) went in sleighs of a much better description. They each hold 5 or 6.
>
> In a few minutes we got the word to start and away we went in single file — 33 sleighs and 212 men.
>
> About noon, we halted at a station in the woods, called Petersville... It is 35 miles from St. John and consists of two or three log huts. [93]

Petersville was located approximately half-way between Saint John and Fredericton and became a convenient stopping place where the troops would sometimes spend their first night in the backwoods. The Scots Guardsman described his experience at that first overnight encampment:

> We arrived at a place called Petersville about 3 p.m.; our quarters was a large log hut, which accommodated 120 of us. There were no beds to sleep on; the floor was covered with branches of the pine tree; each man had only two blankets which we brought with us. The officers had a small hut to themselves, but otherwise they fared no better than we did.
>
> We, as we lay on our backs could see light through the top of the hut,

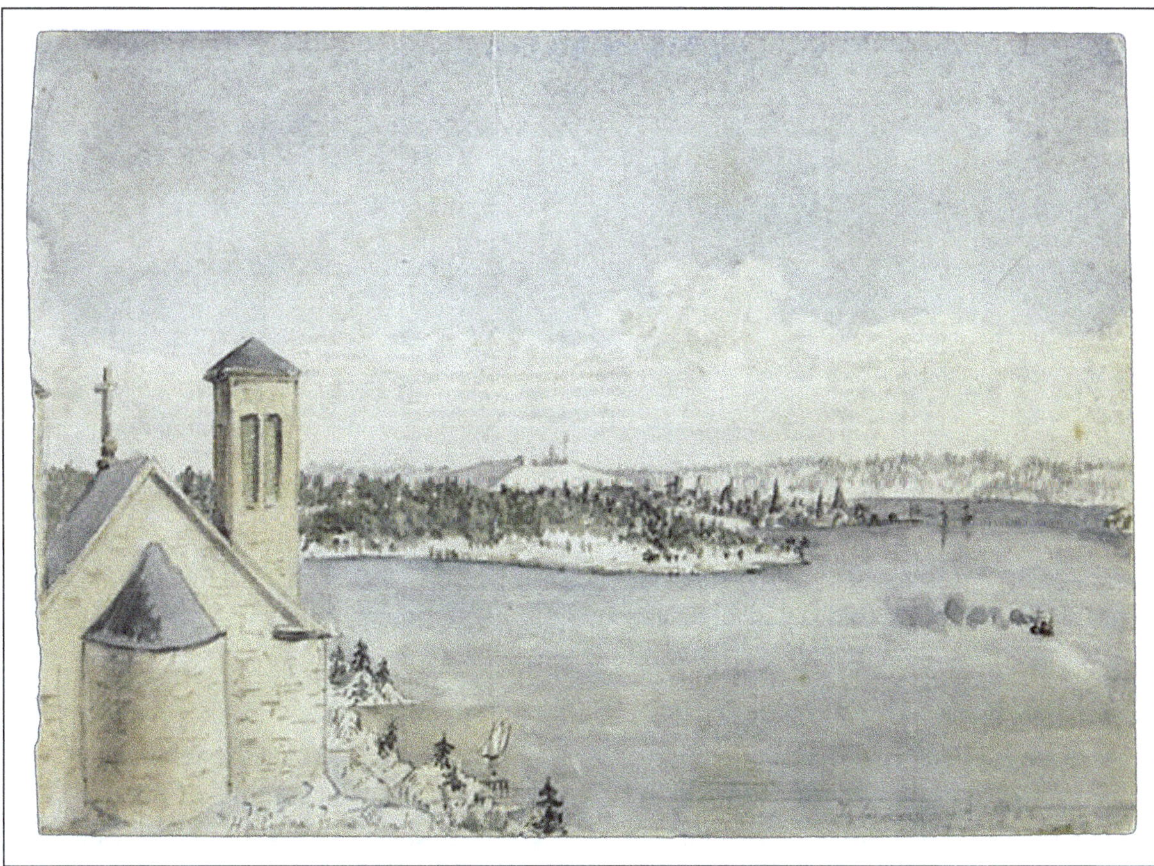

Halifax from York Redoubt, February 7, 1862.
Henry Edward Baines, 1862. Pencil and watercolour on paper.
[Courtesy of Library and Archives Canada.]

From left to right, Baines depicts the Stella Maris Roman Catholic Church, the entrance to the North-West Arm, Point Pleasant and the city and harbour of Halifax. Atop the hill in the background (centre) is the Halifax Citadel.

but although the night was very cold, we did not feel it; a couple of men
were up all night to keep the fires in; there were four stoves in the hut.[94]

The only record left by Henry Baines of his winter march through New
Brunswick is one rough sketch of the soldiers' hut at Petersville.

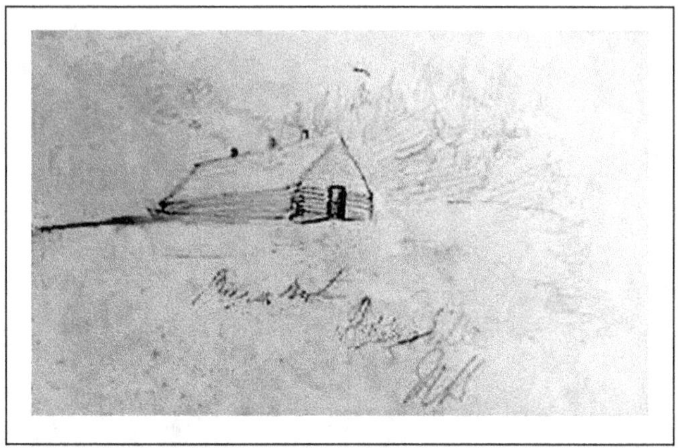

Soldiers Hut, Petersville NB.
Henry Edward Baines, 1862. Pencil on paper.
[Verso of "Halifax from York Redoubt
Courtesy of Library and Archives Canada.]

The sleigh journey typically took ten days to complete; averaging fifty kilometers
every day until Riviere du Loup was reached. From the beginning of January
through to the middle of March, 1862, some 750 soldiers every week successfully
made the cold, snowy journey across New Brunswick. In all, the winter operation
was an overwhelming success, with almost 7,000 soldiers arriving safely in Canada[95].
Upon arrival at Riviere du Loup, No. 5 Battery learned for the first time that their
final destination was to be the City of Toronto in Canada West.

Before proceeding to Toronto, another transportation bottleneck at Riviere du
Loup resulted in further delay as troops waited for the trains that would carry them
westward. After several days, the battery boarded the train for Montreal. An assistant-
surgeon with the Royal Artillery's 4th Brigade described the start of the rail journey:

With a howl from the steam whistle (which is unlike those in England)
we moved off with a sudden jerk. The "cars", as they are called here, are
the same as those used in the United States, and consist of long carriages
with doors at both ends, a passage running through each longitudinally,

with a stove at either end and an iron can containing water for drinking purposes – in addition a portion of each carriage is partitioned off as a saloon. Prefixed to the engine was a snow plough, without which it would have been difficult to make any progress whatever owing to the snow drifts, which always take place when there is any amount of wind. This caused considerable delay, more especially on an incline.[96]

Twenty-five hours later, the train arrived at Montreal. After yet another delay of several days, the officers and gunners of No. 5 Battery left Montreal on the morning of Monday, March 3, on the final leg of their journey. Tremendous snow storms, huge snow drifts and icy tracks forced the train to stop for hours at a time. It took two days to travel the last five hundred kilometers to Toronto. Finally, on March 5, 1862, No. 5 Battery arrived at their final destination. The event was reported in the Toronto *Globe* the following day:

ARRIVAL OF TROOPS.

Last evening, one hundred and ten men and non-commissioned officers belonging to Battery No. 5, 10th Brigade Royal Artillery, under command of Capt. Tweedie, arrived by special train at the Union Depot. They were marched to their quarters at the Parliament Buildings, and are to be permanently located in Toronto. The other officers accompanying the battery, all of whom are staying at the Rossin House, are Lieutenant Baines, Lieutenant Ormsby, Lieutenant Harvey, Dr. Todd and Dr. Woodfield [Woodfull].

The troops left Montreal at half-past eight o'clock on the morning of Monday. The train was much delayed by snow and ice on the track.[97]

Seventy-five days after leaving England, Henry Edward Baines had finally arrived at Toronto, the city that was to be his home for the next three years.

Like most other cities and towns in British North America, Toronto was unprepared for the influx of so many soldiers. The 30th (Cambridgeshire) Regiment, which had been dispatched to Canada aboard the *Great Eastern* the previous summer, had arrived in Toronto in July, 1861. On their arrival, they found there was only accommodation enough for six of the regiment's ten companies. Those quarters consisted of the dilapidated barracks at the Old Fort (now Fort York National Historic Site) situated on the western edge of the city opposite the main entrance to the harbour, and the stone barracks at the New Fort (later renamed Stanley Barracks), located one kilometer further west along the lakeshore on what are now the grounds of the Canadian National Exhibition.[98] The remainder of the regiment had to stay in tents on the Garrison Common (the old Ordnance Reserve, the open expanse of land between the two forts) until the old Parliament buildings on Front Street had been refurbished as living quarters for officers and men.[99]

"E" Battery of the Royal Artillery's 4th Field Brigade had arrived at Toronto in February, 1862. They had been put up at the Parliament buildings until more barracks could be built at the New Fort.[100] When No. 5 Battery arrived in March, the gunners and non-commissioned officers were also housed temporarily at the Parliament buildings while Lieut. Baines and his fellow officers were billeted at the Rossin House, Toronto's premier hotel located three blocks away at the corner of King and York streets. Eventually, the officers and men of the Battery were all moved into barracks at the New Fort.

Two weeks after their arrival in Toronto, on March 20, 1862, No. 5 Battery made their presence officially known in the City of Toronto by mustering the entire unit on the grounds of the Parliament buildings and calling the roll. While all of the officers, sergeants, corporals, bombardiers and gunners were present and correct, the same could not be said of the guns themselves.

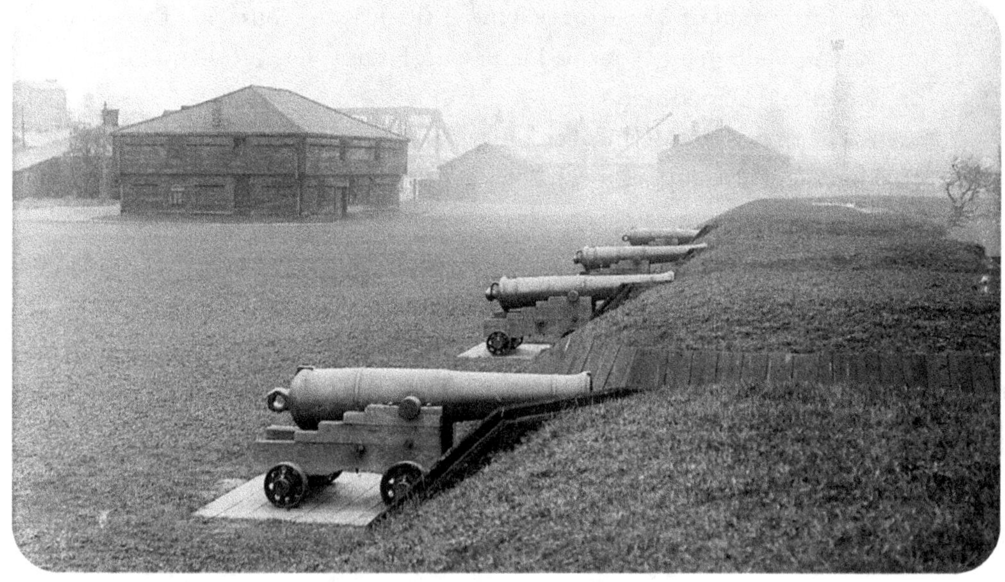

A portion of the 7-gun battery at the Old Fort, Toronto.
Photographer unknown, 1931. Photographic print.
[Courtesy of the City of Toronto Archives. F-16, S71, Item-8577 .]

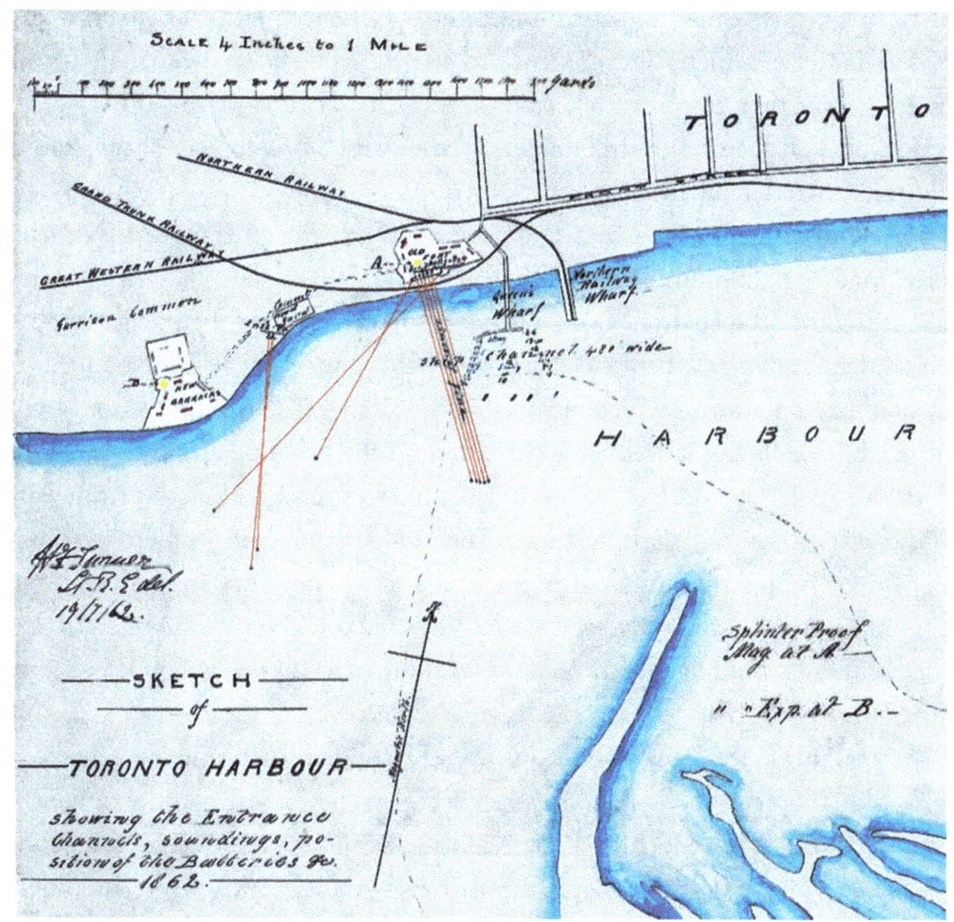

Sketch of Toronto Harbour, 19/7/62 (detail).
Lieut. H.F. Turner, Royal Engineers, 1862. Ink and watercolour on paper.
[Courtesy of Library and Archives Canada.]

This plan shows the "New Barracks" (New Fort) and the Old Fort as well as the gun battery constructed near the wood yard in between the forts. The red lines show the line of fire of the artillery in the batteries. The southern edge of the navigable channel into the harbour is marked with a dotted line. The land at bottom right is the western portion of the sand spit that is now part of the Toronto Islands.

The garrison artillery in place to defend Toronto consisted of only nine serviceable but outdated pieces of ordnance: six 8-inch shell guns and three 32-pounders, all smooth-bore, muzzle-loading guns mounted on fixed platforms in two minor earthwork batteries which were supposed to guard the western entrance to Toronto's harbour.[101] The two gun-batteries, one at the Old Fort, and the other near the garrison wood yard a few hundred meters further west along the lakeshore, had been hastily constructed a few months earlier by soldiers of the 30th Regiment under the direction of an officer of the Royal Engineers.[102] While the guns mounted in the two batteries had a maximum range of more than 2,700 meters — a distance quite sufficient to cover the channel at the entrance to Toronto Bay, the navigable portion of which was situated within 500 meters of the guns — they were mounted on antiquated fixed platforms which meant that they had to fire through embrasures cut in the earthen walls instead of being mounted on the more common traversing type of platforms which would have allowed the guns to fire *en barbette* over the walls of the battery. As a result, the gunners would be unable to reposition their guns quickly enough to keep up a continuous fire on a passing enemy ship. Instead, they would have to wait until the ship sailed across the gun's fixed line of fire at which time each gun detachment would have only one or two chances to hit the target before it sailed past the gunner's sights.

By September, 1862, two more guns would be added to Toronto's meager arsenal bringing the total number of serviceable pieces to eleven. In addition, there were another six guns; three 8-inch and three older 24-pounders, that might be rendered serviceable in a pinch, but since they lacked carriages and platforms they were completely unusable until they could be properly mounted.[103] Lieut. Baines and the thirty men under his direct command would have been responsible for three of the serviceable guns; keeping them well maintained and ready for action at a moment's notice.

With the approach of spring, Henry Baines settled into his Toronto home with its new routines and its potential for new adventures. His greatest challenge however, the one faced by every soldier in a colonial, peacetime garrison, would be dealing with boredom. Henry's solution to this problem would be two-fold: pursuing his long-time love of painting and drawing, and developing a passion for yachting.

Part 2

THE ARTIST

The Toronto that Henry Baines saw when he arrived in 1862 was a small but rapidly growing city. The French had built a fur trading post there in 1750, and John Graves Simcoe, the first lieutenant-governor of Upper Canada, had established the town of York at that location in 1793. Simcoe made York the capital of the province in 1797, but the town remained a provincial backwater until after the War of 1812. In 1834, it was incorporated as the City of Toronto with a population of 9,000. By the time Henry arrived in the city, the capital had been moved to Quebec but Toronto's population had grown to 45,000[1], and the city was prospering with eight banks, twenty hotels, and a wide variety of commercial and manufacturing businesses as well as a university with a school of medicine, two daily newspapers and rail and steamboat connections to all major cities in the province and to many parts of the United States.[2]

During the War of 1812, York had been captured and sacked by American forces. As a result, following the war, the town's defences were strengthened, as were those in other parts of Canada. However, as years of peaceful coexistence with the United States stretched into decades, many of the forts and barracks along the frontier were allowed to deteriorate; the Imperial government having opted to concentrate its limited defence dollars on maintaining the fortifications at Quebec and Kingston rather than on points of lesser strategic importance like Toronto. Acts of armed rebellion in Upper and Lower Canada in 1837 and 1838 spurred some minor military construction projects, including a large barracks at Toronto's Old Fort and a new barracks complex known as the New Fort. However, by 1862, Toronto was, for the most part, utterly defenceless. It was only in the aftermath of the "Trent Affair" that a military commission was hastily formed to draw up plans for new military installations at Niagara, Toronto, Belleville, Kingston, and Quebec City. Even then, the British parliament refused to spend heavily on new colonial defences.[3]

Even though the "Trent Affair" had been officially resolved by the beginning of 1862, relations between Britain and the United States remained strained for the duration of the American Civil War (1861 to 1865). Issues such as continued blockade-running by British-registered ships into Southern ports, and the sale to the Confederacy of British-built ships like the commerce raiders *Florida*, *Georgia* and *Alabama*, kept tensions high between the two countries. In addition, the United States government disliked the British practice of allowing Confederate soldiers and spies to live and move freely in Canada. When this situation led to attacks on U.S. ports on Lake Erie (1863 and 1864)[4] and at St. Albans, Vermont (1864)[5] by Confederate soldiers infiltrating from Canada, tensions mounted further. Meanwhile, Canadians resented the activities of American "crimps" who illegally recruited thousands of British subjects on British territory for service in the United States Army, and Americans resented the British practice of allowing deserters from the Union Army to reside in Canada.

The net effect of these tensions was that the regiments stationed in Canada had to be prepared to be called out for active service on a moment's notice. However, until that callout, the soldiers had to contend with the monotony of garrison duty in Canada. For Lieut. Baines, garrison life in Toronto quickly became a life of predictable routine: Daily assembly of the Battery at reveillé at sunrise and "retreat" at sunset; duty as subaltern-of-the-day, perhaps once a week, mounting the guards at the New Fort and inspecting the soldiers' barracks, cook houses, canteens and reading rooms; church parade every Sunday, and mustering the Battery for inspection once a month.[6]

To relieve the monotony and to keep the gunners sharp, every few weeks No. 5 Battery marched out to the nearby earthwork gun batteries where Toronto's only serviceable long-range artillery pieces were in place to defend the harbour, and there they would engage in gunnery practice; firing on floating targets placed offshore in Lake Ontario.[7] The standard routine of garrison duty was only broken by the occasional field day with the local militia and volunteer forces or by a special garrison-wide parade for a general inspection or a notable occasion such as Queen Victoria's birthday. In all, Lieut. Baines' military duties would have occupied as few as a dozen days every month.

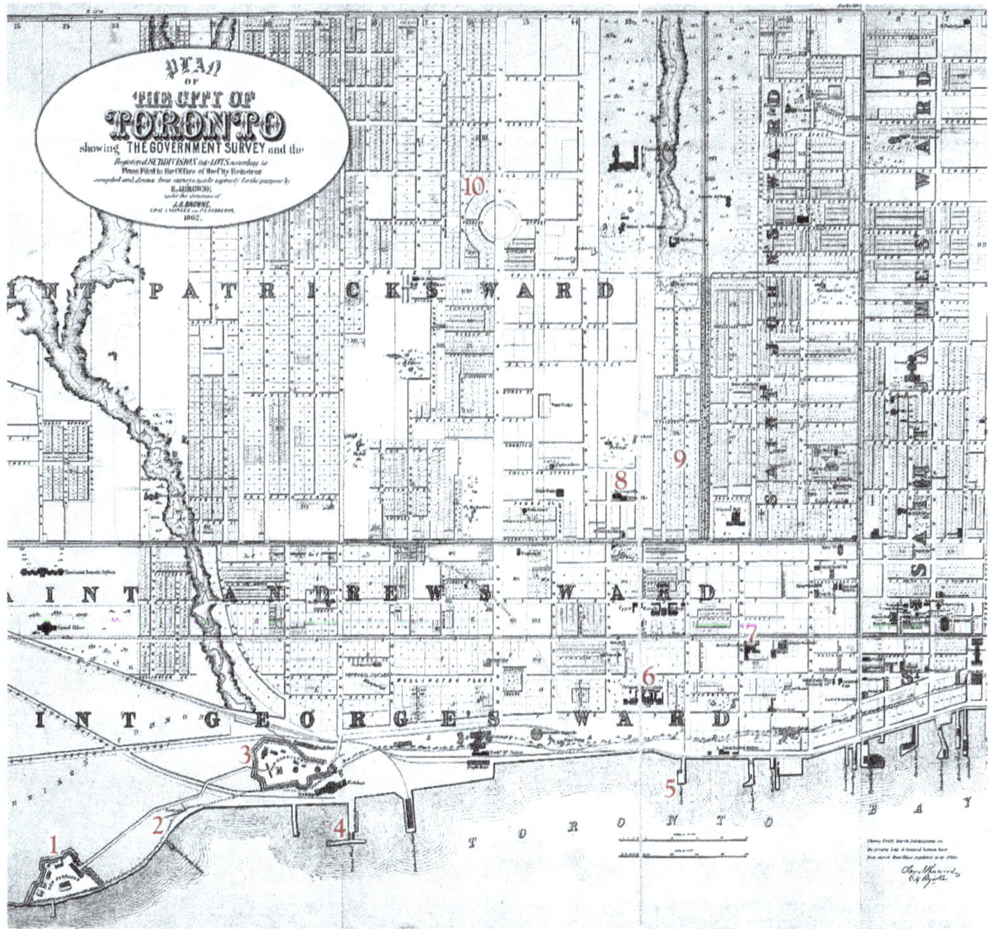

Plan of the City of Toronto, 1862 (detail).
H.J. Browne, 1862. Lithograph
[Courtesy of Toronto Public Library.]

1 - New Fort where No. 5 Battery was in barracks from 1862 to 1865.
2 - Wood Yard battery for two 32-pounders.
3 - Battery at the Old Fort for six 8-inch guns and one 32-pounder.
4 - Queen's Wharf at the foot of Bathurst Street.
5 - Rees' Wharf where the R.C.Y.C. clubhouse was located.
6 - Parliament buildings where the rank and file of No. 5 Battery were first billetted on arriving in Toronto.
7 - Rossin House hotel where the officers of No. 5 Battery were first billetted on arriving in Toronto.
8 - St. George's Church where Capt. Charles Clarkson married Henrietta Coxwell in 1863 and where Isabelle Baines married Alexander Mitchell in 1876.
9 - 30 William St. where Thomas Baines lived with his family and where Isabelle Baines later stayed for a several months.
10 - 81 Wilcocks St. where Isabelle's daughter, Kate Mitchell Boddington, later lived with her husband Dr. David Boddington and their children.

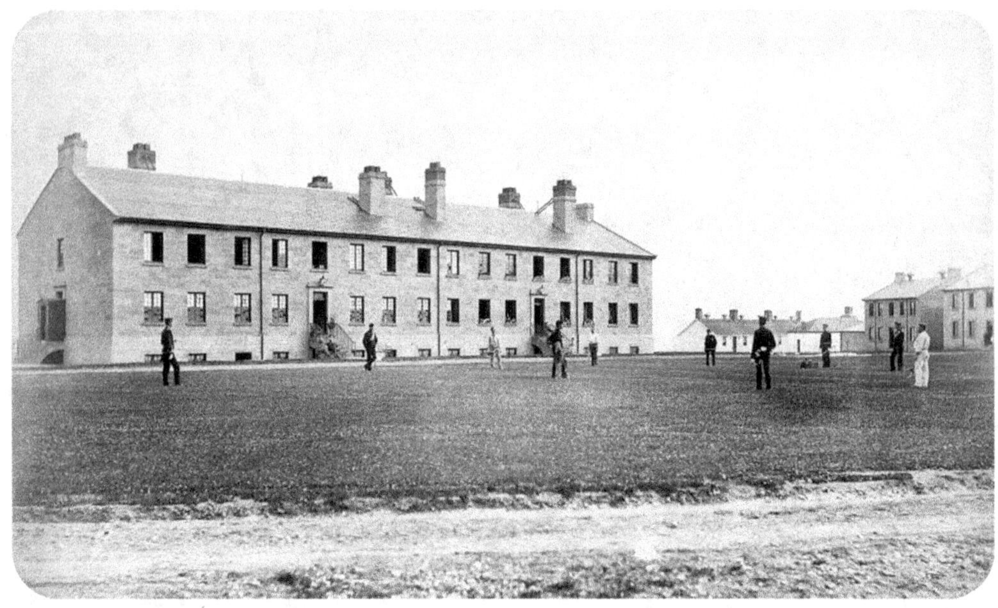

New Fort Barracks Toronto.
Photographer unknown, 1884. Photographic print.
[Courtesy of the City of Toronto Archives, Toronto, Canada. S-327, Sub-1, File-19.]

This photograph shows the officers' quarters at the New Fort where Henry Baines lived
from 1862 until 1865.

Whenever he was not on duty — up to twenty days per month (not including
furloughs) — Lieut. Baines, like the other officers in the Toronto garrison, was free to
partake in the endless rounds of tea parties, soirees, excursions to the countryside,
amateur theatricals and public concerts. The Toronto *Globe* described one ball that
Henry would have attended in September 1862:

THE YACHT CLUB BALL

The company was exceedingly select, and embraced many of the most
respectable of the residents of Toronto, besides many strangers. And besides
being a respectable, it was also an exceedingly brilliant assembly. A large
number of military officers were present, belonging to almost every branch
of the service, so that scarlet and blue were predominant colours. The ladies
turned out in very 'effective' style, and formed a very fair representation of
the beauty of the city. The Music Hall, at which place the ball was held,
was decorated with numerous flags belonging to the Club, and from each
gas branch was hung a cage containing a canary, a novel decoration by the
way, but at the same time a very pretty one.

> Dancing was commenced at half-past nine o'clock, and continued with spirit to the delightful music of the 30th [Regiment] band, until the programme was finished. Refreshments, including supper, were provided by Mr. Webb, of Yonge street.... The wines and refreshments were of first-rate quality, and did the purveyor much credit. All present enjoyed themselves in the highest degree.[8]

Army officers were part of high society in the colonies and they took part in all of the activities expected of that social class. In Toronto, that also meant joining the Tandem Club, the Mechanics' Institute and the Royal Canadian Yacht Club. Sporting activities such as hunting and fishing were also popular among the officers and many of them participated in a variety of team sports, especially soccer and cricket. In the winter, other diversions were available such as skating parties, sleigh rides and ice-boating on Toronto Bay.

Two of Baines' friends, fellow lieutenant Henry Harvey, and Assistant-Surgeon Samuel Woodfull, are mentioned frequently by name in Toronto newspaper notices of theatrical presentations, musical concerts and other events. Many other officers of the Toronto garrison are also mentioned by name as participants in various social gatherings and sporting activities such as cricket matches and soccer games. Henry Baines' name, however is never mentioned. It would appear that Henry had little interest either in sports or in the performing arts. Instead, he preferred to participate in other, less public activities. One of these activities, one which few other soldiers in any foreign garrison could indulge in, was visiting with relatives.

Henry's uncle, Thomas Baines along with his wife and children, lived at 30 William Street (now St. Patrick Street) in Toronto, an easy fifteen-minute carriage ride from the New Fort. Thomas Baines was the older brother of Henry's father, Egerton. Thomas had immigrated to Canada in 1825, and had quickly secured a civil service position with the Crown Lands Office. In 1833, he was appointed secretary of the Clergy Corporation with responsibility for leasing clergy land and collecting rents from tenants. After the corporation's dissolution in 1838, he continued working for the Crown Lands Office as a Land Agent for York County, selling Crown Land to new immigrants to Canada. Thomas was a well-respected resident of Toronto and held a commission as an officer in the 1st West Toronto militia regiment. His meager civil servant's salary was augmented by the profits from several successful business ventures. He established the West Toronto Brewing Company in 1844 and by the 1850's he was on the board of directors of several corporations including the Victoria Mining Company, the Western Assurance Company and the Toronto & Georgian Bay Canal Company.[9]

In 1856, the questionable accounting practices of the Crown Lands Department came under investigation by the provincial legislature. Dozens of Land Agents were found to be in default of remitting payments to the Receiver-General after selling plots of land. Most of the amounts in default were less than £100, and a few were more than £300. Thomas Baines, however, was found to be in default of more than £9,000[10] (the equivalent of more than US$1.2 million in 2016). He was suspended from his position and, in order to prevent further scandal, he resigned as Crown Lands Agent. Many of his assets, however, were seized by the government to make up for the funds that had gone missing.

It is likely that Henry Baines took little notice of Uncle Thomas' legal and financial troubles while spending some of his off-duty hours at 30 William St. While there, he may have spent time painting and drawing with his cousin Egerton.[11] Both Henry and Egerton have left sketches of the house on William Street, and Egerton is also known to have been something of a portrait painter.[12]

Another activity with which Henry occupied many of his leisure hours was going on painting and drawing excursions in and around Toronto, at places such as Dundas near Hamilton, and Niagara Falls. The young artillery officer who had stepped off the train on that cold winter day in March 1862 may have been a soldier by profession, but he was an artist by vocation. Henry had been drawing and painting from a young age, an interest undoubtedly fostered by his mother, Mary, who, like many of her middle-class and upper-class contemporaries in mid-19th Century Britain, had taken up watercolour painting as a recreational pastime.[13]

Mary Rice had grown up in an affluent middle-class family that was well connected to the art world of early 19th Century Britain. Her mother's uncle was the prominent English landscape and portrait artist Henry Edridge (1768-1821). It may have been from uncle Henry, or perhaps from any number of his artist friends such as David Wilkie (1785-1841) or William Collins (1788-1847), that Mary was given formal instruction in painting and drawing.[14] One watercolour by her, a view of the Saint Laurence church at Ludlow, Shropshire, painted in 1847, is in the documentary art collection of Library and Archives Canada.[15]

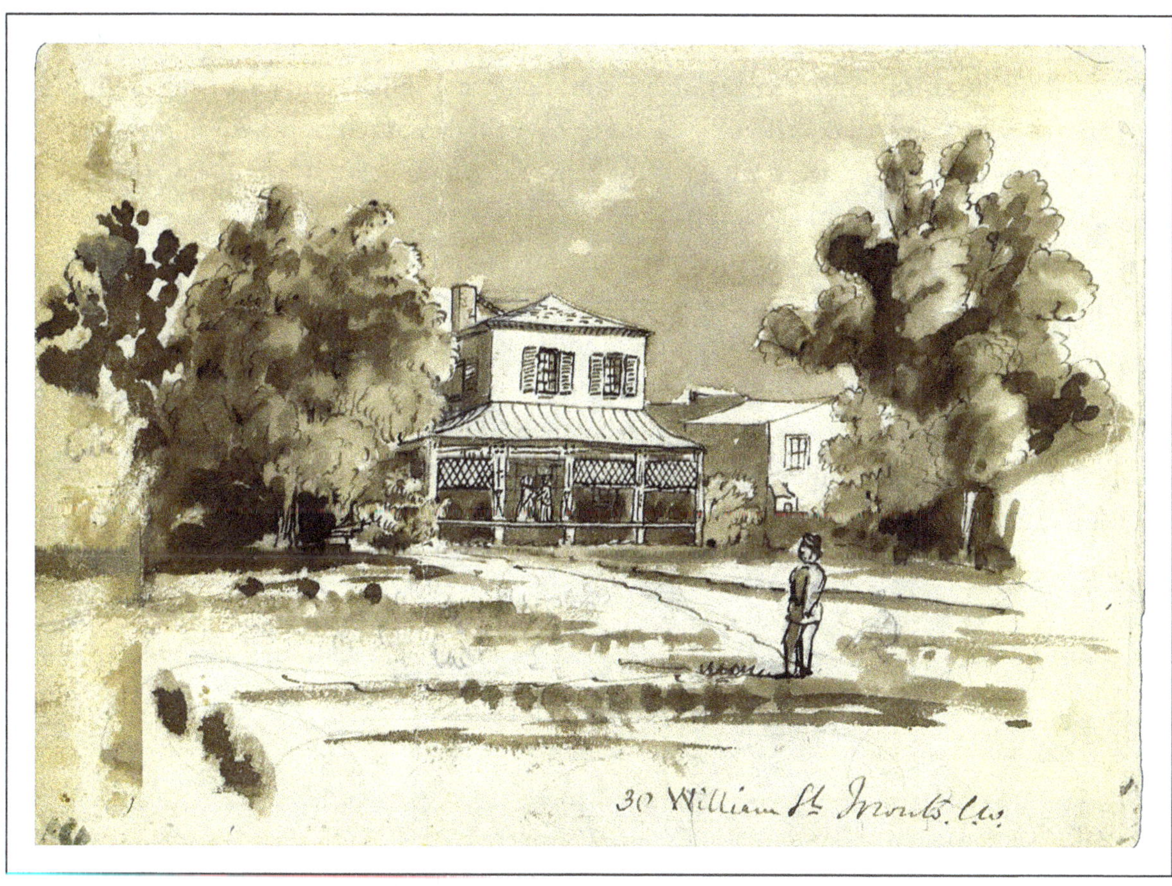

30 William St. Toronto, C.W. (Canada West)
Henry Edward Baines, c.1863. Brown wash over ink on paper.
[Courtesy of Library and Archives Canada.]

It is likely that Mary passed on her painting and drawing skills to her son, who may also have had further art instruction from a professional artist. Any early art training that Henry may have received from his mother or from a drawing master would have had some degree of influenced his later artistic style.

Whatever the source of his drawing and painting skills, Henry's artistic ability may well have been a contributing factor to his being admitted to the Royal Military Academy in 1858 at age eighteen. Not only did candidates for admission to the Academy require a solid grounding in Mathematics, but, at the time, it was strongly suggested that, "... the future studies of each candidate will be very materially forwarded if he has learnt to draw before he is received as a cadet."[16] In addition to drawing detailed plans of fortifications and siege works, the engineers and artillery officers that the Academy produced would be required to accurately depict local topography and troop positions in order to provide military commanders with a view of the ground that might be used as a defensive position or to gain a tactical advantage over enemy forces. For that reason, landscape drawing was part of the

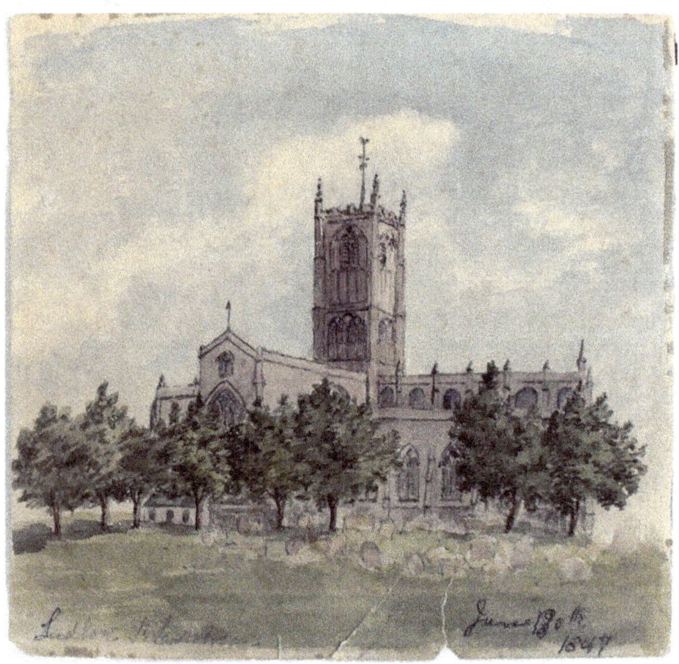

Ludlow St. Laurence, June 13, 1847.
Mary Rice Baines, 1847. Watercolour on paper.
[Courtesy of Library and Archives Canada.]

curriculum at Woolwich, and remained so long after photography was introduced as a "voluntary class" in the Academy's course of instruction in 1865.[17]

Throughout the late 18th and early 19th centuries, a succession of professional civilian artists was employed as landscape drawing masters at RMA Woolwich. These included the renowned English landscape painter Paul Sandby, as well as prominent artists such as Thales Fielding, James Bridges, William Ranwell, Aaron Penley and many others who taught the gentlemen-cadets the fundamentals of landscape drawing and painting.

Over the course of more than a century, the Royal Military Academy produced more than fifty gentlemen-cadets whose artistic talents are known largely by the artwork that they subsequently created while stationed in British North America.[18] From the fall of New France in 1760, to the departure of British troops from the Dominion of Canada in 1871, a total of more than two hundred military men from all branches of the British forces, mostly officers, produced thousands of paintings, drawings and engravings depicting Canadian scenes.

Most of these artist-officers are known only from one or two works that have survived or were used as the basis of engravings to illustrate a published account of travels through Canada. Some sixty of these artist-officers served in the Royal Navy and were stationed either on the Atlantic coast or the Pacific coast, or took part in one or more of the numerous Arctic expeditions of the 19th Century. These included artists such as Richard Short (active 1745-1766) and George Back (1796-1878). Almost one hundred were infantry officers who were either on active service in Canada, stationed in Canadian garrisons, or simply visited North America as tourists. These included James Peachy (active 1773-1797) of the 60th (Royal American) Regiment and Henry Francis Ainslie (1803-1879) of the 83rd Regiment, as well as medical officers such as Edward Walsh (1766-1832) with the 49th (Hertfordshire) Regiment and George Russell Dartnell (1798-1878) with the 1st (Royal) Regiment. Still others were Woolwich-educated officers of the Royal Engineers, numbering more than thirty, including the highly prolific and very talented Philip John Bainbrigge (1817-1881). Artist-officers of the Royal Artillery who served in Canada numbered as few as twenty, but this group includes several very talented men whose work has been well documented such as Thomas Davies (1737-1812), James Pattison Cockburn (1778-1847) and Canada-born John Herbert Caddy (1801-1887).

By the second half of the 19th Century, with photography equipment becoming more widespread and easier to use, there were fewer British Army officers stationed in North America who were painting landscapes to document their time in Canada. Their presence would come to an end altogether in 1871 when the bulk of the British Army left Canada for good. Henry Edward Baines was among the last of the artist-officers of the Royal Artillery known to have produced a significant body of work documenting scenes of early Canada.[19]

Canadian art historians have published dozens of lists of artists who created Canadian art; that is, art produced in Canada or depicting scenes of any place within the political borders of modern Canada. The works of thousands of artists, including many of these British artist-officers, have been meticulously catalogued. Very few of these catalogues, however, include the name of Henry Edward Baines, and those that do typically note only one or two of his works. Even then, they usually wrongly state his name as Henry "Egerton" Baines even though his birth record and all of his military records clearly state his name as Henry Edward Baines.[20] Furthermore, none of these catalogues gives any indication that, during his short life, Henry Edward Baines produced a significant body of work now known to comprise at least one hundred watercolour paintings, pen-and-ink drawings and pencil sketches, mostly Canadian landscapes, created between 1862 and 1866. There is also scant mention in any of these publications that Baines' talent as an artist was only beginning to be developed when he died at Quebec in 1866 at the age of 26. This omission is surprising, especially considering his large body of known work which, in its entirety, clearly places Henry Edward Baines among the ranks of the other important artist-officers who produced a remarkable visual record of Canada in the 18th and 19th centuries. A complete catalogue of his known works is included in the Appendix.

Like his brother officers who painted and sketched Canadian scenes, Baines is classified as an amateur artist; a status more descriptive of his form of paid employment rather than of his artistic ability. While many of these amateur artist-officers were talented, they generally did not present their art at public exhibitions, nor did they create their art in order to earn a living: they were professional soldiers first and artists second. Their drawings and paintings were done largely for their own pleasure.

Professional artists in Canada contemporary with Henry Edward Baines — painters like Cornelius Krieghoff, Paul Kane, William Cresswell, Frederick Verner and many others — made art for a living.[21] They painted landscapes which they showed and sold at public exhibitions, and many of them also painted portraits on a commission basis. Most professional artists were classically trained in drawing, perspective, brush technique, colour, and rendering the human form, and many professionals produced their masterpieces almost exclusively in oil paint on canvas or board. Pencil, pen-and-ink and watercolour sketches in small-format sketch books were reserved for their field work *en plein air*. Some professionals did paint with water-colours, but they usually worked in their well-equipped studios where they often created much larger, finished paintings from their field sketches.

Amateur artists, on the other hand, usually worked with the more portable materials of the watercolour sketch-artist, filling the pages of small sketchbooks with pencil drawings which might later be tinted and embellished with watercolours, or producing fully finished paintings on the spot. This medium, with its easily transported materials — a small box of water-soluble colours, a sketch pad, a pencil, a few paint brushes and a small vessel for water — was much more suited to the active life of a soldier than the oils, pigments, thinners, palettes, canvases and easels used by most professional artists.

In many cases, the artist-officers of the British Army were simply carrying on the English tradition of landscape watercolour painting which had become popular among both professional and amateur artists in Britain during the 18th Century. Highly regarded professional artists such as Paul Sandby (1731-1809), Thomas Girtin (1775-1802) and J.M.W. Turner (1775-1851) had legitimized the use of watercolours as a professional art medium in Britain, and this mode of artistic expression was taken up as a leisure pursuit by many in the British upper classes who were taught landscape painting and drawing by professional artists. Since the majority of officers in the British Army were from this rank of society, those who indulged in art as an amateur pastime likely had some artistic ability as well as some formal training before entering the army. Painting landscapes in watercolour remained a popular pastime in Britain well into the 19th Century, by which time it had been taken up by many in the middle classes as well. In the 1860's, at the height of Henry Baines' artistic career, this "English School" of painting was characterized in the *Illustrated London News* as "... a purely English art which is every day assuming more importance and producing works of wider scope and loftier pretension, arriving at length at the highest poetry of design.... Yea, though applicable with judicious reserve to other purposes, water-colour painting finds its true and widest field in landscape subjects."[22]

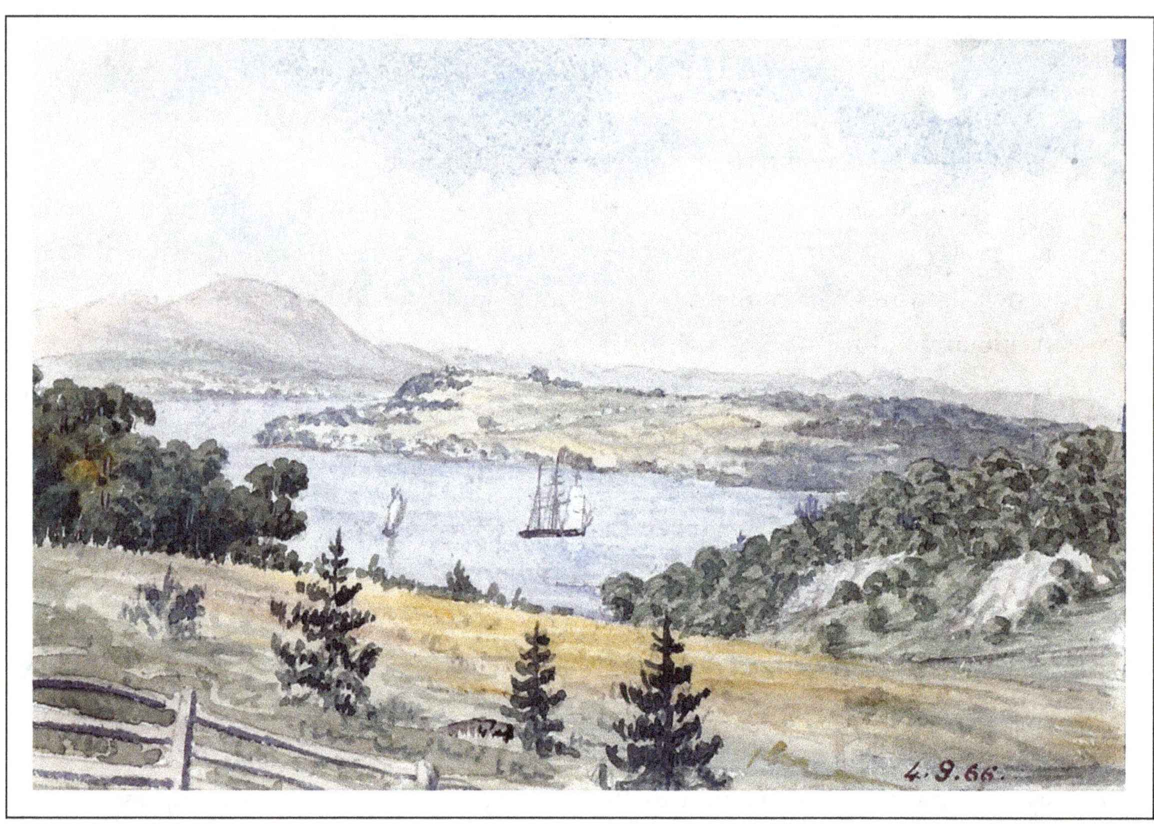

Untitled, 4/9/66 (View of Ile d'Orleans).
Henry Edward Baines, 1866. Watercolour and pencil on paper.
[Donated to Library and Archives Canada by T.B. Cluett, 2017.]

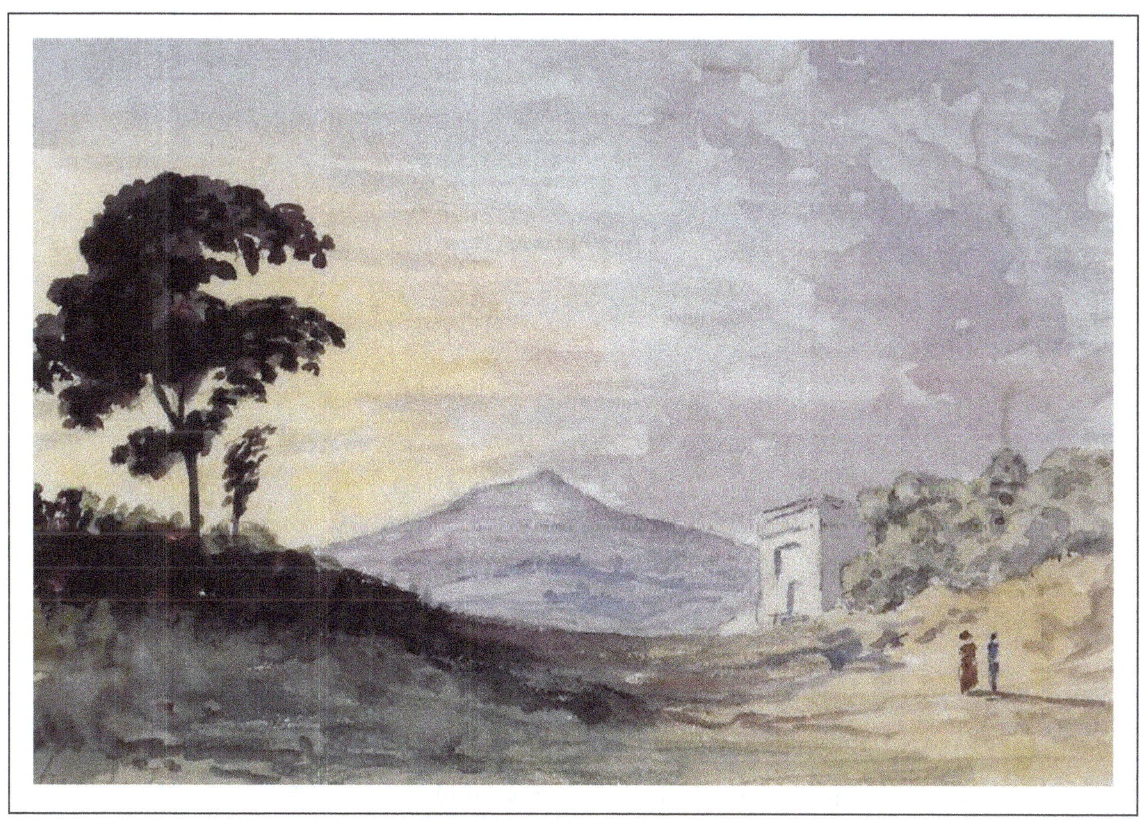

Untitled (Distant view of Mont Ste. Anne).
Henry Edward Baines, c.1865. Watercolour on paper.
[Donated to Library and Archives Canada by T.B. Cluett, 2017.]

Officers of the Royal Artillery and Royal Engineers, many of whom were from the middle classes, had the additional benefit of formal art instruction while attending the Royal Military Academy at Woolwich,[23] so it was not uncommon to find officers from these corps who painted watercolour landscapes of the places where they were stationed. While Henry Edward Baines likely had some training in painting and drawing before entering the Academy, it was at Woolwich where his artistic skills were further developed under the guidance of the Academy's landscape drawing master, the noted watercolour landscape painter James Bridges (1802-1865), who undoubtedly exerted some measure of influence on Henry's developing painting and drawing style. Bridges was known for his Picturesque watercolour landscapes, many of which he had shown at the annual exhibitions of the Royal Academy of Arts in London between 1835 and 1858.[24] It was his skill in drawing and painting landscapes that likely earned him his position as Landscape Drawing Master at the Royal Military Academy.

Like many professional landscape painters of his day, a great deal of Bridges' work conformed to the aesthetic ideal of the Picturesque. The Picturesque was a way of depicting a natural landscape in a coherent, ordered manner, often with distinct tonal planes from darker in the foreground to lighter in the background; the scene frequently being framed by trees or buildings or mountains, and often with a winding road or waterway to lead the viewer's eye along a path to a distant horizon. Any human figures appearing in the painting would usually be seen with their backs to the viewer, directing their gaze toward the horizon and beckoning the viewer to do the same.[25] Bridges would have emphasized the compositional elements of the Picturesque when teaching the gentlemen-cadets at the Royal Military Academy.

Aspects of the Picturesque aesthetic can be seen in several of Henry Baines' paintings. Such works include his "View of Isle d'Orleans" (page 78) and "Distant View of Mont Ste. Anne" (page 79), both painted while he was stationed at Quebec from 1865 to 1866.

The larger part of Baines' known paintings, however, are more exact depictions of the places he visited and the things he saw. Many of his landscapes were painted in a topographical style. These were more accurate representations of a place as he observed it; a quality that would be of greater value for military purposes than the more creative, but perhaps less exact, Picturesque renderings. Where Picturesque works might include elements such as a stream or trees or buildings that had been added to the scene or embellished for effect (but may not really exist in that particular landscape), a purely topographical work depicted the land and its features with greater precision, in as much detail as possible, with geographic and architectural elements placed where they should be, and the entire scene rendered with the proper perspective. The most rudimentary topographical drawings could be simple pencil sketches tinted with light washes of watercolour. More sophisticated topographical paintings were done with light pencil outlines and watercolour more deliberately and exactly applied. These were more typical of Henry Baines' works. Examples of these include "Dartmouth 15 Oct/61" (page 82), painted before he was sent to British North America, and "Port Dalhousie 20/7/63" (page 83), showing the north entrance of the Welland Canal painted two years later. In both of these works, the amount of detail of the land, buildings and ships that Baines captured is notable, and spoke to the topographical tradition.

Generally, Baines' style was highly representational; depicting what he saw, in a precise manner, in order to convey visually as much information as possible. This style would have been in keeping with his occupational training as an artillery officer. In this regard, Henry Edward Baines may have also been influenced by another British artist-officer, Lieut.-Col. Philip John Bainbrigge, who was Professor of Fortifications in the Practical Class at RMA Woolwich while Baines was a gentleman-cadet at the Academy. Bainbrigge had served with the Royal Engineers in Canada from 1836 to 1842, where he painted many landscapes in watercolour.[26] While it is unknown to what extent Lieut.-Col. Bainbrigge may have influenced the art of Henry Edward Baines, many similarities can be seen in several of the paintings of each of these artists.[27]

While landscapes were Henry Baines' preferred subject, he also painted buildings, monuments, steamships, sailboats, and even a few portraits. Henry was not a skilled figurative painter — a trait not uncommon among amateur artists who lacked the rigorous life-drawing lessons of professional artists — but he did execute a number of paintings and drawings which included human subjects, as well as at least two simple portraits. Among these are "Maryborough C.W." (page 155) and "Sodus Point Village, N.Y." (page 177), both painted in 1863 and both showing figures drawn in a simple, naïve manner, and "Portrait of a Woman Reading" (page 85) painted three years later.

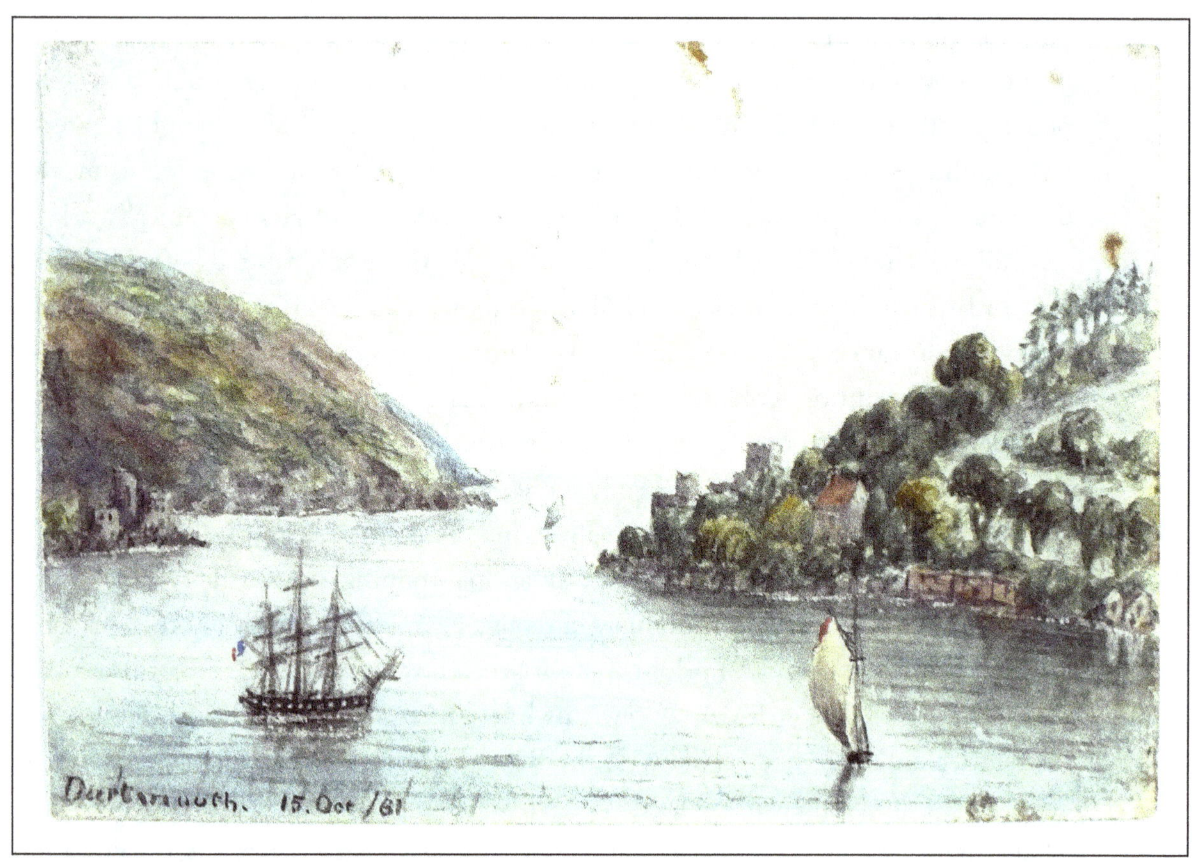

Dartmouth [Devon, U.K.], **15 Oct/61.**
Henry Edward Baines, 1861. Watercolour and pencil on paper.
[Courtesy of Library and Archives Canada.]

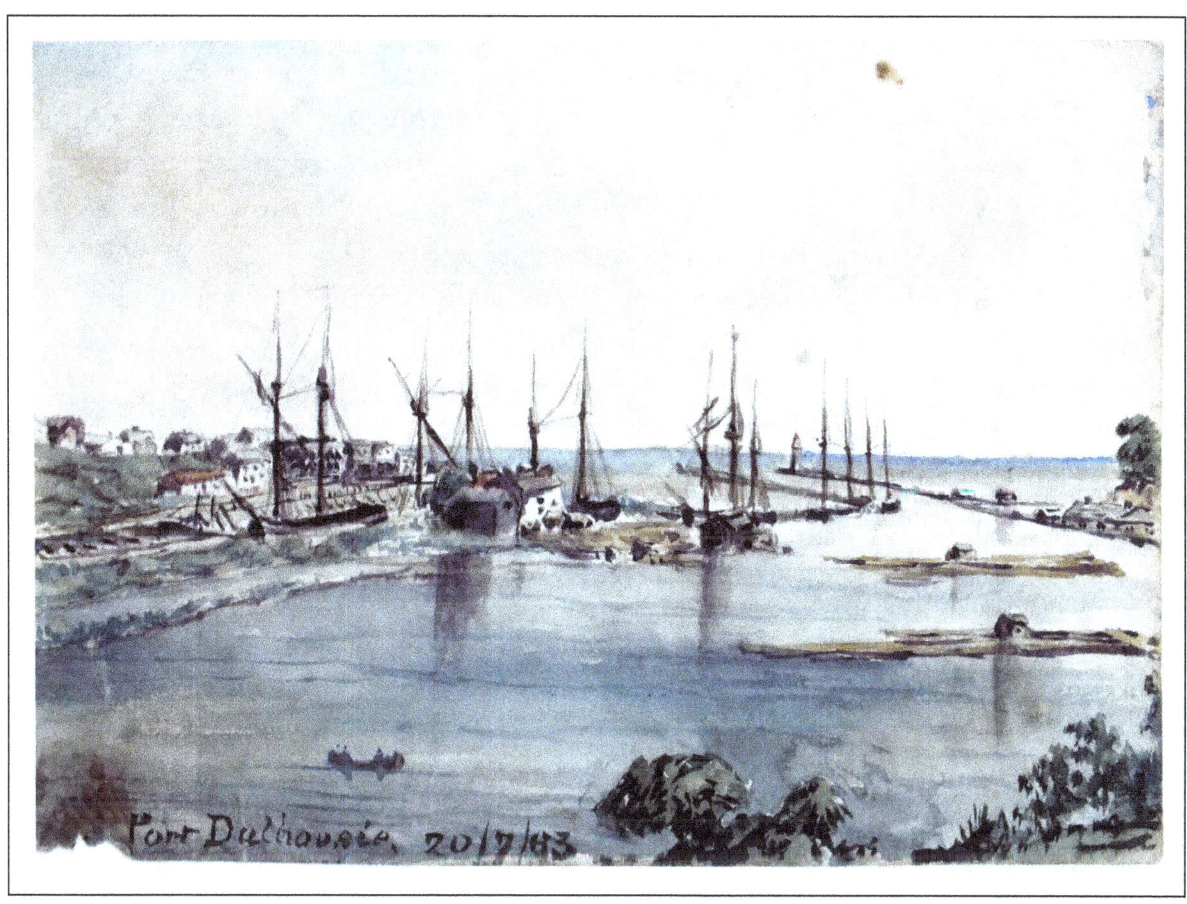

Port Dalhousie, 20/7/63.
Henry Edward Baines, 1863. Watercolour and pencil and ink on paper.
[Courtesy of Library and Archives Canada.]

While the artistic influences from both his childhood and from his time at RMA Woolwich likely shaped Baines' painting style, it is also possible that the work of a variety of professional artists influenced his later works. One of his later water-colours, "Ship sailing past icebergs" (page 86) painted c. 1866, is a highly impressionistic and romantic rendering of a ship in the fog passing close by a number of fantastic icebergs. This work is vaguely reminiscent of some of the "atmospheric" paintings of the British landscape watercolour master, J.M.W. Turner.[28] While still in Britain, Baines may well have been familiar with Turner's work, as well as with the work of many other professional artists.[29]

By the 1860's, an increasing number of professional artists were also working in British North America. Artists such as Paul Kane, Daniel Fowler, William Cresswell and Robert Whale either lived in Toronto or exhibited in Toronto while Henry Baines lived there, so he may have seen their work. Two of Baines' paintings are reminiscent of some of the well known genre scenes painted by renowned artist, Cornelius Krieghoff. Baines' watercolours, "The Tobogganing Party" (page 87) and its companion piece, "Family Snowshoeing in Quebec" (see Appendix), show many compositional similarities to some of Krieghoff's works. It is unlikely that Krieghoff and Baines ever met, but Krieghoff did exhibit in Toronto while Baines was living there, and his paintings were highly praised at the time.[30]

While it is possible that Henry Edward Baines came into contact with, and may have been influenced by some of the professional artists who were working in Canada at the same time that he was stationed in the colony, one professional artist that Baines certainly knew personally was William Armstrong (1822-1914). Armstrong was a railway engineer by training and had started working as a photographer, art teacher and professional painter after he arrived in Toronto in 1851. He was a founding member of the Royal Canadian Yacht Club and was the club's secretary at the same time that Henry was a member of the club. By 1865, just before Lieut. Baines was transferred with his Battery to Quebec, the two men served on the club's executive committee together.[31] Armstrong was a prolific and talented landscape painter, executing magnificent views of Toronto harbour and regattas on Lake Ontario as well numerous detailed transportation scenes and landscapes of the upper Great Lakes when he later accompanied General Wolseley's expedition to the Red River in 1870.[32] To what extent Armstrong influenced Henry Baines' art will remain a matter for speculation.

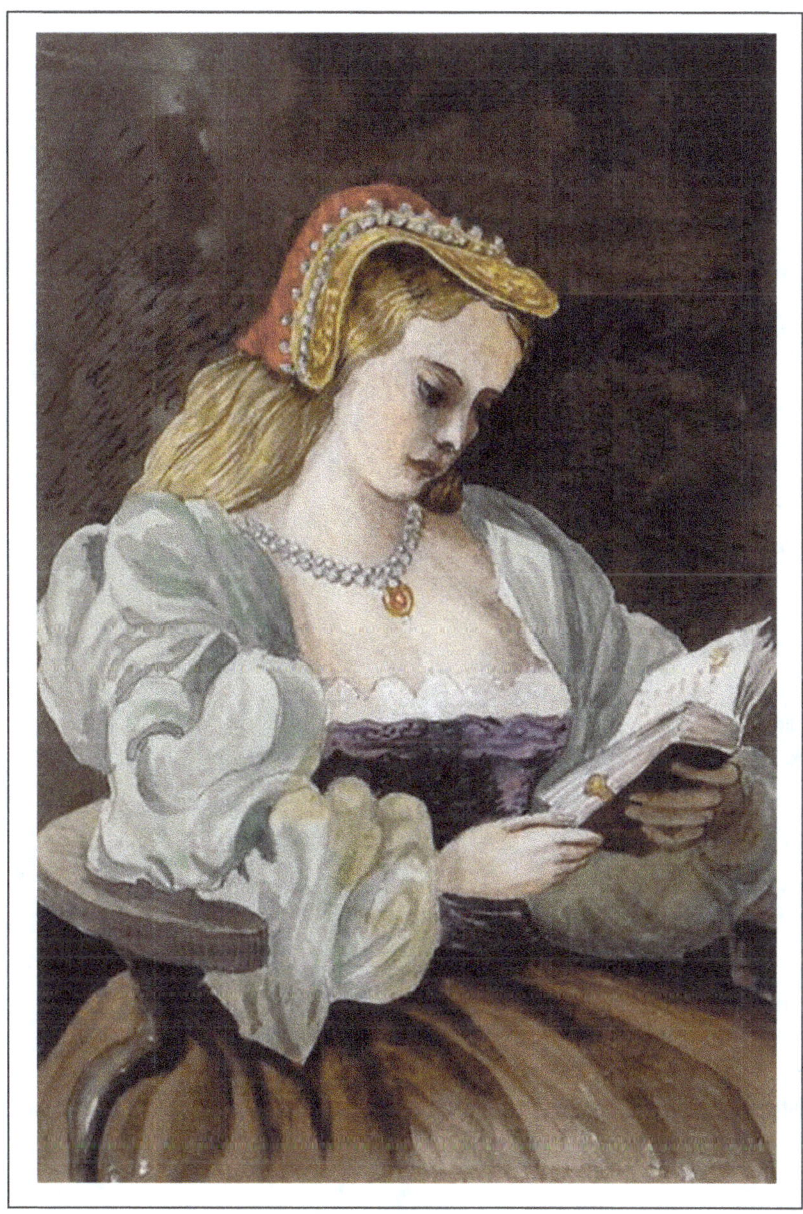

Untitled (Lady Reading a Book).
Henry Edward Baines, c. 1865. Watercolour on paper.
[Donated to Library and Archives Canada by M.C. Seguin, 2017.]

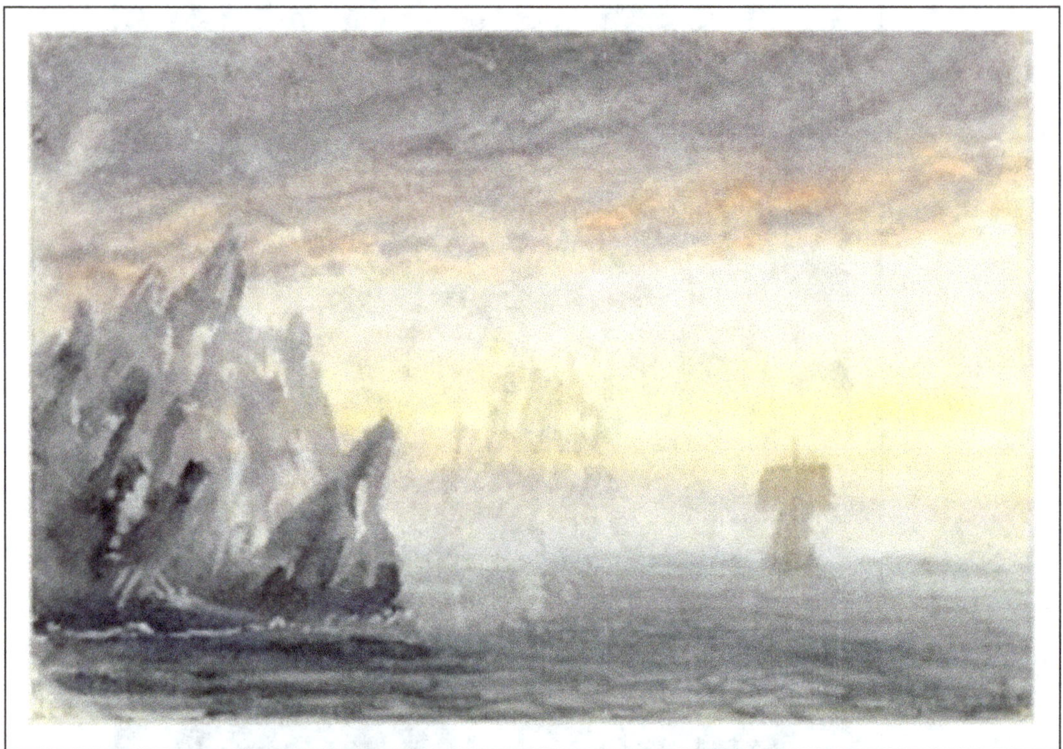

Untitled (Ship sailing past icebergs).
Henry Edward Baines, c.1866. Watercolour on paper.
[Donated to Library and Archives Canada by R.Cluett, 2017.]

This painting is reminiscent of works by English watercolourist J.M.W.Turner.

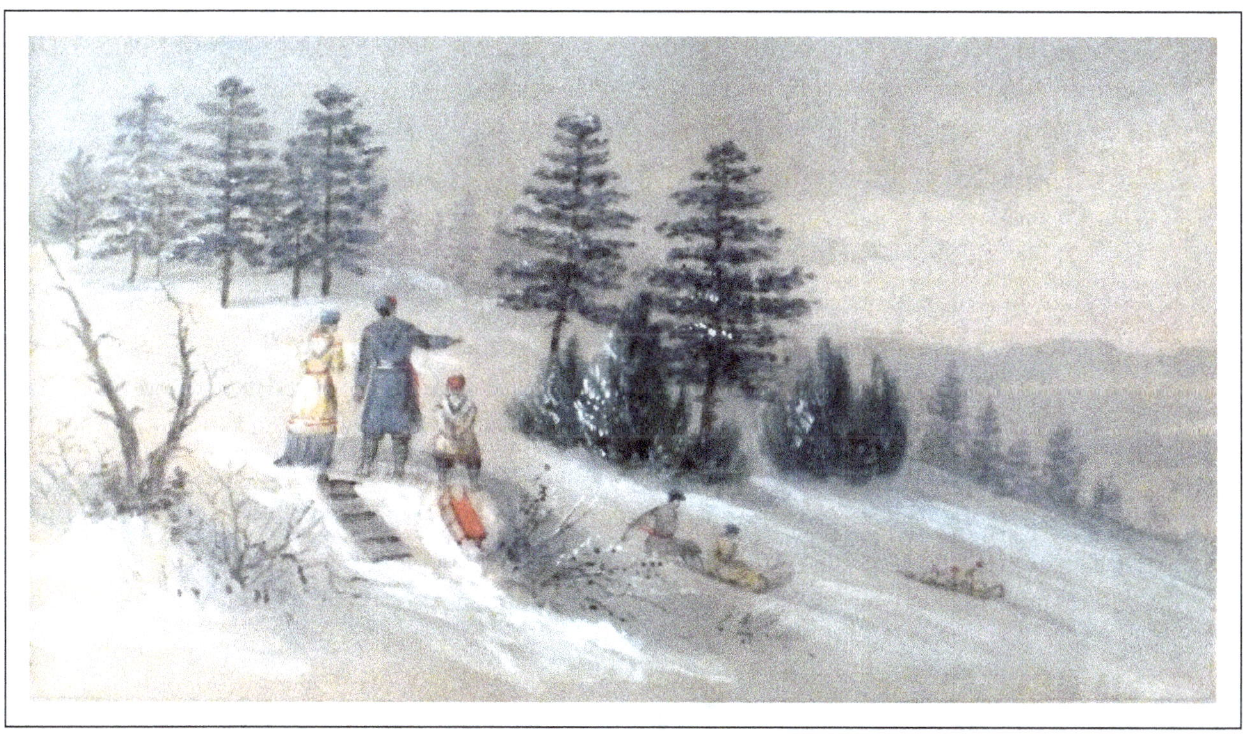

Untitled (The Tobogganing Party)
Henry Edward Baines, c.1865. Watercolour and gouache on paper.
[Courtesy of J. Boddington, Toronto, Canada]

The genre scene may have been inspired by the work of the well-known, professional artist, Cornelius Krieghoff.

The artwork of Henry Edward Baines, while accomplished in its own right, was typical of its time. Most of his art is highly representational as befitted the artist's role as an army officer trained in the topographic style. In those pieces where he adds elements of the Picturesque aesthetic or strays into the Turner-like atmospheric style, his potential as an artist with his own style is seen to be emerging. What makes his artwork remarkable is his use of pencil, paint, ink and paper to capture scenes of mid-19th Century Britain, Canada and America in great detail using a medium that, within a very few years, would give way more and more to photographic images.[33]

While Henry Edward Baines produced numerous sketches and paintings of the places he visited and the things that he saw while in Canada, it appears that none of this artwork was associated directly with his duties as an artillery officer. There is no evidence to indicate that any of his paintings or drawings were done by order of his commanding officer or for any tactical or strategic military purpose. While stationed in Toronto, Henry travelled to Dundas (near Hamilton, Ontario), Port Dalhousie (now part of St. Catharines, Ontario), and Niagara Falls, and his known body of work includes views of all of these places as well as many around the shores of Lake Ontario.

Later, while stationed in Quebec City, Baines painted numerous scenes of the St. Lawrence River and the surrounding countryside. Lieut. Baines' duties as a junior officer in an artillery battery would have been focused largely on keeping his soldiers and his guns ready for action at a moment's notice. If he had any broader responsibilities to which he might be able to apply his artistic talent, such as scouting locations to build additional fortified gun positions or sketching potential fields of fire for the existing gun emplacements, there is no record of this. The available evidence seems to indicate that his paintings and drawings were done simply as a recreational pastime — as a visual record of his travels created for his own pleasure and, perhaps, to give away as souvenirs to his fellow officers.

Painting was one of the few activities that occupied the considerable amount of free time that Henry had in between his relatively infrequent peacetime military duties. One of his other recreational pleasures which Henry enjoyed in his off-duty hours was yachting.

Part 3

THE JOURNAL

Background

Steamboats, ships, schooners, and yachts — these were the subjects of numerous paintings and drawings done by Henry Edward Baines. His keen interest in nautical subjects may have begun when he was a young boy living in the Channel Islands, and then further developed several years later when he was posted there as an artillery officer after graduating from the Royal Military Academy. Eventually, Henry's interest in boats and sailing developed into a passion for yachting.

Not long after arriving in Toronto in 1862, Henry, along with several other officers of the Toronto garrison, joined one of the city's prominent social and recreational clubs, the Royal Canadian Yacht Club,[1] of which Henry's cousin, Willie Baines, was also a member.[2] Soon, Henry had his own sailboat, probably a small, single-masted, gaff-rigged sloop that he sailed in Toronto Bay and along the shores of Lake Ontario.

In the summer of 1863, the commodore of the yacht club, Dr. Edward Hodder, announced that he would take his yacht, *Breeze*, on a three-week cruise around Lake Ontario in August, visiting ports on both the Canadian and American sides of the lake. Henry Baines and two of his fellow artillery officers, Lieut. Henry Harvey and Assistant-Surgeon Samuel Woodfull were invited to accompany him.[3]

Yachting and yacht clubs have a long tradition in the British Isles. The Royal Cork Yacht club was established in 1720, and the Royal Thames Yacht Club in 1775. Across the ocean, the New York Yacht Club was formed in 1844. On the Great Lakes, private yachts had been seen in Toronto as early as the 1830's where owners of these recreational vessels held regattas every summer.[4] By 1852, a formal organization of yachtsmen had been formed in Toronto under the name of the Toronto Boat Club, which became the Royal Canadian Yacht Club (RCYC) in 1854. Early members of the club included many of Toronto's elite: doctors, lawyers, judges and wealthy merchants as well as a number of army officers, artists and sailing enthusiasts from other Canadian ports on Lake Ontario including Hamilton, Whitby, Cobourg, Picton and Kingston, and other members from as far away as Ottawa and Quebec City. The RCYC clubhouse was the old steamer, *Provincial*, moored at Rees' wharf on the Toronto waterfront.[5]

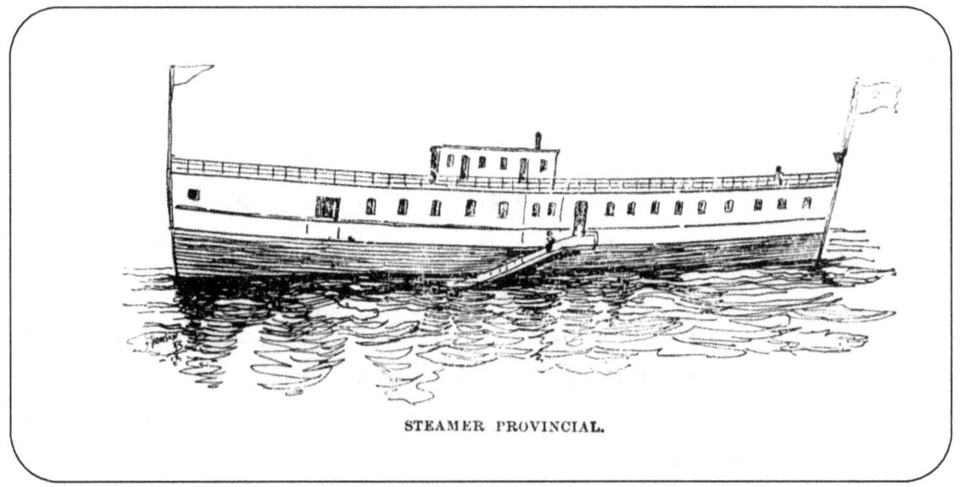

Steamer *Provincial*.
From a sketch by William Armstrong. From *Robertson's Landmarks of Toronto*, vol.2, Toronto, 1896.

The *Provincial* was used as the clubhouse of the Royal Canadian Yacht Club until 1880.

The primary purpose of the RCYC was recreational racing and cruising. Many of the early yacht clubs were also used as proving grounds for hull designs that could potentially be adapted for use by the sailing ships of the Royal Navy. In addition, many of the first RCYC members fancied themselves as a cadre of trained sailors ready to go into action as naval volunteers in the event of another war with the United States. Indeed, many members joined unofficial auxiliary units of the Royal Navy such as the Naval and Pilot Brigade of Toronto which had been established as a result of the "Trent Affair" in 1861, and some of its members saw active service in the Fenian Raids of 1866.[6]

The club's president, always given the title of commodore, was Edward Mulberry Hodder, a prominent Toronto citizen, surgeon and professor. Hodder had been born in Kent, England, and received his early education on Guernsey in the Channel Islands. At age 12, he became a midshipman in the Royal Navy but soon left the service to study medicine in London, Paris and Edinburgh. After becoming a member of the Royal College of Surgeons, he married Frances Tench and together they emigrated to Canada in 1838.[7] Starting in 1856, and for nineteen sailing seasons over the course of the following twenty-two years, Dr. Hodder headed up the Royal Canadian Yacht Club as its commodore.[8]

Commodore Hodder's first yacht, *Cherokee*, was replaced in 1862 with the top-sail cutter, *Breeze*. The *Breeze* was a magnificent, single-masted, cutter-rigged sailboat. She was designed by the RCYC's secretary, the engineer and artist William Armstrong, who modeled her along the lines of the successful British racing yacht *Meta*.[9] The *Breeze* was built in 1861 by the *Meta*'s builder, H. St. Clair Byrne, at his Birkenhead shipyard near Liverpool, England.[10] The *Breeze* carried up to five sails: a large loose-footed, gaff-rigged mainsail and a triangular topsail which could be set on a small spar above the main in good weather; forward of the mast would be the forestaysail; the bowsprit extending beyond the bow of the boat would have carried the jib, and above these forward sails would have flown the jib topsail. Like the *Meta*, the bottom of the deep keel of the *Breeze* was fitted with a retractable centre-board, a technology that, at the time, was becoming outmoded and was being superseded by either a shallow-draught keel with a large centre-board or a very deep, fixed keel with no centre-board.[11]

In the mid-19th Century, many yacht clubs, including the RCYC, classified their racing boats based on a calculated tonnage rather than on hull length or sail area. Until the 1880's, the RCYC used the "Thames Rule" for determining tonnage.[12] This meant that the *Breeze*, classified as a First Class yacht at 17 tons, would have had a length of approximately forty-two feet on deck, a beam of about ten feet and a draught of about six feet.[13]

Dr. Hodder's new boat, the *Breeze*, arrived in Toronto in time for the 1862 racing season. That year, he entered her in the race for the Prince of Wales' Cup from Toronto to Port Dalhousie (St. Catharines) and back. With a total time of 10 hours and 48 minutes for the fifty nautical mile (ninety-two kilometer) round trip at an average speed of about four-and-a-half knots (eight kilometers per hour), *Breeze* showed a disappointing third place after the yachts *Gorilla* and *Rivet*. The *Toronto Leader* newspaper commented at the time that, "Dr. Hodder's yacht, the *Breeze*, is quite a new vessel. She was very carefully built, with the latest improvements faithfully carried out in model and rig, yet she has not fulfilled the expectations formed of her by her builder and owner."[14] Several years later, in 1867, the *Breeze* was lost off the mouth of Toronto's Humber River.[15]

Commodore Hodder was an experienced yachtsman and had been cruising the waters of Lake Ontario since at least 1852 when he joined the fledgling Toronto Boat Club as one of its founding members. His extensive knowledge of the lake was codified in his book *The Harbours and Ports of Lake Ontario*, which he published in 1857. This was the first cruising guide of the Great Lakes and included detailed sailing directions from port to port as well extensive descriptions of every harbour on Lake Ontario, both on the Canadian side and on the American side. In addition, the book contained plans of each harbour well marked with depth soundings and showing all relevant hazards and aids to navigation. Prior to the publishing of

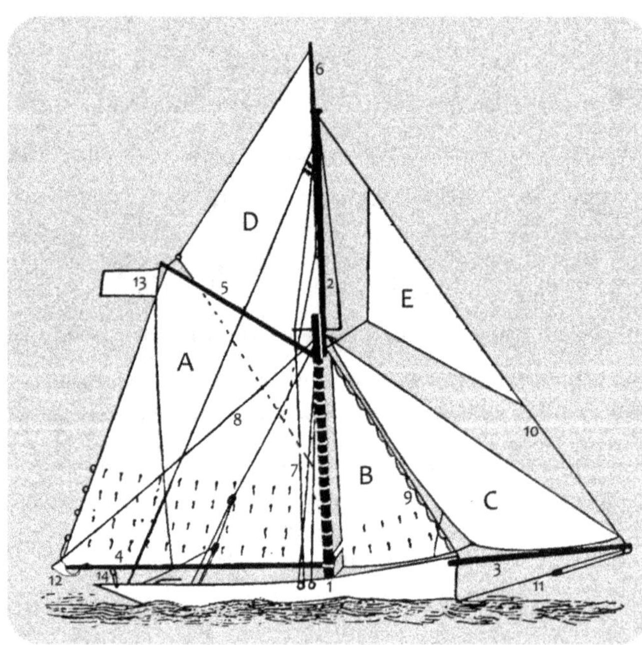

Names of Spars, Sails, Rigging of a Cutter Yacht.
Adapted from *Patterson's Illustrated Nautical Dictionary*, New York, 1891.

The cutter yacht *Breeze* had a sail plan similar to this.

A   Mainsail
B   Forestaysail
C   Jib
D   Sprit Topsail
E   Jib Topsail

1	Main mast	8	Topping lift
2	Topmast	9	Forestay
3	Bowsprit	10	Topmast stay
4	Main boom	11	Bobstay
5	Gaff	12	Reef pennant
6	Topsail sprit	13	Ensign at peak
7	Shrouds	14	Mainsheet

Hodder's book, the only comprehensive survey of Lake Ontario that mariners could rely on was a large nautical chart that had been published two decades earlier by Augustus Ford, a United States Navy officer.[16] Together, Ford's 1836 chart and Hodder's cruising guide remained the only comprehensive navigational references of Lake Ontario until 1877 when the U.S. government's Hydrographic Survey published a detailed chart of the lake.[17]

Accompanying Lieut. Baines on the cruise planned for the summer of 1863 were two of his fellow artillery officers from the Toronto garrison. The younger of the two was Henry Beauchamp Richard Harvey, No. 5 Battery's junior lieutenant. Three years younger than Baines, Henry Harvey had been born in Jamaica and, like Henry Baines, was educated at the Royal Military Academy, Woolwich, where he was a lower classman while Gentleman-Cadet Baines was in his graduating year. At age seventeen, Harvey received his commission in the Royal Artillery and immediately joined No. 5 Battery of the Royal Artillery's 10th Brigade. Baines and Harvey crossed the Atlantic Ocean together on RMS *Asia* from Liverpool to Halifax in 1861. In Toronto, Lieut. Harvey at age eighteen showed a keen interest in the technical side of an artillery officer's work by participating in local trials of improved artillery technology developed by Sir Casimir Gzowski[18]. Later, he would be a student in the Advanced Class of Royal Artillery Officers (Woolwich) studying applied mathematics, metallurgy, chemistry, practical mechanics and physics, a step often taken prior to an appointment as an instructor at the Royal Military Academy.[19] Socially, Harvey was an enthusiastic participant in the Toronto garrison's amateur theatricals and he took part in several performances during his tour of duty there.[20]

The older of Henry Baines' companions on the *Breeze* was Samuel Pratt Woodfull. A native of Kent, England, Woodfull was six years Baines' senior. He had been commissioned in the army's hospital staff corps with the rank of Acting Assistant-Surgeon after graduating from the London Hospital School in 1854. Woodfull served in Asia Minor (Turkey) during the Crimean War after which he was transferred to the Military Train, promoted to Assistant-Surgeon and sent for a short time to Central America.[21] In 1858 he transferred to the Royal Artillery and was attached to the 4th Field Brigade. When the Brigade was dispatched to Canada aboard the SS *Persia* in December 1861, Woodfull missed his boat but he quickly secured passage aboard RMS *Asia* which was leaving from Liverpool a few days later. It was on board the *Asia* that Woodfull would have first met Lieutenants Baines and Harvey. Together, the three officers travelled across the Atlantic Ocean to Halifax, and shared the adventure of the winter sleigh journey through New Brunswick, arriving at Toronto together in March 1862. Once in Toronto, with its small, close-knit medical community, Asst.-Surg. Woodfull came to know Dr. Edward Hodder socially as well as professionally. Woodfull gained valuable surgical experience while performing several operations under Dr. Hodder's supervision.[22] In 1863, Samuel enrolled in the medical school at McGill University in Montreal and graduated as a fully certified M.D. the following year.[23]

On August 3, 1863, Commodore Hodder, Henry Baines, Henry Harvey, Samuel Woodfull and assorted other crew and passengers set off on the *Breeze* — "a summer cruise, a careless sail, that gives material for a careless tale".[24] To record the events of the cruise, Henry Baines kept a handwritten diary of prose and poetry together with a number of simple pen-and-ink drawings chronicling his twenty-five day excursion around Lake Ontario. During the cruise, he also painted two dozen watercolours of the places he visited. After the voyage, it is believed that Henry transcribed the diary (chapters II to VIII), added an introduction (chapter I) and combined these written portions with the watercolours to create a scrapbook or album forming a complete illustrated journal which he titled "A Month's Leave, or, The Cruise of the *Breeze*".

In 1865, an abridged, text-only version of his journal was published in serial form in *Hunt's Yachting Magazine*.[25] In that version, most personal names were omitted and some of the text was altered by the magazine's editors. The pen-and-ink sketches and watercolour paintings that Henry Baines made on the cruise were left out entirely.

In the 1990's, the manuscript journal was housed for a short time in the County of Prince Edward Archives, then located in Picton, Ontario, Canada. While in storage there, a typed transcription of the journal was made, perhaps by A.G.W. Lamont whose name appears in handwriting on the first page of the copy.[26]

The complete illustrated journal of Henry Edward Baines is presented here in its entirety, annotated with explanatory notes about the places he visited, the people he met and the things he did over the course of his summer cruise around Lake Ontario in 1863. Outside of a few of his descendants and a small number of archivists and historians in Canada, the complete journal, "A Month's Leave or The Cruise of the *Breeze*" has, until now, never enjoyed the public attention that it deserves as a remarkable visual and written historical record.

A Note About Reading the Journal

In this annotated version of "A Month's Leave or The Cruise of the *Breeze*", capitalizations and spellings of words and the phraseology of Henry Baines' hand-written manuscript have been kept as close as possible to the original. Punctuation has been changed or added only to provide clarity. Notes in square brackets [ ] and indented annotations marked with a pennant-shaped glyph ◄ have been added by Marc Seguin.

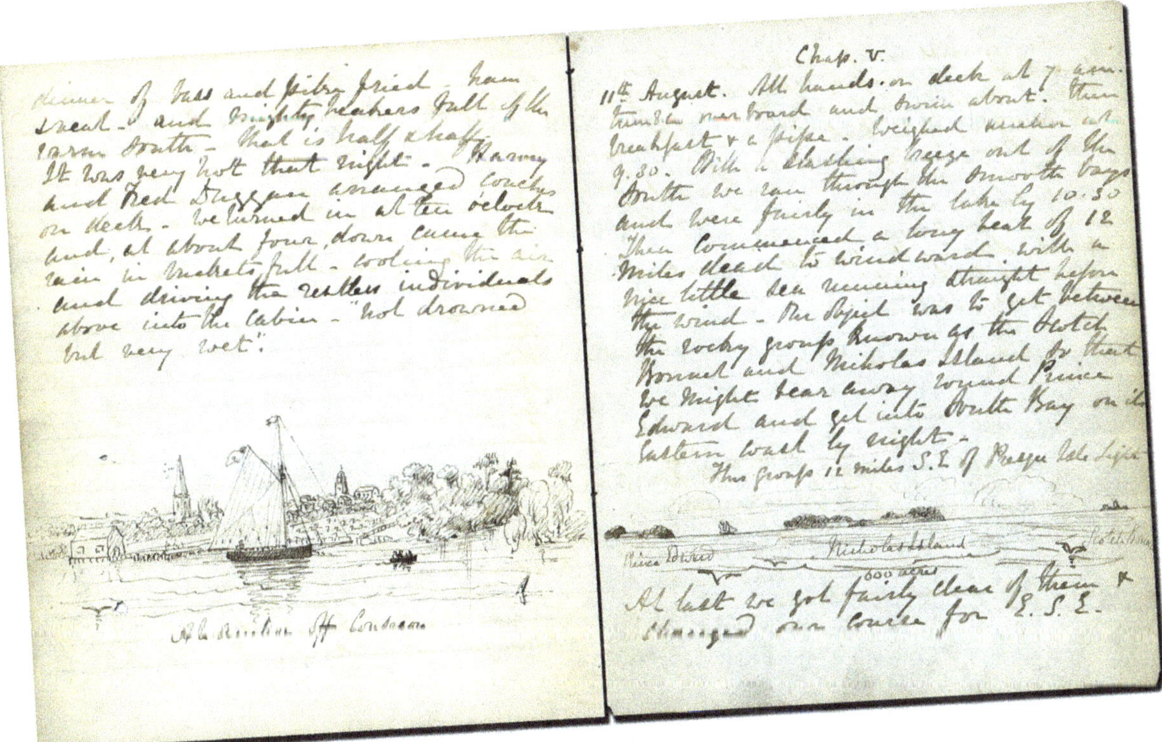

Two pages from the original manuscript of "A Month's Leave or The Cruise of the *Breeze*" by Henry E. Baines, 1863.

Notes About the Artwork in the Journal

All of the artwork has been reproduced here at a size that is very close to that of the originals. The exact order in which some of the watercolours were placed in the original scrapbook is not known because the journal has long since come unbound. Therefore, the images have generally been placed in chronological order to correspond with the written text.

The pen-and-ink drawings have been placed very near their original locations within the body of the text.

Captions have been added under all of the artwork that was included with the original journal, with the exception of the following:

pg. 114   *Harvey bathing in the dinghy (ink on paper)
pg. 118   *Five yachts at Cobourg (ink on paper)
pg. 130   *W. Point, Presqu'Isle (ink on paper)
pg. 135   Consecon Creek (watercolour on paper)
pg. 136   At Anchor Off Consecon (ink on paper)
pg. 136   *12 miles S.E. of Presqu'Isle light (ink on paper)
pg. 147   *May-apple (ink on paper)
pg. 154   View of Waupoose I. and Cape Vesey (watercolour and pencil on paper)
pg. 159   Big Ship House, Sackets Harbor (ink on paper)
pg. 160   *Commodore Tatnall's Giant Shell
pg. 163   *Blockhouse at Sackets Harbor (ink on paper)
pg. 168   *Oswegoite on a Promenade (ink on paper)
pg. 168   *Oswegoite on a Lounge (ink on paper)
pg. 187   Three flags of the RCYC (watercolour on paper
            Left to right the flags are identified as: Commodore's flag (red swallowtail),
            RCYC ensign (blue with a crown in the fly), RCYC burgee (white cross on a
            blue triangle with and crown and beaver).

* Not listed in the Appendix

"A Month's Leave or The Cruise of the *Breeze*" is reproduced courtesy of Library and Archives Canada: Henry E. Baines Fonds, R12032-0-0-E and Henry E. Baines Collection, 122-080218-2. Digitized verstions of some of the original artwork by Henry Edward Baines can be viewed online at http://collectionscananda.gc.ca .

OVERLEAF - **The *Breeze* 17** and title page.
> Henry Edward Baines, 1863. Watercolour and pencil on paper.
> [Courtesy of Library and Archives Canada.]
>
> This is the inside front page and title page of the manuscript journal, "A Month's Leave, or, The Cruise of the *Breeze*".
> The painting shows the 17-ton yacht, *Breeze*, flying the red burgee of the commodore of the RCYC along with the blue RCYC ensign.
> Over the years, some of the ink from the title page has transferred onto the original painting.

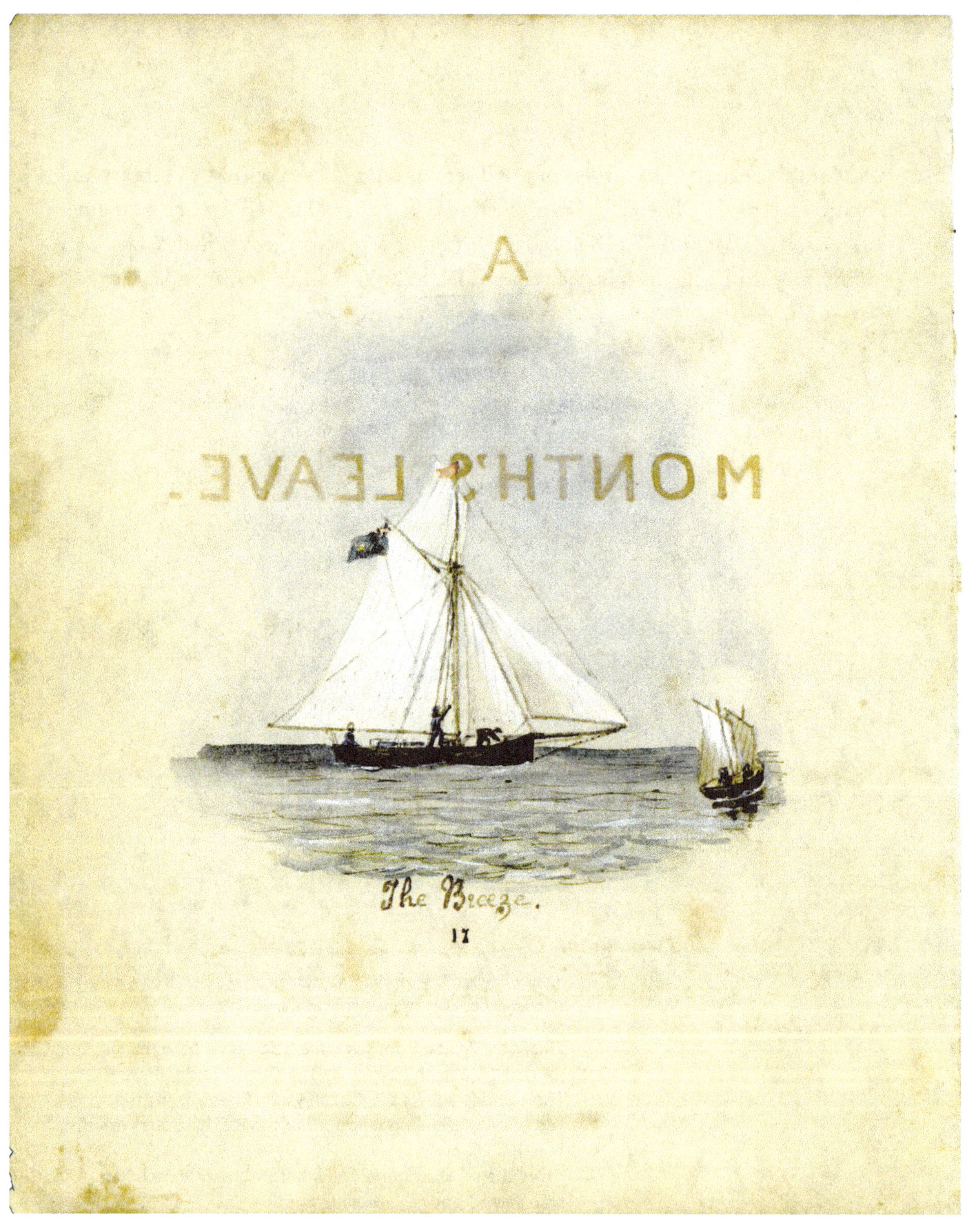

II

A

MONTH'S LEAVE.

OR

THE CRUISE OF

THE BREEZE.

A summer cruise _ a careless sail
That gives material for a careless tale _

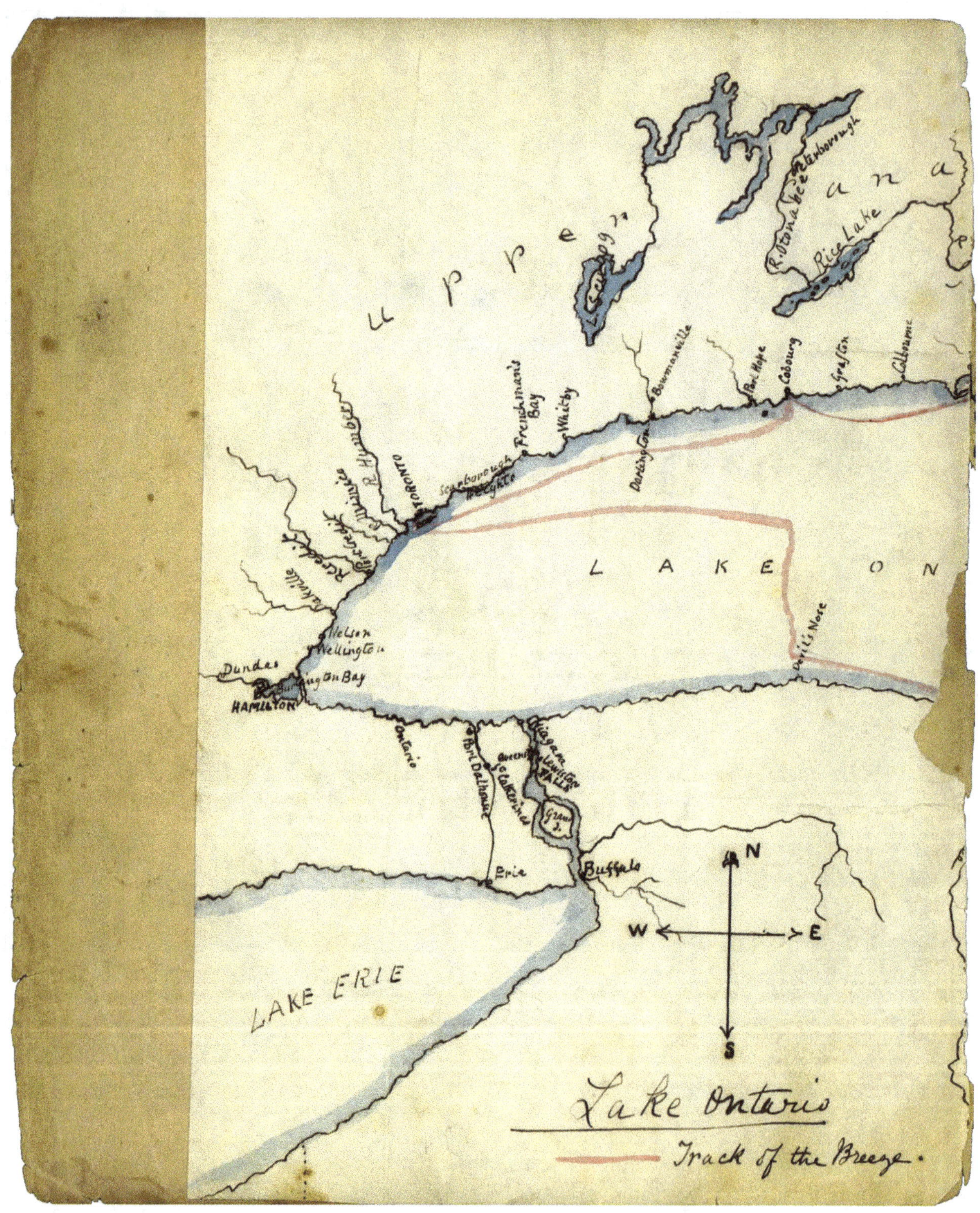

u p p e r
C a n a d a
R. Otonabee
Peterborough
Rice Lake
Scoogog
Bowmanville
Port Hope
Cobourg
Grafton
Colborne
Frenchman's Bay
Whitby
Darlington
Scarborough Heights
TORONTO
R. Humber
R. Credit
Oakville
R. Sixteen
Nelson
Wellington
Dundas
ington Bay
HAMILTON
Devil's Nose
L A K E   O N
Ontario
Port Dalhousie
Queenston
St Catherine
Niagara
Lewiston
FALLS
Grand I.
Erie
Buffalo
LAKE ERIE
N
W
E
S

Lake Ontario
Track of the Breeze.

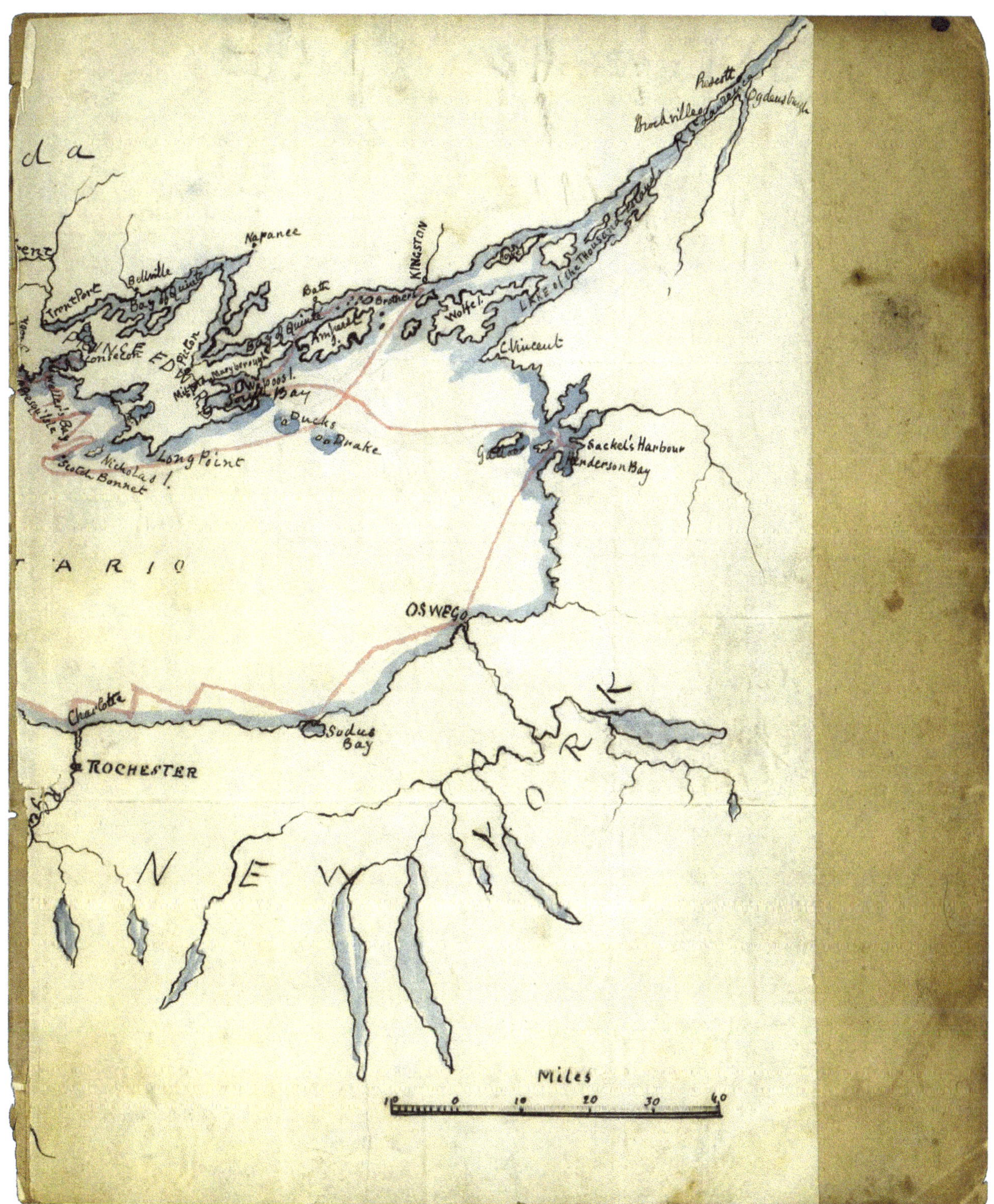

d a
Napanee
Bellville
Trent Port
Bay of Quinte
KINGSTON
Bath
Brother
Wolfe I.
LAKE of the Thousand Islands
Brockville
Prescott
Ogdensburgh
C. Vincent
U N E E ED
Picton
Consecon
Marysburough
Megen
Waupoos I.
Smith's Bay
a Ducks
on Drake
G
Sackel's Harbour
Henderson Bay
Mary's Bay
Bent Isle
Nicholas I.
Scotch Bonnet
Long Point
T A R I O
OSWEGO
Charlotte
Sudus Bay
ROCHESTER
N E W   Y O R K
Miles
10   0   10   20   30   40

PREVIOUS - Lake Ontario
Henry Edward Baines, 1863. Ink on paper with watercolour highlights.
[Courtesy of Library and Archives Canada.]

Map of Lake Ontario showing the track of the *Breeze* during
the cruise, August, 1863.

ABOVE - Signature from the first page of the journal.
Henry E. Baines
R.A. [Royal Artillery]
Toronto - 1863.

Chap. I
Introductory

Lake Ontario is a noble sheet of water on a calm summer day; blue with the deep ultramarine of the Mediterranean, changing in a fresh breeze to bright sunny green with drifting purple cloud shadows and, as the gale grows fierce rising into the power of black blue waves crested with flashing white foam, it is hardly in any one aspect distinguishable from the outer sea. Yet the character of its banks is essentially different. Sloping lawns, hanging woods or else low cliffs of crumbling sand or soft stone surround the Lake. Generally, a narrow strip of shingle or pebbly beach lies neutral between land and water, but in many places the dead trees drifted ashore extend their gaunt limbs far into the fresh green overhanging foliage.

> ◂ Lake Ontario is the most easterly of the Great Lakes of North America, measuring three hundred kilometers long from east to west, and eighty kilometers wide from north to south. The Province of Ontario (called Canada West in 1863) borders the northern and western shores of the lake, and the State of New York borders the southern and eastern shores. The major ports on Lake Ontario in the 1860's were Hamilton, Toronto and Kingston on the Canadian side, and Oswego and Charlotte (the port of Rochester, New York) on the American side.

Many small rivers and brooks empty themselves through reedy marshes into the all receiving Lake. All these contribute to swell the tide which pours eastward to the sea through the mighty St. Lawrence [River], but the chief influx is nearly at the western extremity when the overflow of the inland seas of North America rushes down the famous river Niagara and bursts into the Lake still troubled and impetuous from the great Falls.

The absence of bold capes and abrupt craggy headlands is due to the geological formation of the country. Consequent on this too is the general character of the many harbours which are spacious and shallow rather than deep and intricate. Some of these are naturally secure, landlocked low sandy islands or peninsulas stretching across from cape to cape; others have rough piers formed of cribwork jutting out into the Lake, but all except the few chief ones are slowly wearing away without effort to arrest the gradual progress of decay. This is to be attributed to the railways which obviate the necessity for shipping. In some places, however, when the extensive back country and natural facilities for the operations of commerce have resulted in cities springing up, the harbours are maintained and even added to and thus the cause in one generation has become the effect in the next.

Nor are these havens untenanted. Many a huge steamer, built in tiers like the Tower of Babel in old pictures, churns up the blue water leaving a broad pale foam track as it rushes from port to port. Many a tall white schooner bears to eastern marts the wheat of Michigan or corn from the waving plains of far Wisconsin.

> Despite the growth of railways in British North America throughout the second half of the 19th Century, shipping remained an important part of Canada's transportation network and it was an essential element contributing to the growth of the country, especially in the Great Lakes/St. Lawrence River region. Hundreds of schooners and steamboats plied these waters for commercial purposes in the 1860's, carrying wheat, coal, iron ore, manufactured goods and countless other products. In 1862 alone, these ships handled more than eight million tons of cargo at sixty-three Canadian ports on the Great Lakes.[1]

In rough unwieldy rafts, the massive logs of pine and cedar from the depths of many a dark Canadian forest journey slowly to be broken up under the classic heights of Quebec, and amongst all these flits, from time to time, some trim clean-sailed yacht like a bright careless butterfly hovering in the midst of the busy respectable denizens of a farm yard.

> Huge quantities of timber were harvested in the Canadian hinterland and processed into building materials at sawmills or floated down rivers and streams to Lake Ontario where the logs were bundled into massive rafts. These rafts, each manned by several intrepid raftsmen living in temporary shanties built on top of the rafts, were then floated along the shores of Lake Ontario and down the rapids of the St. Lawrence River to the city of Quebec. In 1862, 40,000 tons of timber and 125,000 tons of sawed lumber were transported in this manner.[2] Quebec was the centre of the Canadian overseas export lumber trade and it was there, under the cliffs of the Plains of Abraham, that the rafts were broken up and the lumber was loaded onto sailing ships for the passage across the Atlantic Ocean.[3]

I am speaking of the Canadian waters. Rarely do we meet a yacht carrying the stars and stripes [the flag of the United States of America] at her peak on Lake Ontario, and even on our own side, these light craft are few and far between — yet there are many wealthy Canadian gentlemen. The old Norse love for wind and wave has by no means died out from among them, and few places on the globe are better adapted for this glorious sport than the wide Lakes of North America. Doubtless then, the cause of so small a number of boats being owned in the principal towns is the want of time under which the gentry labours. Primogeniture and ancestral fortunes are almost unknown in the colonies; the moneyed class is a working class. Few Canadians can take a large share in sport; none can devote themselves entirely to any particular branch of it. From this arises a system of yachting which differs considerably, especially as regards manning the boats, from that prevailing in England.

> ◄ Compared to the number of commercial vessels on the Great Lakes, the number of yachts used exclusively as pleasure craft on the lakes in the mid-19th Century was very small — there would have been only about sixty yachts on all of Lake Ontario, and far fewer on the other Great Lakes.[4] Yachting was a sport reserved for those who had the time and the money to indulge in such a pastime.

The owner of a yacht and his friends sail her themselves. A sufficient number arrange to take their summer holiday together and then start on a cruise of some weeks. During the remainder of the season, they content themselves with afternoon sails or, at most, a run of a day or two from one port to another.

The following log is a record of one of these longer cruises. It is compiled from a book which, with a pencil tied to it, was allowed free range of the ship, and any one of the crew who felt disposed entered therein what seemed good to him. The sketches were all begun and, more or less finished, on the spot. Hence, they do not pretend to do more than give a general idea of the places represented. They are too rough for accurate pictures.

> ◄ Interspersed among the manuscript pages of his journal are a number of watercolours which Baines refers to as "sketches". He is critical of the merit of these "sketches", but to 21st Century art critics and historians alike, Baines' paintings and drawings are a remarkable and skillfully executed record of scenes around Lake Ontario. Perhaps he is not so much criticizing his own work as he is displaying a typical Victorian modesty, with a penchant for understatement, common among many 19th Century English writers.
>
> Henry may have started these paintings, as he says "on the spot", but some of them were likely finished later in his quarters back at the New Fort in Toronto. All of the watercolours appear to have been painted on pages that were initially separate from the written manuscript and inserted later. Since good quality watercolour paper was often hard to come by, some of these paintings were done on the reverse side of other sketches which have no relevance to the cruise. The manuscript also contains several pen-and-ink drawings which are integrated in-line with the handwritten text. They are likely copies of drawings that Henry had included in the original diary that he kept aboard the *Breeze*.

Our yacht was the *Breeze*, a wooden boat, cutter rigged, measuring 17 tons. She was built in Toronto. Her owner and skipper being E.M. Hodder, Esq., the Commodore of the Royal Canadian Yacht Club. Of the crew, three were officers of the Artillery stationed in Toronto and one a law-student of that city who sailed regularly with the Commodore.

> ◀ Here, Baines gives us our first introduction to the yacht, *Breeze*, and her owner, Dr. Edward Mulberry Hodder, Commodore of the RCYC. Baines specifies that the yacht is a "wooden boat" to distinguish her from the few iron-hulled yachts then sailing the lakes, including the *Rivet*. He is mistaken, however, when he says that the *Breeze* was built in Toronto. The commodore's yacht was built in Britain.
>
> The three officers of the Royal Artillery were the writer of the journal (Lieut. Henry Baines) along with Lieut. Henry Harvey of No. 5 Battery, 10th Brigade, and Assistant-Surgeon Samuel Woodfull, attached to the artillery's 4th Field Brigade. The law student mentioned was George Frederick (Fred) Duggan, the twenty-four year old son of Toronto court recorder George Duggan. The RCYC membership roster from 1856 lists a G. Duggan,[5] so it is likely that Fred, and/or his father, were club members.

Except the Commodore and the pilot, none of us were possessed of any particular nautical skills, but we pulled well together and took things as they came with a spirit emulating that of Mark Tapley [a character from Charles Dickens' novel *The Life and Adventures of Martin Chuzzlewit*, first published in 1844.]

Where we went, what we did there and all that we saw will be found fully set forth hereinafter.

The Start and Cobourg
Chap. II

On the morning of [Monday] the 3rd August, 1863, my two brother officers, Woodfull and Harvey and I, left the New Fort with our traps [two-wheeled, horse-drawn carriages]. I took as my equipment a uniform case and busby *ditto* [a busby case, which is a tin hat-box normally used to transport his formal military head-dress, a type of fur hat known as a busby] filled with clothing — a gun and appurts [appurtenances; i.e., accessories], two fishing rods and tackle, a pound of tobacco and plenty of pipes, [books by] Tennyson, Owen, Meredith and Mrs. Browning and a sketch book. My blanket and watch coat were on board. With all our kit, Harvey and I sailed down in my boat; Woodfull rowing in his.

The New Fort was so-called to distinguish it from the old earthen fortifications known then as the Old Fort situated a kilometer closer to Toronto, east along the lakeshore, that had been built during the War of 1812 on the site of Lieutenant.-Governor Simcoe's original 1793 fort.[6] The New Fort was not so much a fortification as it was a group of barracks, storehouses and a military hospital surrounded by a tall wooden palisade. Today, the Old Fort has been restored as Fort York National Historic Site and the only remnant of the New Fort is the stone officers' quarters where Henry Baines once lived, located in what are now the grounds of the Canadian National Exhibition and now known as Stanley Barracks.[7]

At the yacht club, several ladies had assembled to see the last of us and they stood guard over a heap of miscellaneous articles gradually diminishing as our attendant dingies made rapid trips to and fro. On transferring ourselves and luggage to the ship, we found all hands knee deep in a chaotic mass of bottles, demijohns, pies, fishing rods, ropes, great-coats and blankets. Slowly enough, things disappeared into the yawning well or gaping lockers; all hands acting as stevadores and the Commodore working and superintending like two.

Henry and his fellow officers left the New Fort and drove their carriages east along the road, past the 2-gun earthen battery and through the Old Fort to the Queen's Wharf which was located at the foot of Toronto's Bathurst Street. From there, they travelled by boat another one-and-a-half kilometers along the shore of Toronto Bay to the RCYC clubhouse located in the old steamer *Provincial* moored at the Rees Street Wharf. The *Breeze* was moored offshore in the bay, secured to a mooring buoy. As a result, all of their belongings and foodstuffs had to be transported from shore to the yacht in small rowboats known as dinghies.

From his reference to "Mark Tapley", we know that Baines is familiar with the works of Charles Dickens whose most popular novels were published between 1837 and 1865. Here, we also get a sense for Henry's keen interest in poetry; bringing with him on the cruise books by Alfred Lord Tennyson, author of "The Charge of the Light Brigade" among many other poems; George Meredith, the author of several novels and a collection of poems published in the 1850's, and the prolific 19th Century English poet, Elizabeth Barrett Browning. The mention of the author Owen along with these other writers may be a reference to 18th Century Welsh writer, Henry Owen. Other literary and biblical quotations throughout the manuscript indicate that Baines was a well-read individual; typical of an educated, 19th Century Englishman.

At last, every thing was pronounced ready. Our pilot came on board. Farewells got through, sails set and the mooring buoy splashed overboard at 10:15 a.m. — the wind being then light from N.N.W., the thermometer 74° [23° C], barometer 30.3 in [102.6 kPa]. The yacht club ensign was dipped and many white hands [of the ladies on shore] waved whiter cambric; our ensign and brown paws returning the salute. We had on board as passengers for Cobourg, Capt. Morrison M.T. [Military Train], and Mr. Hancock from Toronto. Capt. Clarkson joined as one of the crew, but left us at Cobourg also. The regular hands were the Commodore, Woodfull, Harvey, F. Duggan and myself; Mello Hodder to make himself generally useful, Private Miles of the 30th, and the pilot whose name was Burrel, a strong weather-beaten fellow.

◄ Including Baines, Harvey, Woodfull, Duggan and Commodore Hodder, there were a total of eleven people aboard the *Breeze* during her overnight passage from Toronto to Cobourg. As a result, conditions on the boat would have been very crowded. As we find out later, the main cabin slept six and there must have been accommodation in a forward cabin (the forecastle) for two more. That would still leave three passengers relegated to the deck to stand watch or to make their own makeshift sleeping arrangements.

Baines then proceeds to name the others who are on board as the *Breeze* leaves Toronto:

— Capt. Morrison, M.T. — George P. Edward Morrison was a 20-year veteran of the army. Having purchased his commission as an ensign in the 22nd (Cheshire) Regiment in 1844,[8] Morrison spent most of his military career as an infantry officer in India before being attached to the 3rd Battalion, Military Train (M.T.).[9] The Military Train originated as the Land Transport Corps during the Crimean War and, after 1856, its three battalions were responsible for moving soldiers and military materiel overland anywhere in the world that the British Army was sent.[10] Morrison was also a member of the RCYC and was elected to the position of club captain in 1864.[11]

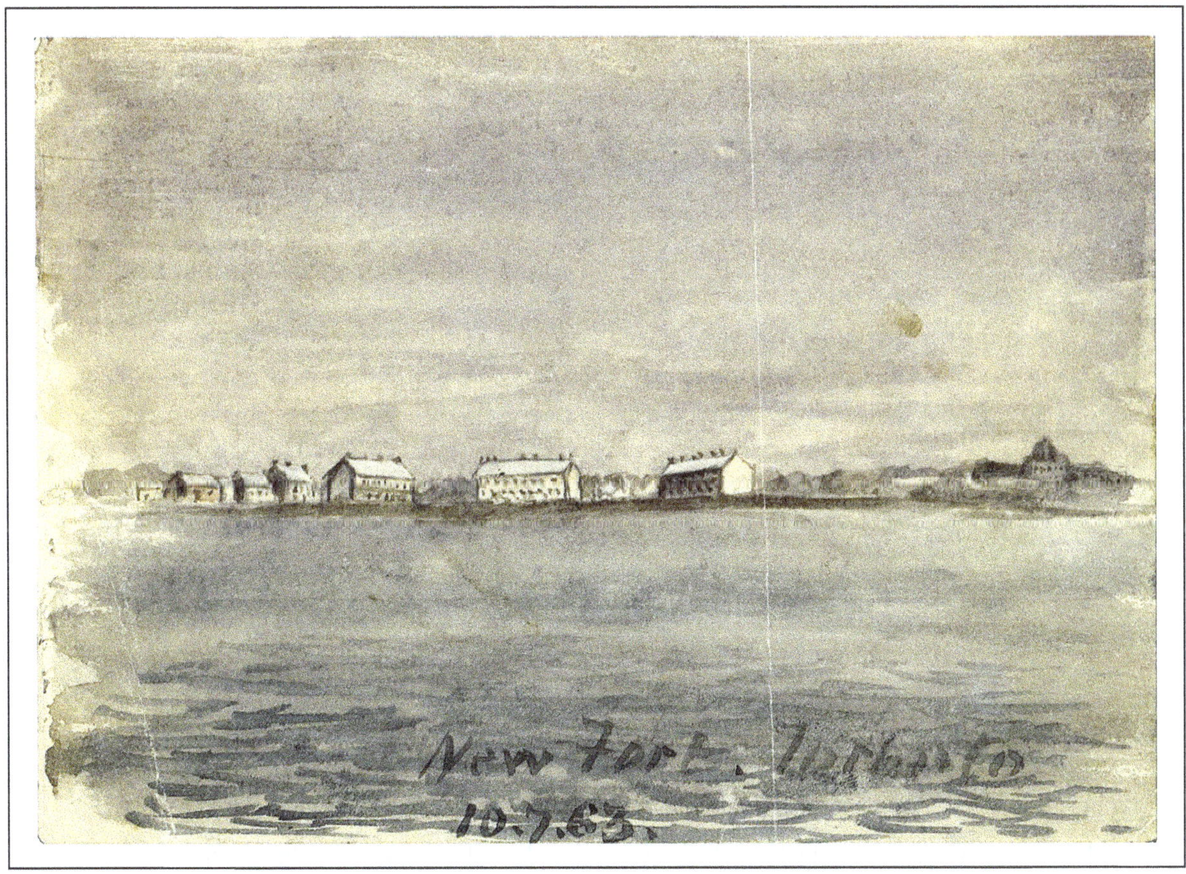

New Fort, Toronto, 10/7/63.
Henry Edward Baines, 1863. Watercolour on paper.
[Courtesy of Library and Archives Canada.]

This is a view of the New Fort as seen from a boat on Lake Ontario. The building at centre is the officers' quarters where Henry Baines lived from 1862 until 1865.

— Mr. Hancock — In later pages, he is referred to as Capt. Hancock. He was probably Robert French Handcock, a officer who had spent fifteen years in the Royal Artillery, stationed mostly in England and in Malta. Handcock rose to the rank of 2nd-captain before retiring from the army on half-pay in 1848.[12]

— Capt. Clarkson — Charles James Palmer Clarkson was an infantry officer in the 30th (Cambridgeshire) Regiment. He joined the army in 1855,[13] and saw service in the Crimea where his regiment fought at Alma, Inkerman and the siege of Sevastopol. After the war, the 30th Regiment was stationed in the Channel Islands before being sent to Canada in the summer of 1861, by which time Clarkson had been given command of a company of the regiment. Unlike the other serving officers on board the *Breeze*, Clarkson had arrived in Canada several months before the "Trent Affair" had prompted the British government to send many more reinforcements to British North America.

— Mello Hodder — Melton St. George Ettrick Hodder was the Commodore's eleven year old son who was taken along on the cruise as the ship's "cabin boy".

— Private Miles — He was a soldier in the 30th Regiment, the same regiment as Capt. Clarkson, and would have been Clarkson's personal servant — in military circles referred to as an orderly, or batman — and he acted as the ship's cook until he parted company with the crew at Cobourg.

— Burrel — He is described as the yacht's "pilot", however, a pilot is usually the term reserved for an experienced seaman who is used exclusively for guiding a ship into and out of port. Baines probably means to indicate that Burrel is a professional sailor, the type that was often hired to act as a yacht's sailing master. Little is known of this character other than the few lines that Baines writes here...

Not like a regular sailor fresh from blue water, this latter was a good type of the better class of Lake hands. During the summer season, he sails in one of the numerous large schooners that carry freight of corn, grain or lumber from one Lake port to another and occasionally venture on a coasting voyage to Halifax [Nova Scotia] or St. John [Saint John, New Brunswick.] His wages might be $35 or $40 *per men* [monthly]. In the winter, when the navigation of the Lakes is rendered impassible by the cold, he betakes himself northward to the unsettled districts and traps the smaller wild animals for the sake of their skins. With tea and tobacco, he said he could rough it anywhere, and I believe him. These Canadian sailors have a good deal of the American versatility in their composition. He was a most useful fellow on board; knowing nearly every harbour on the Lake thoroughly and being a good seaman, though he was not accustomed to small craft. This made him distrust the ship and hesitate about carrying on a good deal at first, but latterly he gained confidence enough and made the most of her.

At noon we were outside [the harbour] and off Gibraltar Point. By way of muster, we produced crackers and cheese and much bottled beer round which all hands speedily gathered and were counted accordingly.

> Hodder describes Toronto's harbour in his 1857 book, *The Harbours and Ports of Lake Ontario:* "This spacious anchorage is without doubt the best natural harbour on Lake Ontario. It is nearly circular, being formed by the main land on the north, and by a long, low, and narrow spit of sand, on the east, south, and south-west, called the Peninsular or Island; it extends in a south-westerly direction from the highlands in the township of Scarboro', and terminates in a point which suddenly turns to the north opposite the Old Garrison [the Old Fort], and upon which trees of stunted growth are thickly scattered; thus is enclosed a beautiful basin of about two and a half miles in diameter, capable of containing a great number of vessels.
>
> The south-west extremity of this island is called Gibraltar Point, on which is erected the Lighthouse [built in 1808 and still standing today; the oldest lighthouse on the Great Lakes[14]], 66 feet high, having a fixed bright light."[15]
>
> Curiously enough, instead of taking the most direct route eastward toward Cobourg, the Commodore chose to sail west, then, once outside the harbour, south past Gibraltar Point, before heading east toward their first port of call. At one time, this was the only route that could be taken to leave Toronto's harbour since a sizeable spit of sand connected Gibraltar Point to the mainland at the eastern end of the city. However, a severe storm in 1857 carved a broad opening to the lake through the eastern end of the spit. Since then, ships were able to pass through this Eastern Gap and shorten their east-bound trips by at least five kilometers.

After tiffin [lunch], pipes and laziness — cloaks on deck and every one still, except when some energetic individual would rise and solemnly turn himself upside down on the shrouds [ropes or cables supporting the mast laterally], quietly resuming his couch and pipe with a grunt of satisfaction at the ceremony. Duggan particularly distinguished himself and was so very active for some ten minutes that it made me quite hot to look at him.

At 1:55, off Scarborough heights [now known as the Scarborough Bluffs] ten miles East of Toronto. These cliffs extend some miles and are almost the only abrupt rise from the Lake on the North shore. They are broken by little vallies and crowned with groups of trees — here and there a farm house standing a little way back from the Lake, or a gentleman's villa near the woods. Beyond this, the shore is low, dotted with farm houses and patches of uncleared woodland, dark against the yellow corn fields or green pasture. At intervals, we see the white puff of an engine on the Grand Trunk [Railway] which runs not far from the water's edge.

It is indeed so close in some places to the Lake that it runs on an embankment rising from the water. In the event of a war, a couple of enterprising Yankees in a small boat could cut this great and only speedy communication between Upper and Lower Canada without difficulty. A moonlight night, a spade and a bag of gunpowder are all they want.

> ◢ The Grand Trunk Railway was founded in 1852 as the "main line" extending across the entire Province of Canada from Riviere du Loup near the New Brunswick border in the east, to Sarnia on the border with the State of Michigan in the west, connecting with dozens of smaller, independent railways in between. In addition, the railway had a line running south from Montreal to the Atlantic Ocean port of Portland, Maine. The Grand Trunk was taken over by the Government of Canada and became the Canadian National Railway in 1920.
>
> Henry's reference here to the possibility of war is the only place in the manuscript that he hints of any potential armed conflict between the United States and Great Britain. It was the threat of war that had originally brought Lieut. Baines and thousands of other British soldiers to Canada eighteen months earlier during the "Trent Affair".
>
> Henry refers to Americans as "Yankees". His frequent use of this pejorative term, in conjunction with other statements about Americans, shows a certain anti-American bias that was shared by many Britons in the 19th Century.

At four o'clock, Port Union was about five miles on the lee beam. It is merely a few stores, some cottages and a wharf of crib work with a wooden storehouse at the end. Scows run in for cargoes of wood or an occasional schooner loads with grain from the country round. The breeze was still light, but steady. Most of us were lying in a group under the mast in the shade of the foresail, half asleep and one or two smoking — the Commodore below looking over the charts.

4:15. Off Whitby, 34 miles East of Toronto. I visited this last year in the *Dart*. The harbour is good and the entrance tolerably deep. Two crib work piers run out from rip-rap breakwaters stretching across the bay. At the head of the harbour inside them is the usual marsh across an arm of which the road to the town of Whitby is carried over a trestle bridge.

> ◢ The *Dart* was the oldest privately-owned yacht known to sail on Lake Ontario. In 1863, the 14-ton yacht was owned by Thomas J. Robertson, former captain of the RCYC, who often sailed her with a crew of six.[16]

Our next excitement was passing a lazy gull perched on a floating log. Woodfull said it ought to be and was, a man in a boat. Some original-minded party produced the glasses [binoculars] and soon Woodfull's "man" got up and flew away. Then came the event of the day — all hands piped to dinner. We rigged up a couple of planks as a table. It fell nearly calm and all our arrangements were perfect. Lamb, salad and condiments went down in silence. Then a huge demijohn of half-and-half, ready mixed, appeared and set our tongues going — then cheese and crackers.

Half-and-half is a beer blend usually made from 50% stout or porter, and 50% pale ale.[17] This is also known today as Black and Tan.

We cast ourselves down on the deck with just enough energy left to fill our pipes and talk lazily about the different directions in which the smoke travelled. By and bye, two or three puffs [of wind] came off the shore, necessitating jibes. The wind at last settling light but steady from the South-West again. We got out lines and tried trolling. Over and over again we tried this in the Lake, but never caught anything. Salmon trout are sometimes taken with a line in the deep water, but the usual mode of fishing there is with a long seine-net. Whitefish as well as salmon trout are taken in this way.

In addition to expressing his creativity in drawing and painting, Baines also wrote poetry. Here he pens a whimsical rhyme, the first of several poems that appear in the journal...

The boat was still – the wind was light – the sky all clear above it.
The water calm and gleaming bright but whiskey would improve it.
Just half the sun above the land – a broad red shining band.
And all around red windless heaven,
This, at a quarter after seven.

A long swell set in off the Lake – and some of us just kept awake
Partly because the ship was rolling – and partly as we went on trolling.
This last amusement "sans" success – for all the fishes seemed to guess
Their chance of getting in a mess.

And all our dodges lost their force – no scaly gills our spoon can tickle.
These being fresh water fish – of course they will not get into a pickle.
The red light quickly fades away and in the West gives place to gray.
The night is fine not wind enough to keep the flapping sails distended
Save now and then a transient puff, and so, our first day out is ended.

We turned in anyhow; no one having any fixed place assigned to him. The cabin is rather confused. Long and interesting stories from Capt. Hancock. There being plenty of volunteers for the first watch, I tell them to call me when I'm wanted and remove my coat and shoes. Peaceful slumber till...

[Tues.] 4th August,   6 a.m. All hands on deck and a variety of dodges for getting a tub were resorted to. The favourite one was to strip to the waist and lean over the rail while some friendly Christian poured buckets of cold Lake water on the head and shoulders. This was very refreshing. Harvey got into the dingy with a towel and a big sponge and, having disrobed, indulged in a regular sponge bath. He looked so pretty that we cast off the painter [the line at the bow of the dinghy connecting it to the *Breeze*] and set him adrift in order to have a good view from a distance. He looked like a mermaid, only rather more so. By half past seven, all hands were ready for breakfast. We were very close to Cobourg pier head, but the wind was light so we were contented to leave the deck to Burrel and Miles whilst we fed. At 8 a.m., we ran between Cobourg piers and met the *Rivet*'s dingy taking their crew out to bathe. We were still at breakfast. Two or three of us went on deck to get the anchor ready just as we entered the inner harbour, but were too late. Burrel, not knowing the way the boat carried, with her luffed up too sharp a puff struck us just before and so we ran straight into the wharf. Luckily, our bowsprit head was higher than the wharf, so the bobstay [the length of rope or chain securing the bowsprit to the boat's hull] lifted us. Loafers on the wharf shoved it off and we anchored all right between *Rivet* and *Palmetto*. The boats in harbour were the *Palmetto* C.B. [C.B. is a Centre-Board boat with a shallow keel or flat bottom] and *Zouave* C.B. of Hamilton, the *Breeze* and *Rivet* d.d. [d.d. is a deep-draught keel, perhaps with a slip-keel] and *Dart* C.B. of Toronto, the *Arrow* d.d. and the *Gorilla*, *Wide-awake*, *Kitten* and *John A. MacDonald* all C.B. of Cobourg.

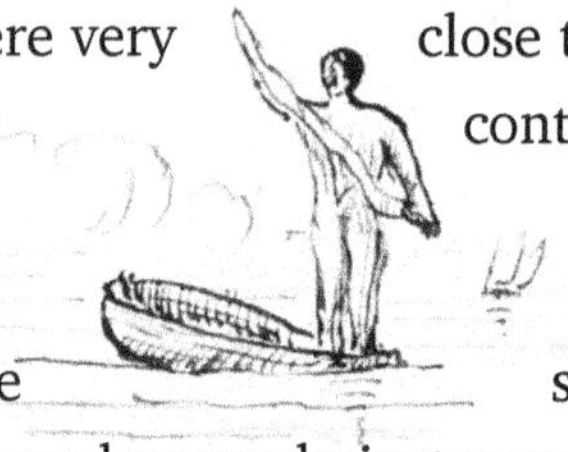

The *Breeze's* sailing time from Toronto to Cobourg was just over 21 hours, making her average speed three knots (5.5 kilometers per hour). Cobourg, with a population of 5,000,[18] was the principal town of Northumberland County, with two banks and ten hotels.[19] Yachts from many ports along the Canadian shore of Lake Ontario had assembled in Cobourg for the annual regatta: two from Hamilton, three from Toronto, and five from Cobourg. In addition, the yacht *Slug* had been transported by rail from Rice Lake. There was also one regatta entry from Kingston, the *Bay Queen*, owned by Ensign Francis Dugmore, an officer in the Royal Canadian Rifle Regiment. However, en route to Cobourg, Dugmore's yacht was wrecked in the treacherous waters off Prince Edward County's Poplar Point. The boat was lost, but all of the crew were saved.[20]

After a pipe, I attired myself and went into town to call on the inhabitants. Did the Barron's, Chatterton's and MacPherson's. The proverbial Cobourg hospitality flourishing like a green bay tree. The others loafed about the town. All assembled at noon for tiffin, except Morrison, Hancock and Duggan. Mr. Barron and Mr. Street visited us.

> While in Cobourg, Baines visited a number of the town's prominent citizens, many of whom he would have known as members of the RCYC. F.W. Barron, was headmaster of the Cobourg Grammar School and owner of the yacht *Donna del Lago*,[21] and Richard D. Chatterton was clerk of the county court and owner of the Cobourg newspaper, *The Cobourg Star*.[22]
>
> Baines then goes on to compare the hospitality found in Cobourg to the proverbial "green bay tree" as referenced in the Old Testament. On the surface, it sounds as though his Cobourg hosts are genuinely hospitable. However, the full biblical reference is "I have seen the wicked in great power, and spreading himself like a green bay tree,"[23] so it may be that Baines is hinting that the rich and powerful of Cobourg share some commonality with the wicked of the Bible.

Dimidium dimidium et [half-and-half] delicious as ever. In the afternoon many of the Cobourg girls assembled on board the *Rivet*. I joined the crew and we had a jolly sail — put down two buoys to mark the course. We had twenty-four on board all told. Not bad for a 16-ton boat. There was plenty of wind and little sea so every one enjoyed it immensely. We got in again at half-past six and I rowing myself on board the *Breeze* just in time to join the rest at dinner. Just as we had finished dinner, the Cobourg band came down and, getting on board the *John A.*, sailed about the harbour playing melodiously the while. All Cobourg turned out to stroll on the pier and enjoy the cool evening breeze. It was very free and easy and also very charming.

The next entry in the log is dated 12:35.
Just returned from the hut of one Cruso — no relation to Robinson — a "big-bug" or sachem in these parts. To the sea rovers gave he a nautch [a dance], likewise beer. Many of the younger and fairer natives were present in their ordinary costume, reserving the full effect of their most gorgeous apparel for the ensuing night. Tattooing does not prevail along this coast. The religion is unknown and it matters not, but I have been credibly informed by some of the more ancient and unmarried females that their fair juniors are much given to the worship of a mysterious deity called the "ossifer."

> As the preamble to this paragraph suggests, this entry in the diary was not written by Henry Baines. Its sarcastic tone is unlike Baines' style. It was likely written by one of the other "Breezers"; someone who had some familiarity with the custom of tattooing in other cultures. This could have been either Capt. Morrison who had

served for several years in India, or Samuel Woodfull who had spent time in Central America.

The writer makes a cryptic reference to Cruso, the prominent Cobourg resident Michael Daintry Cruso, clerk of the divisional court.[24] It may be that the writer was simply trying to be humorous in describing Cruso's home and family as being like those of the native Indians of the area, or perhaps he was trying to express his disdain for Cruso and his four daughters who, as the writer hints, were intent on marrying a rich army officer (the "ossifer").

Young ladies in and around garrison towns often became romantically involved with eligible, wealthy young officers. This practice was usually discouraged by commanding officers, and more than one junior officer had to be sent back home to Britain from an overseas posting for getting too involved with a local girl. A notable exception to this general policy was made in the case of one of the "Breezers", Capt. Clarkson. In September, 1863, just before he was transferred with the 30th Regiment from Toronto to Quebec, Clarkson married his Toronto sweetheart, Henrietta Coxwell. The wedding took place St. George's Church with Dr. Hodder giving away the bride and Hodder's daughter, Olivia, acting as one of the bridesmaids.[25]

Chap. III

[Wed.] 5th August.   Awake at six. Many flies buzzing and biting. The morning bright and warm. No wind. Bathe off the pier head. Oh how cold the water was! Then clear up ship and breakfast at 8 a.m.; pie, rolls, ham, beef, tea and coffee all well furnished, then a pipe. The second class yachts; i.e., those under ten tons, started at 10 a.m.: *Slug*, just brought from Rice Lake on the cars [the railroad cars of the Cobourg Peterboro and Marmora Railway], *Wide-awake, Zouave, Palmetto* and *Kitten*. We then took eight ladies on board, drifted out a little way, then a long rolling swell off the Lake and no wind — so hot ! We got in as soon as we could and saw the first class yachts start at 1 p.m. The start was effected in this way: All the competing boats were moored on the lee of the windward pier, with their mainsails up, in order previously determined by lot. At a given signal, their head sails were hoisted and they were towed out by the bystanders. They got off well, but the *Gorilla* being first had the advantage of a little puff of wind, gained a good deal on the others, maintaining her lead till the end of the day. The others were the *Arrow*, *John A. MacDonald*, *Rivet* and *Dart*. There was a very light wind from the South. All day the race lasted; the wind at times falling altogether then exerting itself enough to give a feeble puff for a few minutes after which it became calm as before. It freshened, however, enough to bring the *Gorilla* in before the time allotted for the race had elapsed, but died away immediately, leaving the *Rivet* just outside. Had the breeze lasted ten minutes longer, the *Rivet* would have saved her time and won the race. The *Wide-awake* carried off the second class prize.

The band played on board the *John A.* as before and we loafed with many ladies on the wharf till they all took themselves off to dress for the ball. Mrs. Stewart, the Misses Hodders and Miss Coxwell arrived by steamer from Toronto and were forthwith conducted to the Globe [hotel.]

> ◄ Commodore Hodder had four daughters; Georgina, Geraldine, Emily and Olivia. Baines does not specify which of the daughters arrived in Cobourg on the steamer from Toronto, but one of them was undoubtedly Olivia who was a friend of Miss Henrietta Coxwell, Capt. Clarkson's betrothed. Mrs. Stewart was probably the girls' chaperone.
>
> One of ten hotels in Cobourg, the Globe was where the annual regatta ball was held.[26] It was reputed to be the finest hotel between Toronto and Kingston. The hotel was destroyed by fire in 1864.[27]

Harvey had taken a room there and I dressed in that. I had to go down to the bar to procure a ticket. It was crowded with loafers, more or less drunk, smoking, chewing and spitting like Yankees. The ball room was dismal, insufficiently lighted and, papered with dark green and brown, it looked like a cavern. The music was bad, the floor was bad and the supper bad. The girls were good though, and that covered nearly all the sins. I was bored into leaving at two. I stood at the door of the hotel, talking for a few minutes, when I noticed two gentlemen coming down stairs in each other's arms, and head foremost. About half way down, the undermost hitched his leg in the bannisters and remained in suspense while the other, shooting ahead, picked himself up and walked away. Imagining this to be a custom of the country, I remained quiescent and observant. Presently, some bystanders disengaged the obfuscated and entangled gentleman and took him into the bar, whence he speedily emerged followed by a fist. This time he fell soft on a group of loafers who scattered in confusion. Much noise and talking, but nothing practical ensued, so I went home to bed. This was not the only row that night.

[Thurs.] 6th Aug.   Could not manage to get up as early as usual this morning. I had, however, my accustomed tumble in off the pier head and performed

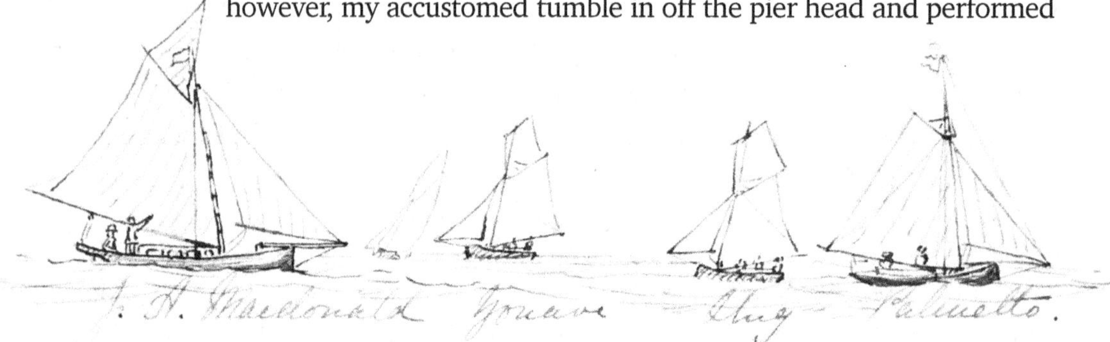

my toilette satisfactorily. I was fortunate enough to possess a small bag in two compartments, originally intended for shaving tackle, but now made to carry brushes and soap. This I slung to a towel and always took with me when I went to bathe. I scrubbed my hands and cleaned my teeth while swimming in the Lake, and brushing my hair was an agreeable pastime on the road back. When bathing off the yacht, we used a tin basin; turn and turn about for any soapy ablutions. One small mirror was provided by the Commodore and it always turned up providentially on our nearing any port with a town attached to it. Elsewhere, it remained *perdu* [lost], as nobody ever looked for it. After bathing this morning I went to a barber, got myself shaved and then joined our party at breakfast at the Globe — then a pipe and a prowl into town. About mid-day, the ladies gathered to the ship and we ran out some seven miles to the southward to watch the race. It was a good sailing day with plenty of wind and, unfortunately, a proportionate amount of sea running. Several of the ladies yielded to the weakness of their dear little interiors, but we never mention names. Mr. Barron, Harvey, Woodfull and Duggan gathered round the weather shrouds and did vocal melody 'an it were any nightingale? (which may have had something to do with the condition of the ladies.) The unfortunate *Rivet* was becalmed between two other boats some few hundred yards on each side of her, both of whom had plenty of wind so, when at last a cat's paw [a gust of wind] came her way, she put about and returned to port. We soon did the same and disembarked our precious freight.

◄ The ladies watching the regatta from the *Breeze* became seasick and several of the gentleman on board sang songs, though rather badly, perhaps, as Baines suggests, because the singers were also feeling the effects of the tossing sailboat. The "nightingale" quote itself is a literary reference that appears to be from the English writer Joseph Addison, dating to 1713.[28]

> Reporting on the yachting events, the *Cobourg Sentinel* commented that, "the lovers of aquatic sports had a fair field for enjoyment during the two days of the Regatta.... The sport was far superior to anything of the kind we ever had the pleasure of seeing."[29]

Then the Toronto party all dined together at the Globe and spent a very pleasant evening at Judge Boswell's. Music and dancing, strolling on the lawns and sitting on the steps; very sociable and jolly.

> ◄ G.M. Boswell was the county court judge for Northumberland County and former member of the provincial legislature. His son Arthur was a law student at the time and subsequently became a lawyer and later served one term as Mayor of Toronto.[30] Arthur Boswell was also a member of the RCYC and succeeded Dr. Hodder as its Commodore in 1878; a post that he subsequently held for seventeen years.[31]

About 1 a.m., we all strolled down to the pier to see Mrs. Parsons off to Toronto. The boat from Kingston came in at two a.m., looking very pretty with her long row of cabin lights and her coloured lamps on each paddle box. Farewells over, I turned in aboard the *Breeze*.

[Fri.] 7th August — Matutinal [morning] swim. Breakfast at the Globe. The Breezers and ladies from Toronto assembled at Judge Boswell's at eleven. Traps and quadrupeds [carriages and horses] were collected and we started for Rice Lake. Arthur Boswell, Bogert and I took the last thing on wheels that appeared. It was a kind of gig [two-wheeled carriage] drawn by the spectre of a horse who appeared ready to go on his knees every day and beg that twenty-four hours more life might be vouchsafed to him. We came up to some others of the party at a public house (or tavern) about half way called Cold Springs. To them we accounted for having brought our beast so far by saying that he luckily fell to pieces near where another of the same class was grazing, so we mended him up with odd bits from this other.

> ◄ Bogert was a member of the Toronto Cricket Club who went to Cobourg for the regatta festivities with his fellow club member Ensign George Cobden of the 30th Regiment.
>
> A plank road ran twelve miles (twenty kilometers) north from Cobourg to the village of Gores Landing on Rice Lake. From there, steamboats ran across the lake and up the Otonobee River to Peterborough. The stagecoach trip from Rice Lake to Cobourg at that time would have taken about ninety minutes. [32] As long as the carriage stayed on the planks, it was a relatively smooth ride. However, once off the

planks, the carriage wheels could easily get bogged down as Baines and his fellow travelers later found. About half-way between Gores Landing and Cobourg was the village of Cold Springs, with a population of 800.[33]

The road was pretty and changing its character constantly — now winding along the foot of a hill, now through deep woods, then emerging into open cultivated country with farmhouses scattered about. There was interest enough to carry us through the twelve miles without our feeling bored. It was a blessed hot day, threatening rain now and then, but the sun always prevented the clouds carrying out their intention. When we arrived at Gore's Landing, we found all assembled in the hotel planning boating expeditions. The greater part of us got on board a small yacht and stood out into the Lake. There was a light breeze just rippling the deep blue water. Some thirty miles in length, the Lake only averages a breadth of three. It is fed by three good sized streams, the largest of which, the Otonabee, falls into it nearly opposite Gore's Landing; the Trent, its great effluent runs out of the East end into the Bay of Quinté at Trentport [now known as Trenton, part of the City of Quinte West, Ontario], but the chief beauty of the Lake is its islands. I do not know how many there are of them, but they are all very lovely, covered with trees to the water's edge, they show every variety of tint in their foliage and stand out well from the more distant wooded capes or lawny meadows on the northern shore. The peculiarity of this Lake to English eyes is the wild rice which grows in the deep water and lifts up its pale green feathery head in thick profusion through beds a mile and more in length. Round the islets and across the rice beds, we cruised till the wind fell and left us fairly becalmed in a rice bed on our way home. A friendly tow brought us to our moorings and we prepared for dinner, noways loth [i.e., without reluctance.] Three of the party had been fishing and had caught some fine black bass, two of which weighed about 4lb. each [1.8 kg]. The first dish at the dinner table was maskinonge [also known as muskellunge], the king fish of these Lakes. It is more like a gigantic pike than any other English fish. This dish received due attention, but did not at all interfere with the rights of those which followed it. The beer was good and plentiful and all things went happily; then pipes, and I made a rough sketch of the Lake from the hill by the hotel. By this time, shawls were being brought out and the horses were put to. Fred Duggan was offered to us in exchange for Bogert, who was wanted to make up a quartette in another carriage. We examined the amount of sitting down room required by each (three in a gig you see) and consented. The dilapidated ground

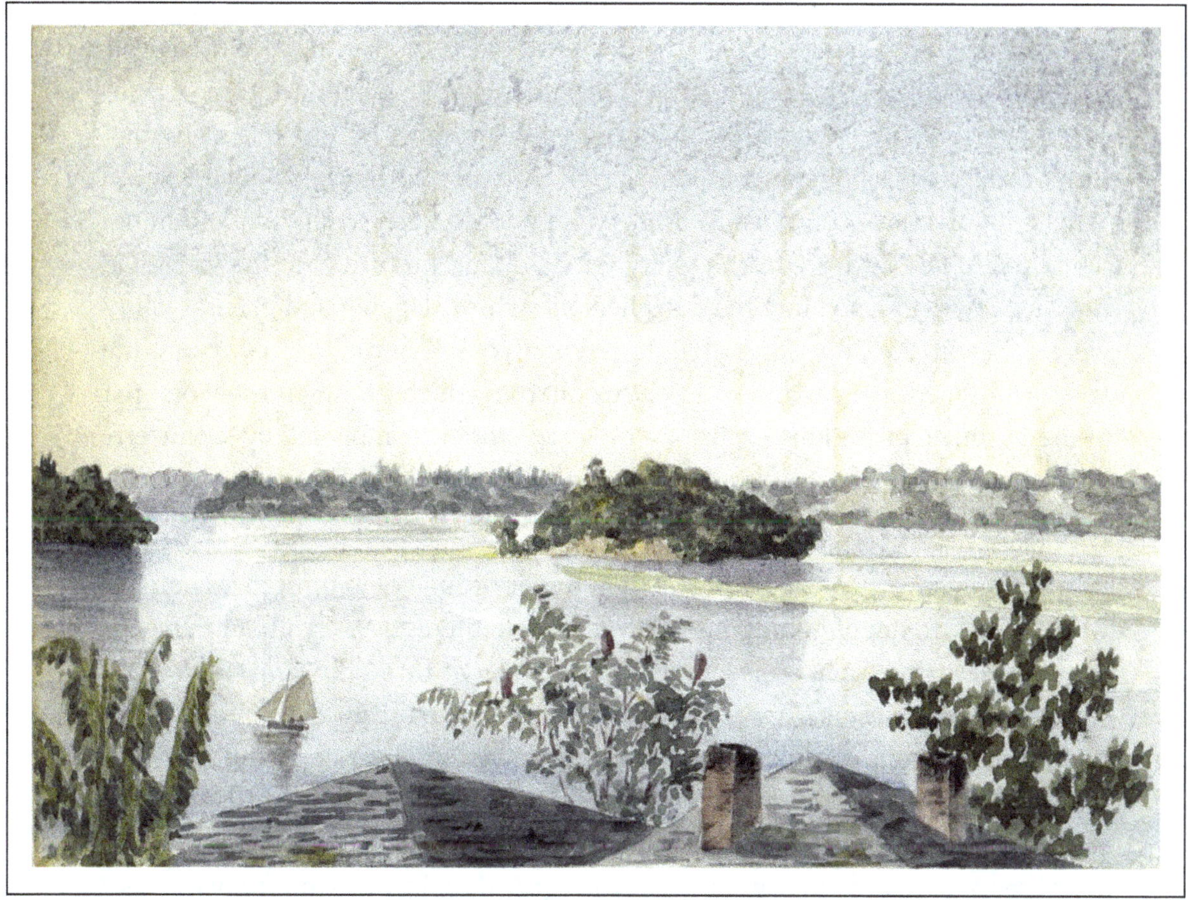

Rice Lake (Pémédashcoutayong).
Henry Edward Baines, 1863. Watercolour and pencil on paper.
[Courtesy of Library and Archives Canada.]

I made a rough sketch of the Lake from the hill by the hotel.

This shows Black Island at left and Sheep Island at centre. In the title of the painting, Baines includes the name that the native Anishnabe people call the lake.

plan of a horse soon fell in rear of the others, though we started him with a spurt and, by the time we got to Cold Springs, it was dark and raining. Damper and darker it grew till we could no longer say whether we were on the road or not, but had to give the perfidious old beast his way. He being probably incited thereto by the fresh smell of a hedge — or rather creepers over a snake-fence, for hedges are not in this country — meandered away till suddenly one wheel went down, the other up and we found ourselves in a heap on the ground. Having taken a wrong turn on entering Cobourg, it was eleven o'clock before we reached Judge Boswell's. What a lot of tea we contrived to drink when we had been wrung out and hung up to dry. At last we were forced to cry out hold, and I returned to the yacht. On my way down, I looked into the Macpherson's where dancing and general jollity were going on. Wet, dirty and tired, I presented myself in the ball room, and the very fact of the large patch of mud on my quarter, which I thought the worst part of the business, proved my excuse for an upset story accompanied by such stern evidence, covered all my sins; lateness and disreputable dishclout [dishcloth] appearance into the bargain.

It is perfectly marvellous how things that, under ordinary circumstances you would never dream of getting into, accommodate themselves to all our personal peculiarities when on a cruise. Judge Boswell's coat fitted me *á merveillé* [marvelously] at tea, and I was equally at home in one of Jim Macpherson's at the party. After awhile, I found myself too limp and tired to be up to the mark so obtained permission to depart. The yacht was some three or four yards from the wharf, so I went to the hotel and had a pipe. Then the ladies had to be put on board the steamer for Toronto. It was blowing and there was a pretty heavy sea running out in the Lake. Consequently, it was three in the morning before the steamer touched the wharf. No berths could be had. Clarkson and Cobden went off with the ladies and we trusted to them to manage. Just had time to run ashore before the gangway was hauled aboard; then back to the hotel, loitering a moment to watch the great lights of the steamer in the long slow heave over each wave till they grew less and less and then went out behind the thick black veil of darkness and rain.

Ensign George Edward Cobden was an officer in the 30th Regiment. He had originally been commissioned in the 46th (South Devonshire) Regiment in November, 1862, but transferred to the 30th Regiment the following month. He arrived in

[Sat.] 8th August.   As several of the visitors attracted to Cobourg by the double event of regatta and ball had departed, I easily obtained a bed in the hotel. Not being likely to enjoy one again for some time, made the most of it and breakfasted pretty late. It was dead calm. I went down to the harbour and had a pipe, then Fred Duggan turned up and we watched the drooping flags and motionless clouds. Consulted Burrel, but got no hope from anything [i.e., there was no hope of sailing that day.] There was a wee wee steamer, about as big as an ordinary row boat, close to us. She had crossed the Lake from Rochester where we met again. A small house in which were two apartments was built in her by way of cabin; aft was the engine and forward two bunks. In the bow, a regular flagstaff with the stars and stripes floating from it. If four fellows had taken her flag, one at each corner, they could have wrapped the boat in it and carried her off bodily.

At last we got tired of watching her manoeuvres and concluded to search for the Commodore. Ran him to earth at Judge Boswell's. We agreed not to go out because there was no wind to take us out, and went through the town in search of tin ware, fishing tackle, etc., etc. Having bought all we could buy, we marched through the streets carrying kettles and pans in regular procession to the ship. We dined on board at six. By the time our pipes were out, Bogert came down attended by ladies. Then the steamer from Toronto arrived. Bogert was put on board and, some how or other, we all found ourselves in sailor costume spending the evening in the judge's drawing-room. That night every one slept on board.

[Sun.] 9th Aug.   At half past six, we shook ourselves out of our blankets and proceeded to tub. Woodfull and I took the dingy to the West pier and had a bracing swim in the clear cold water. While we were dressing and doing toilette, a man bearing the appearance of a half drunk cobbler arrived accompanied by two small boys. He was very loquacious and inveighed against the uncleanly habits of the Cobourg populace who preferred a basin in their own rooms now and then to a daily swim in the big Lake. His own lavatory tendencies he explained by saying he had been a soldier, and then gave us many curious and interesting details of the bathing parades at Gibraltar. Furthermore, he informed us that every English soldier was obliged to learn to swim and that now, regular skating parades for the troops were held in Canada during the winter. We were hungry and preferred breakfast to acquiring more knowledge, so wished him good morning and returned to the ship. After breakfast, we warped out of harbour under sail.

> *Patterson's Illustrated Nautical Dictionary* (1891) defines warping as moving a vessel by carrying out in a rowboat a small iron anchor (a kedge) with a rope tied to it and, after dropping the anchor ahead of the ship, hauling away on the rope from the ship's deck so as to bring the vessel up to the place where the kedge was thrown overboard from the rowboat. [35] This would be repeated many times until the yacht cleared the harbour. The crew of the *Breeze* resorted to warping the yacht to clear a berth or leave a harbour whenever there was insufficient wind to get out of a sheltered port.

The wind was light, but steady from the South-West.
Goodbye to Cobourg.

Chap. IV

When fairly clear of the harbour, our first care was to set things to rights. Private Miles having been ordered home from Cobourg, showed his displeasure thereat by deserting and has not since been heard of. In his place, a boy answering to the name of Alfred was shipped and instructed to make himself generally useful. A cadaverous, loutish looking fellow requiring constant stirring up, he saved us a deal of dirty work in the cleaning and cooking departments.

> It is likely that Private Miles deserted for a reason other than because he had been "ordered home".
>
> Desertion from the British Army was a problem as old as the army itself. Soldiers deserted for any number of reasons as suggested by one officer writing in 1860: "Many desert from being weary of the tiresomeness of a soldier's life in quarters; others desert from regiments in North America from that cause, and the inducements held out by the Americans of land and independence. Others desert from the tyranny of some non-commissioned officer 'clad in a little brief authority'". [36] In British North America, this was exacerbated by the proximity of many of the British Army garrisons to the United States border, across which deserters could

not be pursued by British authorities. This problem was especially acute during the American Civil War when recruiters from the United States routinely crossed the border and tried, often successfully, to entice British subjects, especially experienced soldiers, to join the Union Army with promises of large enlistment bounties and good pay.

During the course of most of the American Civil War, the Federal enlistment bounty for volunteers was $300, and this was often augmented by state and local bounties.[37] A private in the British Army was paid a nominal one shilling per day, but after stoppages for food and clothing, this amounted to only about nine pence per day or annually £13 13s. 9d., equivalent to 96 American dollars per year at the time.[38] Even if the deserter had to split the $300 bounty with the recruiter, $150 represented the equivalent of well more than a year's pay for the average British soldier. Furthermore, pay in the U.S. Army was almost double that of the British Army.[39] Such financial incentives were difficult for many British soldiers to resist.

The practice of recruiting British subjects for a foreign army was strictly illegal in the British colonies. Even in the United States, it was against regulations to allow a deserter from another army to join the regular U.S. Army. These regulations, however, did not apply to the State volunteer regiments that were raised during the Civil War and which made up the vast majority of the fighting units. The recruiters, known as "crimps", were not official agents of the United States government. If they were caught on British territory trying to enlist British civilians into the U.S. Army, they could be charged under the Neutrality laws and the Foreign Enlistment Act. If convicted, they would be subject to fines and time in jail. For that reason, many of the crimps entered Canada under the guise of "employment agents" for companies who needed to hire men as farm labourers or factory workers. Once the recruits were in the United States, they would be taken to the nearest army enlistment office and sworn in. Those crimps caught trying to recruit a British soldier for service in the United States could be charged under the Mutiny Act for enticing a soldier to desert and could face several years in prison.

In January and February of 1862, while the large contingent of British troops was passing through New Brunswick on their way to garrisons in the Province of Canada, a special civilian police force had been set up "in order to check the desertion of the troops while passing the Maine Boundary Line". [40] Nevertheless, eight soldiers — four from the Guards' regiments and four from the 62nd (Wiltshire) Regiment — still managed to desert during this operation.[41] In Canada, special look-out detachments of soldiers watched for deserters at border points, ports and railway stations. Throughout the 1860's, there were regular newspaper reports of soldiers who deserted their regiments and of the capture of some of the deserters and the crimps who assisted them.

In September 1864, the *New York Times* printed a report from Toronto saying "desertions from the British Army, under the Yankee bounty temptation, are so great that near 1,000 of the Queen's troops have left us the past year. Many points on the Canadian lines are watched for deserters. Three were bagged on the

Niagara River last week, and are to be shot at Hamilton next week. An example has to be made, or Her Majesty will have no troops left in six months."[42] Such reports were outright exaggerations. An examination of newspaper articles in the Toronto *Globe* over the course of two years, from the beginning of 1862 to the end of 1863, shows that were no more than thirty-four desertions from garrisons in Quebec, Montreal and Toronto combined (an average of seventeen desertions per year), including several soldiers from Private Miles' regiment, the 30th Cambridgeshires. While many desertions likely went unreported in the newspaper, *The New York Times'* estimate of 1,000 in a single year is a gross overstatement. Furthermore, when deserters were captured and court-martialled, the punishment could be imprisonment for up to ten years, but it was never death. [43]

The fact that Private Miles deserted at all is somewhat surprising. Officers' servants were usually soldiers of good character and among the most trustworthy men in the regiment. Also, if it had been his intention to escape to the United States, it would have been a difficult undertaking to attempt from Cobourg since that town is relatively distant from the U.S. border. First, he would have had to obtain a suit of civilian clothes. Next, he would have to find transport. From Cobourg, the best route would have been aboard a steamboat destined for a port on the New York side of Lake Ontario, such as Charlotte or Oswego.

Whatever his motivations for deserting, Private Miles was never heard from again.

To each man was assigned a resting place. The Commodore had the aftermost berth on the starboard side; I the one forward on the same side; Woodfull opposite the Commodore and Duggan the one forward on the port. Mello turned in with the Commodore, and Harvey spread a mattress between the berths on the floor. His were the most comfortable diggings of all as, no matter which tack we were on, there was no chance of his falling out of bed. As a drawback however, he had only a fluctuating share in the pins over each berth and constantly found his things dispossessed of their hanging room by the occupants of the berths beneath them.

⊲ As tight as sleeping arrangements were in the main cabin of the *Breeze*, Baines makes no reference to where Burrel and the new cook, Alfred, would sleep. Presumably, they could be accommodated in the boat's forecastle where the cooking was also done.

As our uniform cases reposed in the cockpit, we were forced to adopt some dodge to enable us to have an accessible depot for tobacco, pipes, clothing and small deer [insignificant items] generally below. Our plan was to raise the mattress and insinuate our stores beneath it so as to make a pillow. It was a crafty move, but from it came great grief to me hereafter. The tobacco question was simplified

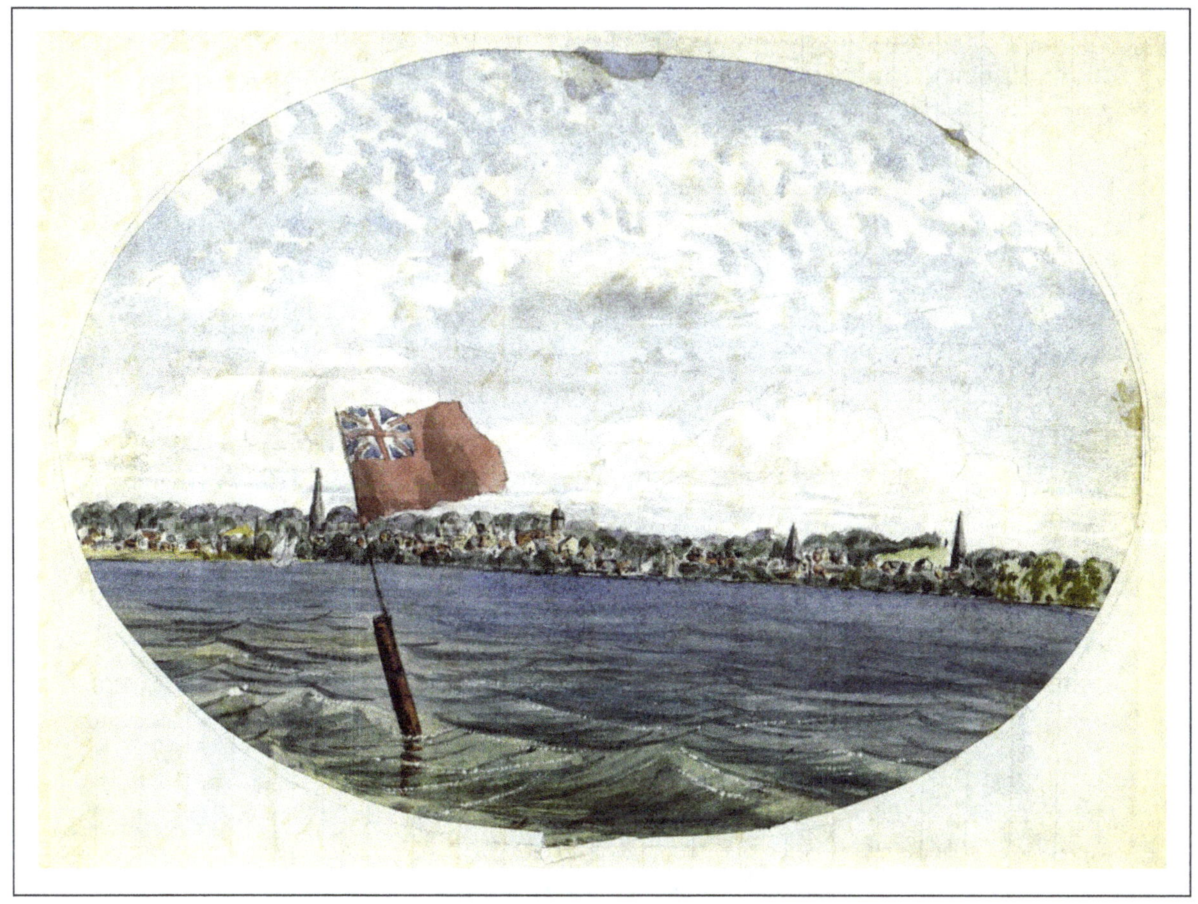

Untitled (Cobourg in the distance).
Henry Edward Baines, 1863. Watercolour and pencil on paper.
[Courtesy of Library and Archives Canada.]

I took a sketch of Cobourg in the distance with one of the regatta buoys in the foreground.
The tall spire on the left is that of the Scotch Church, a handsome new building; that on the right belongs
to the Episcopal Church and the small dome in the centre crowns the town hall.

by the introduction of the principle of voluntary labour. Each had brought a goodly stock with him. A small jar was set apart as a common expense magazine and any one who felt inclined cut up his own tobacco till he was tired and placed the result in the public receptacle.

All things being arranged, we had leisure to look about us. I took a sketch of Cobourg in the distance with one of the regatta buoys in the foreground.

The tall spire on the left is that of the Scotch Church, a handsome new building; that on the right belongs to the Episcopal Church and the small dome in the centre crowns the town hall, a very fine block containing the best ball room I have seen in Canada. It is of this edifice that a certain Yankee is reported to have said to an enthusiastic native who was pointing out its architectural beauties, "Yes sir! A fine taown hall. But Mister, whar the h--l's yer taown?" The truth is that at the time when most of the public buildings in Canada were erected, the projectors imagined their villages would almost immediately swell into cities and designed proportionate accommodation. Swell the frog did, but there was no India rubber in his skin and few classes or localities have yet recovered the effects of "the bad year" when the inevitable squash arrived. Well does jolly hospitable Cobourg deserve its fine town hall, and I only hope that the business downstairs will be as eminently satisfactory to the lawyers and clients as the ball's above have always been to guests and givers.

    ◄ "The bad year" is probably a reference to the Panic of 1857 which saw a major downturn in the United States economy with residual effects in Canada into 1858. Construction of the Cobourg town hall, also known as Victoria Hall, was started in 1856, at a time when the town was prospering and many of the townspeople had thoughts that Cobourg would soon be so large as to be designated a city and, therefore, in need of a suitable city hall. Such was never to be the case. The town never achieved the status of a city but the imposing town hall remains to this day.[44]

From Cobourg, our course lay nearly East to Presqu'Isle, a run of about 25 miles [40 kilometers]. We kept pretty close to shore all the way. A narrow level plateau on the Lake backed by a range of low hills, well cultivated and patched with woods, extended the whole distance. Grafton and Colborne are two villages lying a little way inland and each having a wharf into the Lake for the benefit of schooners loading wood and farm produce.

    ◄ Just to the east of Cobourg, Grafton and Colborne, with a population in the 1860's of 500 and 800 respectively,[45] are some three kilometers inland from the shore of Lake Ontario..

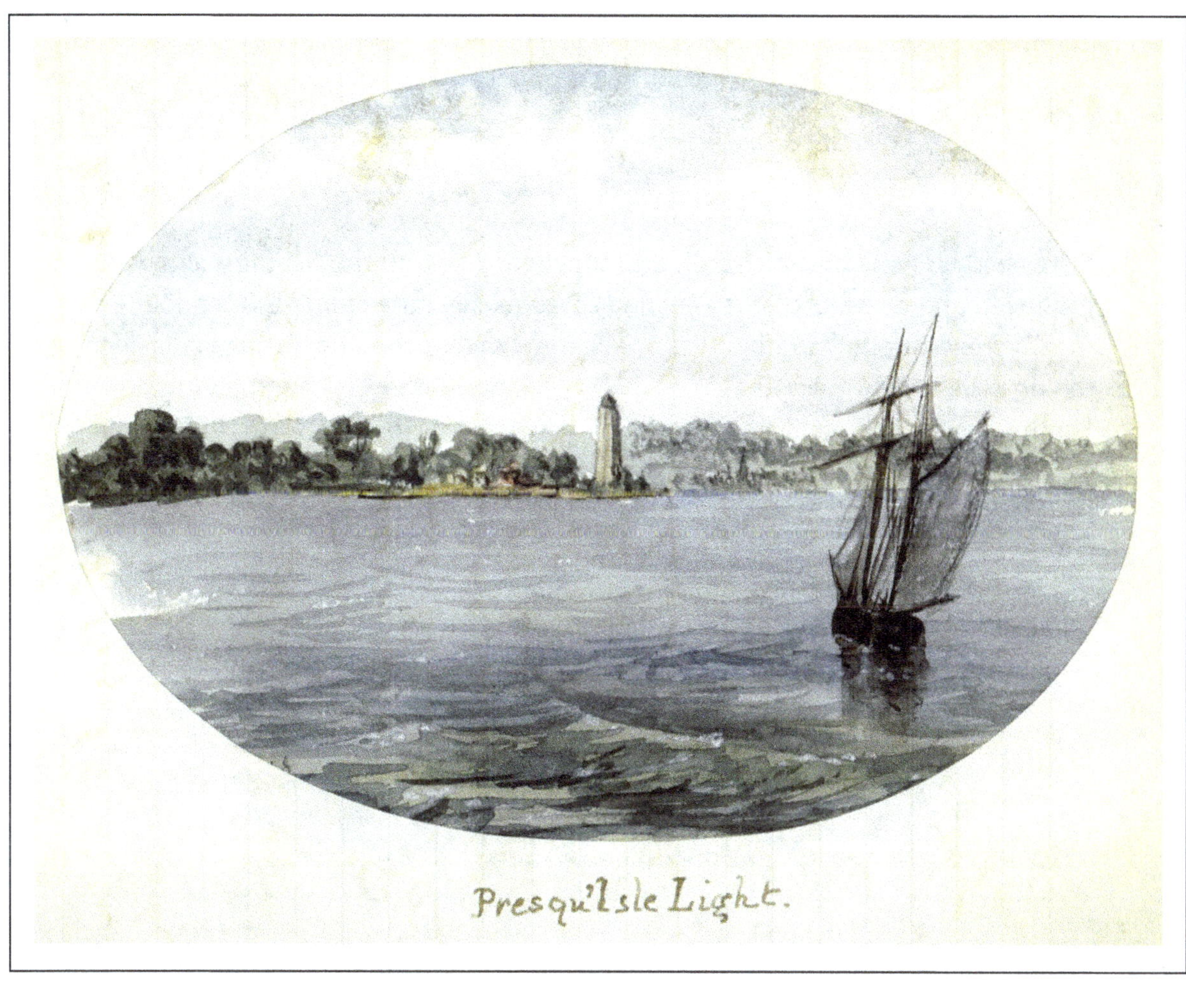

Presqu'Isle Light.
Henry Edward Baines, 1863. Watercolour and pencil on paper.
[Courtesy of Library and Archives Canada.]
This scene shows a two-masted schooner sailing towards the entrance to Presqu'ile Bay which is far to the
right of the lighthouse.

At 1:35, we were one mile South of the western point of Presqu'Isle, a low woody peninsula enclosing the wide harbour. We got up cheese and crackers,

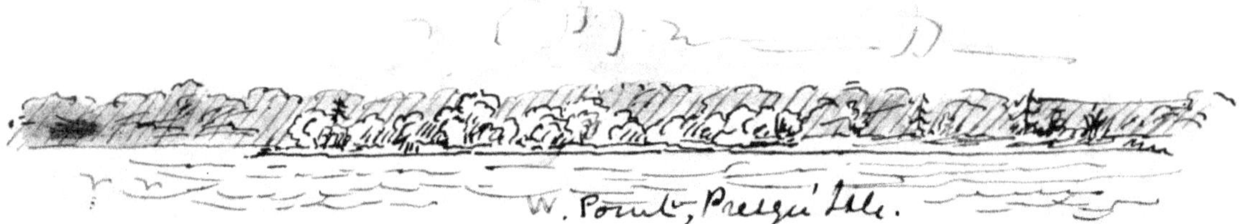

likewise the divine half-and-half, and lunched. Then all the fishing tackle was produced and distributed. We ran along Presqu'Isle, passing the East end at 3:10, then worked through a rather devious channel and anchored a little way inside the first range light [also known as the Salt Point lighthouse.] On the West and South stretched the peninsula and the marshy isthmus; on the North, the mainland with the town of Brighton about two miles inland, and on the East, a low shore, rushy and abounding in small cedar swamps.

> Presqu'ile is a large L-shaped peninsula jutting out some three kilometers into Lake Ontario. At the tip of the peninsula is the Presqu'ile Point lighthouse, built in 1840, where William Swetman had been the lightkeeper since it was built. One kilometer further along the shore, the Salt Point lighthouse, built in 1851, served as the front range light which worked in tandem with another nearby lighthouse to help guide ships through what was then "a rather devious channel." Hodder describes Presqu'ile and its harbour in *The Harbours and Ports of Lake Ontario*: "Twenty-four miles E. ¼ N. of Cobourg is the west or bluff point of Presqu'Isle, well wooded, and with 90 feet water within a short distance of the shore.... Five miles N.E. by E. of this point will bring you abreast of the lighthouse, which is 67 feet high, and upon which there is a very good fixed bright light, that can be seen in fine weather from 12 to 15 miles. Immediately under the lighthouse, to the southward, there is shoal water with boulders; but by keeping half a mile from the shore, this danger is easily avoided.... The channel which leads into this fine harbour now becomes difficult, owing to the shoals which surround it being entirely destitute of buoys or beacons to mark them."[46]
>
> The town of Brighton, situated on the Grand Trunk Railway line three kilometers inland from Presqu'ile Bay, had two mills and four hotels, and a population of 1,182.[47]

The Commodore set off to visit the Light-house. Harvey and I took the dingy to the East side, getting a friendly tow from a sail boat which rushed along at a

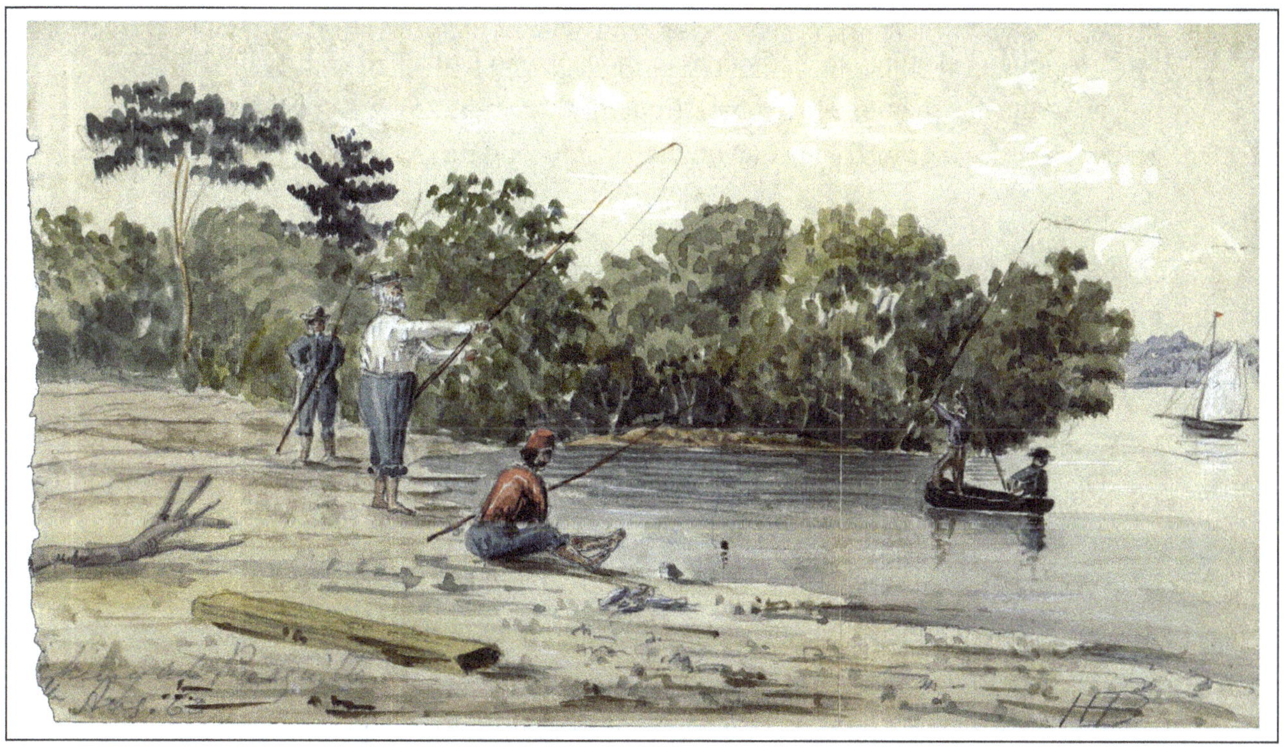

Fishing At Presqu'Isle, Aug. 63.
Henry Edward Baines, 1863. Watercolour and pencil on paper.
[Courtesy of Library and Archives Canada.]

After dinner, we fished off shore and off the ships with small success

The figure in red sitting on the shore may be Henry Harvey. The older man to his left is Commodore Hodder. The boy next to the commodore is likely Hodder's son, Mello. To the right are two men in a dinghy, and at far right is the *Breeze* at anchor in Presqu'ile Bay.

grand pace. We caught one big bass, about 2½ lb. [1.1 kg], while we were being towed, but no more, and after a short time, the flag was hauled down on board the ship as a signal of dinner being ready, and we returned. After dinner, we fished off shore and off the ships with small success. While waiting on the beach for a boat, I met two men belonging to a schooner in the bay who had killed and skinned a racoon in the marsh on their way back from Brighton. Returning on board, we made preparations for a great fishing day on the morrow and turned in early.

[Mon.] 10th Aug.   All hands turn out by five; tumble overboard and swim and then off to fish. We had secured two shore boats in addition to the dingy. Some trolled with the spoon [a type of fishing lure], some moored their boats above a sunken pier and fished with worms, and the others, baiting with eyes and other titbits of the bass caught over night, angled from the ship. By breakfast time, we had a good many pike and bass. Another plunge, then feed, then fish again. While trolling near the first range light, some monster of the deep carried away my favourite spoon by biting the strong wire completely through. Then I fished off the ship. The bottom was covered with long weeds and we dropped our lines in the most open spaces we could find. Burrel hooked a pickerel, but the tackle was too light and, despite the most scientific play, he broke loose just as he got clear of the water.

At two p.m., the Commodore and Woodfull returned from trolling with a boat [full] of fine fish. All smaller ones being thrown aside, we counted our gains and found a satisfactory total of 31 black bass and 8 pike. Then Bologna sausage, biscuits, hymns of triumph and half-and-half. At 2:15, having sent off the shore boats with a bucket of fish to the Light-house keeper, we weighed and stood out of Presqu'Isle with a nice light breeze from the South-West.

We had hardly cleared the entrance of Presqu'Isle when we ran into Weller's Bay; a large but shallow sheet of water bounded towards the Lake by a curious range of sand hills on which grow a few pines and low bushes. The other sides are low and woody, with fields and cottages scattered at long intervals over them. We caught a large bass as we went in with the spoon. Once fairly inside, there is plenty of water and that deep enough, but once we just scraped bottom in the channel. On the South-East, the land was broken by a wide channel leading into Consecon bay.

> During a tremendous storm in 1856, enormous waves carved a channel through the barrier beach of sand dunes separating Wellers Bay from Lake Ontario. This allowed ships to enter the bay as it was one of the only harbours of refuge between Kingston and Toronto. In the 19th Century, this bay was often considered as two separate bodies of water; the smaller portion nearer to Presqu'ile was known as Wellers Bay, and the larger portion was known as Consecon Bay. Today the entire body of water is called Wellers Bay.[48]
>
> Commodore Hodder was familiar with the dangerous shoals leading into Wellers Bay and he commented on them in *The Harbours and Ports of Lake Ontario*: "The shoals opposite the entrance to Weller's Bay are rocky, and have only from 3 to 5 feet water on them; they are also so exposed, that any vessel running ashore on them during a gale, must soon go to pieces."[49] After the *Breeze* scraped bottom, the commodore and Burrel checked the depth of the water using a lead-line; a lead weight attached to a length of rope with markings on it showing the depth of the water.[50] This line, also known as a hand lead, was dropped into the water at intervals to verify that it was deep enough for the *Breeze* to pass safely.

Having anchored and lowered head sails, the Commodore and Burrel took the dingy and lead line and proceeded to examine this opening; soon returning, they reported it practicable. We got under weigh and ran through it. Opening out before us as we advanced lay the pretty land-locked harbour of Consecon. Wooded background, bright green water, meadows and occasional farm-houses slipped rapidly by for about four miles. Then two or three reedy islets were passed and we rounded to, anchored, lowered the ensign and fired a gun as a salute to the inhabitants of Consecon. Two small boys on the wharf uttered a cheer, whereupon a woman appeared and, after a fight, captured one of them and bore him off struggling. Nothing else greeted us and, wondering at the apathy of the inhabitants, we made our toilettes and proceeded on shore.

> Consecon is a village at the eastern end of Wellers Bay in Prince Edward County. The County itself was, and still largely is, an agricultural area occupying a massive peninsula some sixty kilometers across and protruding into Lake Ontario more than twenty kilometers. By the 1860's, Consecon was a growing commercial port. It had a population of 500 along with three churches, two hotels and two mills.[51] In 1876, twenty years after ships began frequenting Wellers Bay, it was officially recognized by the Canadian government as a harbour of refuge and two range lights were constructed to guide ships through its narrow entrance.[52]

Up the road a little way, then turn to the right at the church and down "the long unlonely street," we came upon the tavern with its circumambient loafers and a few stores. The Commodore gave an impetus to the commerce of Consecon by purchasing some pepper and salt at the boot and shoe store, then we turned to the left, crossed a bubbling babbling brook which turned a flour mill, then passed under the bridge and wandered away beneath the trees to the bay; found ourselves in a continuation of the village and, finally, arrived at the top of a little hill. There we stopped to admire the quiet simple view. On one side, the bright calm waters of the bay sparkled in the sun before us. The white houses and gray church of the village peeped out from the sheltering trees. On the right, a stretch of about a mile of green open country ended in the blue of Consecon Lake. The hill on which we were standing forms part of an elevated plateau whose abrupt wooded capes and steep ravines are the chief beauty of the wide pool we gazed at — as a back ground, the blue hills in Northumberland [County] and Hastings [County], and a slight rise of intervening country behind which lay Trentport and the head of the bay of Quinte, distant only four miles [six kilometers].

We bought bread and cheese on our return to the village and also a bucket which was henceforward kept solely for fresh water; a necessary precaution as, though the Lake-water itself is excellent, that in the harbours and rivers is muddy and unfit for drinking.

The principal trade of Consecon seemed to be in lollipops, string and pop corn; at least so one would judge from the contents of the shop windows. There are two Churches; one, the Wesleyan, of stone.

As regards the churches in Consecon, Baines is mistaken. In 1863, there were three churches in the town: the Wesleyan Methodist church (Reverend Joel Briggs) and Holy Trinity Church of England (Reverend H.E. Plees) both on the north side of Consecon creek, and the Presbyterian church (Reverend Thomas Kellough) across the bridge on the south side.[53] Of the three churches, only Holy Trinity was built of stone. The others were wood-frame structures.[54] Only the Methodist church (now the Consecon United Church) is still used as a place of worship. Holy Trinity is now used as the Consecon Public Library, and the Presbyterian church is no longer standing.

The prettiest thing about Consecon was the peep down the brook from the bridge, so I made a rough sketch thereof.

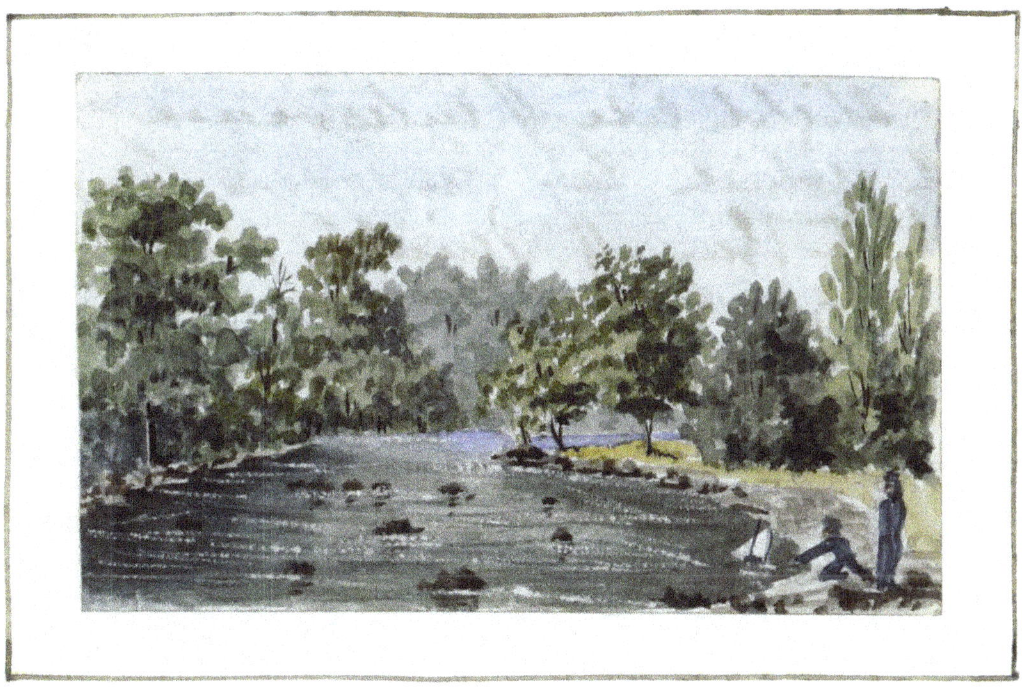

Consecon Creek.

We returned on board, procured fresh water from a well hard by and then gave all our energies to a sumptuous dinner of bass and pike, fried ham and veal, and mighty beakers of the warm south, that is, half-and-half.

◀ Another literary reference, "beakers of the warm south", is taken from the second stanza of the poem "Ode to a Nightingale", published in 1820 by the English poet John Keats (1795-1821)". The entire stanza is as follows:

> O, for a draught of vintage! that hath been
>   Cool'd long age in the deep-delved earth,
> Tasting of Flora and the country green,
>   Dance, and Provençal song, and sunburnt mirth!
> O for a beaker full of the warm south,
>   Full of the true, the blushful Hippocrene,
>   With beaded bubbles winking at the brim,
>   And purple-stained mouth;
> That I might drink, and leave the world unseen,
>   And with thee fade away into the forest dim.[55]

It was very hot that night. Harvey and Fred Duggan arranged couches on deck. We turned in at ten o'clock and, at about four, down came the rain in buckets full, cooling the air and driving the restless individuals above into the cabin; "not drowned, but very wet."

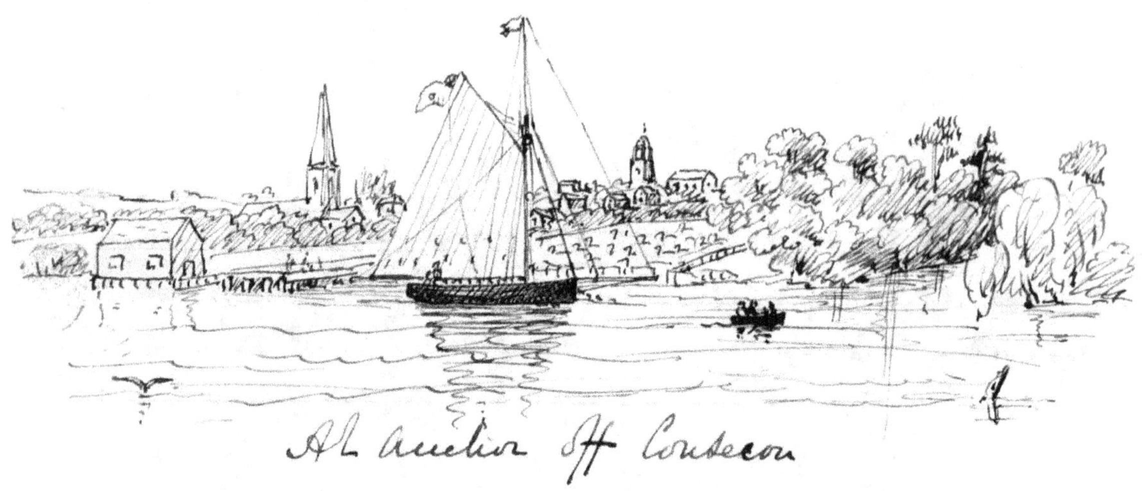

Chap. V

[Tues.] 11th August. All hands on deck at 7 a.m.. Tumble overboard and swam about, then breakfast and a pipe. Weighed anchor at 9:30. With a slashing breeze out of the South, we ran through the smooth bays and were fairly in the Lake by 10:30, then commenced a long beat of twelve miles dead to windward with a nice little sea running straight before the wind. Our object was to get between the rocky group known as the Scotch Bonnet and Nicholas Island so that we might bear away round Prince Edward and get into South Bay, on its eastern coast, by night.

This group 12 miles [19 kilometers] S.E. of Presqu'Isle Light.

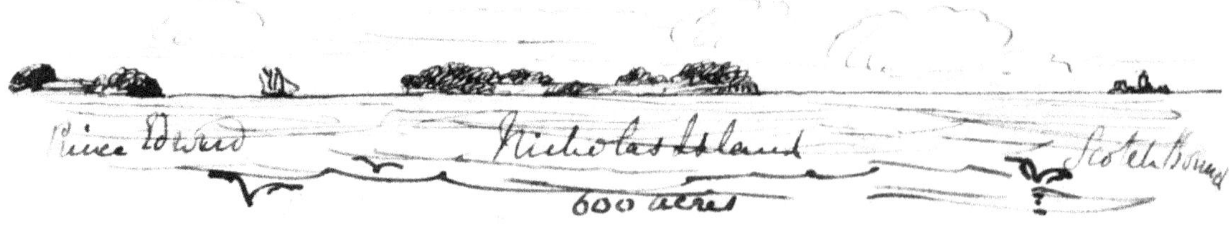

◄ The 200-acre (85 hectare) Nicholas Island, one-and-a-half kilometers west off of Prince Edward County's Huycks Point, is now known as Nicholson Island. Scotch Bonnet Island, a tiny outcropping of rock, hardly more than a meter above lake level, is situated a further one-and-a-half kilometers out in Lake Ontario. This is where the Province of Canada built a masonry lighthouse and lightkeeper's dwelling in 1856.

At last we got fairly clear of them and changed our course for E.S.E. At about five o'clock, we were nearly off Long Point [Point Petre in Prince Edward County.] The wind was steady and there was nothing to do. All at once, the sky clouded over to the South-West. We watched it earnestly and it soon became evident that a pretty heavy squall was coming up. We took in the jib and double reefed the mainsail. One squall passed astern of us towards the North-East. After a very short consultation, the mainsail was lowered and hurriedly stopped [tied with a short length of rope], then the wind fell nearly calm. All the sky was dark with a strange blue tint over it. First, drifted above us, a long line of pale grey clouds with broken streaming edges, then out of the South-West burst three flashes of lightning flooding the whole sky with intense brilliancy. While our eyes were still dazzled with the glare of the last, the squall burst over us — a sudden violent gust of wind, then steady hard blow with thick streaming rain. We knew well enough that coats were useless, so met it in shirts and trousers only; barefooted too. It deluged us at once. The wind was so violent that we could not keep our faces to it. The dark Lake changed to a pale grey with the crests of the waves marked in broad lines of dull blue. Everything on board was snug and fast; Burrel at the helm. We drove through the water under our foresail sheeted down close, at a grand pace. We made a stout rope fast to the dingy and paid out some five or six fathoms [about 30 feet, or 10 meters of rope] that she might be clear of our counter [the boat's transom.] Harder and harder it blew and still we drove before it. A large schooner away to the southward caught it hot and heavy. She let go everything [lowered all sails], but the fore-staysail with a run, and kept the same course as ourselves.

Presently the sea got up, following us at first in short broken waves which, by degrees, grew into long regular masses of dull green water, like billows at sea. The dingy was terribly tossed about. At last, a wave slewed her on one side, the painter slackened, then tautened suddenly. The staple was torn out and our poor little boat was left alone on the wild sea to shift for herself. The first fury of the squall was now spent, but it still blew a gale and the sea grew heavier. From North, South and East, the lightning flashed incessantly overhead. The thunder crashed at short intervals. All the sky was black, except one very beautiful break to the westward; a clear space amongst the clouds, orange, golden, over the blue trees of Prince Edward, reddening upwards to the bright edges of the storm rack beneath which the broad shield of the sun floated in a narrow space of pure white light. Over against this stretched the full arch of a perfect double rainbow. The sun set and darkness came on apace. Again the wind got up. We sighted the Duck's Light [the False Ducks Island lighthouse.] Then our course was altered and it became necessary to set the mainsail. We close reefed it. I had to lay out on the boom to clear the reef pennant which had fouled the cringle [a grommet used for reefing] and, failing to effect this, I got a stop [a short length of rope] and lashed the sail to the spar. The operation reduced me to a state of sea sickness! Here we met the cross sea from the Bay of Quinté [through the Upper Gap between Prince Edward County and Amherst Island], and pretty heavy it was. The boat behaved admirably; not a drop of water but rain or spray came aboard. Like a cork, she rode over the great waves that came rolling up astern threatening to overwhelm us. Once or twice, big schooners appeared suddenly out of the darkness. One showed no light, but just stood across our bows and vanished to the northward. As we got more under the lee of the land, the sea went down. Wet, tired and sick, I turned in and slept till half-past two [in the morning]. We then anchored at Kingston, and ham, biscuits and whisky were going round. I partook slightly and slept again.

The squall was heavy on the Lake. The steamer from Toronto, unable to make Cobourg, ran on to Kingston. The *Banshee,* from Kingston, put back with her bulwarks carried away. Off Port Hope, the *Rivet* lost her mast and, with difficulty, got into Cobourg, half full of water.

◄ The Breezers' intended destination on August 11 was South Bay (Prince Edward Bay) on the sheltered eastern side of the Prince Edward peninsula, however the storm they encountered blew them past their planned anchorage.

The thunderstorm that their yacht weathered that day was severe enough that it was remarked upon by several newspapers around Lake Ontario. From Oswego, New York, the *Oswego Commercial Times* reported: "Shortly after seven o'clock last evening masses of clouds rolled up from the north, west and south-west, bringing with them a gale of wind. The clouds quickly overspread the whole horizon. The scene was impressively grand. The clouds were charged with electricity, and vivid lightning chain and forked, flashed and darted through the air in a terrific manner. We never remember seeing a pyrotechnic displaying the heavens on so grand a scale."[56] Kingston's *Daily News* reported: "The wind gradually increased until,

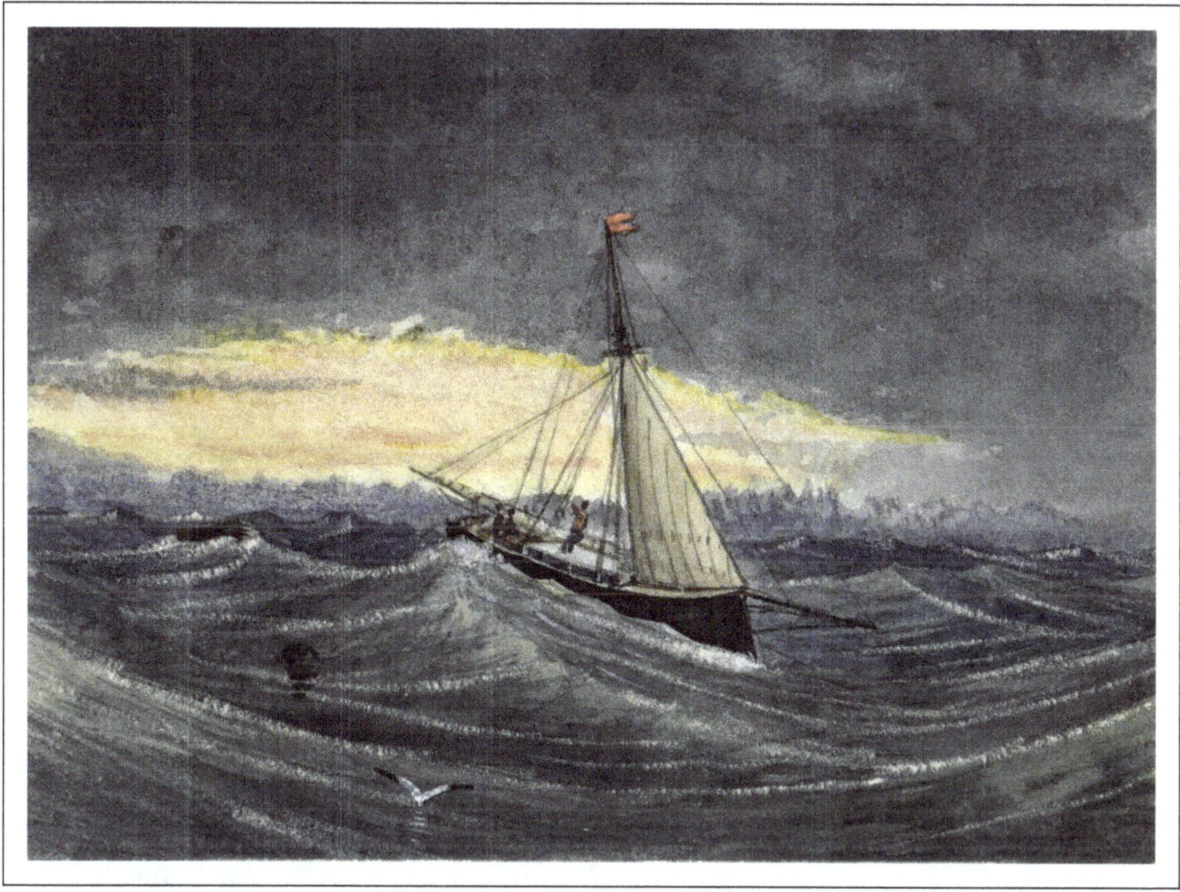

En Route To Kingston.
Henry Edward Baines, 1863. Watercolour, pencil and ink on paper.
[Courtesy of Library and Archives Canada.]

We drove through the water under our foresail sheeted down close, at a grand pace.
All the sky was black, except one very beautiful break to the westward; a clear space amongst the clouds,
orange, golden, over the blue trees of Prince Edward.

shortly before seven, it rose to a furious gale, while the rain came down in torrents. The storm was of brief duration, however, and in about an hour after it began the clouds had passed over and the heavens had assumed their usual aspect."[57]

That same storm system caused a considerable amount of damage all across the Great Lakes, including the spoiling of an estimated one million tons of wheat being carried aboard several ships that were bound to Buffalo, New York[58]. That the *Breeze* was able to endure such a storm with only the loss of her dinghy, attests to the skill of the master and crew, and to the seaworthiness of the vessel.

At the time of the storm, the *Breeze* was sailing through some of the Great Lakes' most dangerous waters. Long Point in Prince Edward County extends from Point Petre eastward to Prince Edward Point where it then becomes mostly submerged to form a line of shoals and rocky islands all the way across Lake Ontario to Stoney Point on the New York shore. Along this line, known by hydrographers as the "Duck-Galloo Ridge", the lake narrows and becomes significantly shallower as it flows toward the entrance of the St. Lawrence River at Kingston. This narrowing and shoaling of Lake Ontario combines to magnify the effects of storms, and this resulted in so many ship sinkings and shipwrecks in the 19th Century that the area became known by mariners as "The Graveyard of Lake Ontario".[59]

Today, most yachtsmen avoid this dangerous coast by passing through the Murray Canal which runs between Presqu'ile Bay and the Bay of Quinte. This route along the north shore of Prince Edward County was opened in 1890 and provides shelter from most of the heavy weather that frequently hits Lake Ontario.

[Wed.] Aug. 12th. Rose at six. As we were anchored in mid-stream and had no dingy, we got up the foresail and dropped alongside Holcomb's Wharf [the Holcomb, Coward & Co. wharf at the foot of Kingston's Gore Street]. Bathing and toilette collected a lot of loafers who peered into the cabin while we were at breakfast. The Commodore went with Duggan to buy a boat for a dingy and we got up sail. A little further up near the bridge was the wharf [the Government Wharf] belonging to the Tête du Pont barracks, which are occupied by the 47th Regt. We moved alongside of this and remained there all the time we were in Kingston. The officers of the 47th were very civil; gave us the use of their rooms and made us feel quite at home with them.

Kingston was originally built around the site of Fort Frontenac, constructed by the French in 1673.[60] With its sheltered harbour and strategic location at the entrance to the St. Lawrence River, Kingston became the largest and most prosperous town in Upper Canada in the early years of the 19th Century. It was incorporated as a city in 1846, and by the 1860's, Kingston had a population of 14,000.[61]

Commodore Hodder described its harbour as, "next to the Bay of Toronto, the best natural harbour on Lake Ontario; the approach to it, however is intricate —

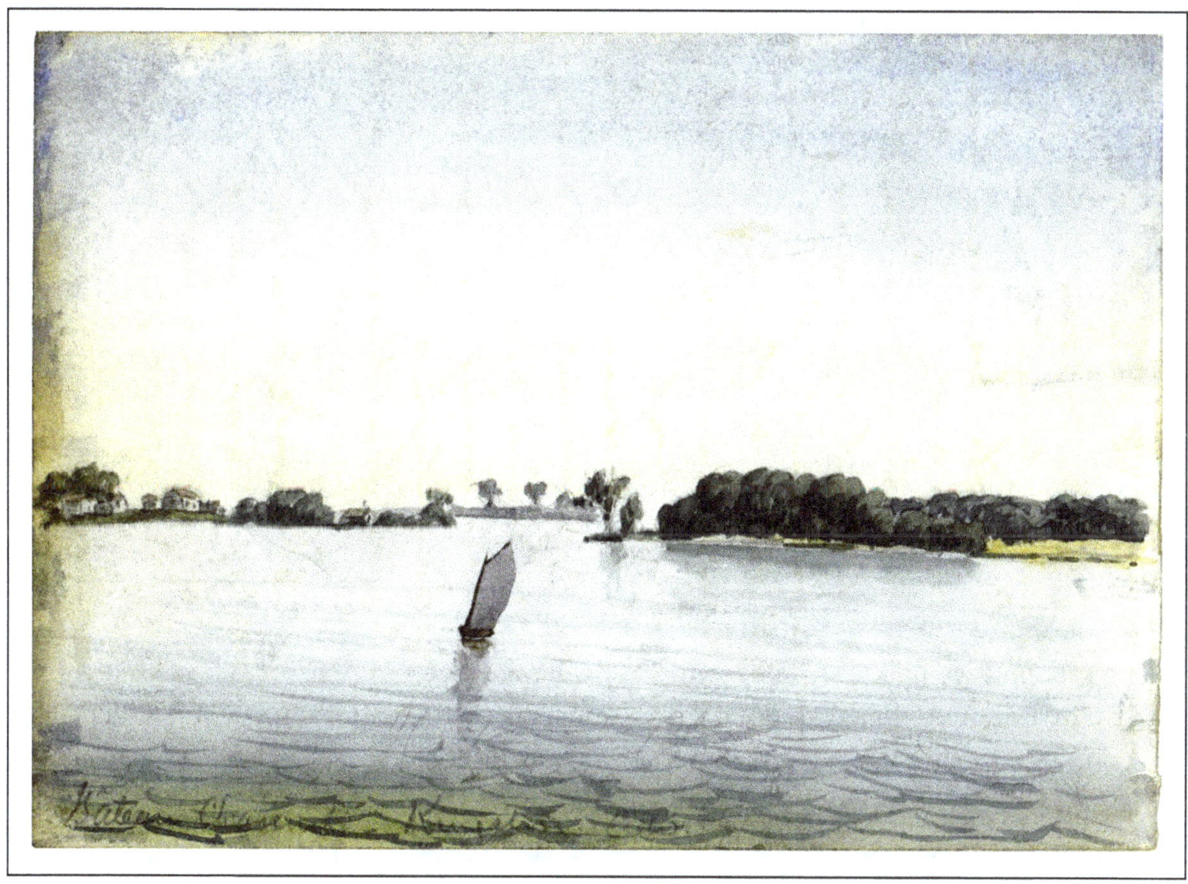

East Entrance to Bateau Channel - Kingston.
Henry Edward Baines, 1863. Watercolour and pencil on paper.
[Courtesy of Library and Archives Canada.]

Sailed in the afternoon toward Bateau Channel, the entrance to which I sketched.

consequently dangerous. There are three channels by which it may be made. 1st, the Bateau Channel between Wolfe or Long Island, and Simcoe or Gage Island. 2nd, South Channel, between Simcoe or Gage Island and Snake Island. 3rd, North Channel, which is the best, having from 4 to 10 fathoms water in it."[62]

Kingston's role as a trans-shipment port for goods moving up and down the St. Lawrence River, combined with its position as the southern terminus of the Rideau Canal connecting north to the Ottawa River, made the town a strategic military centre. After Quebec, Kingston was the most heavily fortified city in the Province of Canada with Fort Henry serving as the city's citadel to protect the harbour and Royal Navy dockyard. A series of artillery batteries and Martello towers augmented the city's defences.

The Tête du Pont barracks was a fortified barrack block built by the British in the 1820's at the western end of the bridge which crossed the Cataraqui River from Kingston to Fort Henry. The 47th (Lancashire) Regiment, an infantry regiment with 1,100 officers and men, had arrived at Quebec aboard the *Golden Fleece* in July, 1861, and was first stationed at Montreal.[63] In May, 1863, the regiment was transferred to Kingston for garrison duty at Fort Henry and at the Tête du Pont barracks.[64]

In addition to the infantry regiment, No. 4 and No. 6 Batteries of the Royal Artillery's 10th Garrison Brigade were also stationed at Kingston along with one troop of the 1st Battalion, Military Train.

As soon as we had dressed decently, we called on the R.A. mess and accepted an invitation to dinner there in the evening. I loafed about the town and called on the Kirkpatricks.

◄ The "R.A. mess" is the Royal Artillery officers' club and dining room that was located at the Artillery Barracks on Kingston's Barrack Street, four blocks from the Government Wharf.

The Kirkpatricks were a prominent Kingston family. Thomas Kirkpatrick was a yachtsman and a lawyer who held numerous civic positions including director of the waterworks. He was also one of the founding shareholders of the Grand Trunk Railway.[65]

Kingston is a solid quiet irregular place, like an English country town. The scenery round is pretty and the number of islands in the river form a great contrast to the wide open Lake outside the other harbours we visited. We had a jolly little dinner in the evening. I was so tired out that I fell asleep soon after mess and only woke when the rest of our party were saying farewell.

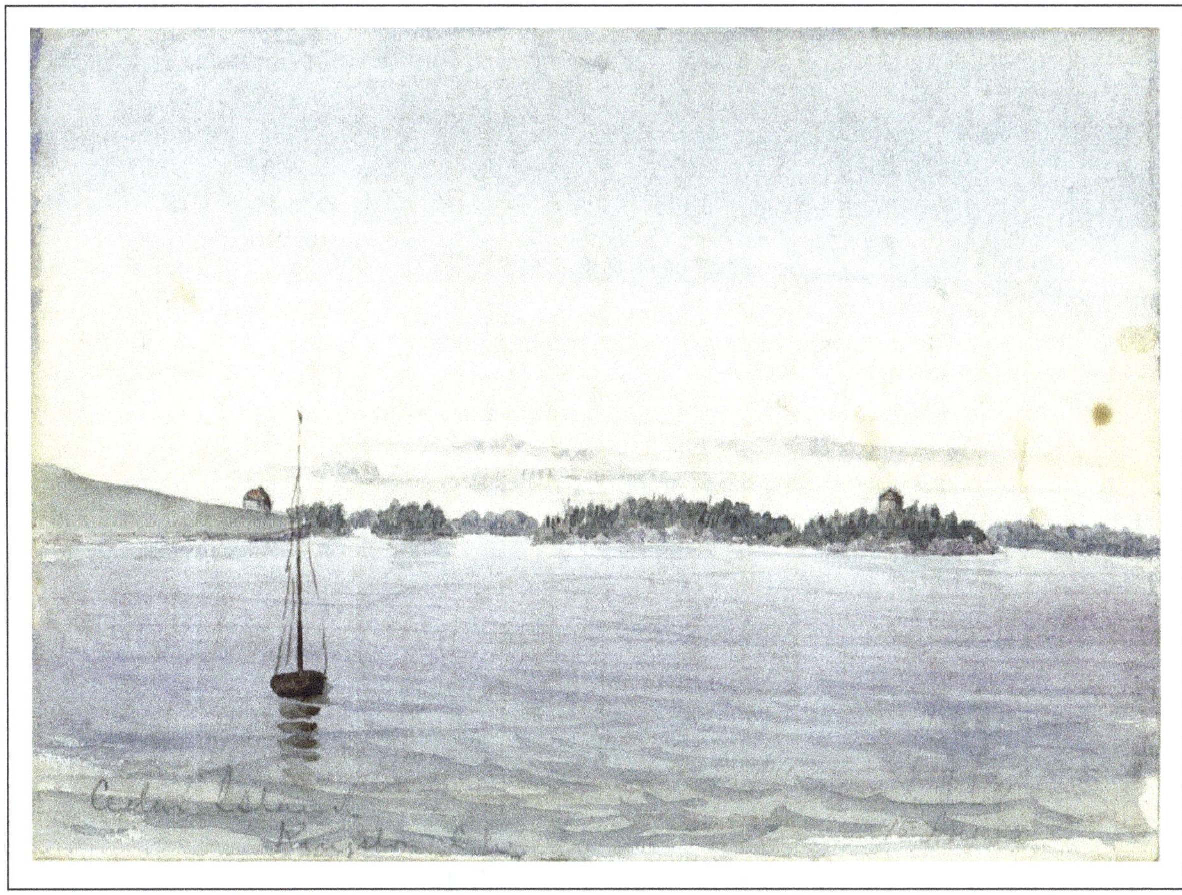

Cedar Island. Kingston C.W. [Canada West]
Henry Edward Baines, 1863. Watercolour and pencil on paper.
[Courtesy of Library and Archives Canada.]

To the left can be seen the top of the East Ditch tower at Fort Henry. To the right is the Martello tower on Cedar Island.

[Thurs.] 13th August.   Up at seven. After breakfast, logging up [writing in his journal] and letter writing. Sailed in the afternoon towards Bateau Channel, the entrance to which I sketched; also Cedar Island, the other side of the Citadel [Fort Henry] from the town. I got a sketch of part of Kingston too, showing the bridge to the Citadel and two of the Martello towers which form part of the defences of the place.

> A Martello tower is a round masonry tower built as a self-contained fort. These towers were generally three stories high: a storeroom on the lower floor for food and ammunition, a barrack room on the middle floor to accommodate several soldiers and usually large enough to also contain a number of artillery pieces, and an artillery platform on the upper floor for one or more guns. There were four Martello towers constructed in Kingston in the 1840's, although they were not fully armed until 1863. The Murney Tower at the south end of the city had three guns, the Shoal Tower in the harbour opposite the city hall had four guns, the Fort Frederick Tower across the harbour at the naval dockyard had eight guns, and the Cedar Island Tower just east of Fort Henry had four guns.[66] All of these towers still stand today.

We tried trolling, but caught nothing. Knox and Robinson were on board, but the Commodore had been obliged to go to Toronto on business and did not return till the 15th. In the evening, Harvey, Duggan and I dined with the 47th [Regiment].

> Baines often mentions individuals without indicating who they are. 2nd-Captain George Uchter Knox was a Royal Artillery officer stationed at Kingston. Formerly with the 6th Brigade stationed in Britain, he had transferred to the 10th Brigade in Canada in November 1862. As for Robinson, here again Baines shows some difficulty with remembering names. There were no military men in Kingston at that time named Robinson. However, there was a young Royal Artillery lieutenant, Robert Henderson Robertson, who had arrived from Britain with the rest of the 10th Brigade at Halifax in January, 1862. This is likely who Baines is referring to.[67]

[Fri.] 14th August.   Woodfull left at six [and would not meet up with his cruising companions again until the following week]. Breakfast at nine, lunch with the 47th and sail with two of them afterwards. It was very squally, so we went above [the] bridge into the river Cataruiqui [Cataraqui River.] We got under the lee of the island [Belle Island] and bathed. No sooner did we show our noses beyond it than the wind caught us again and we went before it some two miles further. Then we anchored and waited till it moderated a little. The boat was very fast and we beat up

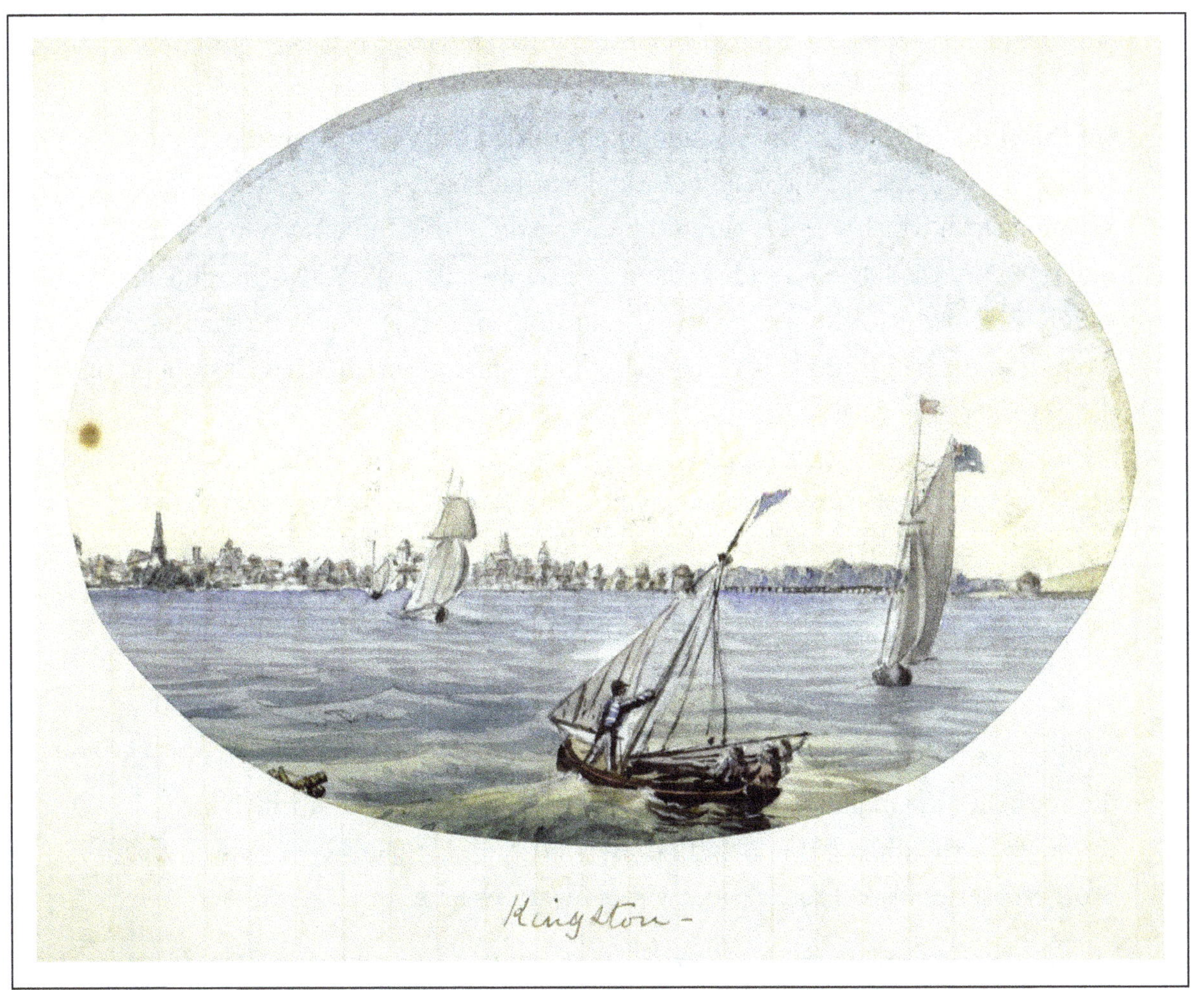

Kingston.
Henry Edward Baines, 1863. Watercolour and pencil on paper.
[Courtesy of Library and Archives Canada.]

I got a sketch of part of Kingston too, showing the bridge to the Citadel and two of the Martello towers which form part of the defences of the place.

At far right is the Fort Frederick Martello tower. To the left of that is the bridge over the Cataraqui River. Just to the left of the sail of the boat in the foreground is the Martello tower known as the Shoal Tower.

rapidly enough, but the weeds were so thick that at every tack we had to raise the centre-board to disengage the weeds collected on it. We met one squall, but, by anchoring and lowering away promptly, lost no ground and only got wet through in less than a minute. I dined with the 47th that night also.

On [Sat.] the 15th Aug., the Commodore returned early in the morning. After breakfast, we did shopping; fishing tackle dear and bad. The Commodore bought a capital stove which was put up in the forecastle. I took the office of cook for that day. At 9:15, having decided that Kingston was played out, we got under weigh. The town looked very pretty with its domed market-place and many spires. We passed the handsome lunatic asylum and the prison which are well situated on the heights to the West of the town.

> The "domed market place" was Kingston City Hall. The city market was attached to the city hall, but behind it and not visible from the water. The provincial penitentiary, situated in the village of Portsmouth on the western edge of Kingston, had been built in the 1830's and served as a maximum security prison until it was closed in 2013. The provincial lunatic asylum, later renamed Rockwood Hospital, was a little further west and was still under construction in 1863.

Through the North Channel we held our course with light wind and smooth water; trolling line out too, but without result. On the port side lay Amherst Island; on the starboard the mainland, wooded to the edge of the low cliffs which form the shore, yet well cultivated and settled. Beyond Amherst Island, we passed the Brothers, several small rocky islets with a few trees on each.

> While sailing back towards Prince Edward County, westward through the North Channel between Amherst Island and the mainland of Addington County (now the County of Lennox & Addington), Baines remarks on a number of sights but, curiously, makes no mention of the town of Bath, the largest and oldest settlement along that shore.

Then all hands prepared for dinner. I cooked a luscious steak; others peeled onions and we opened then the last demijohn of half-and-half.

> Since Baines was now doing the cooking, we are left to wonder what happened to the cook, Alfred, who was taken on at Cobourg.

After dinner, intense laziness, then work up against a light wind in the dark into South Bay. At eleven o'clock, we cast anchor between Wapoos* Island and the main land. Then it came on to rain and we turned in.

Wapoos: Mississiuge [Mississauga Indian word] – Rabbit Island (Ind.)

◀ The large bay, now called Prince Edward Bay, where Waupoos Island is located, was usually referred to in the 19th Century as South Bay. Officially, South Bay is now just the smaller bay at the south-western end of Prince Edward Bay.[68] Waupoos Island itself is an 880 acre island (350 hectares) less than one kilometer off the shore of Prince Edward County. In 1863, as many as ten families owned farms on the island.[69] The bay chosen by Commodore Hodder in which to anchor is well protected and still used as an overnight anchorage by recreational boaters today.

[Sun.] 16th Aug. All hands roused at 5 a.m. to make sail as, in the darkness of the previous night, we had berthed too near shore and, moreover, the sky looked nasty. We ran about a mile to the West and anchored again. Just after we had taken in the sails, the squall burst upon us; thunder, lightning, wind and rain all at once, but there was nothing to do. The boat was watertight so we didn't care a rap, but went quietly to sleep. We breakfasted at nine after the usual bathe. The pretty little skiff the Commodore had procured at Kingston was put into requisition to convey us ashore. We landed on a little point of the mainland [Morrison Point in Prince Edward County]. Mello and I remained ashore and hunted for worms, but found none. Then we turned our attention to fruit and soon got a quantity of large blackberries. We found strange snakes and birds' nests and lots of May-apples.* This is a very strange product of the woods here. It rises from the ground in May, with a single stem at the top of which is a large leaf formed of several small oval fronds radiating from a common centre. Two or three other leaves appear and, about June, a white blossom with yellow centre and a faint sweet smell comes from the main stem between the leaves. In August, the seed ripens in the shape of a yellow ball filled with sweet pulp and small seeds and about four inches in circumference. The plant is about two feet high.

Podophyllum.

Harvey and the Commodore trolled all the morning in a very likely looking bay [probably Smith Bay in Prince Edward County], but only caught one pike, one bass and one perch. We returned on board at 12:30, and found two natives of Wapoos come to inspect us. Their conversational powers had been blighted in youth and had never recovered. At two, we lunched; made a salad of potted lobster, cucumber, onions and tomatoes; also finished the last demijohn of half-and-half, a fact which produced the following elegiac stanzas —

To the Jar.
O fair round jar so true and tried!
That erst hast been so full inside
Useless the cork now guards thy head —
Thy corpse is left. Thy spirit fled.
The last of many a noble jar
Whose memory now glows like a star
That rises o'er the desert past
With brown stout halo, dim and far
Of that great galaxy the Last —
They came — they vanished all too fast!
Thou wert uncorked with hand profuse
What time we lay off Green Wapoos
The skies o'erhead were dull and grey
And wild the storm on broad South Bay
And one by one thy mates laid low
Yielded their life-blood's genial flow
Far on the blue Ontario.

To the Contents thereof.
Type of the holy Marriage rite
Two liquors in thee mingled bright
The brown and sturdy stout the male
The bride bewitching clear and pale —
And most "golumshous", heady ale —
In perfect union these did meet
And formed a tipple all complete
Good to wash down the tasty cheese
With pleasant onion sure to please
Rare products of the graceful hop
How ye embellished mutton chop!

> Bologna sausage found in thee
> A powerful auxiliary.
> Thy froth from well pleased lips we wipe
> What time we smoke the soothing pipe.
> O half and half relapsed at last
> Into the unforgotten past!
> May all thy tribe for me increase!
> Beloved liquor! rest in peace!

After lunch, rain and sleep; consequently small appetite for dinner and restlessness afterwards. This found vent in an expedition to Wapoos Island. Harvey and Duggan rowed me across to a farm house where we were affably received by the old farmer and his better half. We bought chickens, eggs and milk from him and had a long talk. Some heavy smoke we had noticed near Presqu'Isle when on our way thence to Kingston, and again as we were coming in to Wapoos, he accounted for by telling us of a cedar swamp which had caught fire some three weeks before and was still blazing. The tract of marsh and swamp extended for miles. A thousand dollars worth of timber, besides several barns and a few horses, had been destroyed. Then he talked of himself — how he had emigrated when very young to Canada and what a good country it was; how the last wolf on the island migrated to the mainland seventeen years ago; how they caught huge sturgeon in the bay and that it was sometimes called Eel Bay from the number of those fish in it; how there was no church near enough to go to and a clergyman had not been on the island for many a long year. So the old man talked on and the good wife went outside and wrung the necks of some unhappy fowls and the daughters came tittering and rustling down stairs and pushed the door ajar to get a peep at us and fled affrighted when we turned our heads. Then it was time to return to the ship. It blew fresh. The sea was rough and it was some time before we could make out the ship's lights. Harvey and Duggan gave way with a will [i.e., they rowed the dinghy with all their might] and we soon reached her. Having read all our books, we turned in at nine.

[Mon.] 17th Aug.   Turn out at five. The deck was covered with a light white frost. A short angry sea was rolling in from the Lake and the wind pretty fresh. However, we made sail and got outside [out of the channel between Waupoos Island and the mainland]. Here we found the wind dead ahead and the sea so heavy that it was useless to beat against it. Accordingly, we returned to our pristine diggings. Bathe and breakfast. Harvey was anxious to write home in time to catch the mail, so he and I got Mello to set us ashore about nine and we started to walk to Milford where, we were informed, was the nearest post office. Having obtained directions from an old man working in a field, we got on the high road and for two or three miles had a very pretty walk to Maryborough. The high way wound along the foot of a low hill covered with wood, except where a clearing round a cottage or pretentious farm house in the Italian villa style broke in on their cool green solitude. On the other side, low fields of corn or buckwheat alternated with pleasant pasture lands sloping down to the Lake. A little way before reaching Maryborough, the road turned to the right at the mouth of the Black River, on the other side of which was a very pretty wooded bluff which I sketched. Then we followed the course of the stream till we came to a small village having a pretty rustic bridge, a few houses half buried in trees and a schooner nearly ready for launching. This was Maryborough.

> After Mello Hodder rowed the two soldiers to Morrison Point on the mainland of Prince Edward County, they walked three kilometers to the first settlement, the village of Black River, a minor port and shipbuilding centre on the river of the same name. The wooded bluff which Baines sketched is known as McMahon Bluff
>
> Baines writes about the town he calls Maryborough, but he and Harvey were really walking through the township of Marysburgh. This was one of the six townships which made up Prince Edward County at that time.[70].

Here we had the option of two roads to Milford — the upper and lower. Choosing the first, we ascended a hill getting divers glimpses of the Lake, village and winding river between the trees and continued our walk along the crest of the hill which formed one side of the Black River valley. The road was nearly parallel to the stream which curved about beneath the trees; now in still deep pools; now in rippling gleaming shallows almost at our feet.

Three or four miles from Maryborough we came upon Milford, decidedly a "one horse" place. Two taverns, neither of which kept beer, a forge and a dry goods store where was the post-office. The man thereof being interrogated about the mails said, "there was one a week, I knew because the excise officer at Maryborough posted his letters once a week," but what day it went on, could not say.

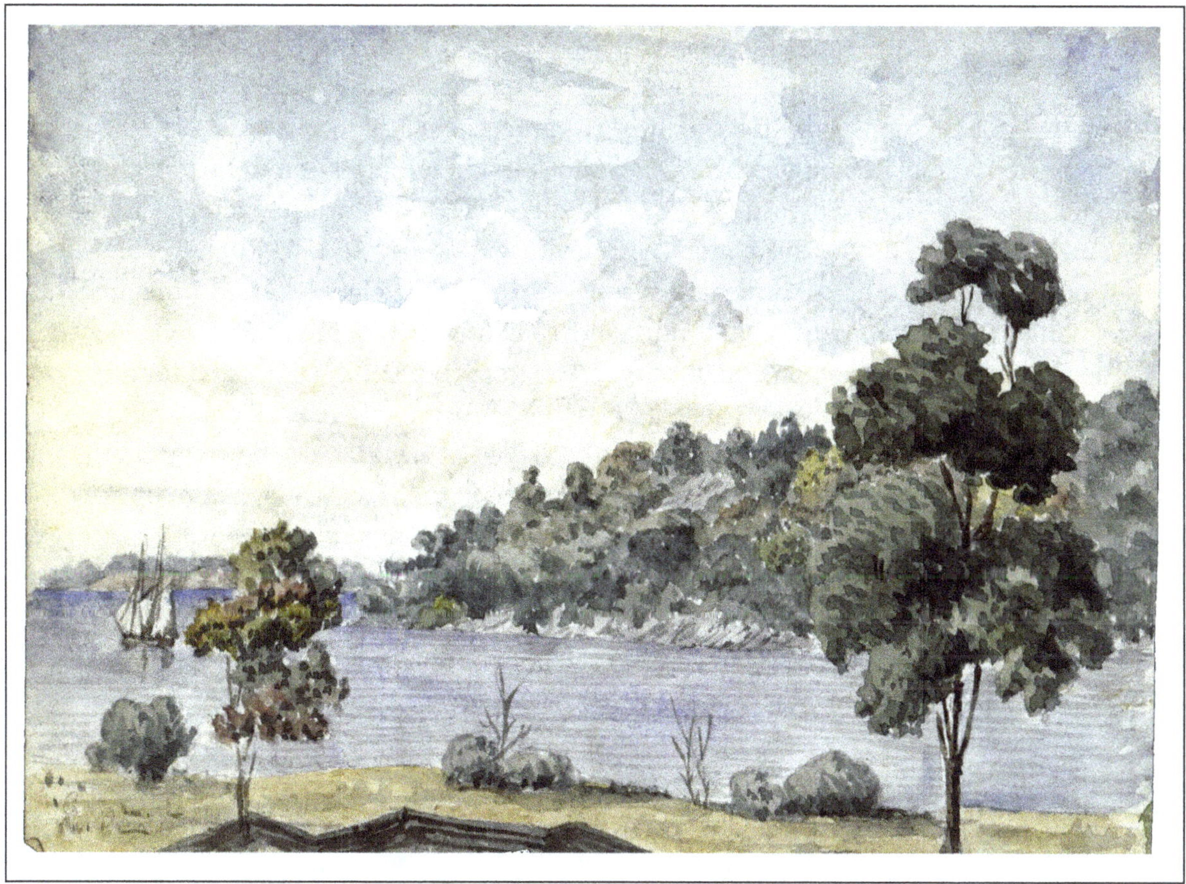

Untitled (Mouth of the Black River).
Henry Edward Baines, 1863. Watercolour and pencil on paper.
[Courtesy of Library and Archives Canada.]

The road turned to the right at the mouth of the Black River, on the other side of which was a very pretty wooded bluff which I sketched.

A schooner is shown at the mouth of the Black River with McMahon Bluff to the right.

◄ After walking a further six kilometers beyond the village of Black River, Baines and Harvey had reached the town of Milford. The town had two hotels, the Milford and the New England, and a population of 300. *Mitchell's Gazetteer for 1864* lists five blacksmiths, three grist mills and eight saw mills in the Milford area.[71]

After one or two unsuccessful attempts, we procured a buggy and good little mare from the blacksmith and drove six miles [9.5 kilometers] on to Picton, the chief town of Prince Edward County. The road was good and the country pretty and undulating, dotted throughout with neat farm-houses and log huts. In one wood, we passed a maple turned scarlet by the frost of the night before. I wondered whether the leaves felt the change in them at night and thought, if not, how deucedly surprised each one must be when he got up in the morning and found his neighbours red and yellow instead of sober accustomed green. We halted on the top of a hill just above Picton [near a spot now known as Macaulay Mountain]. On the left, the river hid under the foliage in the depth of the valley and a bold bluff covered with trees ended abruptly the range beginning at Maryborough. Right ahead in the lowland, Picton, with its gleaming roofs and many churches, stood relieved against the dark hill-side and, on the right, a blue arm of the Bay of Quinte lifted masts and white sails in the midst of an inland landscape. Picton, with a population of two or three thousand, contents itself with one long street, but it has a couple of excellent hotels and some capital shops.

◄ After an hour's drive along what is now the Old Milford Road, Baines and Harvey entered Picton from the east. Situated in a small valley at the end of Picton Bay (part of the Bay of Quinte), Picton was the principal town of Prince Edward County with a population of 2,500. At that time, the town boasted four churches, two hotels (the Globe and the North American) and two weekly newspapers.[72]

We put up at the Globe [hotel], lunched at the farmers' dinner table and had much chat with them, nearly all old-country men [from Britain.] Then Harvey wrote his letter and I strolled forth to do some shopping and inspect the town; bought cheese, matches, light literature and fishing tackle, then drove back to Milford and gave our trap to a woman who assured us she was "all the same as the blacksmith." On our walk back, I stopped to sketch the position of Maryborough. It lies between the Lake and the river and is sheltered by high ground on all sides, but one. We reached the ship in time to enjoy a good dinner at seven. During our absence, the Commodore and F. Duggan trolled long, but unsuccessfully. We could hear the sturgeon leaping near the ship, but we had no intimation of the presence of any other fish.

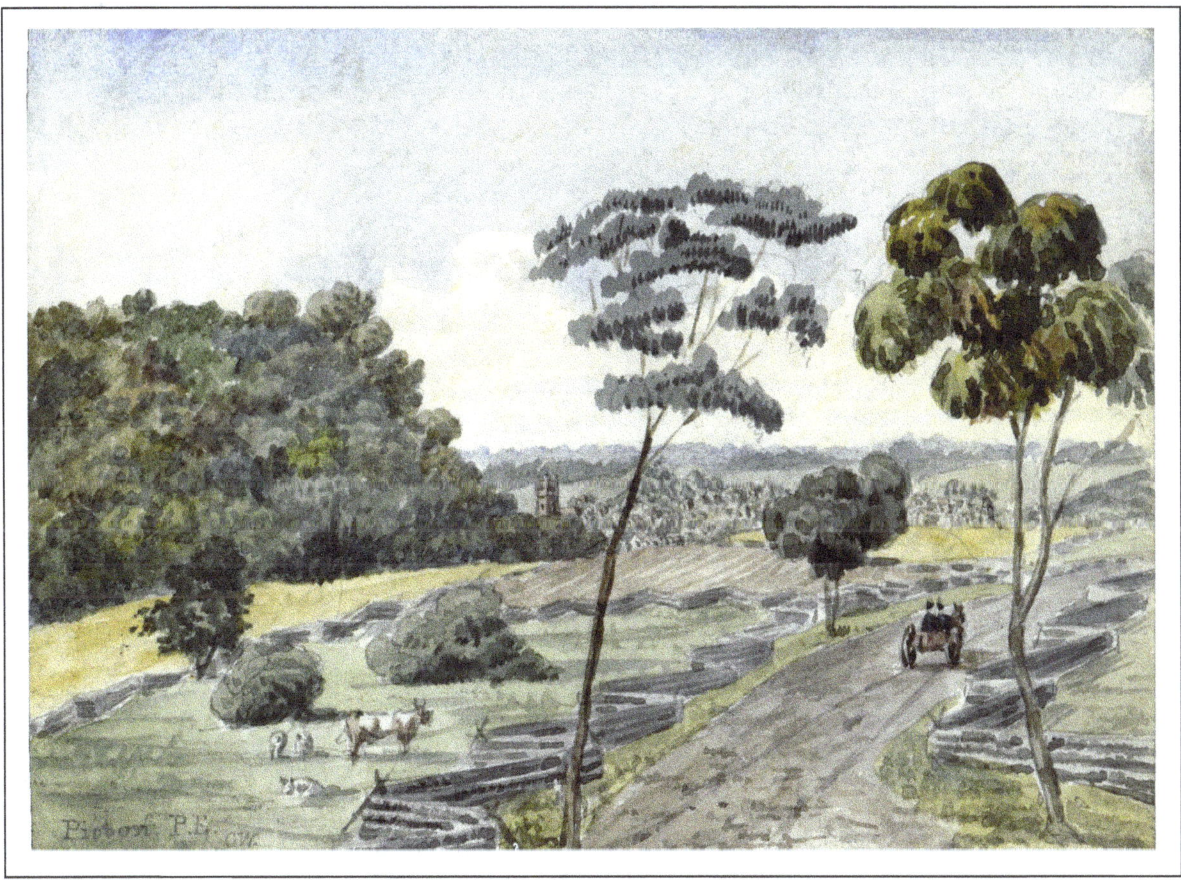

Picton P.E., C.W. [Prince Edward, Canada West]
Henry Edward Baines, 1863. Watercolour and pencil on paper.
[Courtesy of Library and Archives Canada.]

Right ahead in the lowland, Picton, with its gleaming roofs and many churches, stood relieved against the dark hill-side and, on the right, a blue arm of the Bay of Quinte lifted masts and white sails in the midst of an inland landscape..

Chap. VI

[Tues.] 18th Aug.   Got under way at 4:30 a.m. Frost on the deck again. When we got outside of Wapoos, we passed the *Arrow* of Cobourg at anchor; all on board asleep. We started the trolling lines, but caught nothing. Breakfast at 6:30.

◄ The 17-ton yacht *Arrow*, owned by John Wallace of Cobourg, was one of the boats that had competed in the regatta the week before.

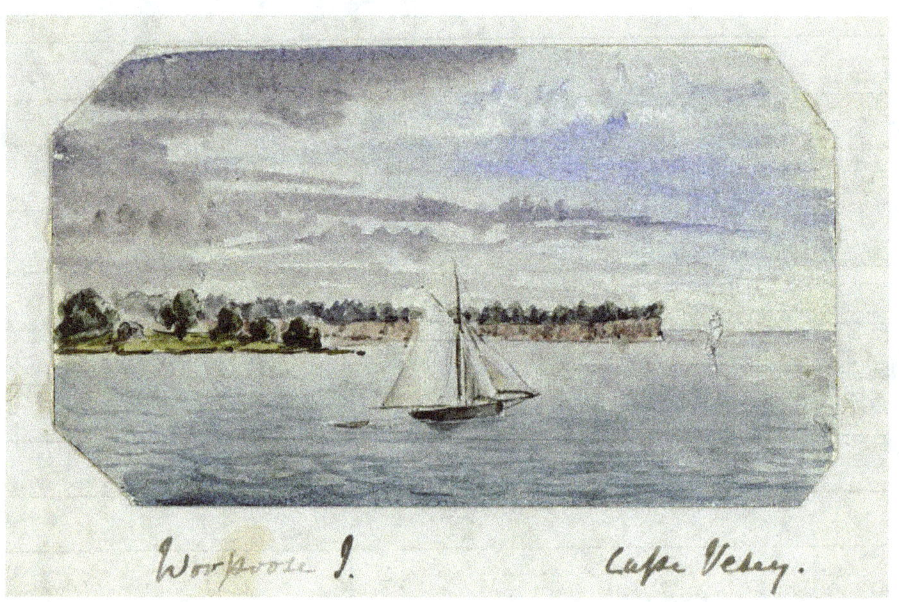

As we passed the last point of Wapoos… Woopoos… Baboos… or whatever it may be, the breeze came up fresh from the South-South-East. We passed the Outer Drake [Main Duck Island]; a low island covered with trees and inhabited by a few fishermen and a farmer or two, then bore away a trifle and went to the northward of Stoney Island [on the New York State side of Lake Ontario].

12:30. When we left this astern, we were fairly in Sacketts Bay. Our course lay straight across to Sacketts Harbour [New York]. On either side stretched a deep inlet — that to the South called Henderson's Bay curves far up into the country between steep banks covered with gloomy pine. At the entrance lay three or four rocky pine clad islets, and on its inland extremity is situated the village of Henderson. On the

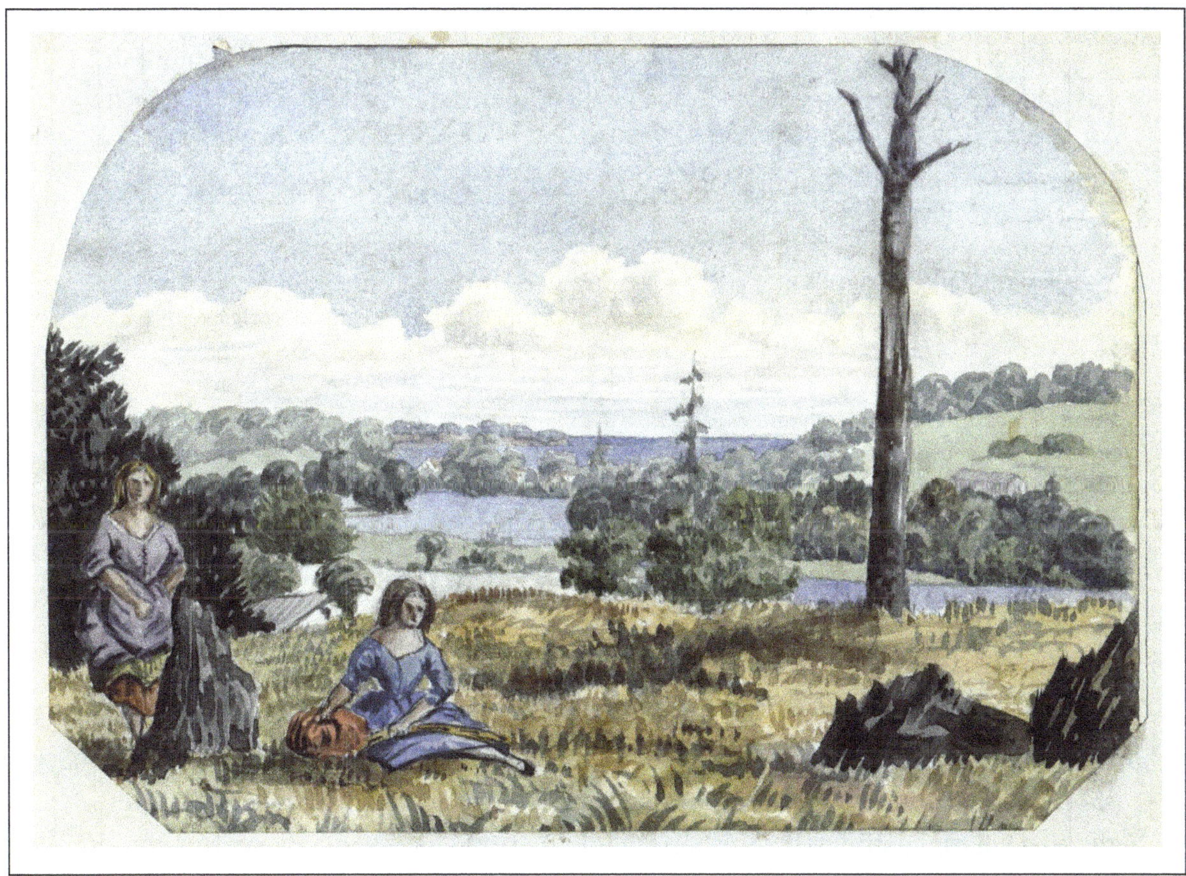

Maryborough, C.W. [Canada West]
Henry Edward Baines, 1863.
Watercolour and pencil on paper.
[Courtesy of Library and Archives Canada.]

I stopped to sketch the position of Maryborough. It lies between the Lake and the river and is sheltered by high ground on all sides, but one.

In his journal, Baines makes no mention of meeting these two young ladies in Marysburgh Township.

other hand, Chamean Bay [Chaumont Bay], winding round Point Peninsula, runs seven or eight miles [13 kilometers] to the northward and loses itself in a marsh through which an intricate channel, some three feet deep, extends to the St. Lawrence beyond Kingston. Here, Burrel told us, Bill Johnson, a notorious river patriot, rebel and freebooter of '37, found refuge and successfully concealed himself. His daughter having eloped some time ago, he followed her and she shot him as he attempted to knife her lover.

Requiescat in Pace! [Rest in Peace]

> ◄ Bill Johnson (or Johnston) was born at Trois Rivieres, Quebec, in 1782. During the War of 1812, he served with the Canadian militia stationed at Kingston. While in Kingston, he was jailed for insubordination, but escaped to the United States and was employed for the rest of the war as a spy for the American army. At the time of the Rebellion of 1837/38 in Upper Canada, Johnson was still living along the St. Lawrence River in New York State, and he and a gang of pirates, pretending to be Canadian rebel patriots, captured the British steamer *Sir Robert Peel* which was passing through the Thousand Islands below Kingston. The gang stole a large amount of currency that was being transported on the ship, and then set the *Peel* on fire. Many of Johnson's gang were captured, but Johnson managed to elude his captors by hiding inside a stone fence for several weeks. Johnson was seen as a folk hero by many on the American side of the St. Lawrence River. He died in 1870, apparently from natural causes. Burrel's story of Johnson being shot by his daughter may be another small part of the larger Bill Johnson myth. [73]

The Yankee coast of the Lake appeared to us to differ from the Canadian in the shore being higher and possessing a back ground of lofty blue table land; part of the Catskill range I fancy. Sacketts Harbour is a small bay with a wharf run out from the southern extremity. On the end of this wharf is a huge shed covering a 120 gun ship, nearly built.

> ◄ Sackets Harbor was first settled in 1801, and became the headquarters of the United States Navy on Lake Ontario during the War of 1812. In 1860, the town had a population of 1,340. [74]
>
> The huge shed or "ship house", was a massive wooden building enclosing the partially built hull of the USS *New Orleans*. Construction of the 87-gun wooden-hulled warship [75] had begun in January 1815, before news of the end of the War of 1812 reached Sackets Harbor. On receiving the news, the ship's builders halted construction. The *New Orleans* was being built to counter the 110-gun British warship HMS *St. Lawrence*, which had been launched at the Royal Navy dockyard in Kingston four months earlier. After the end of the war, the Rush-Bagot Treaty of 1817 between the United States and Great Britain limited the number of naval vessels on

Lake Ontario to one gunboat on each side armed with no more than one 18-pounder cannon. In order to abide by the treaty, the Royal Navy disarmed the *St. Lawrence* and the U.S. Navy built the enormous wooden shed around the *New Orleans*. For many years, each navy kept their ships on Lake Ontario laid up but ready to re-arm at short notice in the event of another war. At the time of the "Trent Affair" in 1861, there was much talk on both sides about naval strategies that might be effected on Lake Ontario, but the Rush-Bagot Treaty was not breached. The USS *New Orleans* remained in the ship house until she was decommissioned and dismantled in 1883.[76]

We rounded this and entered the harbour. As we were about to luff up and anchor, we grounded on a shoal in the middle of the port of the U.S. government; their only arsenal on the Lake too. Her stern held fast, so we all rushed out to the end of the bowsprit and, as she floated, the main sheet was eased off so we cleared it comfortably, anchored inside it, sent down the sails and lay with the stars and stripes at the mast-head and the yacht club ensign (blue ensign with crown in fly) lashed to the topping-lift.

In *The Harbours and Ports of Lake Ontario*, Commodore Hodder admits that he had never visited Sackets Harbour. This may account for the *Breeze* temporarily grounding on a shoal in the harbour. The Commodore does make these observations about the port: "It is not a port of so much importance in a mercantile point of view as many others, although, from the great depth of water in the bay, its secure and sheltered position, and tolerably easy access, it should be ranked amongst the best on the Lake. These recommendations, together with its capabilities of being strongly fortified, have induced the Government of the United States to make it their Naval Depot or Arsenal."[77]

The "Breezers" raised the American flag, the "Stars and Stripes", as a courtesy gesture since they were now in American waters.

We found ourselves anchored nearly in the centre of a wretched little harbour lined with rotten quays and rotting vessels. One large schooner on the stocks and another smaller one, newly launched, were the only signs of real shipping about the place. On our left as we entered the harbour was a big barrack [Madison Barracks] on high ground. Remains of a breastwork along the edge of the low cliffs here and there gave it the semblance of being fortified, but we saw no guns. In front was the town and on the right, the wharf with the ship house, and behind it a small promontory with a few good houses on it. As soon as we had made ourselves decent, we proceeded ashore. The custom house was opposite us and we landed just below it. To our left was what appeared to be a guard house from the number of soldiers lounging about — a long-haired, round-shouldered dirty set of fellows they seemed. The customs office was shut up, but a contiguous loafer "guessed the officer was to the ho'-tel." This being close by, we proceeded thither and found a big square house with soldier-pervaded verandah, but no excise officer. Up and down the single street of Sacketts Harbour, we searched for a butcher all in vain! One store labelled "Meat Shop" we came upon, but it was closed. A fearfully dreary place it seemed to be — two thirds of the shops shut and no one in the remaining ones. All over the town, clustering in knots at the hotel, loafing, chewing and liquoring, we found soldiers. They belonged to a corps being raised in the county whose head-quarters was at the barracks on the hill. Their costume consisted of black felt hat looped up on one side with black feather on the other and gilt cross muskets in front, blue jacket with yellow braid and blue trowsers with yellow stripes. Pink stripes we saw too, but I incline to think they were not regimental. Their boots were of many patterns and some wore spurs. They were called the McClellan cavalry, but were not horsed as yet.

> The soldiers of the United States Army that Baines encountered at Sackets Harbor were recruits for the 20th Regiment, New York Cavalry, a volunteer regiment being raised to fight the Confederates. One source described them as "$1000 bounty men, and many of them were shiftless, good-for-nothing, vagabond fellows who enlisted solely for the bounty, and departed for more congenial climes as soon as it was drawn."[78]
>
> The badges the soldiers were wearing were the crossed sabers of the U.S. Cavalry, not crossed muskets as Baines remembers.[79]

Saving these, we hardly saw a man in the street, and but very few women; nothing approaching to a lady. Several niggers [African-Americans] there were, and particularly careful they were to get out of the way of the soldiers.

> The United States Census of 1860 enumerates thirty-eight African-Americans in Sackets Harbor; nineteen adults and nineteen children.[80]

The attractions of the town were soon exhausted. The hotel, large, dirty and bad, produced no beer. Then we visited the big ship; clambered up from deck to deck by flights of stairs and at last emerged in a small look out station on the top of the building whence there was rather a fine view.

When we came down, I carefully stuck my knife into occasional timbers and satisfied myself that she was not good for much. She is, in fact, rotting from old age.

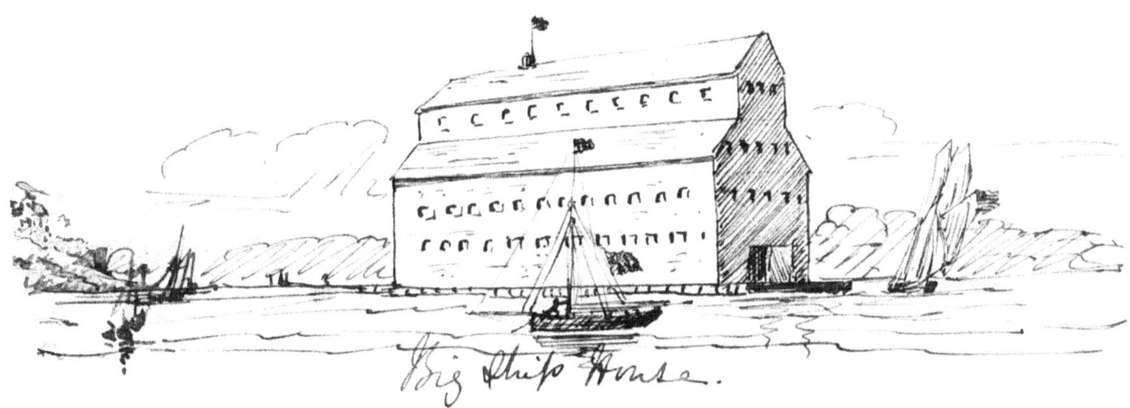

During our last war with the States, she was begun with the design of driving all before her on the Lakes, but Peace came before she was finished and, as one of the stipulations of the treaty provided that neither power should build or keep ships of war on the Lakes, she has remained in *statu quo* ever since. Having done with the big ship, we strolled on the point and back to town — more rambling in search of food. We succeeded in procuring eggs at a linen draper's or dry goods store where they also sold looking glasses, beads and pen-knives. We also talked to the man at the store who had been wounded in the foot at some battle in "the Peninsula" [i.e., during the Union Army's "Peninsula Campaign" in Virginia against the Confederates, March to July, 1862.]

The prevailing desolation of the town is attributable to the fact of the county in which it is situated having sent 2500 men to the war already. Fred Duggan and I strolled a little way out of town. The others joined us and we soon came to a neat wooden church with the door open. Of course we went in, and caught a boy who came to "fix" the windows playing on the organ. Harvey relieved him and, while he was indulging in music, I strolled about the church. On the altar, I found an old *Illustrated London News* [a weekly British newspaper.] As soon as we got through with the church, we voted Sacketts Harbour "played out" and returned on board. On the hill round the town, there are a few good houses which look desolate and the gardens round them dishevelled and untidy. A steak had been raised for dinner, but it was tough; chickens of Wapoos tender. Fred Duggan went on shore after dinner and reported the arrival of more soldiers at the hotel; much drinking and no discipline. We heard shouting, cheering and a low cursing sort of noise. We slept in peace however, till the steamer from Ogdensburgh arrived. The swell she made in the little harbour caused us to bump on the bottom. We had expected Woodfull by this boat, but he did not turn up.

[Wed.] 19th Aug.   Rose at seven. Pulled [rowed the dinghy] to the ship house and bathed on the other side thereof. The water was shallow. The stones at the bottom were slippery, but very sharp. They caught it from living so long with the Yankees. An elderly party warned us against bathing there again. It blew heavily from the South-West so we were unable to get out of harbour. After breakfast, lay down and read *The Castle's Heirs* through.

> *The Castle's Heir: A Novel in Real Life,* was written by the prolific English novelist Ellen Price Wood (Mrs. Henry Wood) and first published in 1861.

As soon as lunch was over, we went ashore, but did not rig ourselves out to such an extent as we did the day before. Our first visit was to the custom's office, the head of which intercepted us on the wharf. He was civil enough and tolerably gentlemanly for a Yankee. The *Breeze* belongs to the Thames Yacht Club and the Commodore carries an Admiralty warrant exempting him from all harbour dues. This considerably surprised our excise friend and he was much confused as to the law. He said, at last, he would write to the Secretary of State at Washington on the subject. Not knowing much of yacht clubs, he had concluded that we came straight out [from Britain] and remarked that the *Breeze* looked small to cross the Atlantic. The Commodore replied that she was a good sea boat and asked him to come on board in the evening. He accepted, but did not come. When we left the office, he took us into a long shed where were stowed immense boxes containing all the curiosities accumulated by Commodore Tatnall, U.S.N. [United States Navy], in his cruise to China and Japan. When Tatnall joined the South [the Confederate States], these were seized by the Yankee authorities and our friend had the duty of opening every case and making an inventory of its contents. The only thing we saw was a pair of shells; a kind of scallop of an enormous size weighing together 350 lbs., about a yard long or more and twenty inches across [approximately 160 kg, measuring one meter by half a meter]. An old U.S.N. officer seeing them remarked they were the largest he had ever met with, except a pair which adorned the door-posts of a Fee-Jee chief [from the South Pacific island of Fiji]. Commodore Tatnall was the man who remarked "blood is thicker than water" when he sent his boats to assist the wounded in our repulse at the Pei-Tso. He was stationed at Sacketts Harbour for some time and they still speak of him with affection in spite of his defection to the rebels.

> A native of Savannah, Georgia, Josiah Tatnall joined the U.S Navy as a seventeen-year-old midshipman in 1812. He saw service in the War of 1812 and in the Mexican War. By 1858, he had achieved the rank of commodore and was given command of the United States naval forces in the East India and China seas, with the USS *San Jacinto* as his flagship. The following year, in a breach of American neutrality during the Anglo-China war, he sent ships to assist the British and French squadrons in their attack on the Taku forts on the Peh Tso River. He was back in the United States in 1860, where his diplomatic indiscretion was punished by being relegated to the command of the naval station at Sackets Harbor. In spite of his anti-secessionist views, when Georgia seceded from the Union in January 1861, Tatnall resigned his commission in the U.S. Navy and returned to Georgia where he was immediately appointed senior flag officer of the Georgia Navy. Soon afterwards, he was commissioned as a captain in the Confederate States Navy. He was captured by Union troops in Savannah in 1864. After the Civil War, he lived in Halifax, Nova Scotia until 1870. He died in Savannah the following year.[81]

We walked over the hill to the S.W. and got a peep at Henderson's harbour. Our path was through a newly reaped corn field. Enough wheat lay about to make the fortune of an English gleaner, but here it was worth nobody's while to pick it up. Turning back, we skirted the rear of the town and reached the gate of the Fort. A sentry leaning on an old Brown Bess [an old flintlock musket], permitted us to enter. I asked for the officers' quarters, eliciting in reply the most laughable "haow?" possible. Passing through the gate we found ourselves in an irregular enclosure of rotten pallisading. Beyond lay the barracks forming three sides of a square. On the Lake side was a large stone building used as a QM's store [a Quarter-Master's storehouse for military equipment]. A lazy kind of drill was going on outside the barracks. Walking along the upper side of the quadrangle, we arrived at the orderly room where we introduced ourselves to Colonel Lord, commanding the regiment. A keen handsome face, soldierlike figure and abruptly civil manner, being up to his eyes in business, he apologised for not being able to attend to us himself and, introducing one of his Captains, desired him to show us over the fort. With this Captain, Heyworth I think his name was, we became very good friends. He was a tall goodlooking fellow, about two and twenty, the son of a farmer near Ogdensburgh. He had been First Lieutenant in the regiment in which Lord was Lieutenant-Colonel, and the latter being sent to raise and command a new corps, he followed him with the rank of Captain. Frank and pleasant, but unmistakeably Yankee, he impressed us favourably, although not what we should consider a gentleman. By himself, he had raised 85 men and had only come into head quarters two days before.

> ◄ The U.S. Army officer who he met at Madison Barracks was not Capt. Heyworth as Baines states, it was Capt. Cudworth. John G. Cudworth had joined the 35th Regiment, New York Infantry, at Elmira, New York as an ensign in 1861. There, he met Major Newton B. Lord. Together, the two officers saw action against Confederate forces in several battles including the Battle of Antietam in September, 1862. By the time the two officers were mustered out of their regiment at the end of their enlistments the following year, Cudworth had achieved the rank of lieutenant and Lord the rank of colonel. Col. Lord immediately set about raising another regiment for service with the Union Army. He sought Cudworth's help to recruit men for the 20th Regiment, New York Cavalry, in which Lord would be the commanding officer and Capt. Cudworth, later promoted to major, would be a company commander. The new regiment was based at Sackets Harbor where all twelve companies were mustered into the service by the end of September 1863. Subsequently, the 20th Cavalry saw action in Virginia and North Carolina throughout 1864. In 1865, the regiment was present at the fall of Petersburg and at the Battle of Appomattox Courthouse where Confederate general Robert E. Lee surrendered to Union general Ulysses S Grant.[82]

Under his auspices, we made the tour of the fort which consists simply of the barracks enclosed in pallisades on the landside and, here and there, a low earthen breastwork towards the Lake. A line of batteries here and a few heavy guns on the promontory at the other side of the harbour would, however, be sufficient to secure the harbour against attack by sea.

> ◄ Here, Lieut. Baines cannot resist giving his expert technical opinion on the best way to position artillery if Sackets Harbor were to be adequately defended.

Resting on skidding in a nook of the breastwork, we found some old guns, howitzers and mortars of strange pattern, and totally unserviceable. As I expressed a wish to see the quarters, we went upstairs into a barrack room. Several men were lying on their beds — wooden trays on posts about 4½ feet high — playing cards. No standing to attention or respect of any kind for their officer. They stared lazily at us when we entered. When we left the fort, several soldiers, some rather drunk than otherwise, were lounging about the gate. One, addressing the captain, asked, "Say Jack! Do you muster in tomorrer?" This man was sober, and Heyworth meekly replied, "Yes."

On the outskirts of the town, we noticed a block house similar in construction to two there are in Toronto. At the dock, we found an old sailor working on the schooner just launched which he owned, commanded and helped to build.

> ◄ A blockhouse is a defensible barrack building, usually a two-storey rectangular structure heavily built of wooden timbers, having loopholes in the walls through which the defenders could fire their rifles at any attackers. The upper storey usually sat square on the lower storey but projected beyond the walls of the lower level so that the defenders could fire through slits in upper level floors to prevent attackers from advancing right up to the walls of the blockhouse. A variation on this form was occasionally built with the upper level rotated so that only its corners overhung the lower level. Three blockhouses of this type had been constructed at Toronto in 1838, and this same type of blockhouse was standing at Sackets Harbor when Baines made a sketch of it in August, 1863.[83]

He talked big about his knowledge of the ports on the Lake, and prized himself in being the possessor of a certain book of them which he described. Harvey quietly took him down by informing him that the Commodore was the author thereof [*The Harbours and Ports of Lake Ontario*, by Edward M. Hodder.] After dinner, Fred Duggan, Harvey and I went ashore and entered the hotel. I noticed that the recruits of the regt. [regiment] had put down their names; places of residence too all right. Under the head of destination, with a fine prescience, they put "HELL." We met Capt. Heyworth, our friend of the morning, and invited him to come on board. He introduced us to Capt. Smith the doctor, and the Commissariat officer whom they call Contractor of his regiment, so we extended the invitation to them. First making us all drink at the bar with them, they followed us to the wharf. Arrived on board, we ushered them below, introduced them to the Commodore, and supplied them with smoking and drinking appliances. We produced some good strong brown sherry and served it out in tumblers. The Contractor remarked as he sipped his allowance, "I wanter know! This is fine drink. What do ye call it?" Heyworth, with much contempt, replied, "Say now, have you never tasted sherry wine?" The doctor and Contractor were loud and snobbish; the soldiers civil, quiet and ready to give us any information in their power.

I had a long talk to Capt. Heyworth who had served under McDowell, McClellan, Pope and Hooker [generals in the U.S. Army]. The raw levies he commanded at Antietam gave him considerable trouble when they were first under fire. He only kept them in the ranks by threatening to shoot them if they bolted. They grumbled and guessed he was no better than they to home, [i.e., in civilian life, the soldiers were the equal of their officer] but stayed nevertheless. Next time, they behaved very well.

> The Battle of Antietam, which took place in the vicinity of the Antietam Creek near Sharpsburg, Maryland, on September 17, 1862, is considered to be one of the bloodiest battles of the Civil War. It has been estimated that in a single day of fighting, a total of 5,510 soldiers were killed, 25,814 were wounded, and 7,043 were listed as missing in action.[84]

The niggers [African-Americans] did not make bad soldiers. They stood round shot [solid, cast iron cannon balls] fairly enough, but always bolted at shell [gunpowder-filled, exploding projectiles], which they called rotten shot.

> More than 180,000 African-Americans served in the Union Army during the Civil War.[85] A limited number of regiments of "U.S. Colored Troops", commanded by white officers, were raised as early as 1862. However, it was not until 1863, after President Lincoln's Emancipation Proclamation, that African-Americans were allowed to volunteer in large numbers for service in the army. Overall, ten percent of the soldiers in the Union Army who died during the war were African-Americans.[86]

On quitting his old regiment, he [Cudworth] had spent a few days at home on leave. At first it was well enough, but his true home, he said, was in the army. The house was very clean and tidy and his mother looked nice by the fire side, but he longed to get back to the trumpets and the noise and "the boys raising hell around generally." A significant fact: Already 700 men were enrolled in the new regiment, chiefly agricultural labourers; fine hardy fellows between 18 and 45. The wages of a farm hand are about 75 cents a day. On entering the army, they get $500, $300 of which is paid down. Their pay is $25 a month in addition to which they receive $40 a year for clothing and a free kit [military equipment]. No wonder that, as he said, they enlist freely. Non-com. officers [Non-commissioned officers; i.e., corporals and sergeants] get their stripes by enlisting men; their rank being proportionate to the number they raise. It they misbehave themselves, it is easy to reduce them to the ranks so the system works well. This regiment was for service in North Carolina. Before leaving, our visitors invited us to dinner next day. We accepted, provided we remained long enough.

We turned in at eleven. Fred Duggan and I had a philological argument. He was strongly phonetic; I hurled French and Max Muller [noted 19th Century philologist] at him, but he did not mind, so I went to sleep. Roused as before by the steamer from Cape Vincent. No Woodfull, so more dormouse [back to sleep, like a dormouse in hibernation].

Chap. VII

[Thurs.] 20th Aug.   All hands made sail at 3:30 a.m. Off at 4. Sails just drawing with a light wind. Turned in again. Woke once and found it dead calm, so we slept till seven, then up and found Sacketts Harbour out of sight.

> At last O Sackett's! Fare you well!
> At last, at last we've burst the spell
> That chained us in thy rotting port
> Between thy rotten ship and fort.
> The languid weariness, doleful dreariness
> That hung like a mist about thy street
> Thy drains all stinking, thy soldiers drinking
> Cursing and loafing the whole day through.
> Where every man that we chanced to meet
> Seemed looking for something or some one to do
> Where women were sighing for drafted males
> And the very dogs seemed ashamed of their tails.
> The pride of thy town is utterly dead
> In grave clothes of dirt and ashes 'tis laid out.
> There's nothing to do there, but turn into bed
> Farewell Sackett's Harbour, thou'rt thoroughly played out.

Douche bath, breakfast, pipe and log up! We went out slowly through the water, close hauled with a light southerly wind, till about eleven. The sky looked bad; black clouds rolling up all round and light scud drifting overhead. We took in jib and mainsail. Light puffs followed in quick succession from S.W., N.W. and N.E., then the squall came fierce with rain and wind from N.E. and we ran before it. The sea got up at once and it became advisable to bring the skiff on board. In getting her alongside however, she swamped and tore away. We were obliged to run on and leave her. As we sighted Oswego, the wind fell so we set the mainsail and got in at 1:05 p.m. This city looks well from the water.

> The French had established a mission at Oswego as early as 1654 that later became a fur-trading post. By the early 18th Century, the area was in British hands and they built two forts, Fort Oswego and Fort Ontario, at the mouth of the Oswego River. After the American War of Independence (1775-1783), Oswego continued to be occupied by British troops even though it was in United States territory. The British finally left Oswego and several other frontier posts under the terms of the Jay Treaty of 1796. During the War of 1812, the British attacked Oswego and destroyed Fort Ontario. After the war, Oswego slowly grew into a major shipping center on the Great Lakes. Oswego was incorporated as a city in 1848, and by 1858 the population was estimated at 18,000.[87] It was the largest port on the American side of Lake Ontario.
>
> In his book, Commodore Hodder comments that, "this excellent Port is in a great measure reclaimed from the Lake by skilful engineering, and at an enormous expense. It is situated at the mouth of the Oswego River, and protected from the heavy seas caused by westerly and north-west gales by walls of solid masonry. Capacious as are the basins, slips, and other parts of the harbour, they are even now barely sufficient for the accommodation of the numerous steamers, propellers, and schooners, which bring their valuable cargoes from all parts of the Upper Lakes to this busy and prosperous city." [88]

On the East side of the town is a fort [Fort Ontario] which commands the harbour. As nearly as I could judge, it is about 120 ft. [36 meters] above the Lake, built on an irregular pentagon. At each angle, a bastion with one embrasure in the flank; no barbette guns visible. The exterior slope of the parapet is revêted [lined] with wood. There is a ditch and glacis, but no outworks. Buildings like barracks occupy part of the enclosure. Crowds of gaily dressed people thronged every available space of the fort and beach below; an excursion from the country we found afterwards.

> Fort Ontario was rebuilt by the American Army in the 1840's, and it was further strengthened during the Civil War. Lieut. Baines' technical training is showing here as he mentions several military engineering terms in describing the features of the fort. Many of the technical terms have their origins in the French language due to the fact that many of the features of 19th Century fortifications were invented in 17th Century France and put into practice by the renowned French military engineer, Sébastien Vauban.[89] Fort Ontario was a five-sided masonry fort. It had bastions protruding from each corner, giving the fort the appearance of a pentagonal star. Bastions were designed to provide flanking fire along the walls, and each bastion protected its two neighbouring bastions to create an effective cross-fire. The masonry

walls were topped by a bullet-proof earthen parapet. Embrasures were cut into the parapet to allow cannons on fixed platforms to fire through them. Barbette guns, which were missing from Fort Ontario, were cannons mounted on sturdy, elevated platforms (*en barbette*) to allow them to fire over the wall. These platforms could be swiveled to change the direction of fire in order to track a moving target such as a sailing ship or a marching column of troops. The ditch is a wide, dry moat, and the glacis is the artificial slope graded from the edge of the ditch away from the fort in order to create a broad, open field of fire devoid of any cover that might be used by an attacking force. Most forts of this type had a number of outlying works such as redans or batteries which were not attached to the main fort but which supplemented the defences. As noted by Baines, Fort Ontario had none of these outworks.[90]

The piers at Oswego run out into the Lake. They are built of the usual cribwork and planked within. The harbour to the West is a small island of cribwork covered with storehouses, etc., that look very strange with masts surrounding them on every side. Higher up, the harbour contracts to a river flowing between quays. Those in the West being lined with stores and hotels, while on the East a fantastic street of elevators [grain elevators], many coloured, clumsy and deformed, rise high above the loftiest mast head in the stream. The river Oswego, the outlet of Lake Oneida, has a fair sized channel. It is deep and full with a strong current. We sailed up the harbour to where a large iron bridge spans the stream and, after much difficulty, succeeded in getting a berth on the West side astern of the schooner *Carthagenian*, 500 tons, and outside a barge manned by French Canadians that was loading with planks.

◄ The 500-ton *Carthagenian*, like many schooners on the Great Lakes at the time, was employed as a bulk-carrier, transporting wheat from western ports to Oswego, where it would be stored in grain elevators before being shipped down the Oswego Canal to the Erie Canal and then onward to eastern markets. The schooner had been built at Oswego in 1858 and suffered the same fate as many other ships on the lakes: in 1867 she was wrecked during a November gale. The ship and her entire cargo of more than 17,000 bushels of wheat, were lost. The captain and his crew of eight were all rescued.[91]

Woodfull stepped aboard as we touched and it began to rain and continued till night. As soon as we had tidied ourselves, I went to the hotel, where Woodfull gave me letters from home he had brought from Toronto.

◄ Woodfull had left the "Breezers" at Kingston six days earlier, but Baines says neither where he had been nor what he had been doing. Earlier, Woodfull had been expected on the steamer from Ogdensburgh, so he may have been coming from the east, likely from Montreal where he had enrolled in the medical school at McGill University. However, Woodfull also had letters with him that he had retrieved in Toronto, indicating that he had also stopped there. As to the letters themselves, Baines leaves us hanging. As usual, he gives us no personal information and refuses to divulge any of the contents of the letters or even who sent them.

The city of Oswego is pretty equally divided by the river. The eastern half is paved and flagged like English towns; the West rejoices in board walks still. On both sides, the shops were poor. One bookstall advertised "Harper for September" [*Harper's New Monthly Magazine.*] Woodfull bought it and found it was September indeed, but 1862. He was disgusted, but it was a cute idea nevertheless. He had been at Oswego waiting for us and, at the hotel, had made acquaintance with a party of young ladies who had come from Rochester to sing at a concert. They were under the charge of their professor and one or two other enterprising Yankees, and through them Woodfull picked up a circle of friends at the hotel, rather numerous than select. He, Harvey and Fred Duggan went to the concert and came back riotous at a late hour. I had turned in long before and slept none the worse for the sound of the constant rain on the deck.

[Fri.] 21st Aug. At six a.m., our friends in the barge slipped off, so we warped into their berth alongside. Then a morning nap till nine. Our tubbing this morning was very slight — no plunge — and the river water looked so brown in the basin that we did not grumble at being prevented jumping overboard. After breakfast, went to the hotel, got shaved and liquored. While at the bar, a man came in, filled a wine glass with bitters and gulped it down without making a face. In the verandah of the hotel were chairs, so we sat there, smoked, watched the passersby and talked to the Yankee loungers.

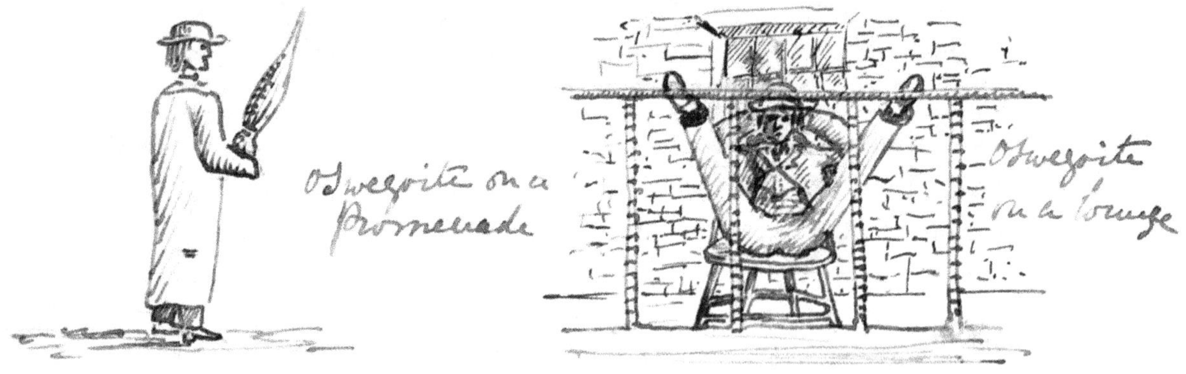

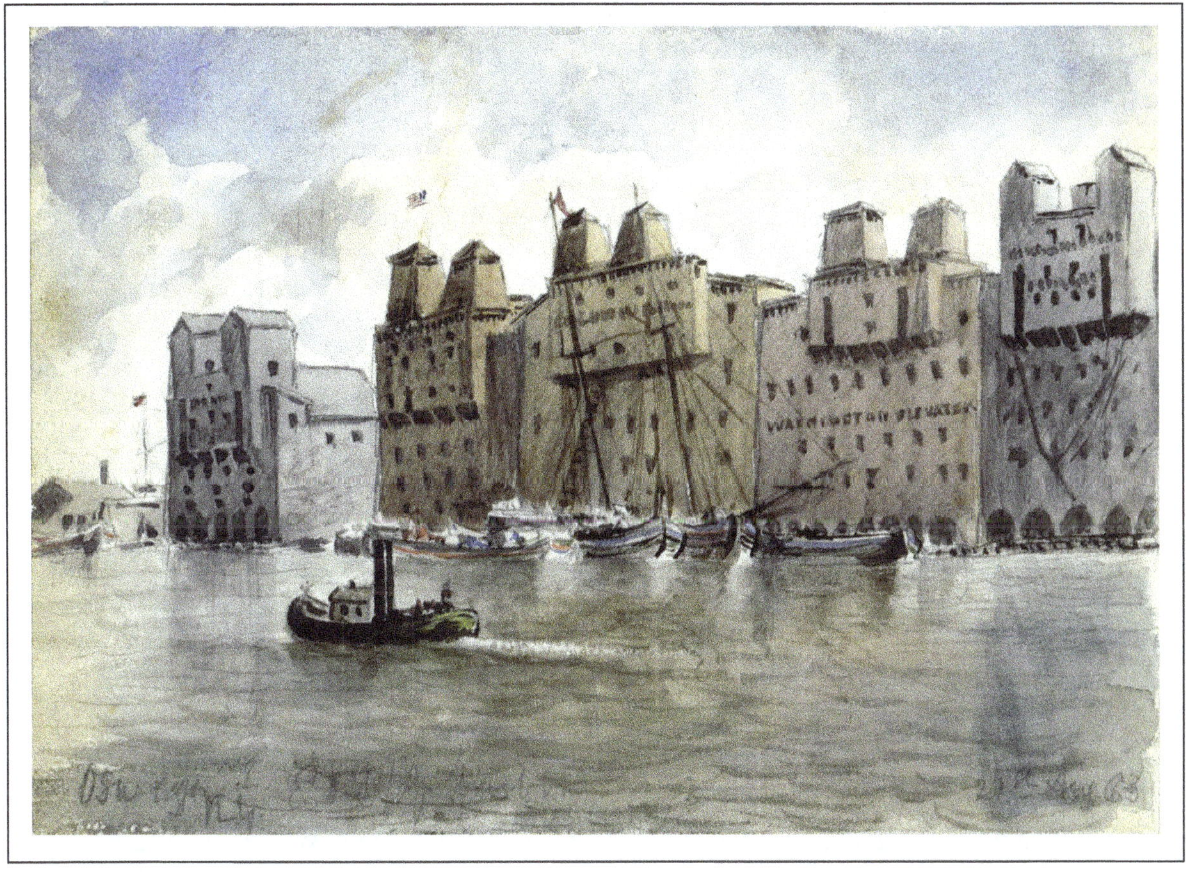

Port of Oswego N.Y. 21st Aug 63.
Henry Edward Baines, 1863. Watercolour and pencil on paper.
[Courtesy of Library and Archives Canada.]

We obtained a view of the city which was singularly bizarre owing to the number of general elevators thronging the foreground.

They had ascertained who we were from Woodfull, and the conversation turned naturally enough on the artillery practice at the siege of Charleston. Said one, "Snakes alive! They've got a 200lb. shell to Charleston." Said another, "What would you feel like if one of the darned things came alongside you ready to burst up!" "J — C — ! Consider me aout!" exclaimed No. 1.

> ◀ While the "Breezers" were on their cruise, the port of Charleston, South Carolina was under siege by Union forces. It was at Fort Sumter in Charleston harbour where some of the first shots of the Civil War had been fired in April 1861, and in August 1863, artillery batteries of the U.S. Army were bombarding Fort Sumter and nearby Fort Wagner, both in the hands of the Confederates, prior to attempting to capture the city of Charleston. During that bombardment, and later during the bombardment of the city itself, 8-inch Parrott Rifles, massive cannons capable of accurately firing a 200-pound projectile at targets up to seven kilometers away, were used.[92] An article in *The Scientific American* magazine from September 1863, reported that "during the furious assault upon Fort Sumter, the first shot fired from the 200-pound Parrott rifle penetrated nine feet into the wall facing Sullivan's Island, after first passing through the gorge wall of the fort; it knocked over a pile of brick upon a steamer outside of the wall, demolished its smoke stack, and caused the boiler to burst, by which casualty four negroes [African-Americans] were killed."[93]

After awhile we all started together to do the town. Our way was along the West bank of the river, but we turned off at the miserable shed dignified with the name of a [railway] station and crossed a bridge over the Oswego river and a double canal [the Oswego Canal, which connected with the Erie Canal thirty-eight kilometers to the south.] Beyond us was another bridge. Leaving the river, we walked through the suburbs on the East. Very pretty and cosy little villas and cottages, wooden, painted bright white or buff, nestled among the trees shrinking back into their own gardens on either side of the road. The grounds were untidy and desolate; the flowers few and common and not a single conservatory. The inhabitants took out the extra dignity in flagstaffs, which started up white and bare all over the town. Woodfull, Harvey and I pursued our peregrinations to the end of the wharf whence we counted twelve schooners leaving the harbour at nearly the same hour.

> ◀ One of the dozen schooners leaving the harbour that day was the *Fleetwing*, bound for Wilson, New York, at the western end of Lake Ontario. Before reaching its destination, Captain Quick's ship was hit by a sudden squall and the schooner capsized. The captain and crew managed to save themselves in a lifeboat, but the ship's cook along with the captain's wife and child were drowned.[94]

From here too, we obtained a view of the city which was singularly bizarre owing to the number of general elevators thronging the foreground. Leaving Harvey with the Commodore, whom we met on the wharf, Woodfull and I wandered away westward along the edge of some low cliffs that overhung the beach. Never had I seen the Lake so nearly resemble the sea. Stretching away in deep blue to the horizon where was no trace of land, its long regular waves came rolling in till they changed to bright green above the sand or burst in sparkling white over the black rocks. Off these, we had a most delicious bathe. On our way back to the ship, we passed through more long shady streets of white villas, each in its own garden. Lunched and spent the afternoon in loafing about the town. Found two more stores for books and stationery. The books were dime novels or reprints of trashy English works. There were no sketching materials, a few cheap photographs in the window and some gaudy prints, bad copies of common English engravings executed for the most part at Leipsic [Leipzig, Germany.] After dinner, we all went to a room fitted up as a theatre where a travelling company performed attenuated versions of "Rough Diamond", "Kiss in the Dark" and "Sam Slick."

> These theatrical productions are all one-act plays written in the mid-19th Century. "A Rough Diamond", first performed in London in 1847, and "A Kiss in the Dark", first performed in 1840, were comedies written by John B. Buckstone. "Sam Slick" was a comedy based on the writings of Nova Scotia author Thomas Chandler Haliburton, published between 1836 and 1860.[95]

It was so absurdly bad. The audience consisted chiefly of recruits and their friends, and the talk ran on the fortunes of the draft. During the afternoon, Harvey and I went into the office where they were claiming exemptions or reporting for service. Everything went on quietly enough; laughing and talking amongst themselves till their turns came.

> In 1861, when President Lincoln called for volunteers to help quell the rebellion of the Southern states, thousands enlisted in state militia regiments. By the end of 1862, however, the number of volunteers for the Union Army had dropped considerably. In order to provide enough soldiers for the army, conscription was enacted by the United States Congress in March 1863. The "Act for Enrolling and Calling Out the National Forces" made all able-bodied males between the ages of twenty and forty-five immediately eligible for enrollment in the Union Army.[96] The provost-marshall's office in Oswego was where the enrollments would take place for men in that district whose names had been drawn for service in the army. That was also where the potential recruits could apply for an exemption from the draft

under certain conditions stipulated in the legislation. Alternatively, the draftee could present a substitute; an able-bodied man who the draftee might pay up to $300 to serve in his place.

After the play, we eat oysters and then turned in.

◄ Oysters were readily available anywhere a rail line connected with New York City, then the oyster capital of the United States. As early as 1857, New York oysters being were served in restaurants as far away as St. Louis, Missouri.[97]

The clock struck twice with an interval of five minutes between the times. This, we found, was a way it had. The fire bell rang from 1:30 to 2:30. All agreed Oswego was played out.

[Sat.] 22nd Aug. — Rouse at 5 a.m. We worked the boat out by lines and a judicious use of the rudder against the stream. At a quarter to six we were under sail and, bowing my farewell to Oswego, I descended to my berth. The wind was South. About eight, we had breakfast — all of us a little seedy. I lay about the deck and read *Davenport Dunn* [a novel written by Charles Lever in 1859]. We jogged on quietly enough till a little before one, when we observed the clouds banking up round us as if they meant mischief. Then the wind hauled round to the South-West. Having taken the jib off her, we double reefed the mainsail and, as the sky looked worse, took it in altogether. Of course, hats and shoes had been sent below at the first warning, so the heavy rain and hard blow which soon overtook us didn't matter. Presently, we took in the foresail and then drove under bare poles [i.e., with no sails at all] some seven or eight knots [twelve to fourteen kilometers]. Before long it was over — wind fell, rain stopped and the sun reappeared bright and warm. Then all hands made sail and we ran between the long crib work piers that form the entrance to Sodus Bay a little before three. We kept close to the East pier till we were inside, then, passing an island on the East, we rounded a low sandy spit with a few trees on it and anchored opposite the town of Sodus Point.

◄ Big Sodus Bay (as distinguished from Little Sodus Bay, twenty-five kilometers to the east) is described by Commodore Hodder as, "the most capacious and best harbour on the south shore of Lake Ontario. It is entered from the Lake by a channel 470 feet wide, between piers which extend out into thirteen feet of water. The lighthouse, which is 66 feet high, is a good revolving light easily seen ten or twelve miles in the Lake. This picturesque and fine harbour runs south or into the land for about six miles."[98] The town inside the bay, Sodus Point, had a population of 200.[99]

Having no dingy, we were obliged to wait till a shore boat came off to us. The interval was employed in getting the rigging covered with our wet clothes, in lunching and in getting a sketch of part of the bay. The whole outline of the coast is very pretty. It is rather hilly, and well-wooded capes jut out far into the calm water, which winds away far to the eastward and loses itself among corn-fields and thick green copses. At six o'clock, we trusted ourselves in a flat-bottomed machine, rather like a boat but still more like a washing tray, and were conveyed ashore. We loafed down the long street of the village and back again. The cottages, for the most part, stand retired in gardens or peach orchards. There are two billiard rooms, a sort of Mechanic's Institute [a precursor to the public library] and a neat little church, all built of wood and painted white. There are lots of visitors lodging in its two hotels as it is a small watering place. They are attracted chiefly by its noble bay, which is about six miles long by three wide and, completely land locked, forms an admirable area for boating. We went on board at seven. Dinner, pipe and turn in at 9:30. At 10:30, a heavy squall of wind and rain with thunder and lightning passed over us. Another like it came on about 2. No harm done to us.

[Sun.] 23rd Aug.   This was a very lazy day. We did not turn out till nine, and then, some of us feeling rather seedy, the number of bathers was limited. We breakfasted at ten, then a pipe. As we had been signally unsuccessful in our search for provisions on shore the previous evening, we made up our minds to start at the first opportunity. The wind was contrary and remained so all day. We fished off a little wharf and I trolled awhile. The latter operation produced nothing but a small perch, but on the wharf we were more successful and caught a few bass and sun fish. These we had fried for dinner at five. The evening we spent in loafing on deck and occasional pipes. Soon after we turned in, there was a tremendous rain squall.

[Mon.] 24th Aug.   We all rose at five. It was blowing pretty fresh so decided on breakfasting at our moorings. Eggs and a biscuit-and-a-half apiece were ready at seven. At eight o'clock, we were under weigh carrying the storm jib and two reefs down in the mainsail. When outside, we found the wind was South-South-West and not so fresh as we had expected. The big jib was got on her and the reefs shaken out. Then we set the topsail. By and bye, the waves began walking on board, so we took in our topsail. It blew harder as we got on and we took in green water [i.e., a large amount of water] over the rail.

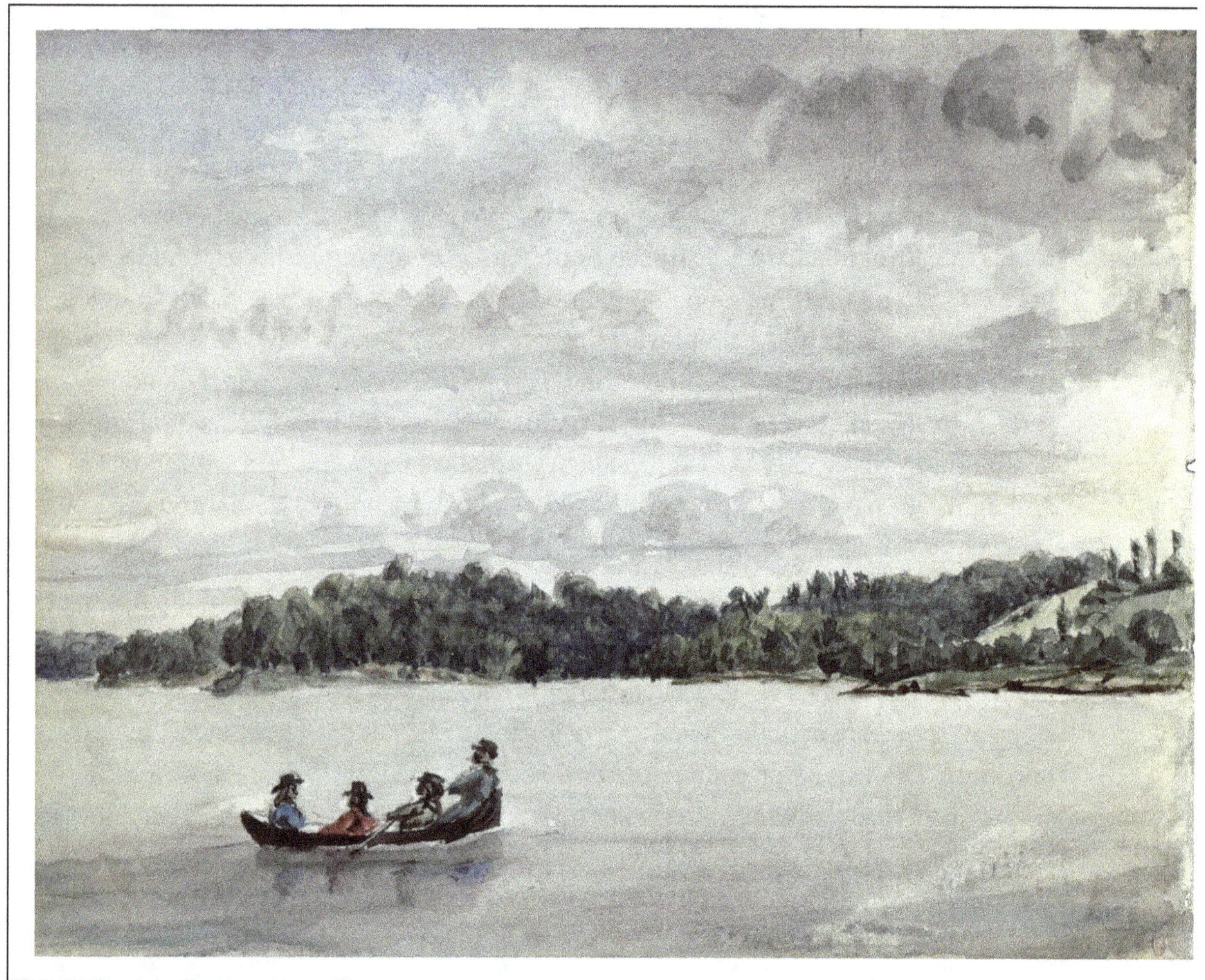

Big Sodus Bay, 22nd Aug 63.
Henry Edward Baines, 1863. Watercolour and pencil on paper.
[Courtesy of Library and Archives Canada.]

The whole outline of the coast is very pretty. It is rather hilly, and well-wooded capes jut out far into the calm water, which winds away far to the eastward and loses itself among corn-fields and thick green copses.

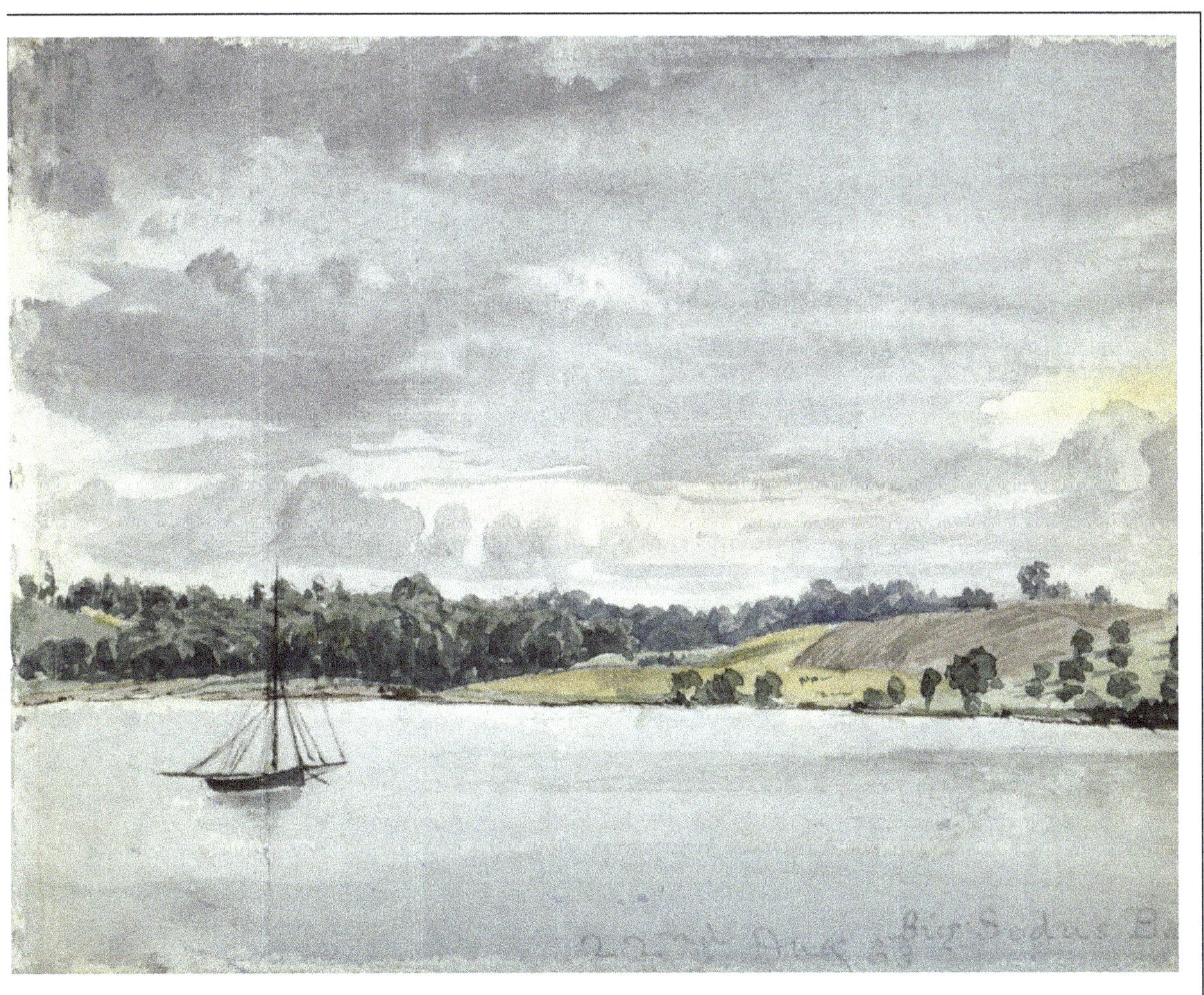
22nd Aug Big Sodus B

She was pretty lively about then, but we took in two reefs in the mainsail and set the storm jib again. By this time we had got past Putneyville [the town of Pultneyville, New York] a small village which struck me as being rather a good type of those generally seen along the Lake, and I made a sketch of it accordingly.

> ◄ Pultneyville was a minor port on Lake Ontario with a church, a sawmill and a number of gristmills. Its population in 1860 was 450.[100]

To the northward of us was a propeller [a steamship with a screw propeller instead of paddlewheels] who did not appear to be making good weather of it. When on our gaining tack, we rather "whipped" her [in a mock race], but we lost again when we stretched in shore, which was occasionally necessary as the wind was against us.

By two o'clock, we had gone through the requisite amount of pitching and tossing and passed the pier heads of Charlotte. These piers run N.E. from the shore — the wind was S.W. — so we were nearly an hour beating up the narrow channel [because they were sailing directly into the wind through a very confined passage]. Harvey and I were at the jib sheets [the lines attached to the forward-most sail, the jib], and my hands did not recover for a week. At three o'clock, we had moored alongside a low wharf just below the railroad station and steamboat moorings.

> ◄ While tacking through the harbour entrance between the long piers at Charlotte, Harvey and Baines positioned themselves at the bow of the boat, one on the port side and the other on the starboard, where they were in charge of controlling the forward-most sail, the jib. Every time the yacht changed direction (tacked), which was many times in such a narrow channel, one of these crew members would quickly haul on the jib sheet on one side of the boat while his partner paid out the other jib sheet on the other side. As soon as one tack was completed, they were forced to tack again so the process was repeated many times, causing the sailors' hands to become badly chafed by the lines they were handling.

Having made the ship snug, I proceeded to get out my best, and my only decent, suit of clothes which had been stowed away under my mattress as before described. I was [not] much pleased at discovering that a bottle of varnish, kept in the adjoining locker, had broken from its moorings during our recent tossing and, streaming through the intervening bulk-head, had thoroughly saturated my coat and, not to put too fine a point upon it, pants. Of course, my hands were covered too, as well

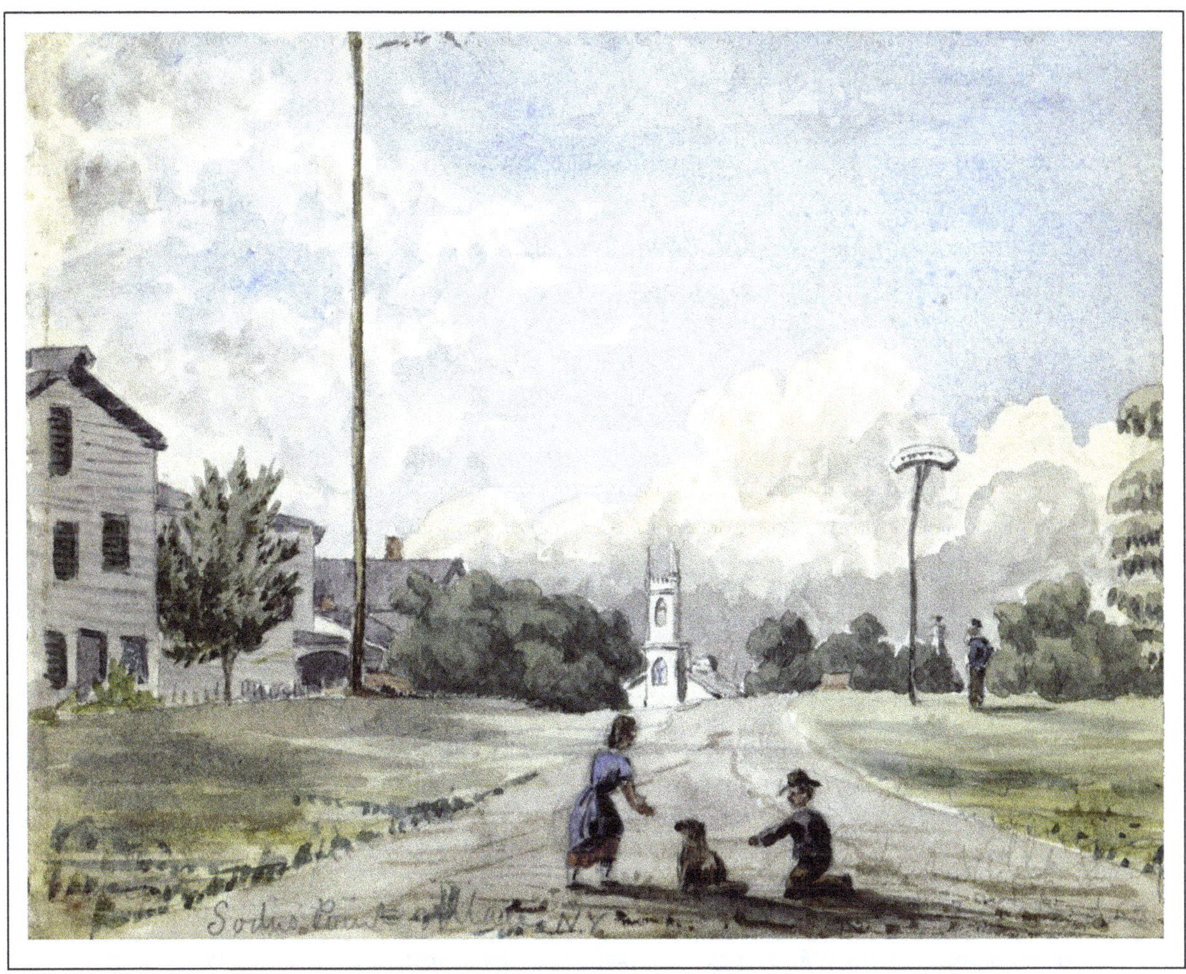

Sodus Point 22 Aug, N.Y. Sodus Village
Henry Edward Baines, 1863. Watercolour and pencil on paper.
[Courtesy of Library and Archives Canada.]

as whatever else was in the neighbourhood of the locker. The varnish was an oily black liquid used for the stays and ironwork of the ship.

I walked through the village to a tavern on the hill kept by two brothers — jolly old fellows very much alike; christened, of course, the Brothers Cheeryble [characters in the Charles Dickens novel, *The Life and Adventures of Nicholas Nickleby*, published in 1839]. Here I laved my paws in fresh butter and soothed my feelings with nice cooling drinks concocted from the wine made in the county. The hotel is called the Stutson House; Stutson being the real name of its owners. From the verandah, we had a jolly view up the river and down the harbour. Charlotte is a small village on the West side of the mouth of Genesee River, about seven miles below Rochester.

> Charlotte, was the lake port for the city of Rochester, ten kilometers up the Genesee River. Charlotte was a thriving town with two churches, a lighthouse, three shipyards, two mills and a population of 400.[101]
>
> In *The Harbours and Ports of Lake Ontario*, Hodder refers to the town as the port of Genesee and describes it as, "protected from the violence of the Lake gales by piers about 2,000 feet [600 meters] long, running N.E. and S.W. into the Lake, and 400 feet [120 meters] apart. the river is narrow and tortuous, rendering it difficult to beat up; but the wharves, when once reached, afford every accommodation and shelter.[102]

The American Company's steamers from Toronto to Montreal touch here [the American Steamboat Company's sidewheel steamers *Bay State, Cataract* and *Ontario*], and another steamer [the sidewheeler, *Rochester*], runs between this and Cobourg. Its only importance is derived from the Lake trade of Rochester which passes through it. We dined at the Stutson House very comfortably, smoked on the verandah afterwards and the musical section of our crew sustained their high reputation. We turned in about ten. During the night, the *Rochester* arrived from Cobourg and her swell caused us to bump awfully against the bottom. Our friend the propeller, which had held on her course when we entered Charlotte, came in too, having been forced to put back off the Devil's Nose [a cape jutting out from the south shore of Lake Ontario, thirty-two kilometers to the west of Charlotte]. It rained heavily before day.

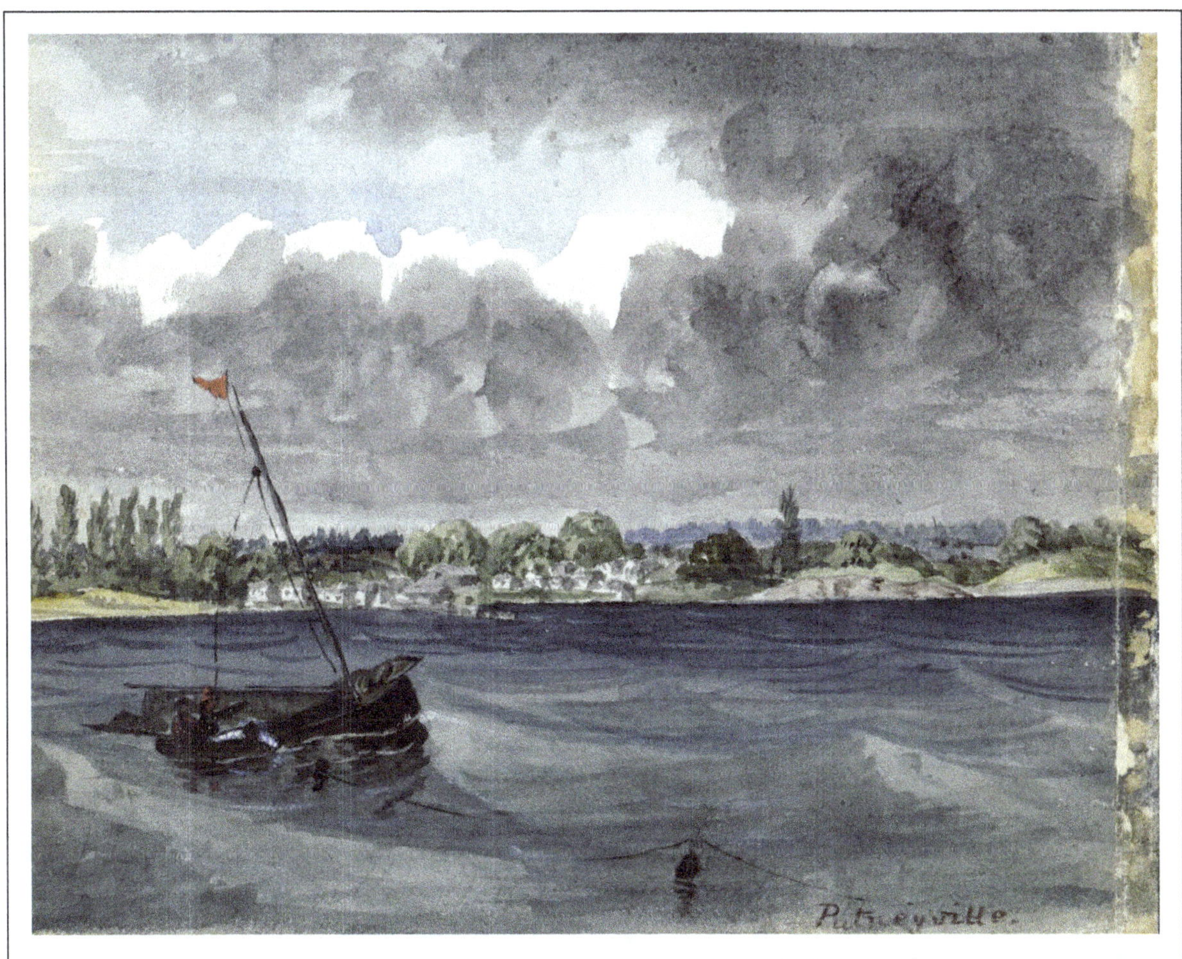

Putneyville.
Henry Edward Baines, 1863. Watercolour and pencil on paper.
[Courtesy of Library and Archives Canada].

Putneyville, a small village which struck me as being rather a good type of those generally seen along the Lake.

Chap. VIII

[Tues.] 25th Aug.   Up at 6:30. While performing our ablutions Mr. Daintry, John
Daintry and Cruso came up. They had arrived in the night. We breakfasted at the
Stutson House. Having made ourselves as respectable as circumstances permitted,
which in my case was not much, we spent half an hour waiting on the platform
[of the railway station] with Mrs. Daintry, Mrs. Stanton and Miss Daintry and their
attendant gentlemen.

> ◄ George S. Daintry of Cobourg had purchased the sidewheel steamboat
> *Rochester* in July 1863, to carry cargo and passengers between Cobourg and
> Charlotte. His son, John, was the ship's captain.[103] In 1864, G.S. Daintry was elected
> mayor of Cobourg. [104]

About half past nine, we all "got on board the cars" [the railway cars of the New
York Central Rail Road] for Rochester. The road [the railroad track] followed the
curves of the river and passed through a rich country of gardens and peach orchards.
Then, entering the city, went down a long street, crossed the principal thorough-
fare and into the station; a huge shed opposite the chief hotel. As a first measure,
we all entered our names in the hotel book and, this done, commenced a prowl
through the streets. Rochester is a fine well-built town — broad streets and tall
brick houses, large shop windows, plenty of people about and things generally
bright and busy. Crossing at right angles, the main streets, State and Buffalo
streets, divide the town into quarters. Secondary streets intersect the rest of the
city and are always parallel to one of these two.

> ◄ The village of Rochesterville was founded in 1817 around the mills that were
> built at the waterfalls along the Genesee River. It was incorporated as the City of
> Rochester in 1834. By 1860, there were twenty-four flour mills operating, and the
> city had forty-six churches and a population of 44,000.[105]

The public buildings are nothing particular. I endeavoured to procure a sketch-
book and one or two colours [of watercolour pigments] at every store I could find
likely to keep them, but it was a vain search. Indeed, I could not make the shop-
men understand what I meant. The bookstores were better than those of Oswego,
but their contents were little more than a larger collection of the same kind of
works. In the "Coffin Stores", I was struck with a peculiarity of Yankee coffins. In
the lid of each, just above where the face of the corpse would come, a small

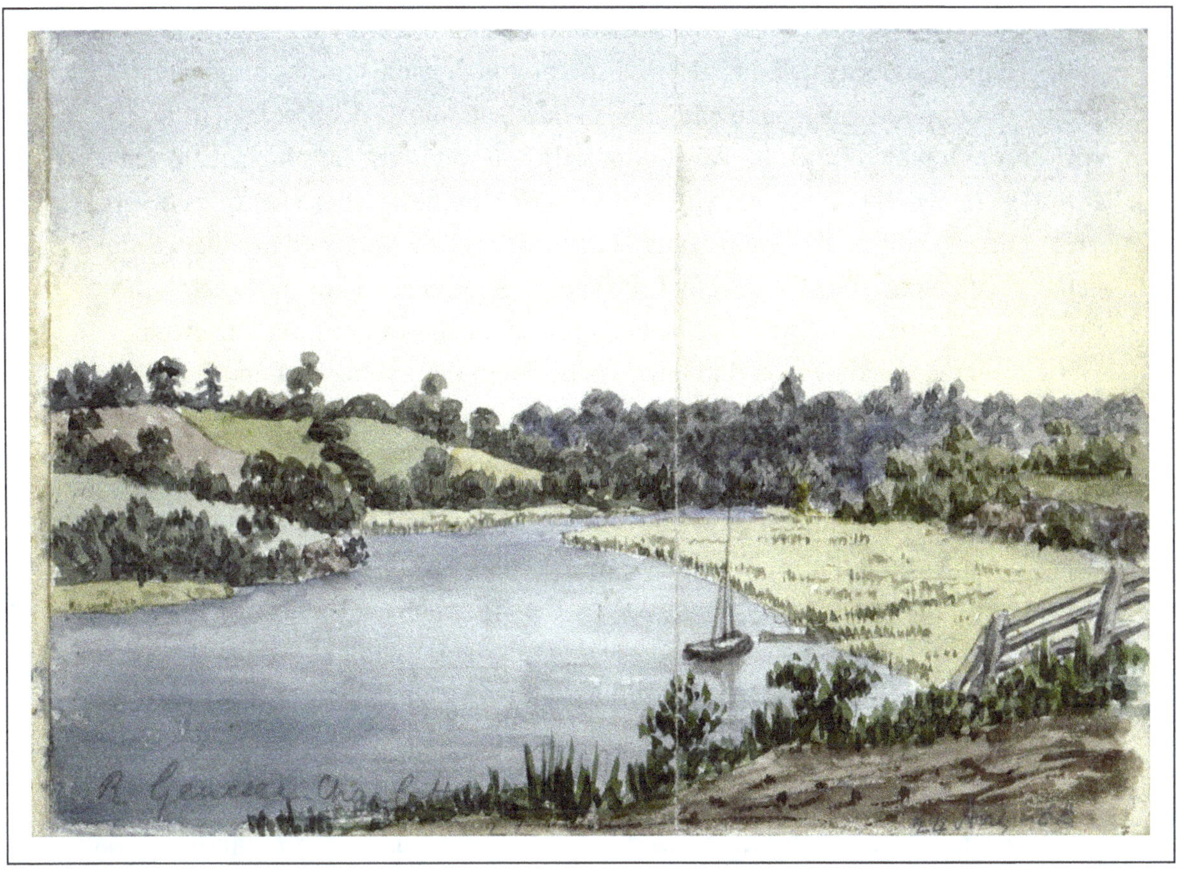

R. Genesee. Charlotte, 24 Aug 63.
Henry Edward Baines, 1863. Watercolour and pencil on paper.
[Courtesy of Library and Archives Canada.]

From the verandah, we had a jolly view of the river and down the harbour.

lozenge of glass about 8 inches long is inserted. I should like to know the origin of this custom.

From ten to twelve, we "did" the city, then we walked a little out of the main avenues and arrived at a field which was situated on the river side just below the Falls. The River Genesee foams down a succession of rapids through the city. It passes under a railway bridge and falls, in one leap, into a deep gorge cut in the rock through which it winds away out of sight. All round the falls are square red factories, many-windowed and with tall smokey chimneys. These factories divert a great part of the water from the falls, returning it to the river in a number of small cataracts all along the cliffs. Partly from this cause and partly from its being the dry season, the falls, though a good height, lose much of their grandeur from want of water, but they would in any case be completely robbed of any claim to picturesque effect by the odious entourage of mills.

Having hurriedly sketched the falls, I joined the rest of the party at the Congress Hall Hotel. Dinner was in full swing when I entered. Such a Babel! I utterly abominate the American system of hotels. In this case, my prejudice was justified. The dinner was pretentious in the multitude of dishes, the attendance was bad and everything half cold. However, I was very hungry and glad to get anything. When we escaped from the noise and confusion of the dining-hall, we took the street cars to Mount Hope, the city cemetery.

The environs of Rochester are rather pretty with their trim white villas, each in its own garden. Here, as before, I noticed the absence of conservatories and the small variety in the flowers. For about two miles, we passed through these suburbs, crossing the Genesee about midway. We entered the cemetery through a large stone gateway. Beyond this was a good sized open space of gravel, then a handsome marble mausoleum, on either side of which gravel roads swept off into the wooded hillocks all round the entrance. We followed the one to the right, which wound about the little hills and valleys and under the trees and then ascended a higher hill than any of the rest, which was crowned by a small wooden tower. The grounds were divided into lots. One, handsomely railed in, was the firemen's lot. It was laid out in distinct plots, one for each of the different companies. A peculiar custom prevails of burying the father and mother of a family side by side and the children around them, all their graves radiating outwards like the spokes of a wheel, each little mound bearing the pet name of the cherub beneath on an oval

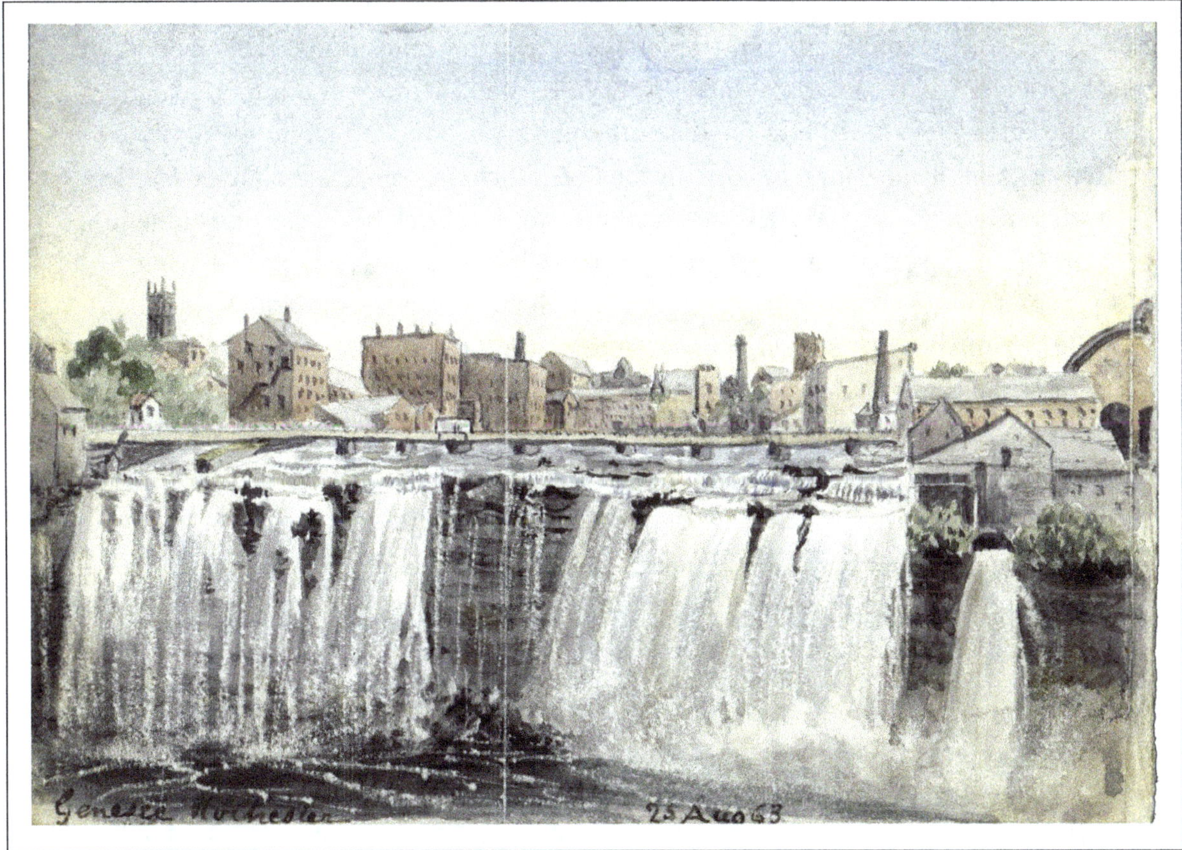

Genesee Rochester, 25 Aug 63.
Henry Edward Baines, 1863. Watercolour and pencil on paper.
[Courtesy of Library and Archives Canada.]

All round the falls are square red factories, many-windowed and with tall smokey chimneys. These factories divert a great part of the water from the falls, returning it to the river in a number of small cataracts all along the cliffs.

ticket of white marble. The system of engraving the pet or Christian name of the occupant on the gravestone is carried to a great extent here, especially when it is near others of the same family. On ascending the tower, we were surprised at the extent and beauty of the view. To the North, the city of Rochester formed the centre of a network of canals and railroads. Beyond it, a few miles of field and wood and then the long blue horizon of Lake Ontario. East and West, without a break, an open fertile plain faded into the distance, but it was bounded along the South by dim distant hills; a spur, I believe, of the Catskill chain. Sprinkled all over the rich level beneath us were white wooden cottages or red brick houses, some alone in their fields or by the wayside, others gathered in little clusters about the white spire of a village church. The patches of woodland seemed dark blue beside the yellow cornfields and brown fallows. Here and there rose the white puff from a train or the sunlight gleamed on a bend in the river. Our ride back to town was continued through the city to Lake View where are some infantry barracks and another fall of the Genesee. Fred Duggan and I, deeming the view obtained from the field above the falls unsatisfactory, descended the cliff and wandered about the river bank. These falls, though not as high as those in the city, are far more picturesque. Only one group of factories is there to attest the Yankee spirit and utter incapability of appreciating any beauty in an uncommercial light.

The river falls into a deep chasm cut in the red sandstone whose rugged walls spring from the bright green banks of the stream beneath. Above and below, luxuriant trees contrast with the red walls which are, in places, completely hidden by the vegetation springing from clefts in the rock. The western portion of the falls is a full deep cascade gleaming vividly white against the gloom of a deep recess scooped in the cliff beside it. The leap is higher on the East, but there is not much water on that side and the black glistening rock peeps in many places through the veil of spray. In the spring, when the river is full from the melting snow, these falls must be very grand. Now they are merely picturesque. We returned to the Congress Hall in time for "tea", which was a good deal more comfortable than dinner. Campbell's Negro Minstrels were in town and we devoted the evening to them.

Minstrel shows were a form of popular entertainment in the United States throughout much of the 19th-century. The shows consisted of the theatrical presentation of elements of African-American life in song, dance, and speech. This was performed by white actors impersonating black men and women by wearing "blackface" makeup — the performer blackened his face with burnt cork and wore

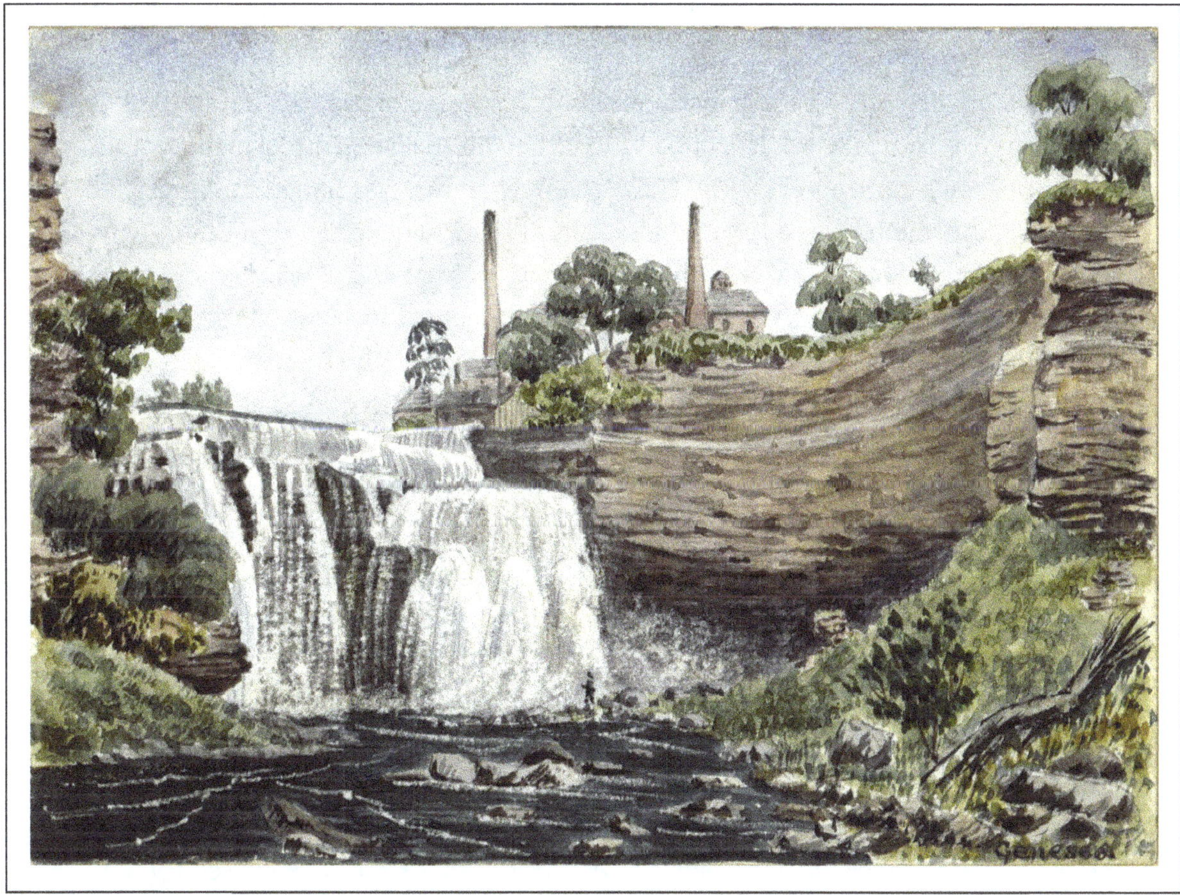

The Lower Falls of the Genesee.
Henry Edward Baines, 1863. Watercolour and pencil on paper.
[Courtesy of Library and Archives Canada.]

The river falls into a deep chasm cut in the red sandstone whose rugged walls spring from the bright green banks of the stream beneath.

costumes that represented a caricature, to the white audience, of the 'typical black' person. The classic age of blackface minstrelsy was from ca. 1840–1870. The original "Campbell Minstrels" were formed in 1847.[106] Subsequently, at least seven other minstrel shows up to the 1860's went by the name of "Campbells". One of those, "Reynolds & Pierce's Campbell Minstrels", gave performances in Toronto where they were on stage for three shows at the St. Lawrence Hall in September, 1862.[107]

Immediately behind us sat a captain and two sergeants of cavalry; soldierlike fellows fresh from service. They talked together till one sergeant espied another man of his own rank entering the Hall. The new-comer was hailed and introduced, "Allow me to introduce Captain So-and-so, Sergeant Such-an-one." "Proud to know you sir." "Glad to make your acquaintance sir." Then they shook hands and talked of friends in the camp. They all seemed to know Nick somebody who "was real pious — always psalm-singin' or prayin'." The new sergeant said, "Nick's gone under" [i.e., he died]. The captain looked profound and said "Wall now, I've met a good many pious fellows like that and they commonly gets hit [by a bullet] or gets fevers, same as other folks — I don't see no good in it all myself." Then the minstrels began and monopolised our attention, except when a drunken fellow tried a stump oration and compared "Canady" [Canada] to the State's prison — said it was an institootion, with a prolonged howl.

We slept at the hotel that night.

[Wed.] 26th Aug.   Returned to Charlotte by the morning train. The wind was North-West, so we could not make our course and had to wait in harbour all day. Fred Duggan and I went to the pier and fished, but there was a heavy sea rolling in and we caught nothing. Then we loafed, had a cocktail and played draughts [a form of checkers played on an 8x8-square board] at the Stutson House, then logged up. It was a fine clear moonlight night. The wind had hauled round to the South so at ten o'clock, we got under weigh and said "good-bye" to Charlotte.

[Thurs.] 27th August.   My watch [duty] ran from midnight till two in the morning. The wind so hauled round that, when we were about abreast of the Devil's Nose, we were obliged to keep away [alter course] for Toronto. Part of the time, indeed, we were steering on Cobourg [due North] till the wind got a little more southing in it and we could bear up again [to head due West.] At six a.m., it was pretty rough and blowing fresh, so all hands were called on deck to send down the top-mast. At twelve noon, we had curaçoa and crackers by way of lunch, and at 1:30 p.m., we anchored off the Yacht Club at Toronto.

The normal cruising speed of the *Breeze* is estimated at less than four knots (seven kilometers per hour). However, on this last leg of the cruise, the yacht sailed 180 kilometers in just over fifteen hours, making her speed on this portion of the voyage twelve kilometers per hour or almost six and a half knots.

Our moorings were soon picked up. Burgess [possibly Lieut. Henry M. Burgess, RA] came on board, then Mr. Holcomb, and we had quite a lively time "packing up." When the *Breeze* passed the New Garrison [the New Fort], she was recognized, and so we found Woodfull's carriage waiting for us. Ourselves and our effects were speedily conveyed to the fort and so …

The Cruise was over.

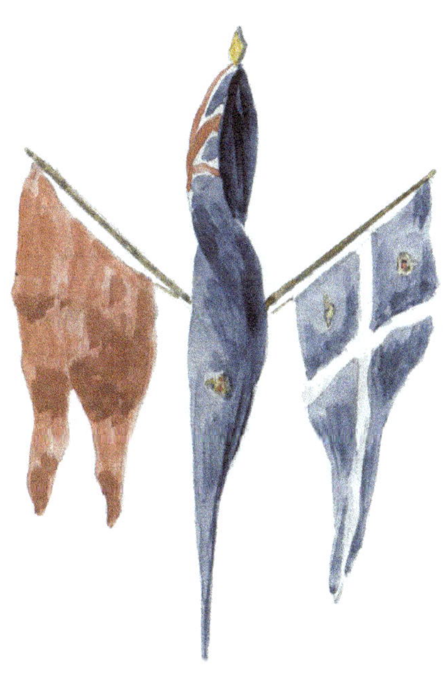

At the end of August, 1863, Henry Baines returned to his life of predictable routine in garrison at the New Fort in Toronto. Given his prolific production of water-colours, he presumably continued his painting excursions around Toronto, however, only two of Henry's paintings from this twenty-two month period (September 1863 to June 1865) have so far come to light (see Appendix).

Henry continued to sail with the Royal Canadian Yacht Club and in March 1865, he was elected as the club's Captain in place of fellow "Breezer", Capt. George Morrison. Baines served on the club's executive committee along with Commodore Hodder, Vice-Commodore G.M. Hawke, Secretary William Armstrong, and Treasurer H.L. Hime.[108]

By the end of spring, 1865, Confederate forces had surrendered to the Union Army and the American Civil War was over. Tensions between the United States and Britain lessened considerably and Britain's War Office started reducing the number of troops stationed in British North America. Some regiments were sent home to Great Britain and others were moved to new stations within Canada. Lieut. Baines and No. 5 Battery received orders to move to Quebec City where Henry continued to draw and paint, and, in all likelihood, continued to enjoy yachting by sailing on the wide expanse of the St. Lawrence River.

Part 4

THE HERO

In May 1865, one month after Confederate general Robert E. Lee surrendered his army to Union general Ulysses S Grant thereby effectively ending the American Civil War, orders arrived from Artillery Headquarters in Montreal: the Toronto garrison was to be reduced to a single battery of field artillery. Lieut. Henry Baines and No. 5 Garrison Battery were to be moved to Quebec City. On May 23, after living in Toronto for more than three years, the officers and men of No. 5 Battery marched out of the New Fort for the last time. Just before 2pm, they boarded the steamer *Magnet* to begin their three-day journey to their new station.

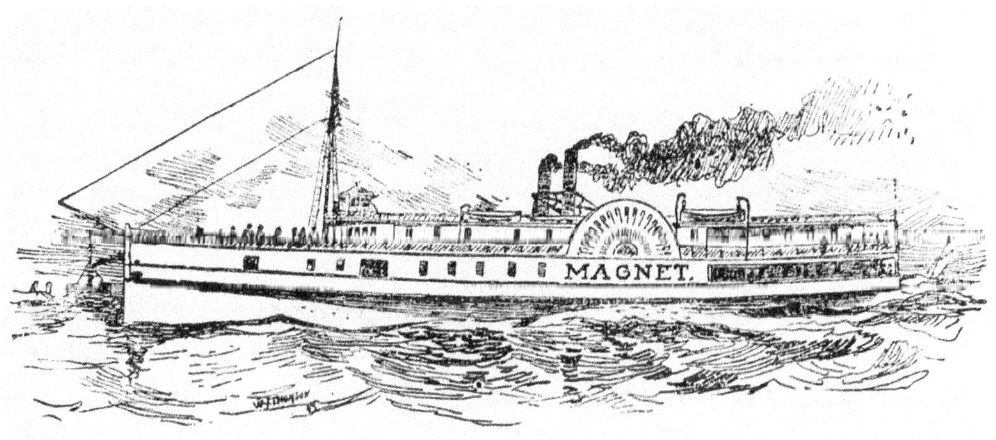

The Steamer *Magnet*.
W.J. Thomson, 1899. Engraving of a sketch.
[From *Robertson's Landmarks of Toronto*, Toronto, 1899.]

As the ship steamed out of Toronto harbour, losing sight of the city as they headed down Lake Ontario, Henry reflected on his time in the city and expressed his feelings in a poem:

On Board the *Magnet*

Far back the low smoke trailing lies,
Back streams the braid white foam,
And backward still I strain my eyes
Towards our three years home.

A black streak on the clear calm sky,
White on the deep blue lake —
'Twixt lake and sky thoughts backward fly,
From foam below, from cloud on high
Their two-fold hue they take

Through dark regret for all I leave,
For hands I clasp no more,
There gleam fresh hopes my fancies weave
From all that lies before.

No more for me the breeze may blow
from sky so clear, o'er lake so blue;
Perchance I ne'er again shall know
A life so calm with friends so true.

As in those years that ran their sand
In bright grains dropping day by day
Where fair Toronto lines the strand
With masts and spires far away,

So far away, and now more far,
Still farther growing — fading still,
The lake verge rises like a bar
'Twixt me and them — they fade until

They die in distance and the sky
Rests all unbroken on the lake —
Three years die with them — so, Goodbye,
New life begins as old links break.

But still where'er my fate may lead,
By Indian palms or dear home shore,
No quiet dreams at even fall,
Old forms will rise — old voices call;
The past will claim my heart, and ah!
The dear old times be mine once more.[1]

His poem was a farewell to the friends he had made in Toronto. Although Henry would never again cross paths with his sailing companion, Samuel Woodfull, and many of his associates from the Royal Canadian Yacht Club, not all of his friends were being left behind. Fellow officer in No. 5 Battery, Henry Harvey, would be with him in Quebec, and there they would meet again fellow "Breezer", Captain Clarkson, who had left Toronto with the 30th Regiment two years earlier when posted to Quebec. Such was a soldier's life — abandoning familiar routines, leaving familiar surroundings, leaving friends and family and moving to a new place, an

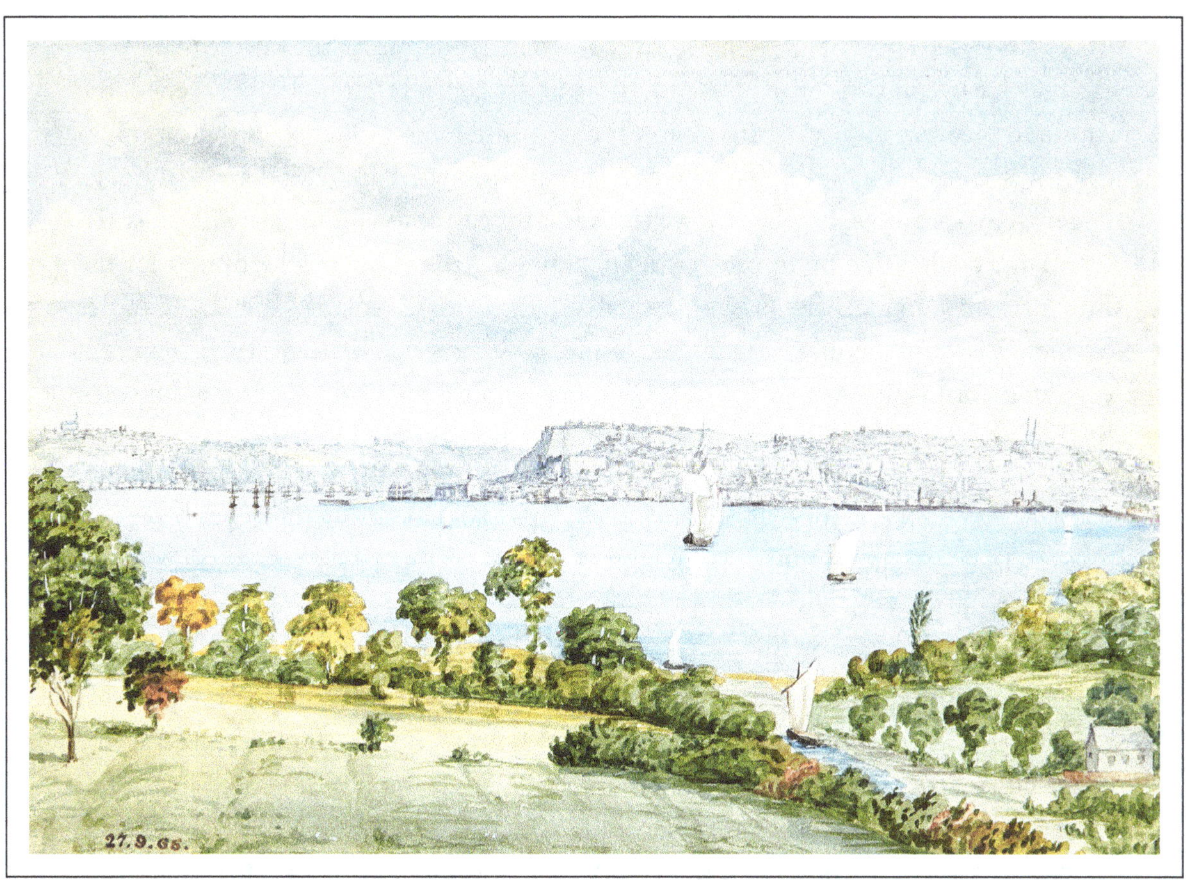

Untitled (View of Quebec from Ile d'Orleans)
Henry Edward Baines, 27 September 1866. Watercolour, pencil and gouache on paper.
[Courtesy of the Art Gallery of Hamilton]

unknown place, but a place that promised new adventures and, in Henry's case, new subjects for his watercolours. Quebec City was such a place.

Founded by the French in 1608, Quebec was originally the capital of the colony of New France. The British captured the colony in 1760, during the Seven Years War. By the Treaty of Paris which ended the war three years later, France ceded the captured territory to Great Britain and the British retained Quebec as the capital of their new colony. By the 1860's, Quebec's population was barely 50,000,[2] marginally larger than Toronto's. Quebec, however, was a much more vibrant city with a social life that exceeded that of Toronto by many times. As the seat of Government for the Province of Canada, the Governor-General of British North America, Charles Stanley Viscount Monck, made his home at Quebec. The Governor-General's entourage of private secretaries, aides-de-camp and senior civil servants along with his Executive Council constituted an informal colonial version of Queen Victoria's court in England. This "colonial court" was augmented by the members of the legislative council and the well-to-do citizenry of Quebec; the judges, doctors, lawyers and wealthy merchants, all of whom added to a rich and varied social atmosphere. The garrison itself, several times larger than that of Toronto, had an equally large cadre of military officers who brought to the city, in the words of one contemporary, "prestige — fashionable circles, wealth and refinement as well as trade and commerce"; the latter to the amount of £100,000 annually.[3] Throughout the 1860's, the economy of the city was booming thanks to its position as a major shipbuilding port and as the centre of the Canadian export lumber trade. Quebec boasted six banks, several fine hotels, daily newspapers printed in both English and French, and a university.

Quebec's picturesque location, high on a plateau dominating the narrow peninsula where the St. Charles River emptied into the St. Lawrence River, presented numerous scenic views of the surrounding country including the suburbs of St. Roch and St. Sauveur, Point Lévis opposite Quebec, the Isle d'Orleans in the middle of the St. Lawrence River, with the falls of Montmorency and the Laurentian Mountains beyond. These views enhanced the architectural charm of the old city walls which encircled the Upper Town with its narrow streets and stone buildings. The Lower Town, a jumble of houses, shops, factories, warehouses and wharfs, occupied the narrow strip of land between the cliff and the banks of the two rivers. High above rose Cape Diamond atop which was situated Quebec's Citadel, a fortress whose guns commanded the river below. The Citadel was the military headquarters of the Quebec garrison

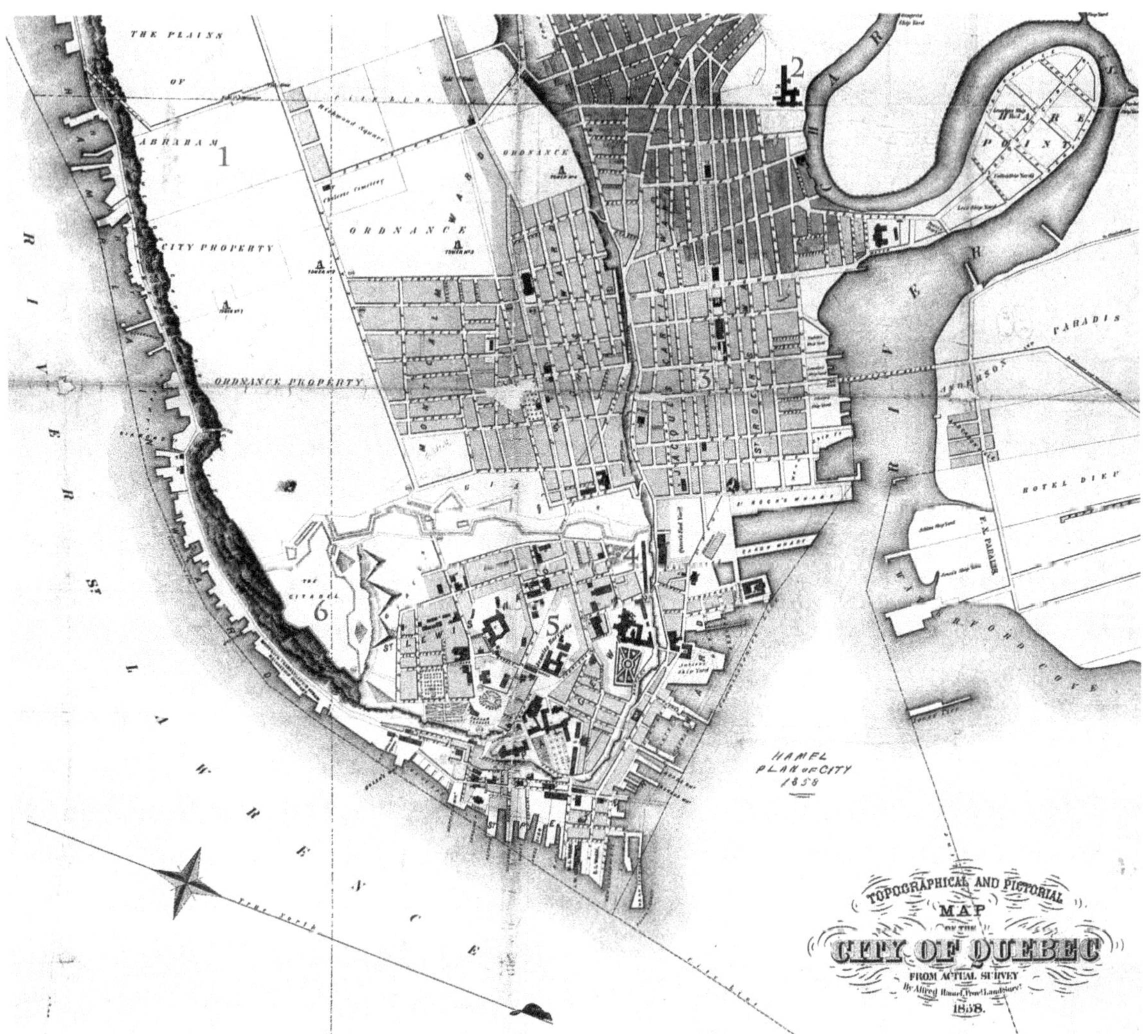

Topographical and Pictorial Map of the City of Quebec, 1858 (detail)
Alfred Hamel. Lithograph. [Courtesy of Library and Archives Canada.]

1 - Plains of Abraham.
2 - General Hospital where Lieut. Henry Baines died.
3 - St. Roch suburb.
4 - Artillery Barracks.
5 - Jesuit Barracks.
6 - Quebec Citadel.

and contained barracks for some of the infantry regiments stationed at Quebec. The nearby Jesuit Barracks in the centre of town housed more infantry, and the Artillery Barracks at the north end of the old walled city where numbers 4, 5 and 6 Garrison Batteries were quartered, provided accommodation for the remainder of the city's troops, numbering more than 2,000 in total. West from the Citadel, the Plains of Abraham, a three kilometer stretch of scenic, rolling meadows, terminated at Spencer Wood, the stately mansion that was the Governor-General's official residence.

From a military standpoint, Quebec was of great strategic importance as a major inland port with direct access to the sea for at least eight months of the year via the St. Lawrence River. The city's primary fortifications, the Citadel and the ramparts surrounding the Upper Town, were augmented by a string of four Martello towers strategically placed on the Plains of Abraham across the neck of the plateau between the two rivers. In addition, three new forts were nearing completion across the St. Lawrence at Lévis where another battalion of infantry was stationed. In all, the city's fortifications were equipped with a total of 198 artillery pieces and another 150 guns, carronades, howitzers and mortars in reserve.[4]

Henry Baines quickly settled into garrison life in Quebec, performing his required military duties, participating in a multitude of social activities and pursuing his passion: watercolours. His painting excursions took him to the locales around the city that presented spectacular views of the St. Lawrence valley and the surrounding countryside. He painted numerous watercolours from the Plains of Abraham, Isle d'Orleans, Lac Beauport and several other locations. From the summer of 1865 through to Autumn 1866, Henry painted more than fifty scenes in and around his new home.[5]

Across the border in the United States, the Union army, which by the end of the Civil War had increased its numbers to more than one million soldiers, had now been largely disbanded. Even though there were still diplomatic tensions over the "Alabama Claims" — claims for losses by the United States against Britain because of the activities of the CSS *Alabama*, one of several Confederate naval vessels which had been constructed in British shipyards and used by the Confederate Navy to attack U.S. commercial shipping during the Civil War[6] — fears of war between the United States and Great Britain had all but disappeared.

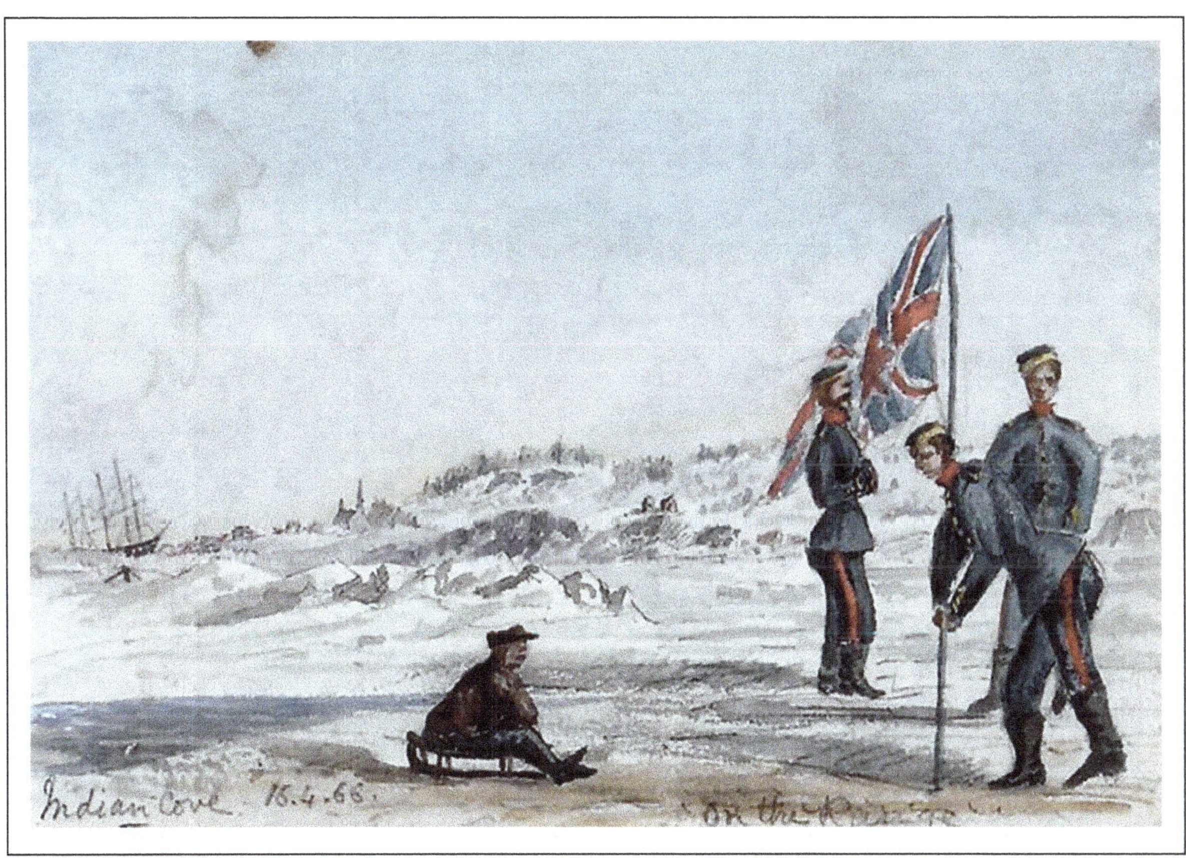

Indian Cove, On the Rouge
Henry Edward Baines, 16 April 1866. Watercolour, gouache and pencil on paper.
[Donated to Library and Archives Canada by Marc Seguin, 2017]

Three officers of the Royal Artillery planting a flag while a boy looks on. This scene is probably near Cap
Rouge, just west of Quebec City

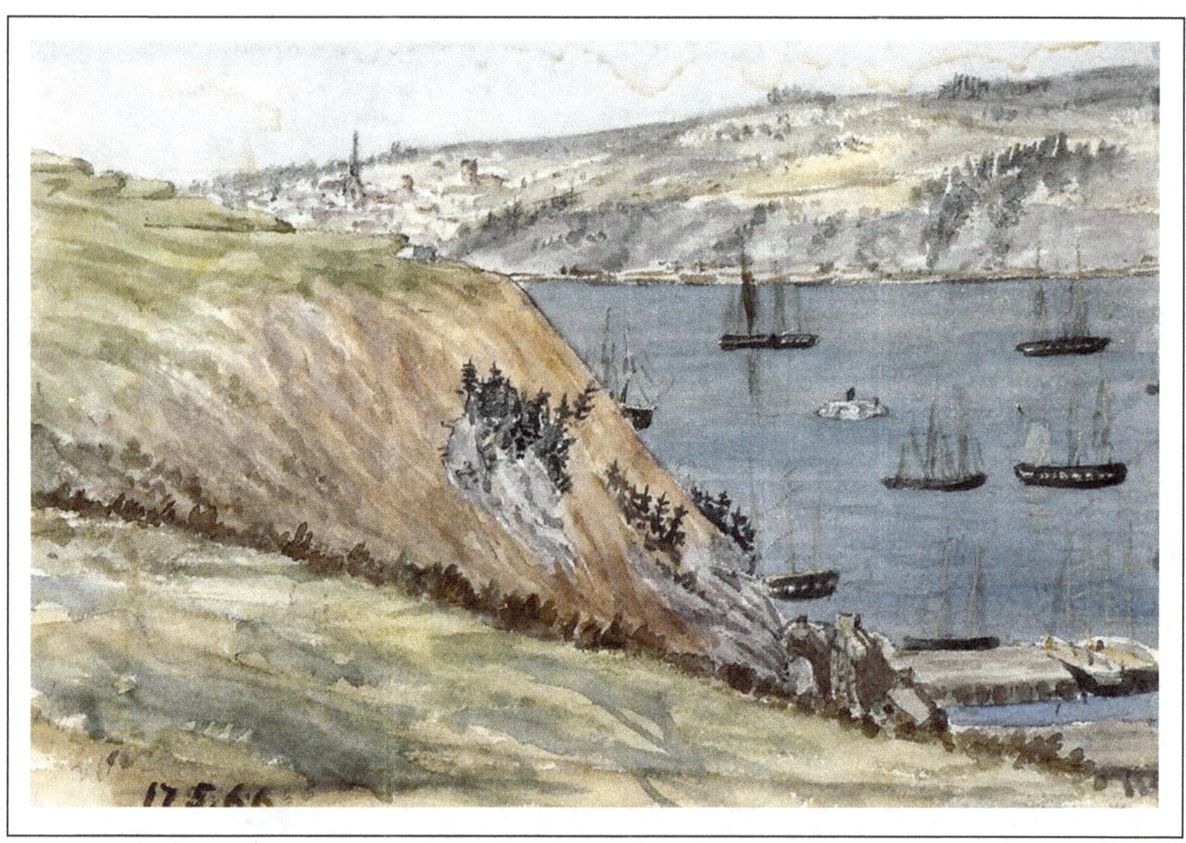

Untitled (View of ships on the St. Lawrence River from the Plains of Abraham)
Henry Edward Baines, 17 May 1866. Watercolour, gouache and pencil on paper.
[Donated to Library and Archives Canada by T.B. Cluett, 2017.]

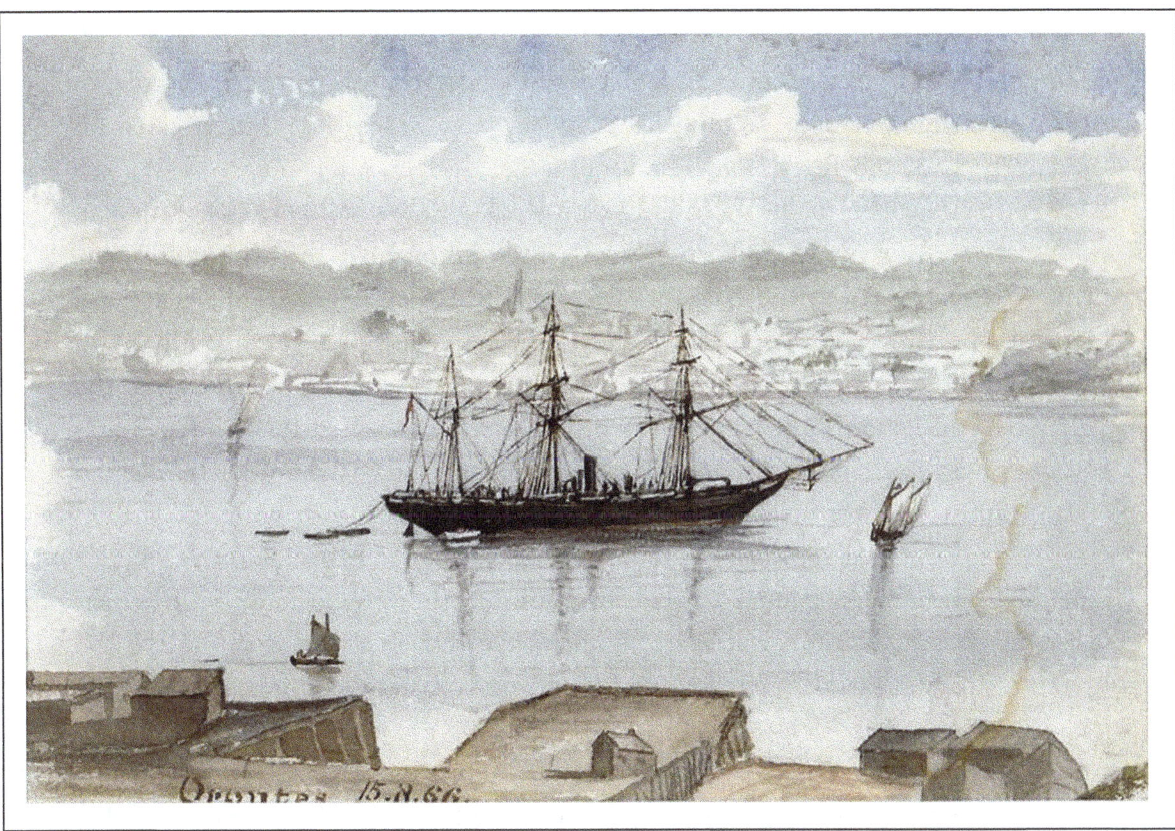

Orontes
Henry Edward Baines, 15 August 1866. Watercolour, pencil and ink on paper.
[Donated to Library and Archives Canada by R. Cluett, 2017]

The troopship HMS *Orontes* is shown anchored in the St. Lawrence River near the wharfs of Quebec's Lower Town. The town of Lévis is in the background.

In the spring of 1866, however, the alarming news of other invaders from the United States had the entire Quebec garrison on edge. The Fenian Brotherhood — Irish-Americans militating for Ireland's independence from Great Britain — had long threatened to form an army to attack Canada in a bid to capture the British colony and hold it for ransom in exchange for Ireland's freedom from British rule. In April, the Fenians raided Campobello Island in New Brunswick, but retreated on the approach of the Royal Navy. In June, large numbers of Fenians crossed the Niagara frontier in Canada West and skirmished with a small corps of Canadian volunteers at Ridgeway near Fort Erie. On the approach of British regulars, the Fenians retreated across the Niagara River to Buffalo. At Pigeon Hill, near Lake Champlain on the Canada-United States border, seventy kilometers south-east of Montreal, three Canadian militia companies guarding the border withdrew at the sight of 1,000 Fenians advancing into British territory. When the United States government stepped in to prevent arms from being sent across the border and Fenian reinforcements failed to arrive from Vermont, the Irishmen withdrew from Canada.[7]

Throughout the summer of 1866, troops all across British North America remained on alert. As summer faded into autumn, however, rumours of Fenian invasions dwindled. Soon, volunteer companies were told to stand down and the British regulars in garrison returned to their normal peacetime military routines.

At 6AM on the morning of Sunday October 14, 1866, the officer of the guard at Quebec's Artillery Barracks sounded the alarm. Officers and men poured out of their quarters into the darkness. Behind them, the early morning sky over the St. Roch suburb just beyond the city ramparts bordering their barracks was lit up and filled with smoke and embers from a fire that was raging through the streets of the crowded, working-class neighbourhood where hundreds of wooden shops and houses were huddled closely together in the St. Chares River valley between the steep escarpment of the Upper Town and the banks of the river less than a kilometer away.

Fire was a constant threat in all 19th Century cities. The use of open flames for cooking, heating and lighting, and the construction of highly combustible wooden buildings in crowded suburbs combined with poorly funded and inadequately trained fire brigades meant that disastrous urban fires were all too common. In Quebec City alone there had been eight major fires in the previous thirty years; two of them in 1845 alone which claimed more than 3,000 houses and left some 21,000 residents homeless.[8]

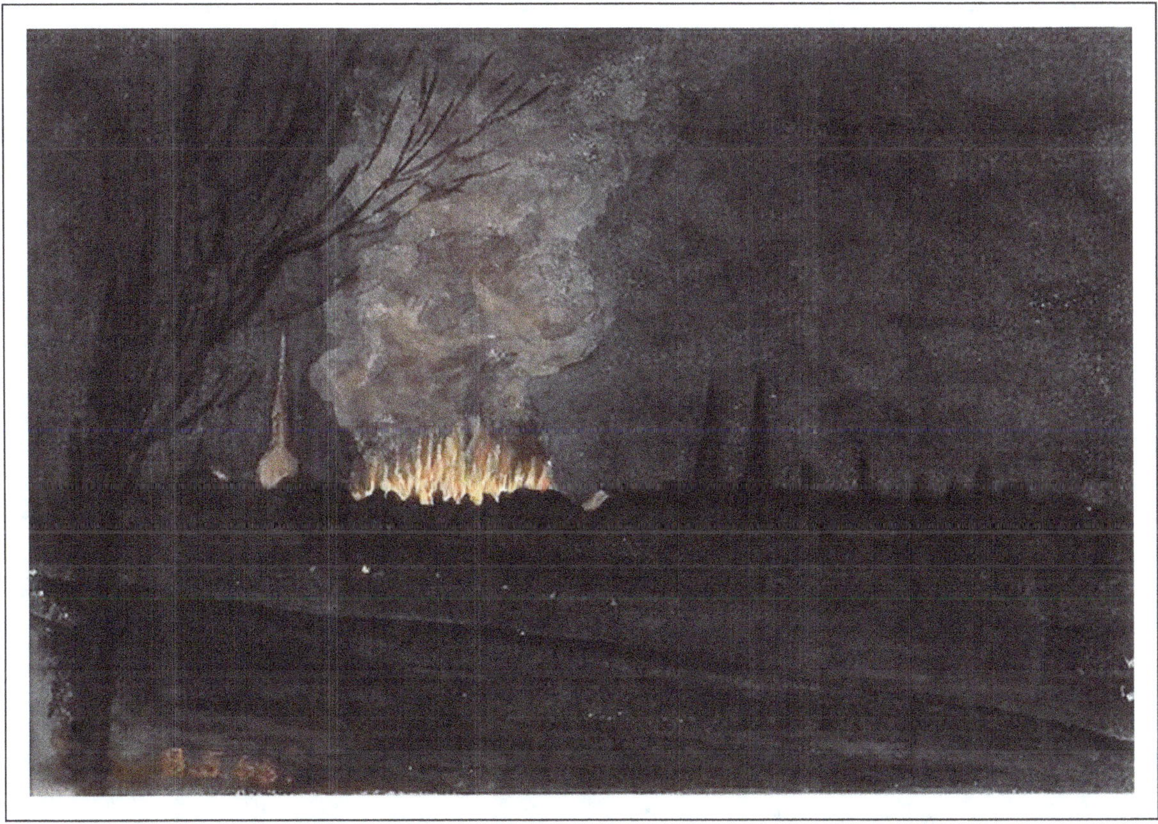

Untitled (Fire near the church)
Henry Edward Baines, 9 May 1866. Watercolour and gouache on paper.
[Donated to Library and Archives Canada by T.B. Cluett, 2017]

This prophetic scene depicts a fire that occurred near the church of Notre Dame de Jacques Cartier in the St. Roch suburb, five months before the Great Fire of Quebec. This view is probably taken from the Royal Artillery barracks located in the Upper Town, just over one kilometer away.[9]

Other cities, too, had seen the devastating effects of major fires. The great fire that swept through Montreal in 1852 left 10,000 people homeless, and just a few months before the fire in Quebec, in July 1866, in the city of Portland, Maine, a fire was started by a firecracker during 4th of July celebrations and 1,800 buildings were destroyed leaving 10,000 people, one-third of its population, without shelter.[10]

In the early hours of that October morning in Quebec, in a back-room gambling parlour at Mr. Trudel's grocery store on St. Joseph Street near the centre of St. Roch, a fire had started around 5A.M. and had quickly spread to the adjacent wooden buildings. The Sapeurs, the volunteer hook and ladder company, were quickly on the scene wielding their axes with great effect to tear down wooden fences and outbuildings to slow the advance of the fire. The city's newly created fire brigade with its water pump and hoses had been called out right away. In the face of strong winds funnelling up the St. Charles River valley from the east, however, the firefighters had little success. Even after the fire brigade arrived, the situation was exacerbated by a lack of water pressure in the fire hoses. Without water to fight the fire, the blaze advanced quickly.

A contemporary account taken from local newspapers gives the details of the start of the Great Fire of Quebec:

> About five o'clock on Sunday morning October 14th, an alarm of fire was heard through the streets of St. Roch's, and on proceeding to the locality, it was discovered to have originated in the house of Mr. Trudel, Grocer, St. Joseph Street, three doors beyond the Jacques Cartier Market. The fire originated in consequence of the prolongation of orgies of carousing far into the night at Trudel's store, where numbers of low characters were in the habit of resorting at night for drinking and card playing. On Saturday night a number of them had congregated there, and notwithstanding the civil regulation for the closing of such places at midnight, Trudel, it is said, allowed them to continue their course far into the Sabbath morning. Owing to the early hour in the morning, there were but few persons about. The wind which had blown half a gale from the eastward all night, had slightly abated; but still it raged with such fury as to cause the most serious apprehensions, which unfortunately were afterwards but too sadly realized. By the time the fire brigade reached the spot Trudel's house was enveloped in flames. The Sapeurs were already there, but there was some delay in laying the hose and getting force enough. The delay, which was not remedied for nearly an hour, enabled the fire to make rapid progress. There were now some ten or a dozen houses on fire, and lumber and wooden sheds, on all sides had ignited.

> By half-past five o'clock more than 80 houses, all wooden, were in a blaze,
> and the flames driven by the wind were spreading in all directions.[11]

The fire brigade found that some of their hoses had been cut by hooligans. While the hoses were being repaired, the fire brigade captain sent for help from the garrison. A messenger was dispatched across town to the officer's quarters near the Citadel where Town-Major, Captain James Pope, the man responsible for the day-to-day military operations in the city, was informed of the urgent need for the army's help. Pope immediately sent messengers to the garrison commandant, Lord Alexander Russell colonel of the 1st Battalion Rifle Brigade, as well as to the commanding officers of the other military units in the city; the Royal Artillery, the Royal Engineers, the Rifle Brigade and the 30th Regiment, and to the 25th (King's Own Borderers) Regiment across the river at Lévis, and even to Captain de Horsey of the Royal Navy commanding HMS *Aurora* docked at the Queen's Wharf in the Lower Town. The unit commanders were respectfully requested to send, without delay, as many men as possible to St. Roch to help fight the fire and to assist the hundreds of civilians who were fleeing for their lives.

At the Artillery Barracks, 10th Brigade commander, Lieut.-Col. McCrea, ordered the alarm sounded and his captains were instructed to distribute several kegs of gunpowder to each of the divisions of their respective Batteries. The divisions, each under the command of their officers, were given orders to use their explosives to demolish buildings in the fire's path to create a firebreak in an attempt to starve the fire of fuel.

The use of gunpowder as a "disruptive agent" was a common practice in fighting urban fires. One Royal Engineer who had experience fighting fires in Montreal explained that, "when fires occur in towns, it is often desirable to make a break in a row of houses, to stop the progress of the flames, and gunpowder may usefully be employed in such cases."[12]

Each of the Battery commanders had their men form up in the Artillery Barracks parade square; some of the gunners shouldering a twenty-five pound (11kg) keg of gunpowder while others were equipped with axes. The commander of No. 5 Battery, Maj. Leslie, gave the order for his Battery to march. At quick-time Lieut. Baines and the other officers together with more than 100 men proceeded out of the barrack yard, through the Palace Gate and down the escarpment along the road into the burning suburb of St. Roch. As they were the military unit closest to fire, the men of the Royal Artillery were the first soldiers on the scene.

The *Quebec Gazette* reported the details of the timely assistance rendered by the Quebec garrison:

Detachments of the Rifle Brigade, Royal Artillery, the 30th Regiment, Royal Engineers, and the crew of the steam-frigate *Aurora* were at the scene of the conflagration, as early as half-past six o'clock. Nothing could exceed the heroism which the gallant fellows displayed throughout the day. Everywhere they were to be seen, officers and men alike, in the midst of danger, while the great majority of citizens stood idly gaping on. The Rifles worked like Trojans; the Artillerymen and Engineers were engaged not only in blowing up houses here and there to arrest the fiery element in its course, but with their axes were mounted on the roofs of houses, while others of them were more humanely employed in assisting the sufferers to save and carry away their furniture. The gallant tars of the *Aurora* also signalized themselves with great credit, running into the most dangerous of spots, and working unceasingly.[13]

Some of the soldiers and sailors were working behind the fire to prevent it crossing back to areas of the suburb that were still untouched by the flames. Others tried to keep the flames at bay while desperate residents tried furiously to save some of their meager possessions. Still others worked at the leading edge of the fire to make a firebreak by demolishing buildings with axes and gunpowder. By 11A.M., the fire had split into three separate blazes, one heading north toward the St. Charles River, one heading further west toward the adjacent suburb of St. Sauveur, and a third one in between, scorching a path directly towards the convent and General Hospital run by the Sisters of St. Augustine. An account from the *Quebec Mercury* fills in the details:

At eleven o'clock in the morning, the whole centre of the district lying between St. Sauveur and the lower streets, running parallel with the river, was a barren waste, with nothing but bare chimneys and smouldering embers. Having nothing to feed on, [the fire] distributed itself in opposite directions. The wind increasing again at this time and blowing in gusts from every direction, three separate conflagrations were observable at once.

St. Sauveur Church, Dunn's soap and candle factory, Rees' rope walk, and other large buildings, were in flames. Along St. Vallier street towards the toll-gate and the streets surrounding the General Hospital and Convent, another terrible fire was raging with greater fury; while at the back of Crown street, along Prince Edward, Jesuit and Ryland streets, the flames were creeping back, enveloping street after street and range after range despite the almost superhuman efforts of the soldiers and seamen of the *Aurora* to arrest it.[14]

The General Hospital was a large stone building inside a walled enclosure situated on the south bank of the St. Charles River. The hospital for the poor and the attached convent of the Sisters of St. Augustine had been built by the French in the 17th Century. On that Sunday morning in 1866, the sixty-five nuns in residence were still at morning prayer when shouts of "fire" were heard in the streets. The patients in the hospital numbered nearly three hundred, all of whom were either too sick or too infirm to be evacuated. Soon, refugees fleeing the fire were pouring through the convent's gates in search of a safe haven from the flames.

Glancing up St. Ours Street (now Boulevard Langelier) from the convent, Vicar-General, Father Cazeau, could see the fire, just eight blocks away, advancing directly toward the hospital. The priest immediately ran for help. He found Lieut.-Col. McCrae and pleaded with him to send some of his soldiers to try to save the General Hospital and its occupants who, by now, numbered more than five hundred. Even though his men were exhausted after having toiled non-stop for more than five hours, the artillery commander quickly dispatched Lieut. Bradley of No. 4 Battery, Lieut. Baines of No. 5 Battery and a detachment of gunners with their kegs of gunpowder to follow Father Cazeau back to the General Hospital. The priest led the way through the smoke-filled suburb to the corner of St. Anselme and Prince

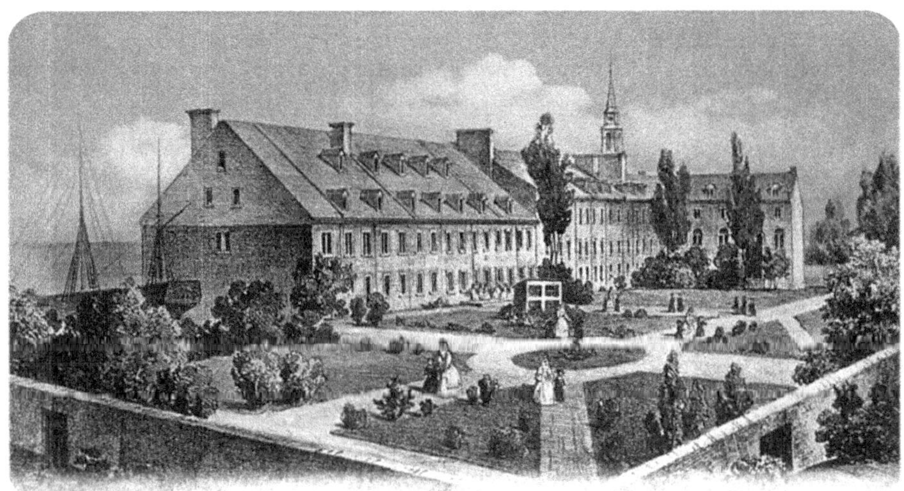

Québec, Hôpital Général. The General Hospital and Convent.
Artist unknown. Lithograph, c. 1905.
[Courtesy of Biblioteque et Archives National du Québec]

The General Hospital and Convent of the Order of the Sisters of St. Augustine was built by the French in the 17th Century. Much of the original building is still standing in 2017.

Edward streets, directly in front of the hospital, where they were to begin blowing up buildings to create a firebreak.[15] This was their last chance to save the hospital, the convent and hundreds of lives.

Lieut. Baines had his gunners place two kegs of gunpowder against the inside wall of a brick house that was in the direct path of the fire immediately across the street from the General Hospital.[16] He ordered his men out of the building just as flames began to engulf the adjacent structure. Henry prepared a long fuse, lit it, and proceeded out of the house. Sparks or flames from the building next door must have reached the powder keg before Henry could find safe cover. The premature explosion threw him thirty feet, landing in the street where his crumpled body was covered with rubble from the demolished building. Another Quebec newspaper, *Le Courier du Canada*, gives this account of Lieut. Baines' heroic actions:

> It was about eleven o'clock, a.m., and the conflagration, after having swept away most of the buildings which lined the streets contiguous to the wall enclosing the Hospital on the eastern side, was on the point of attacking a brick house, situated at less than 20 feet from the large white store of the Hospital. There was not a moment to spare, and the only chance remaining to save the monastery was that of blowing up the threatened building. At this critical moment Lieut. Baines arrived on the spot with his brave Artillerymen; he immediately ordered a keg of powder to be placed in the brick building, and, with intrepidity bordering upon temerity, himself prepared the fuse amid a shower of fiery fragments driven in every direction by the hurricane. The brave Lieutenant had just left the building, and was calmly making his way for cover behind the wall of the Hospital, when a terrific explosion was heard. The brick building was level with the ground, the Hospital was saved, but its rescuer was buried beneath the débris.
>
> Lieut. Baines was immediately carried into a small chamber in the hall of the infirmary, on the first story of the Hospital, where he was laid on a bed, around which were soon gathered the physicians, who pronounced his wounds mortal.[17]

Attended with great care by the nursing sisters, Henry lay unconscious in his hospital bed as the fire continued to burn westward into the St. Sauveur suburb. By five o'clock that afternoon, the fire had burned itself out.

The General Hospital had been saved, but some 20,000 people were now homeless. Quebec's mayor, Joseph Cauchon, quickly ordered temporary shelters to be set up at two militia drill sheds and at the municipal skating rink. He also asked the garrison commander, Lord Russell, to provide army tents to shelter those who had lost their homes. Soldiers of the 25th Regiment and the Rifle Brigade worked into the night setting up hundreds of tents on the open plain west of St. Sauveur. Mayor Cauchon also enlisted the help of the city's bakers who set to work baking hundreds of loaves of bread to feed the homeless. The next day, a general call for financial aid for the victims of the fire was put out to the rest of the city's population as well as to other cities. Numerous officers of the Quebec garrison contributed to the fund and money was received from as far away as Montreal and Boston.

More than a dozen military men who had been fighting the fire had been badly hurt. Lieut. Baines and Sergeant Hughes of the Royal Artillery had both been injured by premature explosions. Hughes was badly burned but survived and was discharged from the army soon afterwards. Also, a naval officer, Lieut. A. Douglas of HMS *Aurora*, along with ten of his men were hospitalized as a result of injuries sustained during the fire. Over the following few days, a tally of the destruction was made: an area of 180 acres had been scorched; more than 1,200 houses and other buildings had been destroyed in St. Roch and another 900 in St. Sauveur at an

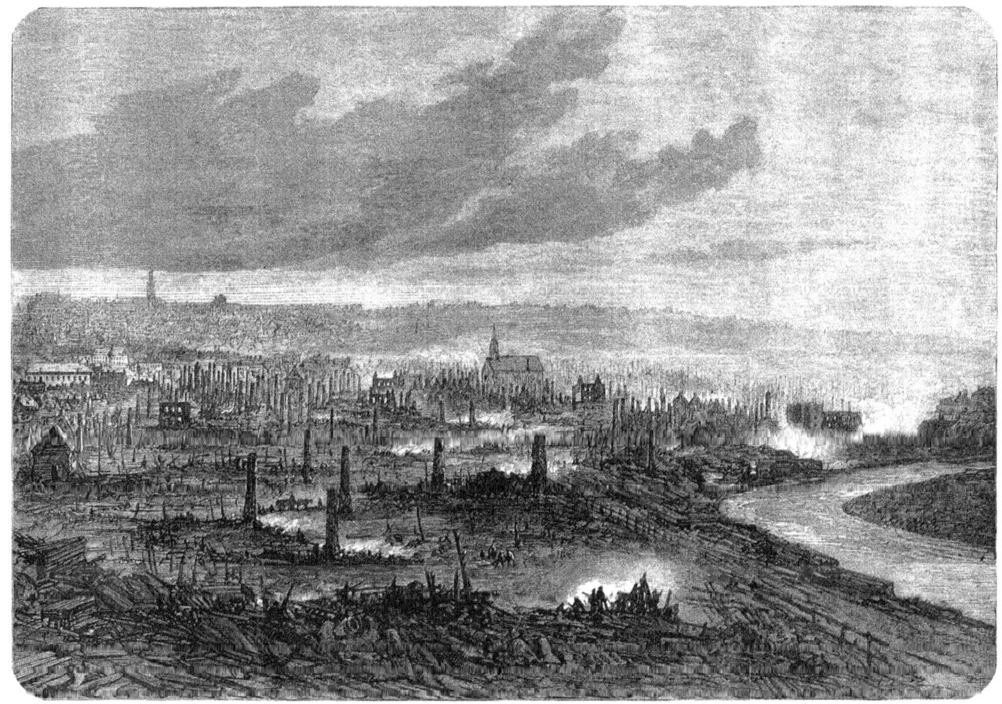

The Great Fire At Quebec.
Artist unknown. Wood Engraving.
[From *The Illustrated London News*, London, 10 Nov. 1866.]

estimated cost of some $3 million. Tragically, the fire had also taken the lives of six of Quebec's citizens.[18]

Meanwhile, Henry Baines remained in the General Hospital under the care of the nursing sisters and attended by three doctors; city physicians Anderson and McKinnon, and the Royal Artillery's Assistant-Surgeon John Adsetts. After a few days, although still in critical condition, Henry showed signs of improvement. He was soon well enough to receive visits from many of his fellow officers including his Battery commander, Maj. Leslie, and his Battery captain, James Barton. Several of the officers' wives also visited Henry in hospital, especially Mrs. McCrea, the wife of the commanding officer of the 10th Brigade, who spent long hours at Henry's bedside.

After twelve days, Henry was able to sit up in bed to write a letter home to his mother. Just as it appeared as though he would fully recover, he contracted Tetanus. Commonly known as lock jaw, Tetanus is a bacterial infection that, at the time, had no cure.[19] Painful contractions wracked his body for two days. During these last days, Captain Barton sat with Henry, read to him and prayed with him until the end.

Henry Edward Baines died just after midnight on Saturday, October 27, 1866. He was twenty-six years old.

The Monday newspapers announced the sad news of the death of the heroic officer. On hearing the news, Mayor Cauchon insisted that the garrison's commandant agree to give the young hero a public funeral with full military honours. In his public announcement, the Mayor declared, "this extraordinary act on my part is justified by the extraordinary circumstance attending the death of this noble-hearted and unfortunate young man. He sacrificed his life to save our properties, and as we cannot do more for him, let us show ourselves at least grateful and sincerely sorrowful by accompanying his mortal remains to their last resting place."[20]

A deep sadness descended upon the residents of Quebec, both military and civilian, on learning of the death of Henry Baines. Many of the artillery officers, including Lieut.-Col. McCrea, Maj. Leslie, Capt. Barton and Assistant-Surgeon Adsetts wrote letters of condolence to Henry's mother, Mary Baines, and his sisters who were then living in the London suburb of Brixton.

In his letter to Henry's mother, Assistant-Surgeon Adsetts gave a sensitive account of her son's heroism:

> Your poor son was engaged on duty in blowing up a house with the object
> of staying the progress of the great fire that was raging at the time, (the
> 14th October,) when unfortunately the charge of powder exploded before
> he could leave the building, and he was hurled for a considerable distance,

a quantity of bricks, part of the wall of the house, falling upon him; he was immediately extricated, and carried to the General Hospital Convent close by; he was immediately attended by a medical man, who found him with his clothes literally torn off him, much bruised, and suffering from violent shock, in fact in a state of deep collapse.

We all hoped, after the first shock was recovered from, that time would restore him, and that he would again take his place amongst us, his improvement up to the tenth day encouraged this idea, but tetanus which then made its appearance, unlooked for, unpreventable, grievously destroyed our hopes, it ran its course rapidly but little controlled by the remedies applied.

During the whole of his illness your son bore himself with courage, patience, and resignation; when first I saw him, and when he knew that our hopes of his living were very faint, he expressed his resignation to the Divine will, he said, "If I die, I die in the performance of my duty, and I thank God that I should so die."

It may be some consolation to you to know what he accomplished by the deed that caused his death; by it he prevented the extension of the fire to a large and valuable public building, the General Hospital Convent, in which were some hundreds of infirm and sickly people, many of whose lives were undoubtedly saved by his prompt and gallant action.

I will not write more now than to tell you that his services were recognized by a public funeral being decreed him, a monument will be erected to his memory, and his name will be gratefully and affectionately remembered for many years to come in this country.[21]

The public funeral of Lieut. Baines, with full military honours, took place on October 31, 1866. At 2pm, the elaborate funeral procession departed from the Artillery Barracks and wound its way through the narrow cobblestone streets of the old city to the Episcopal cathedral, Holy Trinity Church, whose bells of mourning had been tolling for several hours. As a sign of respect, shops in the Lower Town and Upper Town were closed, as were the customs house and other public buildings. All of the ships in port lowered their flags to half-mast. Thousands of people lined the route and watched in sadness as the long funeral procession filed past. The memorial pamphlet, *In Memorium*, compiled some months later, described the scene:

> At two o'clock the mournful procession, which was one of the most imposing and numerous we have witnessed for some time, left the Artillery Barracks, proceeding by way of St. John and Fabrique Streets to the cathedral, in the following order:

Firing party of the Royal Artillery with arms reversed
under command of Lieut. Ormsby.
Band of the Prince Consort's Own Rifle Brigade,
Band of the 30th Regiment,
Band of the Royal Artillery,
playing alternately the solemn and impressive strains of
the Dead March in Saul.
The Undertaker.
THE BODY
upon a gun carriage drawn by four horses, the coffin being
covered with the Union Jack, and surmounted with the hat
and sword of the deceased, and the pall being borne by
Officers of the different corps in garrison.
Col. McCrae, R.A. and Mourners.
Detachment of the P.C.O. Rifle Brigade.
Detachment of Seamen from H.M.S. *Aurora*.
Officers of Royal Artillery.
Detachment of Royal Engineers.
The Royal Artillery commanded by Adjt. Simpson.
Officers of Levis Volunteer Infantry.
Officers of 8th and 9th Battalion Volunteer Rifles.
Officers of Quebec Volunteer Artillery and Cavalry.
Officers of P.C.O. Rifle. Brigade.
Officers of 30th Regiment.
Officers of the Royal Engineers.
Officers of H.M.S. *Aurora*.
Officers of the Royal Artillery.
Brigade-Major de Montenach and Staff Officers of Quebec.
Volunteer and Sedentary Militia.
Lord Alexander Russell, Commandant.
Staff officers of H.M. Land and Naval Forces at Quebec.
His Excellency the Governor-General's Staff.
The Honorable the Judges of the Court of Queen's Bench
and Superior Courts in Quebec.
The Judge of the Sessions.
His Worship the Mayor and Members of the Corporation.
The City Clerk.
Protestant and Catholic Clergy.
The Hon. the Premier of the Government.
The Hon. the Speaker of the Legislative Council.
The Hon. Solicitor-General East.
Members of the Legislative Council and assembly resident in Quebec.
The Collector of Customs.
The President of the Board of Trade.
Magistrates.
His honour the Recorder.
The Batonnier and Members of the Quebec Bar;
and an immense concourse of citizens of all classes.

The whole line of march was crowded with spectators, both in the streets and at the windows, and sorrow was depicted on every countenance.

At the close of the service, the procession reforming in the same order, again took up its line of march through St. Louis Street to the Mount Hermon Cemetery, where the concluding portion of the mournful ceremony, the interment of the remains, and the firing of the usual three volleys in the air, over the grave by the party of forty of the deceased's own regiment, were performed.[22]

Two weeks later, Sister St. Olivier, the mother-superior of the General Hospital convent began a correspondence with Mary Baines to express the sorrow that the nuns felt and to extend their sympathies to the grieving mother:

> Ever since the melancholy events of last October we have felt ourselves drawn towards you, as if by some unaccountable tie of affection. Still as yet we could not find it in our hearts to address you on a subject which we know must re-open the deep deep wound so freshly made. As it is, we come not to speak of comfort to a bereaved mother, but to mingle our tears with her tears.
>
> It was beneath our roof that Lieut. Baines breathed his last sigh.– Oh! dear Madam, if human efforts could have availed; if skill, and kindness, and the most unremitting care could have worked a miracle, your son should not have died.
>
> Oh! the pang that went through every heart when the sad news became known! As for the Sisterhood of this community, we have more reason than all others to deplore the melancholy fate of Lieut. Baines. Was it not while endeavouring to save our monastery from impending destruction that he incurred the fatal accident?
>
> It may bring some solace to your sad heart to know that he felt happy in our midst. He could scarcely find words to express his thanks for what he called our trouble, being so far from his own family, he was at least satisfied that he had here so many mothers and so many sisters, (as he said) to represent the dear, dear mother and fond sisters at home. Indeed if Mr. Baines had been our own brother we could not have been more anxious for his recovery! We could not feel more affected for his untimely death. Long shall the name of the brave young officer be preserved among us, it shall be handed down encircled with dearly bought honour and gratitude to those who will inhabit the monastery in after years.

One more object have we to offer dear Madam, one which we know you will prize as only a mother can prize, it is a lock of your dear son's hair, we caused it to be cut with the express intention of having it conveyed to his family. The locket in which it is enclosed contains also his likeness, the best we could procure. We earnestly request you will kindly accept this slight token of our loving and heartfelt sympathy.

At our special request Major Leslie, R.A. has kindly taken on himself to procure for us a large likeness of Lieut. Baines. The picture will be held in the highest esteem by every member of this community.[23]

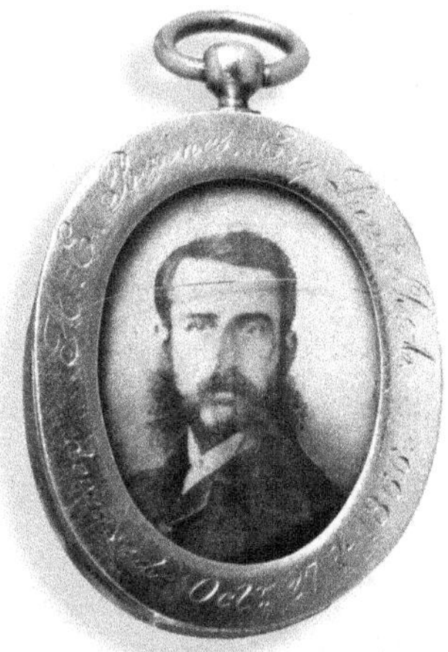

Locket with photograph of Henry Baines.
Artist unknown. Silver and glass with photographic print, 1866.
[Courtesy of B. Selkirk, Grafton, Ontario Canada.]

The locket was a gift to Henry's mother, Mary, from the nuns of the General Hospital. Inside the locket is a snippet of Henry's hair. The locket is inscribed, (recto) "H.E. Baines Esq. Lieut. R.A., deceased Oct' 27th 1866", (verso) "To Mrs. M. Baines. A token of sympathy from the Sisters of the Gen. Hosp. Convent, Quebec."

Mary Baines responded three weeks later to the Mother-Superior's letter:

On Saturday last, I received your truly kind and heartfelt letter with the lines you so thoughtfully copied for me, and the handsome gold locket with my dear son's portrait.

We have felt most grateful to you for your unwearied care and attendance upon him, which all his kind friends have mentioned to us, and which he himself spoke of most gratefully in the few precious lines he was able to write to me in pencil during his illness.

We are thankful that he was permitted to be the means of serving your valuable Institution. He rejoiced in having succeeded in his efforts to do so as he told me in the last few lines he was able to write to me.

The very handsome locket I should indeed prize most heartily not only for its precious contents and as a memento of his brave, heroic act, but for the kind loving sympathising givers of so valuable a treasure which I shall always wear and which my daughters will value when I am no more, its solid workmanship allowing me to count on its long durability.[24]

As a further acknowledgement of the young officer's heroism and the city's gratitude, Mayor Cauchon called for the construction of a fitting monument to be placed in Mount Hermon Cemetery. He arranged for a public fund to be created, and the following year, a large sandstone obelisk, five-and-a half meters tall, was erected to mark the grave of the hero of the Great Fire of Quebec. The coat of arms of the Royal Artillery is carved into the monument and below the carving are inscribed these words:

Erected by the citizens of Quebec
To preserve the memory
and to record their gratitude for the
gallant services of
Lieut. Henry Edward Baines,
Royal Artillery,
whose death was occasioned
by his noble efforts to arrest the progress
of the calamitous fire,
which on the 14th Octr 1866,
destroyed a large portion of the city.
Born at Shrewsbury, England, April 4, 1840.
Died at Quebec Oct. 27, 1866.

The expression of gratitude and admiration felt for Quebec's fallen hero was so great that the monument was over-subscribed. The extra funds were sent immediately to Henry's mother in London where she had a memorial pulpit placed in her church, St. Andrew's Stockwell, near her home in Brixton. In Canada, the officers of the regiment also had a plaque placed in Quebec's Holy Trinity Cathedral.

One resident of Quebec, Mrs. Campbell, was so affected by the death of Henry Baines that she wrote a moving poem and dedicated it to his mother:

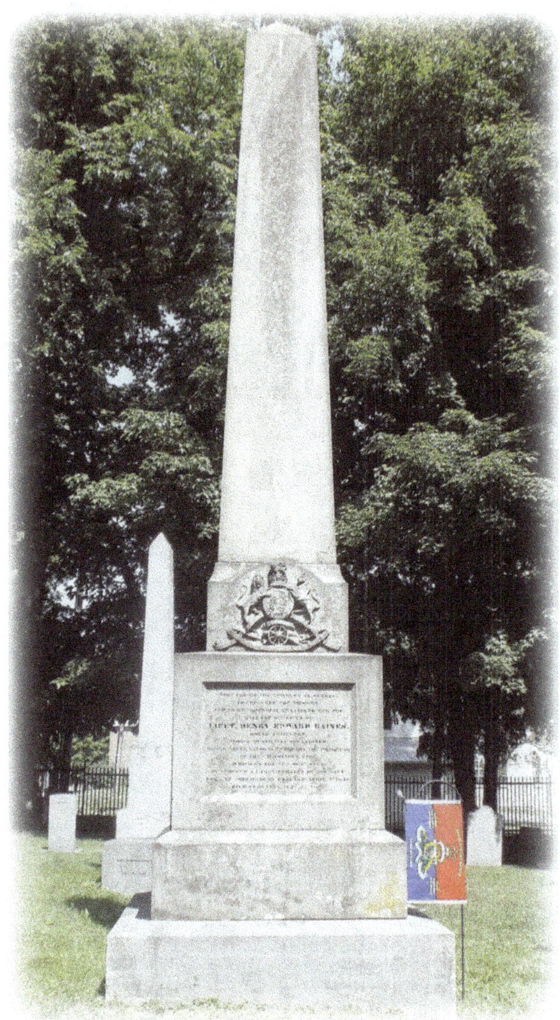

Monument marking the grave of Henry Baines, Mt. Hermon Cemetery, Quebec, Canada, 2016.
Sculpted by Felix Morgan, Quebec, 1867. Carved sandstone.
[Photograph by Marc Seguin, 2016.]

In 2016, the red and blue flag of the Royal Artillery, displaying the crest and mottos of the regiment, was placed at the gravesite of Lieutenant Baines by Marc Seguin and his family to recognize the 150th anniversary of the tragic death of this young soldier. The flag is embroidered with the words, "Henry Edward Baines, Lieutenant, No. 5 Battery, 10th Brigade, Royal Regiment of Artillery. Served 1859-1866."

A VOICE FROM MOUNT HERMON.
Dedicated to Mrs. Baines
by Mrs. A. Campbell.

My dust lies sleeping here,
   Mother dear!
In this far off distant land,
Away from your little band,
And the touch of loving hand,
Your boy lies sleeping here,
   Mother dear!

The Ocean rolls between,
   Mother dear!
You and your own boy's grave,
And the distant rush of wave,
On the pebbly shore to lave,
Is the requiem sung between,
   Mother dear!

Mine is a sweet green spot,
   Mother dear!
And the song of the bird
Is ever heard
In the trees that gird
Us, in this quiet spot,
   Mother dear!

And echo answers here,
   Mother dear!
The tinkle of chapel bell,
And the murmur of its knell,
And the mourners "It is well,"
Echo answers here,
   Mother dear!

To picture my last home.
   Mother dear!
I am laid me down to rest,
Where "Our Father" saw 'twas best;
In this quiet little nest,
For my last home,
   Mother dear!

And my spirit is with Him,
   Mother dear!
In the precious home above,
Where all is light and love,
There rests your own dear dove.
Now with Him,
   Mother dear!

Through Jesus' blood I'm here,
   Mother dear!
In this happy, heavenly land,
One of a glorious band.
Touched by His healing hand,
Through Jesus I am here,
   Mother dear!

So dry that bitter tear,
   Mother dear!
'Twill not be very long
Ere with Jesus you'll sing the song.
Sung by those who to Him belong,
And wipe that bitter tear
   Mother dear! [25]

Mary Baines kept up a correspondence with the Sisters of St. Augustine and expressed many times her wish to visit her son's grave in Canada. She was never able to fulfill her wish. Mary Baines died in December, 1870.

On July 25, 1867, as the troopship, HMS *Simoom*, weighed anchor to begin her long journey up the St. Lawrence River en route to the Mediterranean Sea, the officers and men of the Royal Artillery's 10th Brigade waved farewell to the city of Quebec; many of them, no doubt, with thoughts of their fallen comrade, Henry Baines.

One can imagine that Henry would have delighted in sketching summer landscapes along the river and painting scenic views where the ship stopped in Newfoundland and at Gibraltar en route to the Brigade's new station on the island of Malta. Henry's life did not lead him, as he had hoped, "by Indian palms or dear home shores". Instead, his "path of duty" was the way, not only to glory, but to the loss of his life in the service of Queen, country and the people of Quebec City.

Henry's tragic end at such a young age meant that all of his potential and promise as an artist and a writer would never be fulfilled. The few works that he has left behind testify to this potential, and they now form a unique treasure that give us a glimpse into both his life and into a brief period of British imperial history.

Henry Edward Baines was one of the last artist-officers of the British Army to depict scenes of Canada, for the *Simoom* was one of many British troopships that, over the following three years, would remove all British troops from Canada. The Dominion of Canada, a union of the colonial provinces of Nova Scotia, New Brunswick and Canada (Canada East became the Province of Quebec and Canada West became the Province of Ontario), came into existence as an independent country on July 1, 1867. By 1871, the British Army had turned the defence of the country over to Canadians and all British troops were withdrawn, leaving only a small garrison at Halifax to protect the Royal Navy's dockyard there.[26].

Epilogue

After Henry Baines' death in 1866, his journal and many of his paintings and sketchbooks along with his other personal effects, possibly including other watercolours and drawings, were sent back to England to his mother, Mary, who was living at that time in the London suburb of Brixton with her two daughters Bessie and Isabelle. At some point, the journal and other paintings were brought back to Canada, probably by Henry's younger sister, Isabelle, who, after her mother's

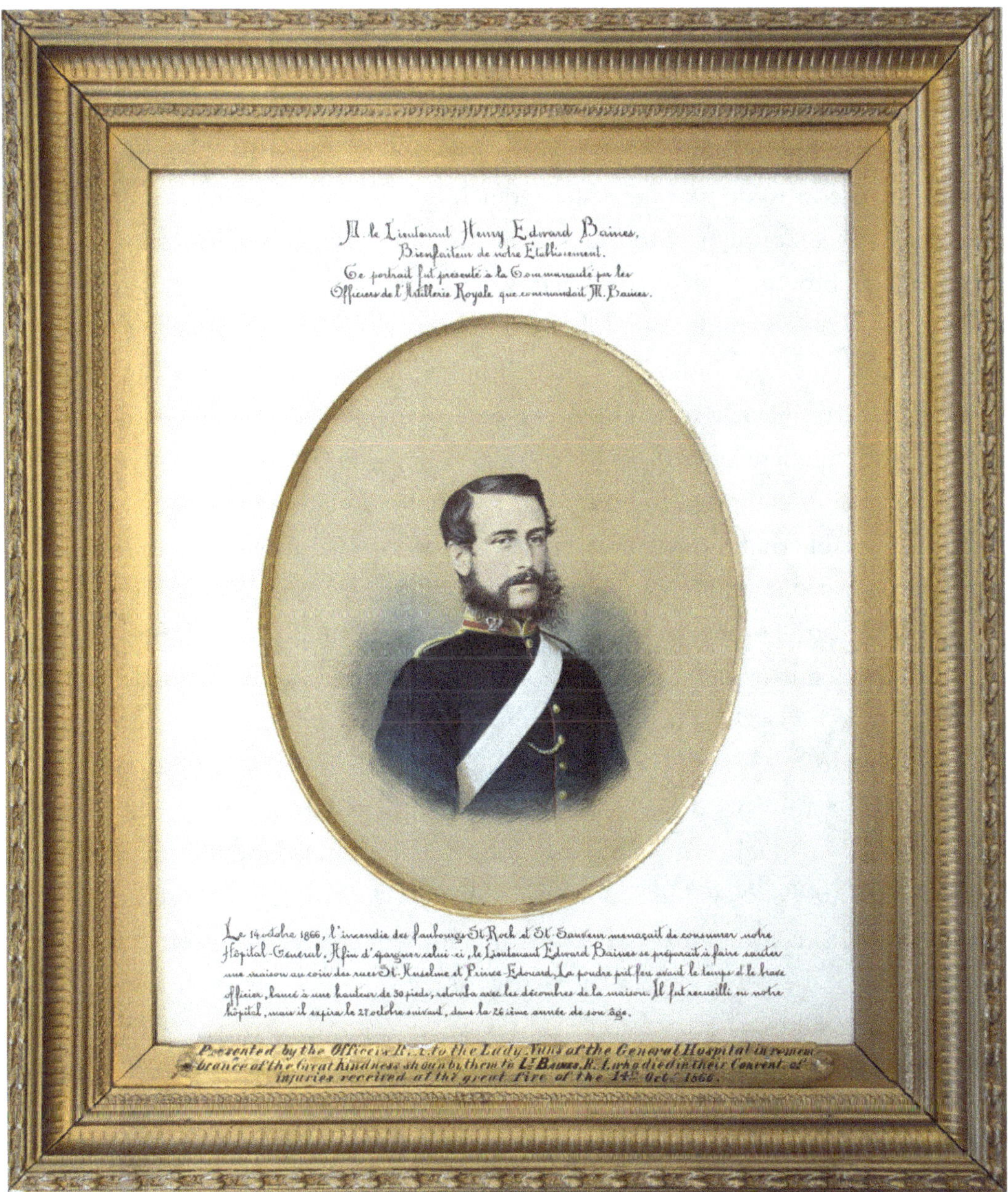

Portrait of Lieutenant Henry Baines, Royal Artillery.
Attributed to the Notman Studio, Montreal, 1867. Gouache over photographic print.
[Courtesy of Archives du Monestere, Quebec Canada]

Inscription on the frame reads, "Presented by the Officers R.A. to the Lady Nuns of the General Hospital in remembrance of the Great Kindness shown by them to L[T] Baines R.A. who died in their Convent of injuries received at the great fire of the 14th Oct[r] 1866."
See note for the text and translation of the inscription on the matte.[27]

death in 1870, emigrated to Canada and lived for a time with her Aunt Catherine, Thomas Baines' widow, and cousin Willie and his wife Anne in the house at 30 William Street in Toronto.[28]

At a wedding ceremony held in St. George's Church in Toronto in 1876, Isabelle married a young farmer, Alexander Mitchell, who lived near the village of Erindale in Peel County just to the west of the city.[29] After Isabelle's death in 1921, many of her brother's personal effects were distributed among the five Mitchell children. The oldest child, Kate, inherited her Uncle Henry's journal and several of his paintings and drawings. Kate Mitchell married Dr. David H. Boddington, and they lived at 81 Wilcocks Street in Toronto. Two of their sons, George and Arthur, donated the complete journal, "A Month's Leave or The Cruise of the *Breeze*", along with a number of paintings, to Library and Archives Canada in 1995.

It is possible that more of Henry Edward Baines' paintings remain in Britain, hanging on parlour walls or forgotten in dusty attics. Henry's older sister Bessie Baines Wilkinson and her descendants may have inherited some of the artwork as well. Other members of the Boddington and Baines families in Canada still own several Henry Edward Baines watercolours, but many others have been sold off over the decades.

One collection of fifty-two watercolours painted by Henry Baines while he was stationed at Quebec in 1865 and 1866 was purchased by the Gerald Peters Gallery of Santa Fe, New Mexico, in the 1990's. Twenty-nine of these pieces were eventually sold to individual collectors and museums over the course of several years. By 2015, there was a block of twenty-three of these watercolours still for sale in the United States.

It was at that time that I began to raise funds to have these paintings repatriated to Canada. As a result of the generosity of the Cluett and Seguin families of Prince Edward County, Ontario, Canada, twenty of these watercolours were purchased from the Gerald Peters Gallery and returned to Canada where they have now been added to the many Henry Edward Baines paintings and drawings in the documentary art collection of Library and Archives Canada in Ottawa. This Canadian institution will preserve these works for the benefit of present and future generations.

Images of some of these watercolours have been reproduced in this book. Eventually all of them will be viewable online at www.collectionscanada.com. It is my hope that all of Henry's original art, along with his other paintings and drawings in the collection, will be exhibited from time to time to allow the public to view these wonderful works in person.

The Appendix that follows lists these watercolours along with all of the other known works of Henry Edward Baines. Anyone with more information about this artist or the whereabouts of any of his artwork is encouraged to contact the author:

Marc Seguin
c/o Ontario History Press
358 Edward Drive, RR3
Consecon, ON Canada
K0K 1T0

marc@ontariohistory.ca
tel. +00+1+613.394.0897

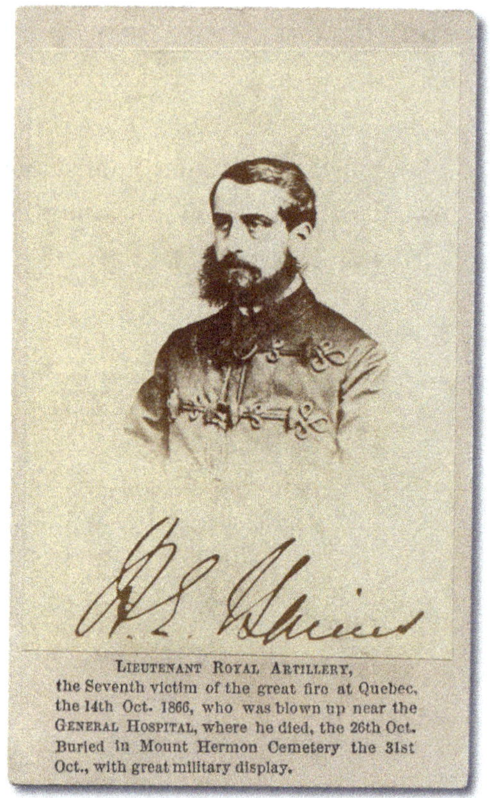

Memorial card with portrait and signature. H.E. Baines, Lieutenant Royal Artillery.

J.P. Fortin, Quebec, 1866

[Courtesy of www.soldiersofthequeen]

Appendix

Catalogue of Known Works by Henry Edward Baines

(as of January 2018)

The minor drawings is this list are not included in the Catalogue of Known Works:

In addition to the 91 watercolours and drawings catalogued here, there are 9 other minor drawings (see previous page) that Henry Edward Baines included in his journal "A Month's Leave or The Cruise of the *Breeze*", making a total of 100 known works of art.

	Date	Title	Medium	Note
	c.1856	Untitled (Possible self-portrait)	Watercolour on paper	Attributed to Henry Edward Baines. Private collection of J. Boddington, Toronto, Canada.
	c.1860	Fruit Schooner Aquila of Jersey, Capt. Long	Watercolour and pencil on paper	Collection of Library and Archives Canada.
	30 May 1861	Untitled (Seascape with sailing vessel.)	Watercolour on paper.	Collection of Library and Archives Canada.
	17 August 1861	Untitled (Church of St. James the Great, East Malling, Kent)	Watercolour on paper.	Collection of Library and Archives Canada.
	15 October 1861	Dartmouth	Watercolour on paper.	Collection of Library and Archives Canada.
	c.1861	Weymouth Bridge from the Barracks	Watercolour on paper.	Collection of Library and Archives Canada.

	Date	Title	Medium	Note
	c.1861	Untitled (Country church with monument.)	Watercolour on paper.	Collection of Library and Archives Canada.
	9 February 1862	Halifax from York Redoubt	Watercolour on paper.	Collection of Library and Archives Canada.
	March 1862	Soldiers Hut, Petersville, N.B.	Pencil on paper.	Collection of Library and Archives Canada.
	1 November 1862	First View of the Falls Taken from Below the Clifton	Watercolour, ink and pencil on paper.	Collection of Library and Archives Canada.
	2 November 1862	R. Niagara	Watercolour and gouache on paper.	Collection of Library and Archives Canada.
	10 July 1863	New Fort, Toronto	Watercolour and pencil on paper.	Collection of Library and Archives Canada. Appears in "A Month's leave or The Cruise of the *Breeze*".
	19 July 1863	Untitled (The Clifton House hotel and the American Falls at Niagara.)	Watercolour and ink on paper.	Private collection of B. Selkirk, Grafton, Ontario, Canada
	20 July 1863	Port Dalhousie, July 20	Watercolour, ink and pencil on paper.	Collection of Library and Archives Canada.

	Date	Title	Medium	Note
	21 July 1863	Port Dalhousie, July 21	Watercolour, ink and pencil on paper.	Collection of Library and Archives Canada.
	August 1863	The *Breeze* 17	Watercolour and pencil on paper.	Collection of Library and Archives Canada. Appears in "A Month's leave or The Cruise of the *Breeze*".
	August 1863	Track of the *Breeze* (Map of Lake Ontario on 2 sheets.)	Watercolour, ink and pencil on paper.	Collection of Library and Archives Canada. Appears in "A Month's leave or The Cruise of the *Breeze*".
	August 1863	Rice Lake, Pémédashcoutayong	Watercolour and pencil on paper.	Collection of Library and Archives Canada. Appears in "A Month's leave or The Cruise of the *Breeze*".
	August 1863	Cobourg	Watercolour and pencil on paper.	Collection of Library and Archives Canada. Appears in "A Month's leave or The Cruise of the *Breeze*".

	Date	Title	Medium	Note
	August 1863	Presqu'Isle Light	Watercolour, ink and pencil on paper.	Collection of Library and Archives Canada. Appears in "A Month's leave or The Cruise of the *Breeze*".
	August 1863	Fishing at Presqu'Isle	Watercolour and pencil on paper.	Collection of Library and Archives Canada. Appears in "A Month's leave or The Cruise of the *Breeze*".
	August 1863	At Anchor Off Consecon	Pencil on paper.	Collection of Library and Archives Canada. Appears in "A Month's leave or The Cruise of the *Breeze*".
	August 1863	Consecon Creek	Watercolour, ink and pencil on paper.	Collection of Library and Archives Canada. Appears in "A Month's leave or The Cruise of the *Breeze*".
	August 1863	En Route to Kingston	Watercolour, ink and pencil on paper.	Collection of Library and Archives Canada. Appears in "A Month's leave or The Cruise of the *Breeze*".
	August 1863	East Entrance to Bateau Channel, Kingston	Watercolour and pencil on paper.	Collection of Library and Archives Canada. Appears in "A Month's leave or The Cruise of the *Breeze*".
	August 1863	Cedar Island, Kingston C.W.	Watercolour and pencil on paper.	Collection of Library and Archives Canada. Appears in "A Month's leave or The Cruise of the *Breeze*".

	Date	Title	Medium	Note
	August 1863	Kingston	Watercolour, ink and pencil on paper.	Collection of Library and Archives Canada. Appears in "A Month's leave or The Cruise of the *Breeze*".
	August 1863	The Mouth of the Black River	Watercolour, ink and pencil on paper.	Collection of Library and Archives Canada. Appears in "A Month's leave or The Cruise of the *Breeze*".
	August 1863	Distant View of Picton, C.W.	Watercolour and pencil on paper.	Collection of Library and Archives Canada. Appears in "A Month's leave or The Cruise of the *Breeze*".
	August 1863	Maryborough, C.W.	Watercolour and pencil on paper.	Collection of Library and Archives Canada. Appears in "A Month's leave or The Cruise of the *Breeze*".
	August 1863	Wapoos Island, Cape Vesey	Watercolour and pencil on paper.	Collection of Library and Archives Canada. Appears in "A Month's leave or The Cruise of the *Breeze*".
	August 1863	Big Ship House (Sackets Harbor, N.Y.)	Pencil on paper.	Collection of Library and Archives Canada. Appears in "A Month's leave or The Cruise of the *Breeze*".
	21 August 1863	Port of Oswego, N.Y.	Watercolour, ink and pencil on paper.	Collection of Library and Archives Canada. Appears in "A Month's leave or The Cruise of the *Breeze*".

	Date	Title	Medium	Note
	August 1863	Putneyville	Watercolour, ink and pencil on paper.	Collection of Library and Archives Canada. Appears in "A Month's leave or The Cruise of the *Breeze*".
	22 August 1863	Big Sodus Bay (2 sheets)	Watercolour on paper.	Collection of Library and Archives Canada. Appears in "A Month's leave or The Cruise of the *Breeze*".
	August 1863	Sodus Point Village, N.Y.	Watercolour and pencil on paper.	Collection of Library and Archives Canada. Appears in "A Month's leave or The Cruise of the *Breeze*".
	24 August 1863	R. Genesee, Charlotte	Watercolour and pencil on paper.	Collection of Library and Archives Canada. Appears in "A Month's leave or The Cruise of the *Breeze*".
	25 August 1863	Genesee, Rochester	Watercolour, ink and pencil on paper.	Collection of Library and Archives Canada. Appears in "A Month's leave or The Cruise of the *Breeze*".
	August 1863	The Lower Falls of the Genesee	Watercolour, ink and pencil on paper.	Collection of Library and Archives Canada. Appears in "A Month's leave or The Cruise of the *Breeze*".
	August 1863	Untitled (Three flags.)	Watercolour and pencil on paper.	Collection of Library and Archives Canada. Appears in "A Month's leave or The Cruise of the *Breeze*".

	Date	Title	Medium	Note
	c.1863	30 William St. Toronto, C.W.	Brown wash and ink on paper.	Collection of Library and Archives Canada. Appears in "A Month's leave or The Cruise of the Breeze".
	c.1863	*Alexandra*, Toronto, Capt. Morris	Watercolour, gouache and pencil on paper.	Collection of Library and Archives Canada.
	c.1863	*Crinoline*, J. Boulton	Watercolour, gouache, pen and pencil on paper.	Collection of Library and Archives Canada.
	c.1863	Signs of the Fall, York County, Upper Canada, Sep 20th	Watercolour on paper.	Collection of Library and Archives Canada.
	c.1863	The Gully, Dundas	Watercolour and pencil on paper.	Collection of Library and Archives Canada. Appears in "A Month's leave or The Cruise of the Breeze".
	c. 1863	Untitled (Paddlewheel steamer)	Watercolour, ink and pencil on paper.	Collection of Library and Archives Canada.
	c.1863	Untitled (Sailing boat sketch.)	Pencil on paper.	Collection of Library and Archives Canada. Appears in "A Month's leave or The Cruise of the Breeze".

	Date	Title	Medium	Note
	c.1863	Untitled (Ships nearing a city)	Watercolour on paper.	Collection of Library and Archives Canada.
	c.1863	Untitled (Sketch of lilies and lily of the valley	Ink on paper.	Collection of Library and Archives Canada.
	22 November 1864	Niagara River	Watercolour on paper.	Collection of Library and Archives Canada.
	c.1864	*Glance, Arrow, Breeze, Rivet, Wide-Awake, Kitten, Gorilla*	Watercolour, ink and pencil on paper.	Collection of Library and Archives Canada.
	29 July 1865	Island of Orleans S.E.	Watercolour and pencil on paper.	Collection of Library and Archives Canada.
	29 July 1865	Untitled (Sailboat Amounin? on the river.)	Watercolour on paper.	Collection of Library and Archives Canada.
	16 August 1865	Quebec	Watercolour on paper.	Collection of Library and Archives Canada.

	Date	Title	Medium	Note
	September 1865	Untitled (Autumn landscape)	Watercolour on paper.	Collection of Library and Archives Canada.
	20 December 1865	Untitled (Seven figures crossing the ice of the St. Lawrence River in a canoe.)	Watercolour on paper.	Donated to Library and Archives Canada by T.B. Cluett, Prince Edward County, Ontario, Canada.
	c.1865	Untitled (Tobogganing in Quebec.)	Watercolour on paper.	Private collection, J. Boddington, Toronto, Canada.
	c.1865	Untitled (Family snowshoeing in Quebec.)	Watercolour on paper.	Private collection, J. Boddington, Toronto, Canada.
	c.1865	Untitled (Shooting ducks at the water's edge.)	Watercolour	Sold by Gerald Peters Gallery, purchaser unknown.
	c.1865	Untitled (Woman pulling a rope at shore, after Punch.)	Ink on paper.	Collection of Library and Archives Canada.
	17 January 1866	Untitled (Ice on the St. Lawrence River at Quebec.)	Watercolour	Sold by Gerald Peters Gallery, purchaser unknown.

	Date	Title	Medium	Note
	17 March 1866	Untitled (People in a horse-drawn sleigh and others walking on a snowy road.)	Watercolour	Sold by Gerald Peters Gallery, purchaser unknown.
	16 April 1866	Indian Cove, On the Rouge (or On the Range), possibly at Cap Rouge, west of Quebec	Watercolour, gouache and pencil on paper.	Donated to Library and Archives Canada by Marc Seguin, Prince Edward County, Ontario, Canada.
	7 May 1866	Untitled (View of the St. Lawrence River showing sailing ships and wharves of Quebec's Lower Town.)	Watercolour and ink on paper.	Donated to Library and Archives Canada by T.B. Cluett, Prince Edward County, Ontario, Canada.
	8 May 1866	Untitled (Night scene of a fire near a church, in St. Roch.)	Watercolour on paper.	Donated to Library and Archives Canada by T.B. Cluett, Prince Edward County, Ontario, Canada.
	17 May 1866	Untitled (Wharves and several ships on the St. Lawrence River as seen from the Plains of Abraham in Quebec.)	Watercolour on paper.	Donated to Library and Archives Canada by T.B. Cluett, Prince Edward County, Ontario, Canada.
	26 June 1866	Untitled (Two boats on a Lake.)	Watercolour on paper.	Donated to Library and Archives Canada by T.B. Cluett, Prince Edward County, Ontario, Canada.
	10 July 1866	Untitled (Montmorency Falls from Ile d'Orleans.)	Watercolour	Sold by Gerald Peters Gallery, purchaser unknown.
	23 July 1866	Untitled (Ships in a river, possibly near Chaudiere Falls.)	Watercolour on paper.	Donated to Library and Archives Canada by M.C. Seguin, Prince Edward County, Ontario, Canada.

	Date	Title	Medium	Note
	15 August 1866	Orontes (The troopship *HMS Orontes* at anchor off Quebec.)	Watercolour and ink on paper.	Donated to Library and Archives Canada by R. Cluett, Prince Edward County, Ontario, Canada.
	4 September 1866	Untitled (Two sailing ships on the St. Lawrence River with Ile d'Orleans and Mt. Ste. Anne in the background.)	Watercolour on paper.	Donated to Library and Archives Canada by T.B. Cluett, Prince Edward County, Ontario, Canada.
	18 September 1866	Untitled (Royal Artillery Officers' Quarters, Quebec)	Watercolour on paper.	Collection of Art Gallery of Hamilton.
	23 September 1866	I. of Orleans (Ile d'Orleans by moonlight.)	Watercolour on paper.	Collection of Royal Ontario Museum.
	27 September 1866	Untitled (Quebec from Ile d'Orleans with bathers.)	Watercolour on paper.	Collection of Art Gallery of Hamilton.
	October 1866	Untitled (View of the St. Lawrence River, possibly from the Governor's garden.)	Watercolour on paper.	Collection of Library and Archives Canada.
	c.1866	Rotten Ice	Watercolour on paper.	Gerald Peters Gallery, Santa Fe, New Mexico.
	c.1866	Untitled (A church steeple, possibly St. Columba's, near a river at sunrise or sunset.)	Watercolour on paper.	Donated to Library and Archives Canada by T.B. Cluett, Prince Edward County, Ontario, Canada.

	Date	Title	Medium	Note
	c.1866	Untitled (Church next to a lake, possibly Lac Beauport.)	Watercolour on paper.	Donated to Library and Archives Canada by M.C. Seguin, Prince Edward County, Ontario, Canada.
	c.1866	Untitled (Full-length portrait of a woman holding a book)	Watercolour on paper.	Donated to Library and Archives Canada by R. Cluett, Prince Edward County, Ontario, Canada.
	c.1866	Untitled (Lower Town, Quebec, from the Citadel. La Basse-Ville de Quebec de la batterie.)	Watercolour, pencil and ink on paper.	Attributed to Henry Edward Baines. Collection of Musée National de Beaux-arts du Quebec.
	c.1866	Untitled (Person near a stone building.)	Watercolour on paper.	Gerald Peters Gallery, Santa Fe, New Mexico.
	c.1866	Untitled (Portrait of a woman reading a book.)	Watercolour on paper.	Donated to Library and Archives Canada by M.C. Seguin, Prince Edward County, Ontario, Canada.
	c.1866	Untitled (Ship sailing past icebergs.)	Watercolour on paper.	Donated to Library and Archives Canada by R. Cluett, Prince Edward County, Ontario, Canada.
	c.1866	Untitled (Three men fishing in a lake.)	Watercolour on paper.	Donated to Library and Archives Canada by R. Cluett, Prince Edward County, Ontario, Canada.

	Date	Title	Medium	Note
	c.1866	Untitled (Two figures in a canoe on a river, possibly the Montmorency River above the falls.)	Watercolour on paper.	Donated to Library and Archives Canada by M.C. Seguin, Prince Edward County, Ontario, Canada.
	c.1866	Untitled (Two figures looking toward a purple sky and mountain, possibly Mt. Ste. Anne.)	Watercolour on paper.	Donated to Library and Archives Canada by T.B. Cluett, Prince Edward County, Ontario, Canada.
	c.1866	Untitled (View of a forest and river with purple clouds.)	Watercolour on paper.	Donated to Library and Archives Canada by M.C. Seguin, Prince Edward County, Ontario, Canada.
	c.1866	Untitled (View of fenced fields with mountains in the background.)	Watercolour on paper.	Donated to Library and Archives Canada by T.B. Cluett, Prince Edward County, Ontario, Canada.
	c.1866	Untitled (View of Quebec from Ile d'Orleans.)	Watercolour and pencil on paper.	Collection of Royal Ontario Museum.
	c.1866	Untitled (View up the St. Lawrence River, possibly from Spencer Wood on the Plains of Abraham.)	Watercolour on paper.	Donated to Library and Archives Canada by T.B. Cluett, Prince Edward County, Ontario, Canada.
	c.1866	Untitled (Wolfe and Montcalm monument, Quebec)	Watercolour on paper.	Gerald Peters Gallery, Santa Fe, New Mexico.

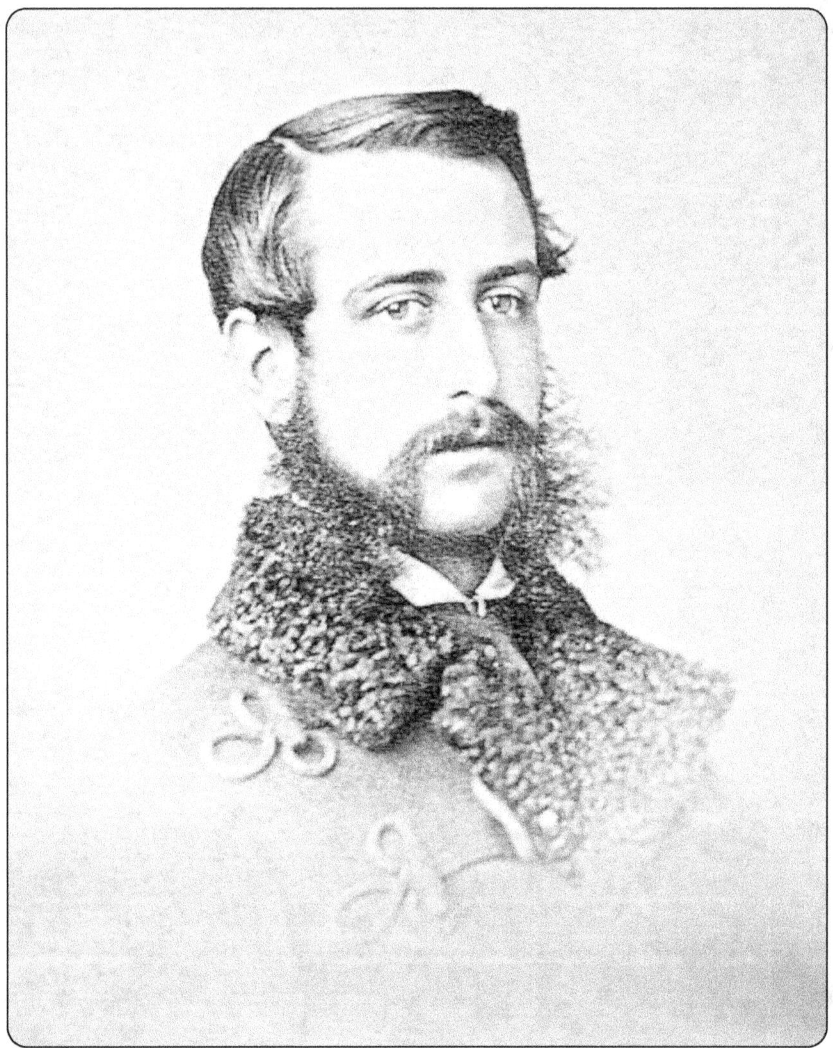

Mr. H.E. Baines
Glass-plate negative. Attributed to W.J. Topley, Notman Studio, Montreal, 1866.
[Courtesy of Library and Archives Canada.]

This positive rendering of a glass-plate negative is catalogued by Library and Archives Canada as a copy dating from 1877. The original photograph could have been taken as early as 1862, when Henry was passing through Montreal on his way to his station at Toronto.
A photographic print of this negative served as the basis for the full-colour portrait of Henry Baines that appears on page 215.

NOTES

Notes: Part 1 – The Soldier

1.   Byron Farwell, *Queen Victoria's Little Wars*, New York, 1972, pp. 1-2.
     See also William H.G. Kingston, *Our Soldiers: Gallant Deeds of the British Army During the Reign of Queen Victoria*, London, 1898.

2.   See Percy M. Thornton, *Some Things We Have Remembered*, London, 1912.
     See also Garnet Gibson, *That Thy Days May Be Long*, Victoria, B.C., 1975.

3.   *Alphabetical List of the Medical Officers of the Indian Army*, London, 1839, pp. 10-11.

4.   Throughout most of the 19th Century, mortality and sickness rates of Indian Army veterans were as much as eight times greater than that of other army veterans, and Egerton Baines may have been one of those soldiers who contracted a tropical disease while stationed in Bengal. See "The Claims of the Indian Medical Department", *Colburn's Untied Service Magazine*, Part III, London, 1860, p. 271.

5.   *The Hereford Journal*, 1 Feb, 1843.

6.   Garnet Gibson, *That Thy Days May Be Long*, Victoria, 1975, p. 59.

7.   There has also been some suggestion that the Baines family moved to the Channel Islands to improve the health of Mary Baines. See Gibson, *ibid.*, p. 13.

8.   "Victorian Forts in Alderney and their Armament in 1859", URL http://www.visitalderney.com/visit/history/alderneys-victorian-history accessed 14 Oct. 2017.

9.   Until the practice was abolished in 1871, most officers' commissions in the British Army were purchased. See Anthony Bruce, *The Purchase System in the British Army 1660-1871*, London, 1980. In the British Army of the mid-19th Century, only a small number of officers were granted commissions without purchase after attending a rigorous course of study at either the Royal Military College, Sandhurst (for infantry and cavalry officers) or the Royal Military Academy, Woolwich (for artillery and engineer officers). Otherwise, infantry and cavalry officers could only become an officer by buying an entry-level commission as an ensign or coronet for not less than £450 (equivalent to US$60,000 in 2016 funds).
     Using a conservative "GDP deflation index", £450 in 1856 would be the equivalent of about £45,300 in 2016. The pound sterling to U.S. dollar exchange rate in 2016 was about $1.35. Therefore, £450 in 1856 would have had similar buying power to US$61,200 in 2016, a factor of approximately 136. This factor is used in all similar monetary comparisons in this chapter. See Lawrence H. Officer and Samuel H. Williamson, "Five Ways to Compute the Relative Value of a UK Pound Amount, 1270 to Present," MeasuringWorth, 2017, URL https://www.measuringworth.com/ukcompare/result.php?year_source=1854&amount=500& year_result=2015# accessed 14 Oct. 2017.

10. See marginal notes in the reprint of "The Cruise of the Breeze", *Hunt's Yachting Magazine*, London, 1865, held by the Toronto Public Library, Call No. 917.1 B115 BR.

11. Augustus Thomas Rice joined the 51st Regiment as an Ensign in 1831. By 1852, he had risen to the rank of captain and was sent with his regiment to Burma at the beginning of the 2nd Anglo-Burmese War. The *New Annual Army List for 1855* summarizes his war service: "Colonel Rice served with the 51st during the war in Burmah from April to August 1852; was on board the E.I.C. [East India Company] steam sloop *Sesostris* during the naval action and destruction of the enemy's stockade on the Rangoon river; served during the succeeding three days operation in the vicinity, and at the storm and capture of Rangoon; also at the assault and capture of Bassein, 19th May (severely wounded). Colonel Rice was mentioned in General Godwin's dispatches as 'deserving the best consideration of Government' for capturing by storm with his company and a sub-division of the 9th Madras Native Infantry the enemy's stronghold, and entrenched position south of Bassein, armed with sixteen guns and twenty gingalls [large swivel-mounted firearms]; honoured with the best thanks of the Governor-General in Council."
H.G. Hart, *The New Annual Army List for 1855*, London, 1855, pp. 571-57m.
As a result of his actions, Captain Rice was promoted to major in his regiment in June 1852. He was then given the brevet rank (temporary rank) of lieutenant-colonel, and then promoted to colonel when he retired from the army on full-pay in 1854.

12. Principal Probate Registry, *Calendar of the Grants of Probate and Letters of Administration made in the Probate Registries of the High Court of Justice in England*, London, 1858-1966.

13. Thornton, *ibid.*, p. 86.

14. Francis B. Head, *The Royal Engineer*, London, 1869, p. 2.

15. See H.D. Buchanan-Dunlop, *Records of the Royal Military Academy, Woolwich*, London, 1892.

16. £101.10s. was the allowance granted to an infantry subaltern on active service who had to re-equip himself in the field after the loss of a substantial portion of his military gear due to enemy action. See Edward Barrington de Fonblanque, *Treatise on the Administration and Organization of the British Army*, London, 1858, p. 291.

17. The pay of a junior artillery lieutenant in 1858 was 5s.6d. per day, amounting to £101 17s. 11d. per year or the equivalent of US$13,850 in 2016. H.G. Hart. *The New Annual Army List for 1858*, London, 1858.

18. Letter, War Office to General Officer Commanding the Troops, Halifax, N.S., 24 Dec. 1861, LAC RG8 C-series microform c-3843/1730-92.

19. "The Pay and Expenses of Officers", *Colburn's United Service Magazine*, Part I, London, 1861, pp. 317-328.

20. Gentlemen-Cadets at RMA Woolwich received an allowance of 2s. 6d. per day which they used to pay for their food. See F.G. Guggisberg, *The Shop*, London 1900.
See also, Royal Artillery Institution, *List of Officers of the Royal Regiment of Artillery*, Woolwich, 1869.

21. Later in 1858, the proposal to amalgamate the two military schools was vetoed by the House of Commons and cadets continued to be admitted directly to RMA Woolwich for many years. It was not until 1939 that RMA Woolwich was fully amalgamated with RMC Sandhurst to become the Royal Military Academy Sandhurst. Royal Artillery, *The Royal Artillery Woolwich: A Celebration*, London, 2008. pp. 62-67.

22. The total enrollment of the Royal Military Academy in 1858 was 137 cadets. Buchanan-Dunlop, *ibid.*, p. 122.

23. *The Belfast Daily Mercury*, May 13, 1858.

24. "French View of Our Military Colleges," *Colburn's United Service Magazine*, 1860, Part III, London, 1860, pp. 367-368.

25. Photography was introduced as a "voluntary class" at RMA Woolwich in 1865. Buchanan-Dunlop, *ibid.*, p. 114.

26. Guggisberg, *ibid.*, pp. 91-93.

27. Buchanan-Dunlop, *ibid.*, p. 121

28. Alfred Lord Tennyson, "Ode on the Death of the Duke of Wellington", London, 1852.

29. A single Coast Artillery Brigade also existed for a short time for service in the British Isles, but was eventually amalgamated with the Garrison Artillery.

30. Individual Horse Artillery and Field Artillery Batteries were identified by letters A through H, while Garrison Artillery Batteries were numbered 1 through 8. See Charles Callwell and John Headlam, *The History of the Royal Artillery from the Mutiny to the Great War*, Vol. 1, Woolwich (facsimile edition).

31. This did not include regiments raised in the colonies strictly for local service such as the Royal Canadian Rifle Regiment, nor did it include colonial militia and volunteer battalions. See J.W. Fortescue, *History of the British Army*, vol. XIII, London, 1930. pp. 524-533.

32. "Stations of the Royal Navy in Commission", a monthly list published by the British Admiralty, indicated that as of July, 1860, the Royal Navy had 246 ships in commission, of which 164 were on foreign stations, including 9 ships in the North American and West Indies squadron. From *The Jersey Independent and Daily Telegraph*, Jersey U.K., 14 July 1860, p. 4.

33. *The Portsmouth Times and Naval Gazette*, April 20, 1861.

34. The first trans-Atlantic telegraph cable had been laid in 1858, but it was operational for only a few days. See Bern Dibner, *The Atlantic Cable*, Norwalk, 1959.

35. U.S. National Archives, Record Group 21, Records of District Courts of the United States, 1685 – 2004, Civil War Prize Case Files Series - Identifier 620244.

36. The 1856 Paris Declaration Respecting Maritime Law stated that "Blockades, in order to be binding, must be effective, that is to say, maintained by a force sufficient really to prevent access to the coast of the enemy". This declaration had been agreed to by all major powers prior to the American Civil War with the exception of Bulgaria, Japan, Mexico, Spain, and the United States of America. In 1861, the U.S. Congress passed a motion to follow the stipulations of the Paris Declaration during hostilities with the Confederate States. See T.G. Bowles, *The Declaration of Paris of 1856*, London, 1900.

37. See E.J. Donnell, *Chronological and Statistical History of Cotton*, New York, 1872.

38. 179 merchant ships, many from the Great Lakes, were commandeered by the U.S. Navy to augment the blockading fleet. *The Evening Standard*, London ,7 Sep 1861, p. 6.

39. As an example, see "Earl Russell on the Blockade of Southern Ports of the United States", *The Daily Post*, Liverpool, 26 Oct 1861, p. 7.

40. *The London Gazette*, 14 May 1861.

41. Amanda Foreman, *A World on Fire*, New York, 2010, pp. 80, 822.

42. *ibid.*, p. 104

43. *The New-York Daily Tribune*, July 09, 1861, Page 7.
John Jay II was the grandson of former U.S. Chief Justice, John Jay.

44. The *Morning Advertiser*, London, 13 June 1861, p. 3

45. The *Morning Post*, London, 12 June, 1863, p. 4

46. "The Military Position of Canada", *Colburn's United Service Magazine*, Part 1, London 1860, p. 429.
'Our conviction is, that at this moment Lower Canada [i.e. Canada East which later became the Province of Quebec] is dangerously exposed and defenceless, and if assailed by a competent force of 20,000 French troops, would again fall under the sway of France'.

47. *The New York Herald*, 23 Sept. 1861, p. 4.
This editorial was directed at all of the colonial powers that had interests in North America: Britain, France and Spain.

48. *The Globe*, Toronto, 1 Oct. 1861.

49. "Neutrality With a Vengeance", *The New York Times*, 20 Sep 1861.

50. Great Britain, Foreign Office, *Papers relating to the blockade of the ports of the Confederate States.* London, 1862.
Some 1,380 incidents of blockade running were listed in British records (one entry to a blockaded port is counted as one incident, and one departure from that port is counted as an additional incident). Of these, 230 incidents involved ships that were either British registered or were arriving from or departing to British ports.

51. *ibid.*, pp. 53, 54, 95.

52. In *The New York Times* article, "Arms From England", 15 May 1861, it is stated that 10,000 Enfield rifles had just arrived from Britain. Another 20,000 British-made rifles were imported by the Union in June, 1861 (*The New York Times*, 10 June 1861).
See also "Arms for the Rebels", *The New York Times*, 1 June 1861, and "Important from the South", *The New York Times*, 27 June 1861.
Hundreds of thousands of these rifles along with millions of rounds of ammunition were imported by both Union and Confederate armies in 1861 alone.

53. Foreman, *ibid.*, pp. 147, 148, 410.

54. Great Britain, Foreign Office, *Papers relating to the blockade, ibid.*

55. Warren F. Spencer, *The Confederate Navy in Europe.* Tuscaloosa, AL, 1983. p. 194.

56. "The Defences of New-York", *The New York Times*, 18 October 1861.

57. "Lake Defences", *The Globe*, Toronto, Nov. 16, 1861. p. 2.

58. *ibid.*

59. "The Search of the Trent – Narrative of the Proceeding from a British Witness. Statement of the Purser of the Trent," appeared in *The New York Times*, December 13, 1861.

60. *The New York Times*, 17 Nov. 1861.

61. *The Globe*, Toronto, Nov. 18, 1861. pg. 2.

62. *The New York Herald*, 27 Nov. 1861, p.5. See also, The New York Times , 3 Dec. 1861

63. *The Evening Standard*, London, Wed. 27 Nov. 1861. p. 4.

64. "Opinions of the Press", *The Morning Chronicle*, London, 29 Nov. 1861, p. 5.

65. *ibid.*

66. Letter sent from London to Washington, Nov. 29, 1861, quoted in Charles Francis Adams, *The "Trent Affair": An Historical Retrospect*, Boston, 1912. p. 11.

67. Letter sent from Edinburgh to New York, Nov. 29, 1861, quoted in Charles Francis Adams, *ibid.*

68. Foreman, *ibid.*, pp. 183-185.

69. Administratively, Newfoundland, was usually considered as separate from the British North American provinces. The Pacific coast colonies of Vancouver Island and British Columbia (later amalgamated into the Province of British Columbia) were also part of "British North America" at the time, but they were not affected by the "Trent Affair".

70. Garnet Wolseley, *The Story of a Soldier's Life*, vol. II, p. 104.

71. M.E.S. Laws, *Battery Records of the Royal Artillery 1859-1877*, Woolwich, 1970.

72. Quoted in Gibson, *ibid.*, pp. 30-31.

73. *Ibid.*, "The sunlight is flooding the atmosphere", p. 42.

74. *Ibid.*, .pp. 38, 39, 40.

75. *Ibid.*, "A Birthday Present", p. 43.

76. A Soldier of the Regiment, *Voyage and Journey of the 2nd Batt. Scots Fusilier Guards*, Montreal, 1862, pp 1-2.

77. "Embarkation of the Staff, &c. for Canada at Liverpool", *The Birmingham Daily Post*, Dec. 23, 1861, p. 4

78. In 1850, RMS *Asia* made the crossing from Liverpool to Halifax in the record time of 8 days, 17 hours, averaging 12.1 knots. See C.R. Vernon Gibbs, *Passenger Liners of the Western Ocean*, 2nd ed. London, 1957. p. 62.

79. *ibid.*

80. Francis Duncan, *Our Garrisons in the West*, London, 1864. p. 222.

81. A Soldier of the Regiment, *ibid.* pp. 3-5.
     The Scots Fusilier Guards were on board ship for 25 days from Southampton to Halifax via the St. Lawrence River.

82. Wolseley, *ibid.*
     The *Melbourne* took 29 days to sail from Woolwich to Halifax, Dec. 7, 1861 to Jan 5, 1862.

83. Duncan, *ibid.* p. 15, aboard the *Lebanon* from Woolwich to Halifax several years earlier.

84. *ibid.*, pp. 227-231.

85. Wolseley, *ibid.*, pp. 108-112.

86. *The British Colonist*, Halifax, Dec. 28 1861, p.2.

87. *The British Colonist*, Halifax, Dec. 31 1861, p.2.

88. Duncan, *ibid.,*. pp. 219-221.

89. *The New York Times*, 1 Jan. 1862.

90. *The Illustrated London News*, London, January 4, 1862.

91. "Memoranda of Embarkation of Troops for British North America", LAC, RG8-C Series, microform c-2849.

92. A Soldier of the Regiment, *ibid.* p. 10.

93. From the "Journal of Lieutenant De la Cherois Thomas Irwin, RA, 1862" quoted by Edgar Andrew Collard in "All Our Yesterdays", *The Montreal Gazette*, Montreal, 30 Aug. 1958.

94. A Soldier of the Regiment, *ibid.* p. 13.

95. In his report to the Assistant Quarter-Master General, Lieut.-Col. Wolseley counted 6,821 officers, non-commissioned officers and soldiers who made the overland journey through New Brunswick that winter. Of those, three men died in hospital along the way. Also, one soldier died "from excessive drinking" and another died "from exposure when drunk". In addition, eight soldiers deserted. See map by G. Wolseley, "Route taken by troops proceeding from St. John New Brunswick to Canada 1862", LAC, NMC-22921.

96. William R. Steuart, "Aldershot to Canada West", *Colburn's United Service Magazine*, 1862, Part II, London 1862, pp. 501-502.

97. "Arrival of Troops", *The Globe*, Toronto, Thursday 6 March, 1861. p. 2.
There is a discrepancy between the number of men of No. 5 Battery that left Liverpool on Dec. 21, 1861 (117 men) and the number that arrived in Toronto on March 5, 1862 (110 men). This may be due to some reports stating the number of "men" and others stating the number of "officers and men".

98. Regimental Committee, *Historical Records of the XXX Regiment*, London 1887, p. 210.

99. The Parliament of the Province of Canada had been moved to Quebec in 1840, and the old Parliament buildings in Toronto remained largely unused until they were occupied by the Legislature of the Province of Ontario in 1867.

100. *The Globe*, Toronto, 19 Feb. 1862, p. 2.

101. Notes by H.F. Turner on "Sketch of Toronto Harbour", 19 July 1862, LAC NMC-4477.

102. "Defences of Toronto", appeared in *The Toronto Leader*, 3 Dec. 1861, and printed in *The British Colonist*, Halifax, 10 Dec. 1861.
The "engineer in charge" was probably Lieut. H.F. Turner, R.E.

103. *Report of the Commissioners Appointed to Consider the Defences of Canada*, London, 1862.
"Appendix No. 7, Return of Ordnance in Charge of Officer Commanding Royal Artillery in Canada", September, 1862."

Notes: Part 2 – The Artist

1. Province of Canada, *1861 Census of Canada*, Quebec, 1862.
    The population of the City of Toronto was 44,821. The population of Canada West was 1,896,091. The population of the entire Province of Canada combined (Canada East and Canada West) was 3,006,955.

2. *Mitchell's Canada Gazetteer and Business Directory for 1864-65*. Toronto, 1864, pp. 783-849.

3. *Report of the Commissioners Appointed to Consider the Defences of Canada, ibid.*

4. See John Bell, *Rebels on the Great Lakes*, Toronto, 2011.

5. Foreman, *ibid.*, pp. 698-699.

6. See *Queen's Regulations and Orders for the Army*, London, 1859.

7. "Correspondence of the Commanding Royal Engineer, Toronto District, 1862", LAC RG8-IB MF C-3833 v.1619.

8. "The Yacht Club Ball", *The Globe*, Toronto, 10 Sep. 1862, pg. 2

9. See the following
    - J. Ross Robertson, *Landmarks of Canada*, Toronto, 1917, pp. 45, 176
    - *The Canada Directory*, Toronto, 1851, p. 412
    - *The Militia Register of Upper Canada*, Toronto, 1839, p. 32
    - "Defalcation of Mr. Baines", *The Globe*, 21 Aug. 1857, p. 2
    - Allen Winn Sneath, *Brewed in Canada*, Toronto, 2001, p. 337.

10. *Report of Commissioners appointed to enquire into the conduct of the late John Clarke, as Agent for Public Lands in Huron*, Toronto, 1857. p. 2.
    Thomas Baines was accused of embezzling a total of £9,497 17s.

11. Egerton Baines (1830-1889) was the son Thomas Baines and his first wife, Catherine Lodge Wilcocks. See Gibson, *ibid.*, p. 109.

12. Egerton Baines painted a portrait of F.W. Barron. See *A Guide to the J. Ross Robertson Historical Collection*, Toronto, 1917, p. 554.
    A lithograph of the house at 30 William St. by Egerton Baines is in the possession of the Toronto Public Library, Baldwin Room, call no. 970-11.

13. Gibson, *ibid.*

14. Gibson, *ibid.*, indicates that Henry Edridge was Mary Rice's uncle, not her great uncle.
    Mary Rice also sat as a model for both David Wilkie and William Collins. See Gibson, *ibid.*, p.92.

15. Watercolour, "Ludlow, St. Laurence", by Mary Rice Baines,1847, LAC Accession no. 1997-107 DAP 00009, Box 001274, Henry Baines Fonds R12032-00-E.

16. Guggisberg, *ibid.*,. p. 45.

17. Buchanan-Dunlop, *ibid.*, p. 114.

18. Art historians have documented 54 graduates of RMA Woolwich who produced artwork of Canadian scenes. Most, but not all of these graduates, were subsequently commissioned in the Royal Engineers or the Royal Artillery. Two noted artists who were educated at the Academy but did not take a commission in the army were George Heriot (1759-1839) and William Roebuck (1796-1847).

19. The last known artist-officer of the British Army stationed in Canada was William Ogle Carlisle (in Canada 1870-73). See J. Russell Harper, *Early Painters and Engravers in Canada*, Toronto, 1970, p. 58.

20. British census records show Henry Edward Baines being born to Philip Ottey Egerton Baines and Mary Rice Baines in 1840. British military records show Henry Edward Baines being commissioned in the Royal Artillery in 1859 and serving until his death at Quebec in 1866. There are no known records of any artist with the name Henry Egerton Baines. Henry did have a cousin, Egerton Robert Baines (1830-1889) of Toronto (son of Thomas Baines and Catherine Wilcocks) who is reputed to have been a portrait painter.
Henry Edward Baines (1840-1866) should not be confused with another English painter, Henry Baines (1823-1894).

21. Frederick Verner served as an officer in the 3rd West York militia regiment in Britain from 1859 to 1862, and also joined the British Legion fighting for Garibaldi's army in Italy before returning to Canada to pursue a career as an artist. He is generally associated with the professional artists of the period rather than with the British artist-officers. See Harper, *ibid.*, p. 316. Another artist, John Herbert Caddy of the Royal Artillery, was a professional soldier in the regular British Army who, after retiring from the army, stayed in Canada and eventually turned to art as a way to make a living, thus becoming a professional artist in later life. See Francis K. Smith, *John Herbert Caddy 1801-1887*, Kingston, 1985.

22. A review of Aaron Penley's book "The English School of Painting in Water Colours" which appeared in *The Illustrated London News*, Jan. 4, 1862, p. 26.

23. Landscape drawing and painting was also part of the curriculum of the Royal Military College, Sandhurst, where a small number of infantry and cavalry officers were educated.

24. Over the course of twenty-four years, from 1835 to 1858, more than a dozen works by James Bridges are listed in the exhibition catalogues of the Royal Academy of Arts. See *The Exhibition of the Royal Academy of Arts*, London, 1835, 1836, 1837, 1841, 1843, 1844, 1845, 1847, 1848, 1850, 1856, 1858.

25. For a comprehensive summary of the Picturesque, see Kamille Parkinson, "Philip John Bainbrigge and the Group of 1838", PhD thesis, Queen's University, Kingston, 2005.

26. *ibid.*

27. To see online images from a collection of Philip John Bainbrigge's works, go to URL http://www.collectionscanada.gc.ca/. LAC, R9266-5-0-E, R3908-0-0-E, R11935-0-4-E.
Specific examples include the following:
– "Beloeil", 1838
http://collectionscanada.gc.ca/pam_archives/index.php?fuseaction=genitem.displayItem&rec_nbr=2833 530&lang=eng&rec_nbr_list=2833530,2896091,2836346,2895235,2833543,2896350,2833580,2896134 ,2896329,2836319
– "Fort Ticonderoga", 1838
http://collectionscanada.gc.ca/pam_archives/index.php?fuseaction=genitem.displayItem&rec_nbr=2833 567&lang=eng&rec_nbr_list=2833567,2896122,2833568,2896121

— "Joachims Portage", 1842
http://collectionscanada.gc.ca/pam_archives/index.php?fuseaction=genitem.displayItem&rec_nbr=2833
558&lang=eng&rec_nbr_list=2833558,2896113,2895543,2895568,2896342,2837826,2836334,2837926,
2833562,2895633

28. Similar works by Turner include "The Blue Rigi", "Sunrise", "Peace—Burial at Sea" and "Norham Castle", in the collection of the J. Paul Getty Museum. California.

29. J.M.W. Turner died in 1851, after which most of his paintings fell into the possession of Britain's National Gallery in London. In December 1859, 103 of Turner's paintings were displayed at the National Gallery's British School in South Kensington (now the Victoria and Albert Museum), just twenty kilometers from where Henry Baines was studying at Woolwich, and it is possible that Henry saw Turner's paintings there. See John Walker, *Turner*, New York, 1982, pp. 31-34.

30. "Those beautiful Krieghoffs should not be permitted to leave Toronto — not one of them; another such collection of painting by European masters may not be met with for years" Report on the Mechanics' Institute Exhibition, *The Globe*, Toronto, 4 Apr. 1865. p.2.

31. C.H.J Snider, *Annals of the Royal Canadian Yacht Club, 1852-1837*, Toronto, 1937, p. 40.

32. See Henry C. Campbell, *Early Days on the Great Lakes: The Art of William Armstrong*. Toronto, 1971.

33. A scrapbook/journal similar to that of Henry Baines' was compiled in 1865 by the British traveller, Mark J. Stewart. Instead of containing paintings and drawings, its 400 pages were illustrated with more than 60 photographs. See "Journal of an American tour extending over four months", LAC, R11884-0-0-E.

Notes: Part 3 – The Journal: Background

1. "Royal Canadian Yacht Club", *Bell's Life in London and Sporting Chronicle*, London, 11 May 1862. "A number of the officers belonging to the regiments now quartered in Canada are amongst the members". p. 6.
Wherever the British Army was stationed, if yachting was possible the officers joined a local yacht club or established one for their own recreational purposes. Such was the case in Montreal in 1863, when the Montreal Garrison Yacht Club was organized by officers of the Grenadier Guards and Scots Fusilier Guards. See I.E.A. Dolby, *The Journal of the Household Brigade for the Year 1864, London, 1864*.

2. A number of RCYC members are identified as stewards at the Yacht Club Ball in September, 1862. Among these is William (Willie) James Baines, son of Henry's Uncle Thomas and Thomas' second wife, Catherine Bancks. See "The Yacht Club Ball", *The Globe*, Toronto, 10 Sep. 1862, pg. 2.

3.   Henry Harvey and Samuel Woodfull may also have been members of the Royal Canadian Yacht Club. This cannot be confirmed since very few comprehensive lists of RCYC members have survived. See Snider, *ibid.*

4.   The earliest known pleasure yacht on Lake Ontario was recorded in 1832, when Captain John Elmsley, a retired Royal Navy officer and member of the Legislative Council of Upper Canada, advertised his 22½ ton cutter-yacht, *Dart*, for sale in Toronto. See Snider, *ibid.*, p. 40.

5.   *ibid.*
The RCYC clubhouse was moved to Toronto Island in 1881.

6.   *ibid.*, pp. 35-36.

7.   Once they had arrived in Canada, Edward and Elizabeth Hodder eventually settled in Toronto where Edward practiced medicine and was one of the founders of the Upper Canada School of Medicine (later incorporated into the medical school of the University of Toronto) where he was Professor of Obstetrics. In addition, he was dean of the medical school, on the board of the Toronto General Hospital, the chief coroner of Toronto, and an officer in the 4th Battalion Toronto Militia with the rank of Surgeon.
See Henri Pilon, "Hodder, Edward Mulberry", *Dictionary of Canadian Biography*, vol. 10, University of Toronto/Université Laval, 2003, URL http://www.biographi.ca/en/bio/hodder_ edward_mulberry_10E.html accessed 14 Oct., 2017.

8.   Snider, *ibid.*

9.   *Bell's Life in London and Sporting Chronicle*, 13 June 1858, p. 7.
The *Meta* was known to be a very fast boat and won many yacht races in her day. She was smaller than the *Breeze*, measuring only 7.5 tons, 33 feet long, 7.5 feet beam and drawing 5.75 feet of water with a deep-draught keel.

10.   *Bell's Life in London and Sporting Chronicle*, 27 Jan. 1861, p. 6.

11.   Snider, *ibid.*, pp. 30-32.
See also Howard I. Chappelle, American Small Sailing Craft, New York, 1951. pp. 266-267.

12.   The Thames Rule, devised originally by the Royal Thames Yacht Club, was used to determine displacement in "tons" (units of cubic feet) as follows: Length minus beam, multiplied by beam, multiplied by half-beam, and divided by 94. A racing handicap of 1 minute per ton was placed on the heavier boats. In 1884, the RCYC adopted the Seawanhaka Rule" which had originated in Ireland but was named for the Seawanhaka Corinthian Yacht Club of Long Island Sound, New York. This rule was expressed as: one half the sum of the waterline length and the square root of the sail area. See Snider, *ibid.*,. pp. 29 and 77.

13.   Sailboats larger than 10 tons were First Class yachts. Smaller sailboats were Second Class yachts. The *Breeze* was registered with the Royal Thames Yacht Club as 18 tons, but with the Royal Canadian Yacht Club as 16 tons. Baines refers to the *Breeze* as a 17-ton yacht.

14.   Quoted in Snider, *ibid.*, p. 38.

15.   After the *Breeze* was lost in 1867, Commodore Hodder replaced her with the 28-ton schooner-yacht *Geraldine* (named after his daughter), in which he won the coveted Prince of Wales' Cup in 1868.
See Snider, *ibid.*, p. 42.

16.   Augustus Ford, *Chart of Lake Ontario from Actual Survey*, New York, 1836. LAC NMC-11314.
For a complete discussion of this nautical chart, see Marc Seguin, *For Want of a Lighthouse*, 2015. pp. 22-28.

17. United States Corps of Engineers, *Lake Ontario*, New York, 1877. NOAA Office of Coast Survey Historical Map & Chart Collection.

18. "The Gzowski Cannon", *The Globe*, Toronto, 4 July 1862. p. 2.

19. H.G. Hart, *The New Annual Army List for 1871*, London, 1871, p. 361.

20. Lieut. Henry Harvey remained with No. 5 Battery, 10th Brigade for his entire military career. After the Battery left Canada for Malta in 1867, Harvey took temporary command of the Battery for several months in 1869 and 1870. While his Battery was still stationed in Malta, Lieut. Harvey left the service in 1872, at age twenty-nine.
See "Statement of the services of Henry B.R. Harvey", U.K. National Archives, WO 76, Regimental Records of Officers' Services 1775-1914.

21. "Statement of the services of Samuel Pratt Woodfull", U.K. National Archives, WO 76, Regimental Records of Officers' Services 1775-1914.

22. Edward M. Hodder, "Cases of Ovariotomy", *The Canada Lancet*, Toronto, Nov. 1871, pp. 104 and 108.

23. McGill University, *Annual Announcement of the Faculty of Medicine*, Montreal, 1864, p. 11. After leaving Canada in 1870, Dr. Woodfull transferred for a short time to the 77th (East Middlesex) Regiment with the rank of staff-surgeon, but then returned to the Royal Artillery before retiring from the army in 1878 with the rank of surgeon-major. See "Statement of the services of Samuel Pratt Woodfull", *ibid.*

24 Henry E. Baines, from the cover of the manuscript "A Month's Leave or The Cruise of the Breeze". LAC R12032-1-2-E.

25. *Hunt's Yachting Magazine*: No. 6, Vol XIV, June 1865 (Toronto to Consecon); No. 7, Vol XIV, July 1865 (Consecon to Picton); No. 8, Vol XIV, August 1865 Waupoos to Oswego); No. 10, Vol XIV, October 1865 (Oswego to Toronto).

26 See LAC, Lamont family fonds, MG25-G424, R5902-0-7-E.

Notes: The Journal – A Month's Leave or The Cruise of the *Breeze*

1. "Statement of the Canadian and American Tonnage" (No. 38), *Tables of the Trade and Navigation of the Province of Canada for the Year 1862*. Quebec, 1863.

2. "Summary Statement of the Welland St. Lawrence and Chambly Canals" (No. 7), *ibid.*

3. See D.D. Calvin, *A Saga of the St. Lawrence: Timber & Shipping Through Three Generations*, Toronto, 1945.

4.   *The Daily British Whig*, Kingston, 5 Sept. 1850, p. 2, lists 24 yachts at Kingston in 1850 and C.H.J. Snider, *Annals of the Royal Canadian Yacht Club, ibid.*, p. 20, lists 25 yachts at Toronto in 1855.

5.   *Laws and Regulations of the Royal Canadian Yacht Club*, Toronto, 1856.

6.   Carl Benn, *Historic Fort York 1793-1993*, Toronto, 1993. pp. 21-40.

7.   See Aldona Sendzikas, *Stanley Barracks: Toronto's Military Legacy*, Toronto, 2011.

8.   H.G. Hart, *The New Annual Army List for 1848*, London, 1848, p. 173.

9.   H.G. Hart, *The New Annual Army List for 1863*, London, 1863, p. 205.
     See also "Statement of the services of George P.E. Morrison," U.K. National Archives, WO 76, Regimental Records of Officers' Services 1775-1914.

10. John Fortescue, *The Royal Army Service Corps: A History of Transport and Supply in the British Army.* London, 1930. p. 157.

11. Snider, *ibid.*, p. 39.

12. Hart, *The New Annual Army List for 1848, ibid.*, p. 479.
     See also "Statement of the services of Robert French Handcock," U.K. National Archives, WO 76, Regimental Records of Officers' Services 1775-1914.

13. Hart, *The New Annual Army List for 1863, ibid.*, p. 285.
     See also "Statement of the services of Charles J.P. Clarkson," U.K. National Archives, WO 76, Regimental Records of Officers' Services 1775-1914.

14. Larry & Patricia Wright, *Great Lakes Lighthouses Encyclopedia*, Erin Ontario, 2006, pp. 50-51.

15. Hodder, *The Harbours and Ports of Lake Ontario, ibid.*, p. 5.

16. Dating from about 1832, the yacht *Dart* was originally owned by Capt. John Elmsley, R.N. See Snider *ibid.* pp. 30 and 40f.

17. Strictly speaking, any 50/50 combination of beers can be called half-and-half. See Frederick Accum, *A Treatise on the Art of Brewing*, London, 1820.

18. Province of Canada, *Census of the Canadas 1860-61*, Vol. 1, Quebec, 1863, Appendix2, shows the population of Cobourg as 4,975.

19. *Mitchell's Canada Gazetteer, ibid.*, pp.119-122.

20. *The Daily News*, Kingston, 8 Aug. 1863, p. 2.

21. See Edwin C. Guillet, *Cobourg 1798-1948*, Oshawa, 1948, p. 144.
     Barron had formerly been the headmaster of Toronto's Upper Canada College.
     See also Snider, *ibid.*, p. 30

22. *Mitchell's Canada Gazetteer, ibid.*, p. 121.

23. Syndics of the Cambridge University Press, *The Holy Bible Containing the Old and New Testaments*, Cambridge, 1962, Psalm 37:35.

24. J. Riordans, *The Upper Canada Law List and Solicitor's Agency Book*, 5th Ed., Toronto, 1866, p. 32.

25. *The Globe*, Toronto, 16 Sep. 1863, p. 2.
    Coincidentally, the Coxwell's were neighbours of Thomas Baines on William Street in Toronto, and both the Baines and Coxwell families attended St. George's Church. In 1877, Henry Baines' sister, Isabelle, who had emigrated to Canada several years earlier, was married in St. George's Church to Alexander Mitchell. One of the witnesses at that ceremony was recorded as O.S. Hodder. "Registrations of Marriages, 1869-1928", Archives of Ontario, Series: MS932; Reel: 26.

26. Guillet, *ibid.*, p. 113.

27. *Ibid.*, p. 103.

28. J & R Tonson, *The Works of Joseph Addison*, Vol. IV, 1761, p.190.

29. *The Cobourg Sentinel*, as quoted in *The Daily News*, Kingston, 11 Aug. 1863, p. 2

30. Russell, *Mayors of Toronto*, Erin Ontario, 1982, pp. 109-110.

31. Snider, *ibid.*, p. 103.

32. C.M. Strickland, *Twenty-Seven Years in Canada West*, Vol. I, 1853, p. 64.

33. *Mitchell's Canada Gazetteer, ibid.*, p. 123.

34. See *The Army and Navy Gazette*, London, 20 Dec. 1862, p. 4
    See also *The Globe*, Toronto, 24 July 1863, p. 2

35. Howard Patterson, *Patterson's Illustrated Nautical Dictionary*, New York, 1891, p. 192.

36. An Old Dragoon, "Suggestions for Preventing Desertion from the Army", *Colburn's United Service Magazine*, 1860, Pt. 1, p.272.

37. Dorothy O. Pratt, "Bounty System", *Encyclopedia of the American Civil War*, D.S. Heidler and J.T. Heidler editors, New York 2000, pp. 256-257.

38. The exchange rate of pounds sterling to U.S. dollars in 1863 was $7.08. Lawrence H. Officer, "Dollar-Pound Exchange Rate From 1791," MeasuringWorth, 2017, URL http://www.measuringworth.com/exchangepound/ accessed 14 Oct. 2017.

39. Baines states later on in the journal that the pay in the U.S. Army is $25 per month. Other sources state that privates in the U.S. Army were paid $13 per month. See Steven J. Ramold, "Pay, USA", in *Encyclopedia of the American Civil War, ibid.*, p. 1465.

40. Letter, War Office to G.O.C. Halifax, 15 March 1862, LAC, RG8 C Series, reel C-3843, p. 1401.

41. Notes on the map drawn by Garnet Wolseley, "Route taken by troops proceeding from St. John, New Brunswick, to Canada, 1862", LAC NMC 22921.

42. *The New York Times*, 8 Sep. 1864.

43. See *The Globe*, Toronto, various issues, 1862 to 1863.
    In September 1864, two deserters who shot at soldiers pursuing them were originally sentenced to death for attempted murder, but the sentence was commuted to imprisonment for life *The Globe*, Toronto, 5 Sep. 1864, p. 2.

44. Randall White, *Ontario 1610-1985: A Political and Economic History*, Toronto, 1985, p. 110. See also http://www.heritagetrust.on.ca/en/index.php/properties/victoria-hall accessed 14 Oct. 2017.

45. See Seguin, *ibid.*, pp. 108-130.

46. Hodder, *The Harbours and Ports of Lake Ontario, ibid.*, p. 13.
The channel into Presqu'ile Bay was straightened in 1890 after the opening of the Murray Canal connecting the bay with the Bay of Quinte. See Seguin, *ibid.* pp. 299-302.

47. *Mitchell's Canada Gazetteer, ibid.*, p. 71.

48. Geographical Names Board of Canada, "Wellers Bay" URL http://www4.rncan.gc.ca/search-place-names/unique/FDBYR accessed 14 Oct. 2017.

49. Hodder, *The Harbours and Ports of Lake Ontario, ibid.*, p. 15.

50. Patterson, *ibid.*, p. 84.

51. *Mitchell's Canada Gazetteer, ibid.*, p. 132.
See also Richard Lunn and Janet Lunn, *The County: The First Hundred Years in Loyalist Prince Edward*, Picton, 1967, pp. 219-222.

52. Seguin, *ibid.*, pp. 207-235.

53. *Mitchell's Canada Gazetteer, ibid.*

54. Patricia C. Taylor, *History of the Churches of Prince Edward County*, Picton, 1971.

55. John Keats, *Poems Published in 1820*, Project Gutenberg, 2007, p. 51.

56. *The Oswego Commercial Times*, Oswego, 12 Aug. 1863.

57. *The Daily News*, Kingston, 13 Aug. 1863, p. 2

58. *The Globe*, Toronto, 17 Aug. 1863, p. 3

59. Seguin, *ibid.*, pp. 6-33.

60. Department of National Defence, *A History of Fort Frontenac*, Ottawa, 2014.

61. *Mitchell's Canada Gazetteer, ibid.*, p. 285.

62. Hodder, *The Harbours and Ports of Lake Ontario, ibid.*, pp. 15-16.

63. *The Globe*, Toronto, 6 July 1861, p. 2.

64. *The Globe*, Toronto, 28 May 1863, p.4.

65. Mitchell & Co., *General Directory for the City of Kingston*, Toronto, 1865, p. 5.

66. In addition to the four Martello towers at Kingston, two other taller towers, known as the East Ditch tower and West Ditch tower, were built on either side of Point Henry to serve as auxiliary defences for Fort Henry. Ivan J. Saunders, "A History of Martello Towers in the Defence of British North America 1796-1871", *Occasional Papers in Archeology and History*, No. 15, Ottawa, 1972, pp. 52-74.

67. See H.G Hart, *New Annual Army List for 1864*, London, 1864.
See also H.W. Askwith, *List of Officers of the Royal Regiment of Artillery 1716 to 1899*, 4th ed. London, 1900, pp. 73-74a.

68. Geographical Names Board of Canada, "South Bay", URL http://www4.rncan.gc.ca/search-place-names/unique/FCQDG accessed 14 Oct. 2017.

69. See *Tremaine's Map of the County of Prince Edward Upper Canada*, Toronto, 1863.

70. In 1871, Marysburgh was divided into two separate townships, North Marysburgh and South Marysburgh, making a total of seven townships in Prince Edward County.
See H. Belden, *Illustrated Historical Atlas of the Counties of Hastings and Prince Edward*, Toronto, 1878, p. xvi.

71. *Mitchell's Canada Gazetteer*, ibid., p. 410.

72. *ibid.*, p. 556.

73. *The New York Times*, 3 Sep. 1852.
See also, *The Oswego Advertiser & Times*, 21 Oct. 1870, and Samuel W. Durant and Henry B. Pierce, *History of Jefferson County New York*, Philadelphia, 1878. pp. 413-414.

74. United States Government, *Population Schedules of the Eighth Census of the United States, 1860*, New York, U.S. National Archives, Vol. 27, Roll 762, Jefferson County.
H. French, in *Gazetteer of the State of New York*, Syracuse, 1860, p. 358, states that the population of Sackets Harbor was only 994. p.358.

75. Other sources say that the USS *New Orleans* was capable of carrying more than 110 guns.
See Durant and Pierce, *ibid.*

76. United States Navy, *Dictionary of American Naval Fighting Ships*, Vol. 5, Washington, 1970, p. 66.

77. Hodder, *The Harbours and Ports of Lake Ontario*, ibid., p. 17.

78. *History of Jefferson County New York*, ibid., p. 397.

79. The crossed muskets insignia was used at a later date, but only by the U.S. Infantry, and only after 1875. Prior to that time, the infantry used a hunting horn as their badge. The badge of the U.S. Cavalry was always crossed sabres.
See Institute of Heraldry, United States Army, URL http://www.tioh.hqda.pentagon.mil/ Catalog/Heraldry.aspx?HeraldryId=15286&CategoryId=9362&grp=2&menu=Uniformed%20Services&ps=2 4&p=0&hilite=cavalry accessed 14 Oct. 2017.

80. United States Government, *5th Census of the United States, 1860*. U.S. National Archives, RG 29.2.1.

81. See J. Thomas Scharf, *History of the Confederate States Navy*, New York, 1887.

82. National Park Service online database "The Civil War – Search For Soldiers",
http://www.nps.gov/civilwar/search-soldiers.htm accessed 14 Oct. 2017.

83. Benn, *ibid.*, pp. 102 & 104.

84. Benson J. Lossing, *A History of the Civil War 1861-65*, New York, 1895, p. 192.

85. See William A. Gladstone, *United States Colored Troops 1863-1867*, Gettysburg, 1996.

86. Lossing, *ibid.*, pp. 370 & 480.
A total of 359,528 soldiers died from all causes during the war, including those killed in action, those who died of wounds received in action, those who died of disease, those who died in prison camps and those who died from accidents and other causes. Included in that number are the deaths of 36,847 "U.S. Colored Troops".

87. H. French, *Gazetteer of the State of New York*, Syracuse, 1860, pp. 519-524.

88. Hodder, *The Harbours and Ports of Lake Ontario, ibid.*, p. 19.

89. Association des Amis de la Maison Vauban, *Vauban: sa vie, son oeuvre*, France, 1984.

90. John T. Hyde, *Elementary Principles of Fortification*, London, 1860.
Compare Fort Ontario with a similar pentagonal fort, Fort McHenry in Baltimore, which has a number of outworks, see URL https://www.nps.gov/media/photo/gallery.htm?id=1C27E1E2-155D-451F-6739965D63726B10 accessed October 2017.

91. Robert Thomas, *Register of the Ships of the Lakes and River St. Lawrence 1864*, , Buffalo, 1864, p. 23.
The *Carthagenian* was wrecked less then two kilometers east of the entrance to Oswego harbour during the gale of November 29, 1867. *The Detroit Free Press*, 6 Dec. 1867

92. John Johnson, *The Defense of Charleston Harbor 1863-1865*, Charleston, 1890. pp. 115-132.

93. "Tremendous Force of Rifled Projectiles", *The Scientific American*, New York, 5 Sept. 1863, p. 154.

94. *The Buffalo Daily Courier*, 26 Aug. 1863, p. 2

95. See John B. Buckstone's published works: *A Rough Diamond*, London, 1847, and *A Kiss in the Dark*, London, 1852.
See also Ray Palmer Baker, *Sam Slick by Thomas Chandler Haliburton*, New York, 1923.
pp. 413-415.

96. United States Congress, "An Act for enrolling and calling out the national Forces, and for other Purposes," *Congressional Record*, 37th Cong. 3rd Sess. Ch. 74, 75. 1863, March 3, 1863.

97. Mark Kurlansky, *The Big Oyster: History on the Half Shell*, New York, 2006, p. 207.

98. Hodder, *The Harbours and Ports of Lake Ontario, ibid.*, pp. 20-21.

99. French, *ibid.*, p. 694.

100. *ibid.*

101. *ibid.*, p. 399.

102. Hodder, *The Harbours and Ports of Lake Ontario, ibid.*, p. 21.

103. *The Daily News*, Kingston, 2 July 1863, p. 2.

104. Guillett, *ibid.*, p. 253.

105. French, *ibid.*, pp. 403-404.

106. "Minstrelsy, American", Oxford Music Online, URL http://www.oxfordmusiconline.com /public accessed 14 Oct. 2017.

107. *The Globe*, Toronto, 6 Sept. 1862, p. 3.
See also advertisements in the New York Herald, 13 Dec. 1862, p. 7.

108. Snider, *ibid.*, p. 40.

Notes: Part 4 – The Hero

1.   Gibson, *ibid.*, pp. 46-47.

2.   The population of Quebec in 1861 was 51,109. Province of Canada, *1861 Census of Canada*, Quebec, 1862.

3.   J.M. LeMoine, *Quebec, Past and Present*, vol. II, Quebec, 1876, p. 306.

4.   *Report of the Commissioners Appointed to Consider the Defences of Canada, ibid.*

5.   Henry Edward Baines' scrapbook containing 52 watercolours of this Quebec period was sold to the Kennedy Galleries in New York City and then in 1995, it was sold at auction by Eldred's Auction House to the Gerald Peters Gallery in Santa Fe, New Mexico. By 2015, only 23 of the original 52 paintings in this collection were still for sale by the Gerald Peters Gallery.
In 2017, 20 of these 23 were purchased from the Gerald Peters Gallery by the Cluett and Seguin families of Prince Edward County, Ontario, Canada, and donated to the documentary art collection of Library and Archives Canada.
Of the other 29 works, 6 are known to have been sold to private collectors in the Province of Quebec, and 5 others are thought to be in the collections of Canadian museums: 2 at the Royal Ontario Museum in Toronto, 2 at the Art Gallery of Hamilton and 1 at the Musee National de Beaux-arts du Quebec. In addition, there are 5 more in the collection of Library and Archives Canada.

6.   See Thomas W. Balch, *The Alabama Arbitration*, Philadelphia, 1900.
The "Alabama Claims" were not settled until 1872, when Britain agreed to pay the United States $15,500,000 in compensation.

7.   See John MacDonald, *Troublous Times in Canada: A History of the Fenian Raids of 1866 and 1870*, Toronto, 1910

8.   City of Quebec historical display, Boul. Langelier, August, 2016.
The following list indicates the year of the fire and the effects:
    1836 60 houses, 6 stores, 6 schooners, 100 families homeless
    1845(two fires) 3,130 houses, 21,000 people homeless
    1846 Saint-Louis theatre, 50 fatalities
    1854 Quebec Legislature
    1861 47 houses, 87 families homeless
    1862 191 houses, 280 families homeless
    1865 150 buildings, 600 families homeless.
In May, 1866, a smaller fire destroyed fifty houses in the St. Roch suburb. "Destructive Fire in St. Rochs, *The Quebec Gazette*, Quebec, 9 May 1866. p. 2.

9.   The fire in May 1866 in the St. Roch suburb was described in *The Quebec Gazette* the following day:
     Last night between eight and nine o'clock, a destructive fire broke out in St. Rochs. It originated, we believe, in a joiner's work-shop. The church of the Congregation [Notre Dame de Jacques Cartier] was in great danger but through the exertions of the firemen was saved without having received any damage. Viewing the fire from an elevated position, we were reminded of the eventful conflagration which some years ago [1845] swept over the whole suburb. Before the fire of last night was subdued, about fifty houses were destroyed.
     "Destructive Fire in St. Rochs", *The Quebec Gazette*, 9 May 1866. p. 2.

10.   George Varney, *A Gazetteer of the State of Maine*. Boston, 1886. p.465.

11.   "From a Canadian Paper, Quebec Oct. 15th, 1866.", printed in the pamphlet *In Memorium*, Quebec, 1866.
This may have been a composite account compiled from several newspapers including *Le Canadien*, *Le Courier du Canada*, *The Quebec Gazette* and *The Quebec Mercury*.

12.   Captain Schaw, "Gunpowder as a Disruptive Agent", *The Journal of the United Service Institution*, vol.2. London, 1859. p. 275

13.   "Terrible Conflagration", *The Quebec Gazette*, Oct. 15, 1866, p. 2.

14.   *The Quebec Mercury*, October 15, 1866.

15.   See Réligieuses Hospitalieres de la Miséricorde de Jésus, Ordre de Saint-Augustin, *Monseigneur de Saint-Vallier et L'hopital General de Quebec*, Quebec, 1882, pp. 555 - 564.

16.   Newspaper accounts mention only a single powder keg, but Captain Schaw, *ibid.*, indicated in his article on the subject that at least 50 lbs of gunpowder (two 25-pound kegs) were necessary to demolish a building.

17.   Translation of "Mort de Lieut. Baynes", *Le Courier du Canada*, Oct. 29, 1866, from *In Memorium*, *ibid.* pp. 12-13.

18.   *Le Courier de Canada*, 17 Oct. 1866, p. 2.

19.   Centers for Disease Control and Prevention, *Epidemiology and Prevention of Vaccine-Preventable Diseases*, 13th ed., Atlanta, 2015.
It was after World War I before an effective Tetanus vaccine was developed.

20.   *Le Courier du Canada*, 29 Oct. 1866, translation from *In Memorium*, *ibid.* p.15.

21.   *In Memorium*, ibid pp. 21-24.

22.   ibid pp. 16-19.

23.   Extracts from a letter, Sister St. Olivier, Quebec, 15 Nov. 1866 to Mary Baines, London, from *In Memorium*, *ibid.* pp. 24-27.
The locket mentioned by Sister St. Olivier is still in the hands of the descendants of Henry Baines' sister, Isabelle. The portrait mentioned of Lieut. Baines is reproduced on page 215.

24.   Extracts from a letter, Mary Baines, London, to Sister St. Olivier, Quebec, Dec. 6, 1866, Archives du Monastere, Quebec.

25.   Campbell, A., "A Voice From Mount hermon", from J.M. Le Moine, *Picturesque Quebec*, Montreal, 1882, pp. 360-361.

26.   On November 11, 1871, the last of the British troops defending Canada marched out of the Quebec Citadel and boarded the troopship HMS *Orontes* to sail back to Great Britain. Only a detachment of Royal Engineers at Quebec remained in Canada along with a small garrison at Halifax to protect the Royal Navy's dockyard.

27.   The original photographic print of Henry Baines showed him in a plain frock coat (see the illustration on page 234). After his death, the officers of his Battery had the photograph overpainted to depict him in his full-dress uniform. In March, 1867, his portrait was presented to the nuns of the General Hospital Convent who had cared for Henry during his final days.

Inscription on the matte of the portrait:
  M. le Lieutenant Henry Edward Baines, Bienfaiteur de notre Etablissement. Ce portrait fut

présenté a la Communauté par les Officiers de l'Artillerie Royale que commandait M. Baines. Le 14 octobre 1866, l'incendie des fauborgs St. Roch et St. Sauveur menaçait de con sumer notre Hopital-Général. Afin d'épargner celui-ci, le Lieutenant Edward Baines se pré- parait a faire sauter une maison au coin des rues St. Anselme et Prince-Edouard. La poudre prit feu avant le tempest le brave officier, lancé a une hauteur do 30 pieds, retomba avec les descombres de la maison. Il fut recueilli en notre hopital, mais il expir le 27 octobre suivant, dans la 26ieme anné do son age.

English translation:
Lieutenant Henry Edward Baines, benefactor of our establishment. This portrait was pre- sented to the Community by the officers of the Royal Artillery who commanded Mr. Baines. On October. 14, 1866, the fire in the St. Roch and St. Sauveur suburbs threatened to con- sume our General Hospital. After arriving here, Lieutenant Baines prepared to blow up a house at the corner of St. Anselme and Prince Edward streets. The gunpowder ignited pre- maturely and the brave officer, thrown to a height of 30 feet, fell back with the rubble from the house. He was taken to our hospital, but he expired on the following October 27, at age 26.

28. Gibson, *ibid.*, p. 13.

29. While on her honeymoon in 1876, Isabelle Baines Mitchell travelled to Quebec to thank the nuns at the General Hospital Convent for caring for her late brother, and to visit the his grave in Mount Hermon Cemetery.
See correspondence between Isabelle Baines and the Sisters of St. Augustine, Archives du Monestere du Quebec.

BIBLIOGRAPHY

Archive and Unpublished Sources

Archives of Ontario
- Legislative Assembly. "Return to an Address, report of Commissioners appointed to enquire into the conduct of the late John Clarke, as Agent for Public Lands." Toronto, 1857. Pamph 1857, #3, c1.
- Registrations of Marriages, 1869-1928. Series: MS932, Reels 26 and 145.

Gloucestershire Archives. Parish Registers. P78/1 IN 1/66

Jenkins, Danny R. "British North Americans Who Fought in the American Civil War, 1861-1865", (unpublished master's thesis). University of Ottawa, 1993.

LDS Family Search. Select Birth and Christenings 1539-1975. Salt Lake City, 2013.

Library and Archives Canada.
- Baines, Henry E. Fonds. R12032-0-0-E.
- Census Returns for 1861. Roll C-1101-1109
- "Correspondence of the Commanding Royal Engineer, Toronto District, 1862", LAC RG8-IB MF C-3833 v.1619.
- Ford, Augustus. *Chart of Lake Ontario from Actual Survey*, New York, 1836. LAC NMC-11314.
- Lamont family fonds, MG25-G424, R5902-0-7-E
- Maps, Plans and Charts, R12567-0-7-E, NMC 1177.
- "Memoranda of Embarkation of Troops for British North America", LAC, RG8-C Series, microform c-2849.
- Stewart, Mark J. "Journal of an American Tour. R11884-0-9-E. Volume/box number: 1
- Turner, H.F. "Sketch of Toronto Harbour", 19 July 1862, LAC NMC-4477.
- War Office letter to G.O.C. Halifax, 15 March 1862, LAC, RG8 C Series, reel C-3843, p. 1401.
- War Office letter to General Officer Commanding the Troops, Halifax, N.S., 24 Dec. 1861, LAC RG8 C-series microform c-3843/1730-92.
- Wolseley, G. "Route taken by troops proceeding from St. John New Brunswick to Canada 1862", LAC, NMC-22921.

London Metropolitan Archives. P82/GEO2, various items.

Parkinson, Kamille. "Philip John Bainbrigge and the Group of 1838",(unpublished PhD thesis), Queen's University, Kingston, 2005.

Toronto Reference Library, Baldwin Room. Baines, Henry Edward. "A Month's Leave or Cruise of the Breeze", extracted from Hunt's Yachting Magazine, with marginal notes by Col. Rice.

United Kingdom National Archives
– Calendar of the Grants of Probate and Letters of Administration made in the Probate Registries of the Hight Court of Justice in England. London.
– "Statement of the services of Officers". U.K. National Archives, WO 76, Regimental Records of Officers' Services 1775-1914.
– War Office Records, WO 10/2602-2613. Artillery Muster Books and Pay Lists.

United States National Archives. *Records of District Courts of the United States, 1685 – 2004*, Civil War Prize Case Files. U.S. National Archives, Record Group 21, - Identifier 620244.

Books

A Soldier of the Regiment. *Voyage and Journey of the 2nd Batt. Scots Fusilier Guards*. Montreal, 1862.

Accum, Frederick. *A Treatise on the Art of Brewing*. London, 1820.

Adams, Charles Francis. *The "Trent Affair": An Historical Retrospect*. Boston, 1912.

Alphabetical List of the Medical Officers of the Indian Army. London, 1839

Art Gallery of Hamilton. *Canada in the Nineteenth Century: The Bert and Barbara Stitt Family Collection*. Hamilton, 1984.

Askwith, H.W. *List of Officers of the Royal Regiment of Artillery, 1716 to 1899*. 4th ed. London, 1900.

Bailliere, H. *The New World or The United States and Canada Illustrated and Described*. London, 1859.

Barnard, George. *The Theory and Practice of Landscape Painting in Water-Colour*, 3rd ed. London, 1885.

Barnes, R. Money. *A History of the Regiments and Uniforms of the British Army*, 6th ed. London, 1967.

Bell, John. *Rebels on the Great Lakes: Confederate Naval Commando Operations Launched from Canada 1863-1864*. Toronto, 2011.

Bell, Michael. *Painters in a New Land, from Annapolis Royal to the Klondike*. Toronto, 1973.

Benn, Carl. *Historic Fort York 1793-1993*, Toronto, 1993.

Bowles, T.G. *The Declaration of Paris of 1856.* London, 1900.

Browne, James A. *England's Artillerymen: An Historical Narrative of the Services of the Royal Artillery.* London, 1865.

Bruce, Anthony. *The Purchase System in the British Army 1660-1871.* London, 1980.

Buchanan, Alexander C. *Canada, 1862: For the Information of Emigrants.* Quebec, 1862.

Buchanan-Dunlop, H.D. *Records of the Royal Military Academy Woolwich.* London, 1892.

Callwell, Charles and John Headlam. *The History of the Royal Artillery from the Indian Mutiny to the Great War*, Vol. I. London, 1931.

Calvin, D.D. *A Saga of the St. Lawrence: Timber & Shipping Through Three Generations.* Toronto, 1945.

Campbell, Henry C. *Early Days on the Great Lakes: The Art of William Armstrong.* Toronto, 1971.

The Canada Directory. Toronto, 1851.

Carmen, W.Y. *Richard Simkin's Uniforms of the British Army.* Exeter, 1985.

Chappelle, Howard I. *American Small Sailing Craft.* New York, 1951.

Chartrand, René. *Canadian Military Heritage*, Vol. 2. Montreal, 1995.

Cooke, W. Martha E. *W.H. Coverdale Collection of Canadiana: Paintings, Watercolours and Drawings.* Ottawa, 1983.

Costi, Michele. *Memoir on the Trent Affair.* Washington, 1865.

de Fonblanque, Edward Barrington. *Treatise on the Administration and Organization of the British Army.* London, 1858.

de Pencier, Honor. *Posted to Canada: The Watercolours of George Russell Dartnell, 1835-1844.* Toronto, 1987.

Dibner, Bern. *The Atlantic Cable.* Norwalk CT, 1959.

Dickens, Charles. *The Life and Adventures of Martin Chuzzlewit.* London, 1844.

Dolby, I.E.A., ed. *The Journal of the Household Brigade for the year 1864.* London, 1864.

Donnell, E.J. *Chronological and Statistical History of Cotton.* New York, 1872.

Drayson, A.W. *The Gentleman Cadet: His Career and Adventures at the Royal Military Academy, Woolwich.* London, 1875.

Duncan, Francis.
    – *Our Garrisons in the West: Sketches in British North America*. London, 1864.
    – *History of the Royal Regiment of Artillery*, vol. II. London, 1873.

Duyckinck, Evert A. *National History of the War for the Union, Civil, Military and Naval*. New York, 1865.

Farwell, Byron. *Queen Victoria's Little Wars*. New York, 1972.

Foreman, Amanda. *A World on Fire: Britain's Crucial Role in the American Civil War*. New York, 2010.

Fortescue, J.W.
    – *A History of the British Army*. London, 1899-1930.
    – *The Royal Army Service Corps: A History of Transport and Supply in the British Army*. Cambridge, 1930-31.

French, H. *Gazetteer of the State of New York*, Syracuse, 1860,

Gibbs, C.R. Vernon. *Passenger Liners of the Western Ocean*, 2nd Ed. London, 1957.

Gibson, Garnet. *That Thy Days May Be Long*. Victoria BC, 1975.

Gooding, S. James. *An Introduction to British Artillery in North America*. Bloomfield ON, 1965.

Graham, C.A.L. *The Story of the Royal Regiment of Artillery*. Woolwich, 1962.

Greene, George Washington. *The Works of Joseph Addison*, Vol. IV. Philadelphia, 1880.

Griffiths, F.A. *The Artillerist's Manual and British Soldier's Compendium*, 7th ed. London, 1859.

Guggisberg, F.G. *The Shop: The Story of the Royal Military Academy*. London. 1900.

Guillet, Edwin C. *Cobourg 1798-1948*. Oshawa, Ontario, 1948.

Harper, J. Russell.
    – "A Study of Art at the Upper Canada Provincial Exhibitions, Ontario Painters 1846-1867". *National Gallery of Canada Bulletin* 1(I:1, May 1963). Ottawa, 1963.
    – *Early Painters and Engravers in Canada*. Toronto, 1970.
    – *Everyman's Canada: Paintings and Drawings from the McCord Museum of McGill University*. Ottawa, 1962.
    – *Painting in Canada: A History* (2nd ed.). Toronto, 1977.

Harpers Magazine. *Harper's Pictorial History of the Civil War*. Chicago, 1866.

Hart, H.G.
    – *The New Annual Army List*. London, 1840.
    – *The New Annual Army List for 1848*. London, 1848.
    – *The New Annual Army List and Militia List for 1855*. London, 1855.
    – *The New Annual Army List and Militia List for 1856*. London, 1856.
    – *The New Annual Army List and Militia List for 1858*. London, 1858.

Hart, H.G (continued)
- The *New Annual Army List and Militia List for 1861*. London, 1861.
- The *New Annual Army List and Militia List for 1863*. London, 1863.
- The *New Annual Army List and Militia List for 1864*. London, 1864
- The *New Annual Army List and Militia List for 1866*. London, 1866.
- The *New Annual Army List, Militia List and Indian Civil Service List for 1871*. London, 1871.

Head, Francis B. *The Royal Engineer*. London, 1869.

Headley, John W. *Confederate Operations in Canada and New York*. New York, 1906.

Heidler, D.S. and J.T. Heidler (ed.). *Encyclopedia of the American Civil War*. New York, 2000.

Hind, Henry Youle et al. *Eighty Years' Progress of British North America*. Toronto, 1863.

Hodder, Edward M. *The Harbours and Ports of Lake Ontario*. Toronto, 1857.

Hogg, Ian V. *A History of Artillery*. London, 1974.

Holley, Alexander L. *A Treatise on Ordnance and Armor*. London, 1865.

Hunt & Son.
- *Hunt's Universal Yacht List for 1852*. London 1852.
- *Hunt's Universal Yacht List for 1857*. London 1857.

Hutchinson, Thomas. *Hutchinson's Toronto Directory, 1862-63*. Toronto, 1863.

In Memorium. Quebec, 1866.

Kane, John. *List of Officers of the Royal Regiment of Artillery from the 1716 to the Present Date*. Rev. ed.
      Woolwich, 1869.

Kingston, William H.G. *Our Soldiers: Gallant Deeds of the British Army During the Reign of Queen Victoria*.
      London, 1898.

Kirby, James (ed.). *The British North American Almanac and Annual Record for the Year 1864*, Vol. I.
      Montreal, 1864.

Laws, M.E.S. *Battery Records of the Royal Artillery, 1859-1877*. Woolwich, 1970.

Le Moine, James M. *Quebec, Past and Present: A History of Quebec, 1608-1876*, vol.2. Quebec, 1876.

Leather, John. *Gaff Rig*. Camden, Maine, 1970.

Lefroy, J.H. *On the Probable Number of the Native Indian Population of British America*. Toronto, 1852.

Litchfield, Norman E.H. *Badges & Insignia of the Royal Artillery*. Derby, 1981.

Lossing, Benson J. *A History of the Civil War*. New York, 1912.

Lovell, John.
- *The British North American Almanac and Annual Record for the Year 1864.* Montreal, 1864.
- *Mackay's Montreal directory for 1863-64.* Montreal, 1863.
- *Mackay's Montreal directory for 1866-67.* Montreal, 1866.

Macdonald, John A. *Troublous Times in Canada: A History of the Fenian Raids of 1866 and 1870.* Toronto, 1910.

MacDonald, R.J. *The History of the Dress of the Royal Regiment of Artillery, 1625-1897.* London, 1899.

MacDougall, P.L. *Forts Versus Ships: Defence of the Canadian Lakes and Its Influence on the General Defence of Canada.* London, 1862.

McGill University. *Annual Announcement of the Faculty of Medicine 1864-65.* Montreal, 1864.

McMann, Evelyn. *Biographical Index of Artists in Canada.* Toronto, 2003.

Mitchell, J.L. *Mitchell's Canada Gazetteer and Business Directory for 1864-65.* Toronto, 1864.

Mockler-Ferryman, A.F. *The Life of a Regimental Officer During the Great War 1793-1815.* London, 1913.

Morrison, John. *A Treatise on Tetanus.* Newry, 1816.

Owen, C.H. *The Principles and Practice of Modern Artillery.* 2nd ed. London, 1873.

Partridge, Colin & Trevor Davenport. *The Fortifications of Alderney.* Alderney, Channel Islands, 1993.

Patterson, Howard. *Patterson's Illustrated Nautical Dictionary.* New York, 1891.

Public Archives Canada. *The Painted Past: Selected Paintings from the Picture Division of the Public Archives of Canada.* Ottawa, 1984.

Punch Magazine. *Cartoons from Punch,* vol. 2. London 1906.

Regimental Committee. *Historical Records of the XXX Regiment.* London 1887.

Reid, Dennis.
- *A Concise History of Canadian Painting* (2nd ed.). Toronto, 1980.
- *Lucius R. Obrien: Visions of Victorian Canada.* Toronto, 1990.
- *Our Own Country Canada.* Ottawa, 1979.

Religieuses Hospitalieres de la Misericorde de Jesus Ordre de Saint-Augustin. *Monseigneur de Saint-Vallier et L-Hopital Général de Québec.* Quebec, 1882.

Riordans, J. *The Upper Canada Law List and Solicitor's Agency Book,* 5th Ed. Toronto, 1866.

Robertson, J. Ross.
- *Landmarks of Canada.* Toronto, 1917.
- *Robertson's Landmarks of Toronto,* Vol. 2. Toronto, 1896.

Roy, Pierre-Georges.
- *Bulletin des Recherches Historiques*, vol. 29. Quebec, 1923.
- *Les Monuments Commemoratifs de la Province de Quebec.* Quebec, 1923.

Royal Academy of Arts. *Exhibition of the Royal Academy of Arts.* London, U.K. Catalogues for 1835, 1836, 1837, 1841, 1843, 1844, 1845, 1847, 1848, 1850, 1856, 1858.

Royal Artillery. *The Royal Artillery Woolwich: A Celebration.* London, 2008.

Royal Artillery Institution.
- *List of Officers of the Royal Regiment of Artillery.* Woolwich, 1869.
- *Minutes of Proceedings*, Vol. VI. Woolwich, 1870.

Royal Canadian Yacht Club. *Laws and Regulations of the Royal Canadian Yacht Club.* Toronto, 1856.

Royal Gun Factory. *Treatise on the Construction and Manufacture of Ordnance in the British Service.* London, 1877.

Russell, Victor L. *Mayors of Toronto 1834 1899.* Erin ON, 1982.

Russell, William Howard.
- *My Diary North and South.* Boston, 1863.
- *Canada: Its Defences, Condition and Resources.* London, 1865.

Seguin, Marc. *For Want of a Lighthouse: Building the Lighthouses of Eastern Lake Ontario, 1828-1914.* 2015.

Sendzikas, Aldona. *Stanley Barracks: Toronto's Military Legacy.* Toronto, 2011.

Smith, Francis K. *John Herbert Caddy 1801-1887.* Kingston, 1985.

Sneath, Allen Winn. *Brewed in Canada.* Toronto, 2001.

Snider, C.H.J. *Annals of the Royal Canadian Yacht Club, 1852-1937.* Toronto, 1937.

Spencer, Warren F. *The Confederate Navy in Europe.* Tuscaloosa AL, 1983.

Spendlove, F. St. George. *The Face of Early Canada: Pictures of Canada which have helped to make history.* Toronto, 1958.

Strickland, C.M. *Twenty-Seven Years in Canada West*, Vol. I. London, 1853.

Swayze, David D. *Shipwreck: A Comprehensive Directory of Over 3,700 Shipwrecks on the Great Lakes.* Boyne City, Michigan, 1992.

Syndics of the Cambridge University Press. *The Holy Bible Containing the Old and New Testaments.* Cambridge, 1962.

Tennyson, Alfred. *Ode on the Death of the Duke of Wellington.* London, 1852.

Thomas, Robert. *Register of the Ships of the Lakes and River St. Lawrence, 1864.* Buffalo, N.Y., 1864.

Thompson, Joshua. *Militia List for Canada West*. Toronto, 1852.

Thornton, Percy Melville. *Some Things We Have Remembered*. London, 1912.

Timbers, Ken (ed.). *The Royal Artillery, Woolwich: A Celebration*. London, 2008.

Tonson, J. & R. *The Works of Joseph Addison*, Vol. IV. London, 1761.

Toronto Public Library.
– *A Guide to the J. Ross Robertson Historical Collection*. Toronto, 1917.
– *Landmarks of Canada: A Guide to the J. Ross Robertson Canadian Historical Collection in the Toronto Public Library*. Toronto, 1967.

Tunstall, W.C.B. "Imperial Defence, 1815-1870", Chapter XXII, *The Cambridge History of the British Empire*, vol. II. Cambridge, 1968.

Vieth, Frederick H.D. *Recollections of the Crimean Campaign and the Expedition to Kinburn in 1855*. Montreal, 1907.

Walker, John. *Turner*. New York, 1982.

Wheater, W. *A Record of the Services of the Fifty-First (Second West York) the King's Own Light Infantry Regiment*. London, 1870.

White, Randall. *Ontario 1610-1985: A Political and Economic History*. Toronto, 1985.

Wilkinson, J. *The Narrative of a Blockade-Runner*. New York, 1877.

Wolseley, Garnet J.
The Soldier's Pocket Book for Field Service, 2nd ed. London, 1871.
The Story of a Soldier's Life, vol. II. Toronto, 1904.

Wright, Larry & Patricia. *Great Lakes Lighthouses Encyclopedia*. Erin ON, 2006.

Government Publications

Adjutant-General's Office. *The Queens Regulations and Orders for the Army*. London, 1859.

Canada House of Commons. *Return for copies of correspondence relating to the Defence of the Frontier, 1863-64 and representations relating to the Rebellion of the Southern States*. Ottawa, 1869.

Dominion of Canada. *Sessional Papers*, Vol. VI, Session 1869. Ottawa, 1870.

Gordon, John W., *et al. Report of the Commissioners Appointed to Consider the Defences of Canada*. London, 1862.

Great Britain, Foreign Office, *Papers relating to the blockade of the ports of the Confederate States.* London, 1862.

Halifax Regional Municipality. "H00373: Substantial Alteration, 4 York Redoubt Crescent". Halifax, 2013.

Principal Probate Registry, *Calendar of the Grants of Probate and Letters of Administration made in the Probate Registries of the High Court of Justice in England.* London, 1858-1966.

Province of Canada.
- *Census of the Canadas, 1860-61: Personal Census,* Vol. I. Quebec, 1863.
- *Provincial Statutes of Canada.* Toronto, 1851.
- *Report of Commissioners appointed to enquire into the conduct of the late John Clarke, as Agent for Public Lands in Huron.* Toronto, 1857.
- "Report of the Commissioners Appointed to Report a Plan for the Better Organisation of the Department of Adjutant General of Militia". Sessional Papers, vol. 4, Session 1862. Quebec, 1862.
- *Report of the Select Committee to Whom was Referred the Annual Report of the Chief Emigration Agent.* Quebec, 1860.
- *Statutes of the Province of Canada.* Toronto, 1856.
- "Statement of the Canadian and American Tonnage" (No. 38), Tables of the Trade and Navigation of the Province of Canada for the Year 1862. Quebec, 1863.
- "Summary Statement of the Welland St. Lawrence and Chambly Canals" (No. 7), ibid.
- *1861 Census of Canada,* Quebec, 1862.

United States Corps of Engineers, *Lake Ontario,* New York, 1877. NOAA Office of Coast Survey Historical Map & Chart Collection.

Upper Canada. *The Militia Register of Upper Canada,* Toronto, 1839.

Internet Sources

Baines genealogical records. http://search.ancestry.ca . Accessed 20 May 2016.

Blouin Art Sales Index. . http://artsalesindex.artinfo.com/Henry-Egerton-Baines-7528-results.action Accessed 7 Oct. 2016

Canadian Military History Gateway. http://www.cmhg.gc.ca/cmh-pmc/page-480-eng.aspx . Accessed 18 Oct. 2017.

Clyde Built Ships. http://clydeships.co.uk/view.php?year_built=&builder=&ref=21921& vessel=ASIA - . Accessed 7 Oct. 2016.

Clyde Site. http://clydesite.co.uk/clydebuilt/viewship.asp?id=17208 . Accessed 26 Apr. 2016.

David Swayze Great Lakes Shipwreck File. http://www.baillod.com/shipwreck/swayze/ . Accessed 18 Oct. 2018.

Geographical Names Board of Canada, "Wellers Bay" http://www4.rncan.gc.ca/search-place-names/unique/FDBYR . Accessed 18 Oct. 2018.

Gerald Peters Gallery, Santa Fe New Mexico. http://www.gpgallery.com/artists/henry-baines . Accessed 18 Oct. 2017.

Getty Research Institute.   http://www.getty.edu/vow/ULANFullDisplay?find=turner&role=&nation=&prev_page=5&subjectid=500026846 . Accessed 18 Oct. 2017.

Great Lakes Vessels Online Index. http://greatlakes.bgsu.edu/vessel/view/005737 and http://greatlakes.bgsu.edu/vessel/view/004541 . Accessed 18 Oct. 2017..

Henri Pilon, "Hodder, Edward Mulberry", Dictionary of Canadian Biography, vol. 10, University of Toronto/Université Laval, 2003, URL http://www.biographi.ca/en/bio/hodder_ edward_mulberry_10E.html . Accessed 14 Oct., 2017.

Indian Army, Assistant-surgeon Philip Ottey Egerton Baines. http://discovery.nationalarchives.gov.uk/details/rd/3f85f3ae-7415-4095-bf42-9c5036f8bd53 . Accessed 18 Oct. 2017.

Lawrence H. Officer and Samuel H. Williamson, "Five Ways to Compute the Relative Value of a UK Pound Amount, 1270 to Present," Measuring Worth, 2017, https://www.measuringworth.com/ukcompare/result.php?year_source=1854&amount=500& year_result=2015# accessed 14 Oct. 2017.

Lawrence H. Officer, "Dollar-Pound Exchange Rate From 1791," Measuring Worth, 2017, http://www.measuringworth.com/exchangepound/ . Accessed 14 Oct. 2017.

Library and Archives Canada. http://www.collectionscanada.gc.ca/lac-bac/results/arch?module=arch&action=results&Languageeng&PageNum=1&SortSpec=score+desc&SearchIn_1=&SearchInText_1=bainbrigge&Operator_1=AND&SearchIn_2=&SearchInText_2=&Operator_2=AND&SearchIn_3=&SearchInText_3=&Level=&MaterialDateOperator=after&MaterialDate=&DigitalImages=1&Source=&ResultCount=10&BIGipServerWEBSITE_V41XAPPS_SERVER=1361792654.20480.0000&_ga=GA1.3.765568287.1495732198&_gid=GA1.3.1852882864.1495732203&_gat_UA-27341782-2=1&Media%5B%5D=1100 . Accessed 14 Oct. 2017.

National Gallery Glossary. http://www.nationalgallery.org.uk/paintings/glossary/ . Accessed 18 Oct. 2017.

Ontario Heritage Trust http://www.heritagetrust.on.ca/en/index.php/properties/victoria-hall . Accessed 14 Oct. 2017.

Pentagon Institute of Heraldry. http://www.tioh.hqda.pentagon.mil/Catalog/Heraldry.aspx?Her-aldryId=15286&CategoryId=9362&grp=2&menu=Uniformed%20Services&ps=24&p=0 &hilite=cavalry . Accessed 18 Oct. 2017.

Quebec City history. https://www.ville.quebec.qc.ca/EN/touristes/connaitre/histoire/1756-1867.aspx . Accessed 18 Oct. 2017.

Soldiers of the Queen. http://www.soldiersofthequeen.com/Canada-HenryEdwardBaines.html . Accessed 18 Oct. 2017.

Thomas Baines 1799-1867. https://en.wikipedia.org/wiki/Thomas_Baines_(Ontario) . Accessed 7 Oct. 2016.

Toronto Plaque, E.M. Hodder. http://www.cabbagetownpeople.ca/person/ edward-mulberry-hodder/ . Accessed 18 Oct. 2017

U.S. Center for Disease Control. http://www.cdc.gov/vaccines/pubs/pinkbook/tetanus.html . Accessed 14 Oct. 2017.

U.S. National Park Service, Civil War, Search for Soldiers. http://www.nps.gov/civilwar/ search-soldiers.htm . Accessed 18 Oct. 2017.

Victorian Forts in Alderney and their Armament in 1859, http://www.visitalderney.com/visit/ history/alderneys-victorian-history . Accessed 14 Oct. 2017.

Newspapers

Army & Navy Gazette. London, U.K.
- 10 Aug. 1861
- 20 Dec. 1862
- 9 Feb. 1867.

Bath Chronicle & Weekly Gazette. Bath, U.K., Thur. 14 Mar. 1861.

Belfast Daily Mercury. Belfast, Thur. 13 May 1858

Belfast Morning News. Belfast, Tue. 9 Sept. 1862

Bell's Life in London and Sporting Chronicle. London, U.K.
- 13 June 1858
- 1 July 1860
- 27 Jan. 1861
- 11 May 1862
- 5 Oct. 1862.

Birmingham Daily Post. Birmingham, U.K., Mon. 23 Dec. 1861.

Birmingham Journal and General Advertiser. Birmingham, U.K., Sat. 14 Nov. 1829.

British Colonist, Halifax
  - 10 Dec 1861
  - 28 Dec 1861
  - 31 Dec 1861

Canadian Illustrated News. Hamilton, Canada West., Sat. 29 Nov. 1862.

Canadien. Quebec, Canada East, 15 Oct. 1866.

Charleston Daily News. Charleston, U.S.A., 16 Oct. 1866.

Chester Chronicle. Chester, U.K., Sat. 30 Oct. 1858.

Cobourg Sentinel. Cobourg, Canada West
  - Sat. 1 Aug. 1863
  - Sat. 8 Aug. 1863
  - Sat. 22 Aug. 1863.

Daily British Whig. Kingston, Canada West
  - 5 Sep. 1850
  - 20 Aug. 1851
  - 15 Mar. 1860
  - 4 Dec. 18678.

Daily Mail. Toronto, Canada 5 Apr. 1894

Daily News. Kingston, Canada West
  - 14 Aug. 1862   - 14 Aug. 1863
  - 8 Aug. 1863   - 15 Aug. 1863
  - 11 Aug. 1863   - 10 Sep. 1863
  - 12 Aug. 1863   - 14 Oct. 1863
  - 13 Aug. 1863   - 7 Sep. 1869.

Daily Post, Liverpool, 26 Oct 1861

Dublin Evening Mail. Dublin, Ireland, Wed. 25 Feb. 1857.

Evening Standard, London
      7 Sep 1861
      27 Nov 1861

Evening Telegraph. Philadelphia, U.S.A., 15 Oct. 1866.

Globe. Toronto, Canada West
- 21 Aug.1857
- 17 Mar. 1858
- 6 Mar. 1861
- 27 June 1861
- 7 Aug. 1861
- 5 Sep. 1861
- 10 Sep. 1861
- 14 Sep. 1861
- 19 Sep. 1861
- 21 Sep. 1861
- 1 Oct. 1861
- 16 Nov. 1861
- 18 Nov. 1861
- 2 Jan. 1862
- 4 Jan. 1862
- 14 Jan. 1862
27 Jan. 1862
- 19 Feb. 1862
- 26 Feb. 1862
- 3 Mar. 1862
- 4 Mar. 1862
- 6 Mar. 1862
- 7 Mar. 1862
- 10 Mar. 1862
- 4 July 1862
- 31 July 1862
- 10 Sep. 1862
- 7 Feb. 1863
- 9 Apr. 1863
- 24 July 1863
- 16 Sep. 1863
- 22 Sep. 1863
- 5 Sep. 1864
- 4 Apr. 1865
1 Nov. 1866.

Globe and Mail. Toronto, Canada. 5 May 1961.

Halifax Morning Chronicle. Halifax, Nova Scotia
- Wed. 1 Jan. 1862.
- 6 Feb. 1862

Hereford Journal. Hereford, U.K., Wed. 1 Feb. 1843.

Illustrated London News. London, U.K.
- 18 May 1861
- 26 Oct. 1861
- 30 Nov. 1861
- 7 Dec. 1861
- 14 Dec. 1861
- 21 Dec. 1861
- 28 Dec. 1861
- 4 Jan. 1862
- 11 Jan. 1862
- 23 Aug. 1862
- Vol. XLII, Jan. to June 1863
- Vol. XLIII, July to Dec. 1863
- 8 May, 1869.

Jersey Independent and Daily Telegraph. Jersey, Channel Islands
- Sat. 14 July 1860
- Fri. 10 Aug. 1860
- Wed. 9 Jan. 1861

Kentish Independent. London, U.K.
- Sat. 15 Jan. 1853
- 11 Dec. 1858.

Liverpool Mail. Liverpool, U.K., Sat. 12 June 1858.

London Daily News. London, U.K., Thur. 4 Mar. 1858.

London Evening Standard. London, U.K.
- Wed. 12 May 1852
- Sat. 13 Mar. 1858
- Mon. 4 Oct. 1858
- Sat. 10 Dec. 1870.

London Gazette. London, U.K.
- 31 Aug. 1847
- 29 Feb. 1856
- 28 May 1858
- 14 May 1861
- 29 May 1861
- 14 Jan 1862
- 29 Nov. 1870
- 7 Mar. 1871
- 20 Sep. 1872
- 12 July 1878.

Manchester Weekly Times. Manchester, U.K., Sat. 14 Dec. 1872.

Montreal Daily Witness. Montreal, Canada. 20 Feb. 1878.

Montreal Gazette. Montreal, Canada
- 30 Aug. 1958
- 6 Sep. 1958
- 13 Sep. 1958.

Morning Advertiser. London, U.K.
- 1 Mar. 1856
- 6 Jan 1860
- 13 June 1861

Morning Chronicle. London, U.K.
- 27 Feb. 1856
- 29 Nov. 1861.

Morning Post. London, U.K.
- Tue. 19 May 1835
- Sat. 2 Dec. 1854
- Sat. 6 Dec. 1856
- Thur. 12 Aug. 1858
- Sat. 14 Dec. 1858
- Mon. 1 Aug. 1859
- Wed. 4 Jan. 1860
- Fri. 12 June 1863.

New Orleans Daily Crescent. New Orleans, U.S.A., 16 Oct. 1866.

New-York Daily Tribune. New York, U.S.A., 9 July 1861.

New York Herald. New York, U.S.A.
- 28 June 1861
- 23 Sep. 1861
- 27 Nov. 1861.

New York Times. New York, U.S.A.
- 12 Oct. 1852
- 28 May 1861
- 10 June 1861
- 24 June 1861
- 27 June 1861
- 11 Sep. 1861
- 20 Sep. 1861
- 18 Oct. 1861
- 28 Oct. 1861
- 17 Nov. 1861
- 18 Nov. 1861
30 Nov. 1861
- 3 Dec. 1861
- 6 Dec. 1861
- 13 Dec. 1861
- 16 Dec. 1861
- 19 Dec. 1861
- 20 Dec. 1861
- 22 Dec. 1861
- 23 Dec. 1861
- 24 Dec. 1861
- 25 Dec. 1861
- 26 Dec. 1861
- 27 Dec. 1861
- 29 Dec. 1861
- 1 Jan. 1862
- 3 Jan. 1862
- 9 Jan. 1862
- 20 Jan. 1862
- 19 Apr. 1862
- 9 Aug. 1862
- 10 Aug. 1862
- 9 Sep. 1862
- 6 Nov. 1862
- 16 Nov. 1862
- 24 Apr. 1863
- 26 June 1865
- 8 Sep. 1864
- 1 July 1864
- 18 Sep. 1866
- 3 May 1894

Newry Telegraph. Newry, Ireland, Thur. 13 Mar. 1862

Oswego Palladium. Oswego, U.S.A., 14 Aug. 1856.

Ottawa Citizen. Ottawa, Canada West, 4 Jan. 1862.

Portsmouth Times & Naval Gazette. Portsmouth, U.K.
- Sat. 20 Apr. 1861
- Sat. 27 Apr. 1861.

Potter's Electric News. Haverford West, U.K., Wed. 12 Mar. 1862

Quebec Gazette. Quebec, Canada East
- Mon. 15 Oct. 1866
- Wed. 17 Oct. 1866
- Mon. 29 Oct. 1866.

Saunders's News-Letter and Daily Advertiser. Dublin, Ireland, Wed. 8 Jan. 1862.

Sheffield & Rotherham Independent. Sheffield, U.K., Sat. 21 Dec. 1861.

Sheldrake's Aldershot and Sandhurst Military Gazette. Farnham, U.K., Sat. 3 Nov. 1866

Standard. London, U.K.
       – Mon. 7 Jan. 1850
       – Sat. 29 Apr. 1871.

Tyrone Constitution. Omagh, Ireland
       – Fri. 18 Apr. 1851
       – Fri. 15 June 1855.

Warder. Dublin, Ireland, Sat. 14 Dec. 1861

Worcester Herald. Worcester, U.K., Sat. 14 Nov. 1829.

Periodicals

Archivia: The Journal of the Association of Canadian Archivists. Burant, Jim. "The Military Artist and the Documentary Art Record", #26, Summer 1988. Ottawa, 1988.

Army Doctrine and Training Bulletin, vol. 2, no. 4. Campbell, W.E. "The Trent Affair of 1861". Winter. Ottawa, 1999.

Blackwood's Edinburgh Magazine, vol. XCI. London, U.K., 1862

Canada Lancet. Edward M Hodder, "Cases of Ovariotomy". Toronto, Nov 1871.

Colburn's United Service Magazine and Naval and Military Journal. London, U.K.
       – Part 3, 1857
       – Part 2, 1859
       – Part 1, 1860
       – Part 3, 1860
       – Part 1, 1861
       – Part 2, 1862
       – Part 3, 1862
       – Part 1, 1863
       – Part 3, 1863
       – Part 1, 1867.

Hunt's Yachting Magazine. London, U.K.
>- Vol. XII, 1863
>- No. 6, Vol. XIV, June 1865

Hunt's Yachting Magazine (continued).
>- No. 7, Vol. XIV, July 1865
>- No. 8, Vol. XIV, Aug 1865
>- No. 10, Vol. XIV, October 1865.

Hunt's Yachting Magazine (reprint) "The Cruise of the Breeze", London, 1865, held by the Toronto
>Public Library, Call No 9171 B115 BR

Journal of the United Service Institution. Vol. II. London, U.K., 1859.

Urban, Sylvanus. *The Gentleman's Magazine*, vol. XII, January to June. London, 1862.

LIST OF MAPS AND ILLUSTRATIONS

(HEB - art by Henry Edward Baines)

INDEX

See "Artists" to find individual artists, "Ships" for names of ships, and "Yachts" for names of yachts.

Abbreviations used:
CE – Canada East (now Quebec)   CW – Canada West (now Ontario)   RA – Royal Artillery
RE – Royal Engineers   RN – Royal Navy   USN – United States Navy   App. – Appendix.

B

D

E

F

G

O

P

This book is available at most book stores and through online booksellers.
It is also available directly from Ontario History Press at www.ontariohistory.ca

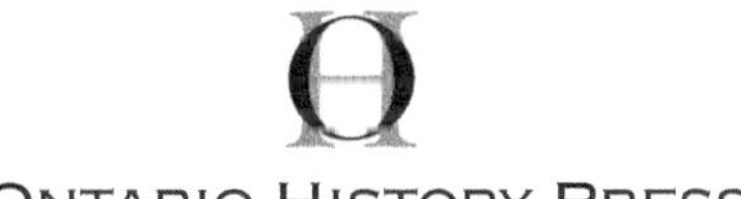

ONTARIO HISTORY PRESS

www.ontariohistory.ca

www.ingramcontent.com/pod-product-compliance
Lightning Source LLC
Chambersburg PA
CBHW080512030726
47592CB00012B/3328